MEDIA OF THE MASSES

Stanford Studies *in* Middle Eastern
and Islamic Societies *and* Cultures

MEDIA OF THE MASSES

Cassette Culture in Modern Egypt

Andrew Simon

STANFORD UNIVERSITY PRESS
Stanford, California

Stanford University Press
Stanford, California

Printed in the United States of America on acid-free, archival-quality paper

Library of Congress Cataloging-in-Publication Data

Names: Simon, Andrew (Andrew G.), author.

Title: Media of the masses : cassette culture in modern Egypt / Andrew
Simon.

Other titles: Stanford studies in Middle Eastern and Islamic societies and
cultures.

Description: Stanford, California : Stanford University Press, 2022. |
Series: Stanford studies in Middle Eastern and Islamic societies and
cultures | Includes bibliographical references and index.

Identifiers: LCCN 2021054255 (print) | LCCN 2021054256 (ebook) | ISBN
9781503629431 (cloth) | ISBN 9781503631441 (paperback) | ISBN
9781503631458 (ebook)

Subjects: LCSH: Audiocassettes—Social aspects—Egypt—History—20th
century. | Sound recordings—Social aspects—Egypt—History—20th
century. | Cassette tape recorders—Social aspects—Egypt—History—
20th century. | Mass media—Social aspects—Egypt—History—20th
century. | Egypt—Social life and customs—20th century.

Classification: LCC TK7881.6 .S56 2022 (print) | LCC TK7881.6 (ebook) |
DDC 621.389/324—dc23/eng/20211116

LC record available at https://lccn.loc.gov/2021054255

LC ebook record available at https://lccn.loc.gov/2021054256

Cover art: Erika Iris
Cover design: Rob Ehle

Contents

Figures

Acknowledgments

MEDIA OF THE MASSES IS THE PRODUCT OF MANY VOICES THAT EX-
panded my horizons over the years. Without Radouane Nasry, a charismatic in-
structor who introduced me to Arabic and a part of the world I never imagined
exploring during my senior year of high school in Connecticut, it is likely that
this book would not have come to be. If my knowledge of the Middle East started
to take shape in New England, it grew by leaps and bounds in North Carolina.
At Duke University, I had the great fortune of learning from miriam cooke, Shai
Ginsburg, Kelly Jarrett, Bruce Lawrence, Mbaye Lo, Ellen McLarney, Ylana Miller,
and Rebecca Stein, scholars whose passion for engaging students, as opposed to
merely lecturing, made classroom discussions immensely rewarding. I owe a
special note of gratitude to miriam and Bruce, who not only supervised my senior
honors thesis, which, at the time, felt like a book, but also inspired me to craft
stories worth telling. To this day, I am fortunate to count both of you as mentors
and friends.

Outside of the United States, I owe a debt of gratitude to the Yemen College
of Middle Eastern Studies in Sanaa, the nearby Democracy School, a nongov-
ernmental organization committed to advancing children's rights in the midst
of many obstacles, and the al-Diwan Language Center in Cairo. All three places
elevated my Arabic skills, which proved essential to conducting the research for
this book and prepared me to embark on a yearlong fellowship at the Center for

Arabic Study Abroad in Egypt, where I witnessed the downfall of Husni Mubarak. It was at mass demonstrations in Tahrir Square that I realized the power of sound, mass media, and Egypt's expressive culture. To Sayed Daifallah, Dina Bashir El Dik, and Wael Farouq, thank you for demonstrating how learning Arabic need not be limited to grammar or vocabulary exercises. Your presence, patience, and passion for teaching created a community I will not soon forget.

At Cornell University, my graduate studies benefited greatly from the wisdom, guidance, and generosity of several individuals, including Ross Brann, Ibrahim Gemeah, Ali Houissa, Kholoud Hussein, Jeanette Jouili, Mostafa Minawi, Lauren Monroe, Viranjini Munasinghe, David Powers, Deborah Starr, Jonathan Tenney, and Shawkat Toorawa. Thank you all for your support. To my adviser, Ziad Fahmy, I wish to convey my deepest appreciation. Whether keeping your door always open, taking the time to discuss countless cultural productions, or exploring the culinary scenes outside of conferences, you have taught me what it means to be a mentor. I hope to have the same impact on students that you have had on me. To the institutes that sponsored my early research, the Mario Einaudi Center for International Studies, the Society for the Humanities, and the Graduate School, thank you for your belief in this project's potential.

As for my research in the Middle East, the American Research Center in Egypt and the Social Science Research Council lent invaluable support. Generous fellowships from each of these entities made much of my fieldwork possible and enabled me to forge new contacts, revisit familiar sites, and gain a greater understanding of Egypt's recent past and my potential contributions to it. On these fronts, I am indebted to Mansur ʿAbd al-ʿAl, Djodi Deutsch, Sayyid ʿInaba, Amira Khattab, Muhammad Lutfi, Esmat al-Nimr, Nermine Rifaat, Muhammad Sadiq, ʿAbbas Muhammad Salama, and many others who played a key part in this journey. Youssef Fouad, thank you for being such a wonderful friend and for reminding me to take a break from work. Ahmad, Hossam, and all the other book vendors at Sur al-Ezbekiya, thank you for your willingness to support my scholarship and for encouraging me to write the book I wished to find on your shelves. This is that book. To the Netherlands-Flemish Institute in Cairo, the American University in Cairo Library, the Music Library, and the Arabic Press Archives at Tel Aviv University, I am grateful for your assistance.

At Dartmouth College, I have been fortunate to find a vibrant intellectual community. Tarek El-Ariss, Jim Dorsey, Dale Eickelman, Chad Elias, Ezzedine Fishere, Levi Gibbs, Susannah Heschel, Kevin Reinhart, and Jonathan Smolin have made Hanover feel like home. My students, meanwhile, have inspired me to ask bigger questions and reassess why this history matters. Working with all of you has been a source of great joy. There is then the Leslie Center for the Humanities, which enabled me to hold a manuscript workshop. I am hard-pressed to think of a more productive day and am grateful beyond words for the feedback provided by Walter Armbrust and Joel Gordon, two scholars whose commitment to enriching the work of others is unparalleled. To the Middle East Studies Association, the American Historical Association, the International Journal of Middle East Studies, and the Tunisian Academy of Sciences, Letters, and Arts, thank you for providing opportunities to discuss parts of this book. I look forward to sharing it with even wider audiences going forward. In this regard, I am thrilled to be working with Stanford University Press. Kate Wahl's insights have transformed this project, Caroline McKusick has lent welcomed support, Katherine Faydash has offered no shortage of thoughtful suggestions, and the remarks of reviewers have pushed me to reconsider what I thought I knew. As for the book's cover, I am honored to feature an image crafted by Erika Iris, an artist whose captivating canvases I have long admired and whose work with cassettes I find inspiring.

Last, I am grateful for the unwavering support of friends and family. Jonathan Cross, Evan Langenhahn, and Michael-Weston Murphy have served as trusted sounding boards. My parents, Rob and Lori, have always pushed me to pursue my dreams wherever they should lead. Thank you both for always being there and believing in me. My sister, Amanda, has brought much happiness to my life and reminds me that she, an MD, should be the only one in our family to respond to requests for "a doctor" on flights. My grandmother Frances challenged me to write a book that would hold her attention from the first few pages, while my grandmother Grace taught me how to think outside of the box at an early age. My grandfather Walter, who always enjoyed hearing about my experiences abroad, is the first relative I know to have traveled to the Middle East, and I will continue to treasure his memories of the region. To my partner, Frances, who now knows more about Egypt's cassette culture than she likely ever wished, your love, sense of humor, and spirit of adventure never cease to astound me. Thank you for everything. I hope this book makes all of you proud and that this story proves to be as enjoyable to read as it was to write.

Note on Transliteration

I HAVE FOLLOWED THE GUIDELINES PROVIDED BY THE *INTERNA-
tional Journal of Middle East Studies* (*IJMES*) for the transliteration of words in
classical Arabic (*fusha*). With the exception of the letter *'ayn* (') and the *hamza*
glottal stop ('), I have elected to omit all other diacritical marks for the purpose of
expediency. In terms of songs and other materials in colloquial Egyptian Arabic
(*al-'ammiyya al-misriyya*), I have slightly modified the IJMES system by writing
the letter *jim* (j) as *gim* (g) and by replacing the consonant *qaf* (q) with a *hamza* (')
when appropriate. Proper names and places with well-known English spellings,
such as Sadat or Cairo, have been maintained, while the Arabic titles of commercial ventures, like Sawt al-Qahira, have been preserved in transliteration. Unless
otherwise noted, all translations are my own.

MEDIA OF THE MASSES

INTRODUCTION

IN THE CAIRO SUBURB OF MAADI, A SMALL SIDEWALK KIOSK, KNOWN locally as Farghali, supplied passersby with basic goods in the summer of 2015. Bags of potato chips blanketed the sidewalk, soft drinks filled a wall of refrigerators, and cartons of cigarettes lined the shelves. Of all the products at the makeshift market, one, in particular, seemed to be of noticeably less use. Below boxes of Johnson's baby wipes and behind bags of sunflower seeds, a crowded glass case, no less than six feet tall, housed hundreds, perhaps thousands, of cassettes covered in a thick coat of dust (fig. 1). The audio recordings on display, unlike the store's other wares, varied widely. Everyone from 'Amr Diab, a pop-music icon, to 'Amr Khalid, a popular Islamic preacher, to a British rock band by the name of the Beatles endured as material traces of a once-robust cassette-tape culture.

Like the sounds they carried, the costs of the cassettes varied. Recordings of Umm Kulthum, an iconic singer known simply as "the lady" (*al-sitt*) across the Middle East, sold for as much as E£25, while albums featuring Ahmad 'Adawiya, a pioneer of popular (*sha'bi*) music, fetched as little as E£15, or about $2. According to Nasir, the stand's manager, these prices were well within reason since companies had ceased to manufacture cassettes. "The age of cassettes," the proprietor emphatically exclaimed, on more than one occasion in the same conversation, "was over" (*'asr al-kasit khalas*)! Once an ordinary object, cassette tapes, he contended, had become a collector's item. Although cassettes certainly no longer enjoyed

1

FIGURE 1. A collection of cassette tapes at a Cairo
kiosk, 2015. Photo by the author.

the same degree of popularity they once did, one thing held true: the history of
audiocassette technology in Egypt had yet to be written.

Media of the Masses offers the first in-depth engagement with Egypt's cassette
culture. In focusing on the social life of a single mass medium, this book presents
a panoramic history of a modern nation through the lens of an everyday technology. Over the course of six thematic chapters revolving around the ideas of
consumption, the law, taste, circulation, history, and archives, it places cassettes,
cassette players, and their diverse users into direct dialogue with broader cultural,
political, economic, and social developments unfolding in the mid- to late twentieth century. Accordingly, a wide array of actors, from singers and smugglers to
politicians and police officers, surface in this investigation, which contributes to
debates on sound, technology, and archives in and outside of Middle East studies.
In the process of discovering what the vibrant biography of one technology can
teach us about a society's dynamic past, this history, in many ways, serves as
extended caption to the photograph of the cassette case in figure 1.

Over the pages to follow, we will explore how cassette technology decentralized state-controlled Egyptian media long before the advent of satellite television and the internet, enabling an unprecedented number of people to participate in the creation of culture and the circulation of content. In these regards, cassettes and cassette players did not simply join other mass media like records and radio; they were the media of the masses. In the midst of investigating these forgotten developments, this book presents a novel approach to the study of Middle Eastern media, proposing that media technologies and the stories they tell may assist us in radically reenvisioning the making of modern nations. Accordingly, in the case of Egypt, we will consider how cassette technology may serve as a historical window onto everyday life. It is in this context that we will encounter both elite and ordinary Egyptians who came into contact with the technology once it shifted from being a concept to a commodity. By placing cassettes and cassette players into constant conversation with Egyptian society and its members, broader historical developments, such as the fashioning of black markets and the forging of "modern" homes, come into relief. The resulting story features two complementary parts. In part 1, "Cassette Culture, Mass Consumption, and Egypt's Economic Opening," we will unpack the birth of Egypt's cassette culture in relation to the creation of a wider culture of consumption. In part 2, "Making Sense of a Medium: The Social Life of Audiocassette Technology," we will uncover the impact of cassettes and their users on the creation of culture, the circulation of content, and the writing of history.

ORDINARY OBJECTS: MASS MEDIA AND MIDDLE EAST HISTORY

Upon entering the Philips Museum in Eindhoven in the Netherlands, one encounters a timeline celebrating the electronics company's many accomplishments. The commanding display spans the length of a long glass hallway and highlights the development of several technologies for all to see. Among the devices of note is an instrument whose origins may be traced back to 1963, the year Philips introduced the compact cassette and consequently set the "global standard for tape recording."[1] The man behind this breakthrough was Lou Ottens, a Dutch engineer. As the head of product development at Philips' factory in Hasselt, Ottens was determined to design something that was cheaper, smaller, and easier to use than the reel-to-reel tape recorder, a device that left much to be desired in his eyes.[2] To ensure that this sound-system-to-be satisfied these aims, Ottens proposed that spools of magnetic recording tape be contained within it.

This recommendation became a reality in the world's first compact cassette and its player: the EL-3300. In the operating instructions for the new machine, the emphasis placed by Ottens on usability and portability is immediately evident. "Now that you are the proud owner of this handy pocket recorder," the opening lines of the manual read, "you can record and play back wherever or whenever you wish."[3] Much like the entry on the Philips Museum timeline, many historical accounts of the cassette tend to conclude here, with the item's invention comprising the entirety of its biography. A technology's creation, however, is only one small part of its story. As we will see, once cassettes and cassette players came into existence, they traveled well beyond the walls of their workshop in Europe.

In Arjun Appadurai's seminal edited volume *The Social Life of Things*, Igor Kopytoff makes a provocative observation concerning objects. "Biographies of things," the anthropologist proposes, "can make salient what might otherwise remain obscure." To assist readers in imagining what such an account may look like in practice, the writer briefly introduces the example of cars in Africa. By exploring the foreign technology's transfer, purchase, use, and movement, he maintains, one would be able to "reveal a wealth of cultural data."[4] Since the publication of Kopytoff's remarks, scholars working in multiple disciplines and localities have demonstrated what such biographies may contribute to our understanding of diverse historical contexts. To recognize only a few, more recent, examples, Carl Ipsen has engaged cigarettes to cast new light on twentieth-century Italian society, Kerry Ross has employed cameras to unpack the making of an everyday activity in Japan, and Marie Gaytán has harnessed tequila to chart the rise of a national emblem in Mexico.[5] Meanwhile, in Middle East studies, academics have detailed the social life of olive oil, an ancient statue, and a sought-after stone when empires prevailed.[6] Taking a cue from the theoretical frameworks of these accounts, we will consider what the journeys of everyday technologies may add to our understanding of Middle East history. In the spirit of uncovering the "wealth of cultural data" to which Kopytoff alludes, we will explore what the untold story of one mass medium may teach us about the history of modern Egypt.

According to David Nye, historians of technology generally fall into two camps. Those in the first group, "the internalists," play the part of the inventor's assistant, witnessing and recording their every action and thought, while those in the second cohort, "the contextualists," concentrate on those who encountered things once they became available, documenting the use and reception of inventions.[7]

As David Edgerton has explained, this second perspective, which he calls the "history of technology-in-use," liberates researchers by enabling them to look beyond a limited set of dates, places, and people. "In the innovation-centric account," Edgerton forcefully contends, "most places have no history of technology. In use-centred accounts, nearly everywhere does."[8]

Historians of the Middle East have crafted detailed accounts of technologies in action. Covering devices we seldom contemplate, as well as enterprises that command our attention, they have scrutinized the social life of widely varying instruments. Cameras, timepieces, telegraph lines, dams, printing presses, and means of transportation, all surface in this body of literature, which transcends any single historical genre, spanning the local and the global, the national and the imperial, the social and the cultural, the intellectual and the environmental.[9] Collectively, the thoughtful case studies at the heart of this corpus evidence how the trajectories of technologies, small and large, are integral to the making of the modern Middle East. One area of inquiry that remains on the relative margins of this scholarship, however, is mass media, or, more specifically, media technologies predating the internet and satellite television.

Scholars have spilled no shortage of ink on social media and its significance in relation to the mass uprisings that shook the Middle East nearly a decade ago. Indeed, a quick survey of recent publications reveals that Facebook, Twitter, and other online platforms have supplanted al-Jazeera, a transnational news channel based in Qatar that became a household name in the early 2000s, as the subject of choice for many studies on the region's media.[10] Although offering key insights into the intersections of activism, authoritarianism, and contemporary politics, these works unanimously lend the impression that only the most recent media matter in Middle East studies. This notion, to be certain, is not restricted to accounts of the Arab Spring. Perceptive treatments of Israel's occupation and military culture, dissent and solidarity during Iran's Green Revolution, and virtual Muslim communities similarly foreground social media, while astute examinations of reality shows, Ramadan programs, and religious broadcasts spotlight satellite television.[11]

What might be gained by reorienting such discussions of media in the Middle East? How might we expand the conventional parameters of media studies? And in what ways might we begin to question the "newness" of new media? In the chapters to follow, we will attempt to address these inquiries by venturing beyond satellite television and the internet to an earlier mass medium whose connections to politics, culture, and everyday life in Egypt remain largely unknown and whose ability to serve as a productive point of entry into one society's past waits to be uncovered. In the process of utilizing cassettes and cassette players as a historical lens, we will bridge close readings of cultural products performed by anthropologists and broader investigations of mass media generated by historians in Middle East studies.[12] Attuned to both content and context, the resulting account reveals how one might reimagine a nation through an everyday technology.

To date, scholars have illuminated only selected aspects of Egypt's cassette culture. Contemporary writers have noted the role of audiotapes in the revitalization of local culture in the Western Desert, the exchange of personal messages between Egyptian migrants in the Gulf and their loved ones back home, and the presence of censored music in Cairo's kiosks.[13] Additionally, academics have tried to periodize the advent of cassettes, usually dating their emergence to the late 1960s or, more often, the 1970s. By the mid-1980s, one author estimates, Egypt's cassette industry encompassed "close to four hundred cassette companies."[14] These formal outlets produced and released thousands of songs, which were joined by countless other recordings on pirated tapes, and cassettes continued to be popular in Egypt after the arrival of compact discs.[15] Together, these enticing observations offer a small glimpse into a more expansive cassette culture.

Indeed, the most extensive study of audiotapes in Egypt to date is limited to Islamic sermons. In *The Ethical Soundscape*, Charles Hirschkind deftly complicates discussions of cassettes as vessels for militant messages by scrutinizing the technology's part in the fashioning of moral sensibilities. He situates cassette sermons in relation to Egypt's wider Islamic revival and sheds valuable light on the "ethical labor" undertaken by ordinary Muslim listeners in Cairo in the mid-1990s.[16] Undoubtedly an important dimension of public piety, the cassettes introduced by Hirschkind account for only a fraction of the tapes circulating in Egypt at any one time.[17] In an effort to render a more panoramic picture of cassette technology and its users, this book navigates a wide array of audio content across multiple decades. At the same time, our discussion of Egypt's cassette culture builds on a few other foundational explorations of the technology further afield, such as Peter Manuel's work in India, by elucidating not only the "effects" of cassettes and the materials on them but also broader historical matters, a number of which, at least at first glance, may appear to have little or nothing to do with the mass medium.[18]

This approach to an everyday technology in the context of Egypt's past is perhaps best illustrated in a photograph that appeared on a popular Instagram page, Everyday Egypt, in 2017. In the black-and-white shot, a young boy, no more than

FIGURE 2. A boy behind a broken television, 2015. Photo by Mohamed Mahdy.

ten years of age, plays on a concrete rooftop in the seaside city of Alexandria (fig. 2). A "Blackstripe 3 System" Toshiba television accompanies the child and surfaces in the image's foreground. No longer possessing a screen, the aged object, acting as a window, perfectly frames the picture's subject, capturing an ordinary moment in the child's life that appears to be a scene from a show. Much like the television set in this photo, we will mobilize cassette technology as a window onto everyday life in this study. Instead of privileging engineers, investors, and inventors like Ottens, we will prioritize a wide range of Egyptians who came into contact with cassettes and cassette players once they existed. As one sociologist has observed, "objects do not speak for themselves."[19] The burden of imbuing inanimate things with a voice falls upon people. This book takes up this challenge by recounting some of the stories cassette technology would tell if it could speak in modern Egypt.

SOUND STUDIES AND SILENT SCHOLARSHIP

I was studying Arabic in Cairo during the downfall of Husni Mubarak. Just beyond the walls of the American University's downtown campus, I listened to millions of Egyptians express their frustrations with the present and their aspi-

rations for the future. In Tahrir Square, I witnessed scenes that came to charac-
terize these mass demonstrations in the eyes of many people: an effigy of Egypt's
president hanging from a traffic light; colorful graffiti criticizing a repressive
regime; signs asserting demands, calling for unity, and mocking political authorities; and citizens from all walks of life risking bodily harm in the pursuit of
meaningful change. These sights were arresting, but the sounds accompanying
them also played a pivotal role in what was taking place: protesters ordering a
helicopter to "leave" as it hovered overhead in a failed show of force; poets con-
fronting poverty, corruption, and hypocrisy in rhyming couplets atop makeshift
stages; children reciting subversive slogans whose meaning likely eluded them
but whose words they easily memorized; and the rise of new voices, like Ramy
Essam, who amplified the chants of his compatriots, alongside the revival of
others, like Shaykh Imam, who challenged those in positions of power decades
earlier. Egypt's revolution was far from a silent affair, and its acoustic elements
opened my ears to the significance of sound and the senses in understanding the
present as well as the past.

In an article published in 1994, George H. Roeder Jr., a prominent scholar
of visual culture, encouraged his fellow historians to pay more attention to the
sensory elements of the past. "Ours is a nearly sense-less profession," he boldly
declared in the *Journal of American History*.[20] Nearly fifteen years later, Mark
Smith, a leading advocate of sensory history, responded to this call on the pages
of the same publication. In the introduction to a roundtable titled "Still Coming
to 'Our' Senses," he pointed to the "explanative power" of the senses, which had
come to captivate historians with a wide array of interests.[21] Likely much to the
delight of both Roeder and Smith, an increasing number of scholars have begun
to take touch, taste, sight, smell, and hearing more seriously in their work since
the turn of the century. Indeed, in the inaugural issue of *The Senses and Society*,
an academic journal launched in 2006, the anthropologist David Howes went as
far as to proclaim that a "sensorial revolution" was under way in the humanities
and social sciences.[22] One key aspect of this "revolution" and resulting wave of
scholarship is sound.

As early as 1977, R. Murray Schafer, in *The Tuning of the World*, introduced the
term "soundscape" to a wider audience, a concept he defines as "any acoustic field
of study."[23] It was not until the past couple of decades, however, when "sound studies," whose participants routinely cite Schafer's monograph as a foundational text,
came to constitute a better-defined field of interdisciplinary inquiry. Historians

have played an incremental part in this development. Whether uncovering past acoustic terrains, charting the trajectories of technologies, or teasing out the intersections of sound, noise, science, politics, and culture, they have shed light on "the audible past."[24] Although these investigations, along with many others, have led one scholar to claim that "auditory history has entered the discipline with a vengeance," the history of the Middle East remains firmly on the margins of this growing body of scholarship.[25] This fact, perhaps, is no more apparent than in multiple "sound studies" readers, which neglect the region's acoustic past.[26] To begin to redress this imbalance, we will examine the materiality, making, and meaning of sounds through the lens of audiocassette technology and its users in modern Egypt.

Historians of the Middle East have long overlooked the acoustic as a site of serious engagement. Ziad Fahmy, for example, has called attention to the "soundproof, devocalized narratives of the past" produced by historians of the Arab world, and Andrea Stanton and Carole Woodall have questioned how sound may feature more prominently in Middle East studies.[27] In the case of Egypt, the ease with which many academics write about society, culture, and everyday life without interrogating the auditory is especially striking. To consider only one notable example, in his sweeping history of Egyptian culture Paul Starkey cites no fewer than ten periodicals and fifty literary works, but he references only two radio stations and three singers. In the event that theater surfaces in his authoritative discussion, it is often in relation to the texts penned by playwrights rather than the performances of them.[28] Ultimately, such one-dimensional narratives reveal only a fragment of people's sensory worlds, since, as Steven Connor correctly observes, "the senses are multiply related," and as such, "we rarely if ever apprehend the world through one sense alone."[29] Building on the recent efforts of scholars undertaking audible histories of the Middle East, we will investigate how Egypt's cassette culture may serve as a springboard for writing a multisensory history of the modern nation.[30] In so doing, we will break new ground for a still-nascent "acoustic turn" in Middle East historiography and contemplate how the study of sound can significantly enrich our understanding of the Middle East and the world around us.

To be certain, Middle East studies is not a noiseless enterprise. Anthropologists, (ethno)musicologists, and religious studies experts have exhibited a greater interest in sound than historians have, especially in relation to Islam and state-sanctioned culture. Since the turn of the century, discussions of "audible Islam" have assumed multiple forms.[31] Building on earlier accounts of Muslim preachers and Qur'anic recitation, scholars have unpacked specific sounds, such as the call to prayer (al-adhan), in addition to the formation of pious communities.[32] The resulting analyses introduce us to preachers, performers, and ordinary believers in mosques, festivals, and several other settings where sound and Islam intersect around the world. With respect to the Middle East, academics have illuminated the responses of Muslim authorities to music and new technologies, the productive power of mass media in the cultivation of religious sensibilities, and the ways everyday objects transmit and reshape the ethics-laden messages they relay.[33] Whether embracing the idea of a "Muslim public sphere," a "Muslim cultural sphere," an "Islamic counterpublic," or another faith-centric framework, writers have regularly adopted Islam as an overarching reference that demarcates the boundaries of their scholarship and, ultimately, limits the scope of their contributions to the study of the Middle East and its acoustic terrains.[34] Although enjoying a disproportionate amount of attention from scholars, "Islamic sounds," in the case of Egypt's cassette culture, have constituted only a small percentage of the content available to listeners at any given time. Audiotape technology, therefore, presents a valuable opportunity to look and listen beyond Islam when unpacking Egypt's soundscape.

In addition to reorienting discussions of sound and Islam, this book strives to enhance prevailing treatments of cultural production in the Middle East. At the start of her seminal study on Umm Kulthum, a leading emblem of "high" Egyptian culture, Virginia Danielson makes a simple yet significant observation. "Listening," she states, "begins with the choice to pay attention to certain sounds rather than others."[35] In Middle East studies, state-sanctioned musicians, from Fairuz to Muhammad 'Abd al-Wahhab, have inspired numerous explorations that evidence a clear preoccupation with the same individuals deemed important by ruling regimes.[36] Collectively, this literature succeeds in highlighting the fashioning of select entertainers as national icons, the development of music industries, and the relationships between performers and political elites who benefited from one another's presence. The limited breadth of this scholarship, however, begs this question: what about artists who were not routinely praised but were nevertheless popular in the Middle East?[37] In the spirit of broadening the parameters of these works, *Media of the Masses* offers a counterhistory of cultural production in modern Egypt. By placing subversive and state-sponsored voices into conversation with one another, and by bringing into the historical fold performers and producers who do not enjoy exhaustive biographies, public monuments, or an enduring presence in state-controlled media, a more nuanced picture of Egypt's acoustic culture is possible.

One of the instruments at the center of this acoustic culture is radio. From the late 1920s to the mid-1930s, around a dozen different independent radio stations, run by individuals, existed in Egypt.[38] The freedom enjoyed by this small community of broadcasters, however, was not destined to last. In 1932, Egypt's minister of transportation declared that one could no longer set up a radio and a receiver without a license.[39] Shortly thereafter, he presented the government's plan to establish a state-operated channel, at which point all other stations would be compelled to close. Over the following two years, radio entrepreneurs resisted this looming silence.[40] Their opposition, though, was ultimately in vain. By 31 May 1934, private airwaves fell quiet in Egypt, and the government's station, with the support of the British Marconi Company, issued its first broadcast, signaling the official start of state-controlled Egyptian radio. In the years to come, the relationship between radio and Egypt's ruling regimes would only deepen. In 1952, a group of men within the military, known as the Free Officers, seized control of the radio's headquarters in Cairo and announced the overthrow of Egypt's monarch King Farouk (r. 1936–1952).[41] A few years later, when Gamal Abdel Nasser became Egypt's second president, the radio's reach expanded dramatically under his watch and at the leader's behest. A brilliant orator, Nasser relied extensively on the medium to relay his beliefs to a mass audience.[42] It is against this historical backdrop that cassette technology and its users would later democratize sound, subvert state-controlled Egyptian radio, and decentralize other "big media" dominated by local gatekeepers.[43]

In the preface to the English translation of *Les cloches de la terre*, Alain Corbin, a pioneer in the field of sensory history, entices readers with a curious opening comment. "Many will be astonished," he suggests, "at the idea of treating bell ringing as a subject of historical investigation, and yet it offers us privileged access to the world we have lost."[44] Corbin's remark, which precedes his now-foundational exploration of bells and their significance in nineteenth-century France, resonates with the historical study at hand. Set in a different place, at another point in time, this book strives to provincialize several histories of recorded sound that prioritize the "West" and demonstrate how the social life of a second technology may offer "privileged access" to a recent period of Egypt's past that, in many ways, remains unchartered waters for historians.[45]

ASSEMBLING EVIDENCE: EGYPT'S "SHADOW ARCHIVE"

Missing documents, censored periodicals, restrictive research clearances, and shuttered state archives are among the myriad obstacles inevitably faced when writing histories of Egypt after the ascent of the Free Officers in 1952. In light of these challenges, it is not surprising that earlier periods of Egypt's past, such as the British Occupation, have received considerably more attention from historians than the second half of the twentieth century. In the spirit of illustrating how one may paint a richer picture of Egypt's recent history in the absence of the Egyptian National Archives (Dar al-Watha'iq al-Qawmiyya), where records following the fall of the monarchy are unavailable to researchers, this study considers a number of pressing questions.

What "alternative archives" are available to historians of modern Egypt and how might the events, actors, and ideas surfacing in these collections enrich and transform accounts of the country under Gamal Abdel Nasser, Anwar Sadat, and Husni Mubarak? How might those working outside formal repositories contribute to discussions of archives, official histories, and counternarratives in the case of Egypt as well as other contexts? And how might we think more critically about archives, the sources that constitute them, and the sorts of scholarship they impede or enable by navigating materials from a wide range of sites? With these inquiries in mind, this book sets out to catalyze a conversation on archives and the writing of history in Middle East studies by demonstrating how one may unpack an era of Egypt's past that has yet to be sufficiently explored.

With a few notable exceptions, scholars of the modern Middle East have yet to join their colleagues working on places as disparate as Indonesia, Peru, and France in what Ann Laura Stoler has termed the "archival turn," a theoretical shift from treating archives as "sources" for producing scholarship to positioning archives as "subjects" of scholarship.[46] Historians, in particular, engage surprisingly little in what Kirsten Weld has called "archival thinking," an interdisciplinary mode of analysis that treats archives as an area of inquiry rather than the subject of footnotes.[47] In the event that historians of the modern Middle East do address archives at any length, it is often in the context of absence, scarcity, or the security sector. As early as 1975, Ibrahim 'Abduh described the difficulties of writing on Nasser's Egypt, a task plagued by "lost" papers, inaccessible archives, and scattered materials monopolized by individuals.[48] For all these reasons, 'Abduh pointedly contended, it is a "history without documents" (*tarikh bila watha'iq*). More recently, Anthony Gorman has similarly identified a "dearth of documents" when it comes to historicizing postmonarchical Egypt, Khaled Fahmy has highlighted what is lost when historical research is a matter of "national security" in Egypt, and Omnia El Shakry has discussed the "impermeability" of postcolonial archives across the greater Middle East.[49]

In conversation with these scholars, we will consider the opportunities inspired by these obstacles. More specifically, this book introduces and navigates Egypt's "shadow archive," a constellation of visual, textual, and audio materials that exist outside of the Egyptian National Archives. Drawing inspiration from an article by Jean Allman on Ghana's shadow archive, which consists exclusively of "formal" holdings in foreign archives, libraries, and research centers, my use of the term departs from hers insofar as it encompasses primary sources from both "official" and "informal" settings, ranging from street markets and public libraries to private holdings and commercial enterprises.[50] In so doing, this history endeavors to craft a richer picture of Egypt's past and to expand the methodological horizons of Middle East scholarship.

One of the sources at the center of this shadow archive is the state-controlled Egyptian press. Over the past decade, historians have increasingly turned to magazines and newspapers to make sense of modern Egypt. Building on Beth Baron's pioneering analysis of women's journals, Hanan Kholoussy, Ziad Fahmy, and Michael Gasper, for example, have availed themselves of Arabic-language periodicals to rethink gender, nationalism, and collective identity under British colonial rule.[51] In an effort to show what the press stands to offer to a more recent period of Egypt's past, we will conduct a sustained reading of two leading state-controlled magazines, which covered a wide array of cultural, political, economic, and social affairs on a weekly basis during the final three decades of the twentieth century.[52] By utilizing both periodicals, it is possible not only to overcome the absence of the Egyptian National Archives but also to explore a series of topics that often escaped "official" records altogether. The first of these magazines, *Ruz al-Yusuf*, surfaced in 1925, having adopted the name of its actress-founder.[53] Initially committed to artistic matters, the publication began to devote more attention to politics by 1926 and soon became one of the most prominent magazines in Egypt. This success, in part, was due to its editor, Muhammad al-Tabi'i, who ultimately left *Ruz al-Yusuf* in 1934 to establish a second weekly, *Akhir Sa'a*, which similarly amassed a large audience.[54] On 24 May 1960, both periodicals were nationalized under Nasser in accordance with Law No. 156 for the "organization of the press" (*tanzim al-sahafa*).[55]

As a result of this legal measure, which ushered in a new era of direct oversight, the Egyptian press, one scholar mourns, "becomes less valuable as a source for critical commentary."[56] What was once a "voice," another historian laments, turned into an "echo."[57] Notwithstanding such negative assessments, this investigation illustrates how state-controlled magazines, like *Ruz al-Yusuf* and *Akhir Saʿa*, may be read against the grain to reveal valuable insights into Egyptian society. What this reading looks like in practice will gain greater clarity in the chapters to follow, but, for the time being, one example is perhaps beneficial. Consider two letters to the editors. The first appears in *Akhir Saʿa* on 18 May 1988.[58] Its author, one Salah Mutawalli, resides at a distance from Cairo in the province of al-Sharqiyya. The subject of the document is Cairo Radio. Like the Egyptian town, Salah explains, Cairo Radio has transformed from a producer into a consumer. Instead of creating new content, he claims, it "lives on the melodious morsels of the giants of *tarab* who have since left our world."[59] To redress this situation, Salah urges Cairo Radio to return to being a producer of "refined" songs. Less than two months later, a second note on the same topic ran in *Ruz al-Yusuf*.[60] In fact, with the exception of the title and the author, the item matches the earlier text in *Akhir Saʿa* to the letter. What could explain this puzzling occurrence?

Although it is possible that the citizen behind the more recent message read Salah's letter and agreed with his critique to such an extent that he decided to resubmit it, nearly verbatim, it is more likely that the two documents originated from the editors, not the readers, of the state-controlled magazines. As will become clear in chapter 3, *Ruz al-Yusuf* and *Akhir Saʿa* both popularized attacks on audiocassettes deemed to be "vulgar" by Egyptian critics, who, at times, looked to state-controlled Egyptian radio as a means to protect and elevate "public taste." Thus, what appears at first glance to be a simple case of plagiarism may actually serve as a window onto a larger discussion concerning cultural production, media technologies, and public taste in Egypt.

If not for an in-depth, issue-by-issue reading of *Ruz al-Yusuf* and *Akhir Saʿa*, over an extended period of time, it is all too likely that the similarities between the aforementioned letters would have gone unnoticed. More important, the full potential of the Egyptian press as a historical source would remain unrealized. Drawing on extensive runs of magazines from multiple collections, including the Moshe Dayan Center's Arabic Press Archives in Tel Aviv and the library of the Netherlands-Flemish Institute in Cairo, we will mobilize editorials, advertisements, crime reports, cartoons, celebrity news, court cases, and pictures,

FIGURE 3. *Sur al-Ezbekiya* paper market in downtown Cairo, 2019. Photo by the author.

among other items in the popular press, to chart broader historical debates and developments that often rest on the margins of secondary literature. Looking beyond state-controlled Egyptian periodicals, we will also employ films, memoirs, foreign newspapers, consular reports, personal photos, private papers, and oral interviews. Likewise, we will make use of cassettes, the colorful sleeves that encase them, the catalogs that market them, and the diverse places that contain them. Collectively, these multisensory materials converge to constitute Egypt's shadow archive.

On many occasions, the sources at the heart of this project surfaced in a haphazard manner, whether turning up in a pile of personal ephemera at the Ezbekiya Wall (Sur al-Ezbekiya), a sprawling paper market atop a bustling metro station in downtown Cairo, or appearing in kiosks, bookstores, or antique shops across the capital (fig. 3). In this regard, Lucie Ryzova's concept of the "Ezbekiya methodology" is particularly poignant. Instead of directing historians to things they "*should* look for after defining a research project," this approach, she explains, "gives one a fairly good idea of what there *is*: what generations of people left behind."[61] Expanding this concept beyond the paper market after which it is named, *Media of the Masses* draws on sources that escape formal collections as well as those that complete them. In the process of doing so, this interdisciplinary endeavor bridges multiple sorts of sites and types of materials while also challenging conventional understandings of what constitutes an "archive" in Middle East studies and calling attention to the kinds of alternative histories that such a rethinking may make viable. By offering a methodological opening to democratize historical research in a time of overzealous gatekeeping and an intellectual opportunity to pursue new topics, Egypt's shadow archive in this book enables us to reconsider the writing of the recent past and our collective knowledge of it.

SETTING THE STAGE: EGYPT'S RECENT PAST

The distant past, present, and future of the Middle East have been discussed and debated by scholars at length. The recent past, in comparison, has merited less attention from experts, who are perhaps waiting for more time to pass before revisiting and reinterpreting this important period. The reasons for this imbalance are twofold. First, serious restraints on archival resources across the Middle East and lengthy declassification procedures abroad limit public access to key historical documents, making relatively recent matters all the more difficult to decipher. Second, few disciplines focus on the recent past. Weary of encroaching on the present and eager to utilize traditional archives with accessible sources, historians generally gravitate toward what happened long ago, whereas anthropologists, sociologists, political scientists, and media experts mainly research what is happening now. In theory, religious studies and literature scholars should be less preoccupied with the passage of time than their peers, but they tend to examine particular processes, like radicalism, and selected genres, such as the novel, that circumscribe the scope of their analyses. By offering an expansive engagement with Egypt's recent past, free of conventional categories, this history extends an invitation to reconsider the types of materials we explore and the disciplinary conventions we follow in the spirit of opening new frontiers in Middle East studies.

Since the Arab Spring, a growing number of scholars have started to reassess aspects of Egypt's modern history. In the case of Gamal Abdel Nasser's rule (1954–1970), researchers have documented and detailed the gendered politics of nation building, the Egyptian army's ill-fated intervention in Yemen's civil war, and the not-so-clear divide between Islamism and Arab nationalism.[62] Building on these explorations, we will venture beyond Nasser to explore a more recent period in Egypt's past that witnessed a series of significant developments. During the final three decades of the twentieth century, these changes included the demise of one authoritarian ruler and the rise of two others in his wake, the renewal of war and the forging of peace with Israel, a shift from state-sponsored socialism to open-market economics to neoliberalism, and the revival of Islam in public and political life.[63] Egypt, in short, was evolving.

Following Egypt's defeat to Israel in the 1967 war and Nasser's death three years later, Anwar Sadat came to power (1970–1981). Having strengthened his immediate foothold through a corrective movement targeting those in positions of influence whose loyalty was deemed to be suspect, Sadat strove to enhance his legitimacy and establish a legacy. In 1973, he resumed armed conflict with Israel. A military stalemate, the ensuing October War provided Egypt's president with a significant political victory. Sadat marshaled his newfound currency as the "Hero of the Crossing" to chart a different course for Egyptian society. In 1974, he released the "October Paper." One key element of his exposition was the *infitah*, or the "opening up" of Egypt's economy. Egypt's move from state-sponsored socialism to open-door capitalism was intended to generate foreign investment, strengthen private enterprises, and curtail state intervention in economic matters. This transition was not without tribulations, and Sadat would pass before it fully took shape. Shortly after signing a peace treaty with Israel in 1979, Sadat was assassinated by a group of Islamic militants in 1981. This irony was not lost upon observers. One of the entities behind the assassination, Egyptian Islamic Jihad, surfaced under Sadat, who strategically empowered Islamists and paved the way for a broader Islamic revival in Egypt.

After Sadat's sudden demise, Husni Mubarak became Egypt's fourth president (1981–2011). Unlike both of his immediate predecessors, who had tried to refashion Egyptian society, Mubarak often prioritized stability above all else. To consolidate his authority from the outset, Mubarak swiftly restored Egypt's state of emergency. On paper, emergency law targeted terrorism and ensured security. In practice, it often served a different purpose. By magnifying the powers of the police and suspending the constitutional rights of citizens, the law permitted Mubarak to rule in an increasingly oppressive manner. Six years after Sadat's assassination, Mubarak ran unopposed for a second presidential term. Following his reelection, by referendum, he set out to revive regional relationships and to further cement his authority at home. The Arab League readmitted Egypt in 1989, and Mubarak led a nationwide crackdown on religious militants in the 1990s. Mubarak's stability and Egypt's renewed centrality in regional affairs drew the interest of Western powers. Intent on identifying a Middle Eastern partner, foreign leaders routinely bolstered Mubarak's autocratic rule, which was extended three more times between 1993 and 2005. Despite growing repression, stalled reforms, and the failure of neoliberalism to benefit the masses, Mubarak ultimately presided over Egypt for thirty years before resigning amid a revolution in 2011.

In navigating a dynamic time in the making of modern Egypt, which routinely serves as "historical context" for later mass uprisings rather than an avenue of inquiry in its own right, this book departs from traditional themes to tell a different story. First, we will redirect accounts of momentous affairs, like armed conflicts, to more mundane matters, such as music. Second, instead of detailing the consolidation of power, we will call attention to its contestation. Last, we will look past the religious to the profane, harnessing Islam as but one of many lenses to make sense of Egypt. The result is a more grounded, rhizomatic history that moves beyond political programs, watershed events, religious movements, and intellectual debates. It is a history that weaves together widely ranging developments that rarely surface in concert to illuminate how Egyptians from all walks of life experienced a changing society.

Egypt's cassette culture lends itself particularly well to rethinking the nation's modern history. In 1963, Philips introduced the very first compact cassette player at the Berlin Radio Exhibition. The mass medium did not make waves in Egypt, though, until the 1970s. Over the course of Sadat's tenure, cassette technology flourished. Bolstered by mass consumption, cassette culture boomed and continued to gain ground long after the dawn of the compact disc in the early 1980s and its subsequent spread in the 1990s. In fact, cassettes remained popular well into Mubarak's rule in the 2000s. *Media of the Masses*, accordingly, treats the decades leading up to Mubarak's downfall not as a mere precursor to a revolution but as its primary focus. Rather than summarizing away a key period in the making of modern Egypt to contextualize one chapter of the Arab Spring, we will take this era seriously. Unencumbered by the burden of big ideologies, like secularism and sectarianism, neoliberalism and nationalism, Islamism and authoritarianism, we will strive to transcend the confines of conventional concepts to undertake a more expansive exploration of one nation's recent past and the lives of those who occupied it.

MEDIA OF THE MASSES: A MIX TAPE

In lieu of adopting a rigid chronological approach to Egypt's recent past, this book operates as a mix tape, with each track, or chapter, revolving around a particular theme. Starting with side A, the first of two complementary parts, we will explore how the advent of cassette technology in Egypt coincided with the creation of a wider culture of consumption under Sadat, the face of Egypt's economic opening. The story of the *infitah* rarely departs from the realm of elite politics. Part 1 of this study, though, presents a novel social history of economic developments. In detailing the making of Egypt's cassette culture, we will shed new light on a vibrant era and its wide-reaching impact on the everyday lives of countless Egyptians.

In chapter 1, I begin to unpack the making of Egypt's cassette culture through a low-resolution photograph of three men posing with a cassette radio. After charting the image's recent circulation on social media, I consider how the picture's untold story and the curious scene it presents may serve as a point of departure for writing a social history of Sadat's *infitah* and its initial aftermath under Mubarak. In the course of exploring how ordinary and elite Egyptians came into contact with cassette technology—in print, abroad, and at home—I demonstrate how the mass medium's commercial life may elucidate wider historical phenomena. These matters range from the making of the "modern home" and the material impact of migrant workers to the creation of "coveted" commodities and the crossroads of leisure and technology. By unraveling these interconnected topics, this chapter offers an alternative history of economic change, spotlights the origins of Egypt's cassette culture, and advances discussions of consumers and consumption, which generally take a back seat to workers and work, in Middle East historiography.

If chapter 1 prioritizes the outward appearance of a robust commercial landscape for cassette technology, chapter 2 illuminates some of its inner dynamics in relation to the law. Paying particular attention to the "criminal biography" of cassette technology, I scrutinize two practices: theft and smuggling. From a counterreading of "popular crime reports," I show how stories praising the security sector and publicizing the downfalls of thieves in the press actually reveal a thriving black market for cassette players that proved difficult to police. This theme of the law and its limits carries over to my discussion of smuggling, where I explore how citizens wielded and flouted the law to smuggle cassette players across Egypt's national borders. Through navigating places like Port Saʿid's free zone and Cairo's airport, I follow a portable technology on the move and reorient drug-centric accounts of smuggling in the Middle East by uncovering the suspect transit of ordinary things. In addressing both theft and smuggling, this chapter enhances the making of Egypt's cassette culture as well as discussions of the *infitah* and mass consumption.

Having unpacked the advent of Egypt's cassette culture in the context of a wider culture of consumption, side B considers the impact of cassette technology and its operators on Egyptian society. In decentralizing state-controlled media, cassettes and their users inspired important changes in the domains of culture, politics, and history. In part 2, we will investigate the impact of this mass medium and those who wielded it on cultural production, contemporary politics, and Egypt's historical record in order to demonstrate how everyday technologies and the stories told by them may assist us in better understanding the making of modern nations.

Starting in chapter 3, I target the crossroads of class, culture, and politics in Egypt. By enabling any citizen to become a cultural producer, as opposed to a mere cultural consumer, audiotape technology and its users sparked significant anxiety in the mid- to late twentieth century, when cassettes carrying content local gatekeepers considered "vulgar," most notably *sha'bi* music, were censured by several critics for poisoning public taste, undermining high culture, and endangering Egyptian society. This chapter breaks down those arguments and shows that tapes actually broadcast a vast variety of voices. Thus, underlying many criticisms of cassette content was not simply a concern for aesthetic sensibilities, but a struggle over what constituted Egyptian culture and who had the right to create it during a time of tremendous change. By navigating and elucidating Egypt's "vulgar soundscape," this chapter presents a fresh counterhistory of Egyptian cultural production that casts new light on the cultural politics of Sadat's economic opening.

If cassettes and their users significantly expanded the creation of Egyptian culture, the technology and its operators also broadened the circulation of cultural content. Piracy, as a popular practice, began not with digital files online but with magnetic tape reels decades earlier. In chapter 4, I scrutinize how a wide range of Egyptians, from private citizens to state employees, copied sounds in the mid- to late twentieth century. I open with a long-forgotten court case pitting two leading artists against a third performer who managed to legally "steal" their music. Once unpacking this fascinating confrontation, I historicize the steps taken by musicians, police officers, and company executives to eradicate counterfeit cassettes across Egypt and well beyond its borders, before detailing how multiple forms of piracy hampered these efforts. As will become clear, copying sounds was not simply a matter of replicating recordings. This mundane activity, at a more fundamental level, radically altered the very movement of cultural material by empowering anyone with a tape recorder to become a cultural distributor at a time when recording labels reigned, mass media was state-controlled, and elite artists enjoyed great power in Egypt.

The creative power and circulatory potential of audiotapes are no more evident than in the case of Shaykh Imam, a blind Egyptian singer whose informal cassette recordings unsettle Egypt's historical record. In what is widely regarded as one of the warmest receptions an American president ever received overseas, Richard Nixon landed in Cairo in the summer of 1974. In chapter 5, I examine the writing and rewriting of this historic event. Once unpacking what I call a "sonorous spectacle," I explore how one contemporary song, "Nixon Baba" (Father Nixon), directly challenged the Egyptian government's "official story" of the state visit. To make sense of this subversive soundtrack, I start with its singer, Shaykh Imam, an "ordinary icon" whose voice spread near and far on noncommercial cassettes created and circulated by individual listeners. After elucidating Imam's historical trajectory and the centrality of audiotapes to his career, I illuminate the movement and lasting resonance of "Nixon Baba," which witnessed a resurgence during the Arab Spring. In so doing, I illustrate how cassette technology served as a powerful tool not only to criticize ruling regimes but also to counter the very narratives crafted by their advocates.

The sounding of some stories and the silencing of others continue to gain greater clarity in chapter 6, which brings this history of Egypt up to the twenty-first century by contemplating the material remnants of a once-lively cassette culture. Following in the footsteps of anthropologists who have utilized oral interviews to write innovative histories of the Middle East, and taking a cue from historians who have made use of ethnographic methods to uncover a more vivid picture of the past, I draw on the voices of a religious scholar, a library director, and an electronics dealer, among others, to provide a microhistory of cassette technology that offers insights into the production, preservation, and study of Egypt's acoustic past. Two inquiries guide these case studies. What questions do contemporary cassette collections raise? And which kinds of histories do these alternative archives and their attendant voices make viable? In covering the lives of audiotapes and their ordinary users, this chapter rethinks "the archive" in Middle East studies and paves the way for future ethnographies of sound that are historically rigorous.

Last, in lieu of simply ending a conversation, the conclusion of this book strives to spark future exchanges. Opening with the physical traces of a once-vibrant cassette culture introduced in chapter 6, I return to the Cairo kiosk at the very start of this introduction and investigate the recent disappearance of its cassette recordings. Using this curbside stall as a starting point, I consider the opportunities afforded by sound and the senses, everyday technologies in action, and shadow archives in the field of Middle East studies. Ultimately, I conclude by placing *Media of the Masses* into conversation with the Modern Egypt Project, an ongoing undertaking led by the British Museum in London to present and reimagine Egypt's recent past through the window of the country's everyday artifacts. With this mix tape in mind, let's begin to consider how the most ordinary things may yield the most surprising insights.

Part I

CASSETTE CULTURE, MASS CONSUMPTION, AND EGYPT'S ECONOMIC OPENING

Chapter 1

SELLING

Leisure, Consumer Culture, and Material Terrains

AT 7:41 IN THE MORNING ON 9 JANUARY 2017, A LOW-RESOLUTION, black-and-white photograph surfaced on Old Things (Hagat 'Adima), a popular Egyptian Facebook page committed to showcasing "all that is beautiful enough to stir the sorrow of all generations."[1] In the grainy shot, three men, sporting loose-fitting robes, pose with a cassette radio. The scene seems to be staged and its subjects show little emotion. Two of the figures stand rigidly in the back before a blank canvas, while the third sits in front of them with the tape player atop his lap. As much as the shot reveals, it also conceals. The subjects remain anonymous, the location mysterious, and the motivation for taking such a picture in the first place unknown. A comedic caption accompanying the picture provides little in the way of answers. "People photographing holding an iPhone 6," the writer jests, "will see themselves like this after a couple of years."

Once posted online, the photograph of the three men snowballed. Countless Facebook users circulated it near and far, "sharing" the item more than fifteen thousand times in a matter of days. One of the settings where the intriguing picture reappeared was Farouk of Egypt (Faruq Misr), a second Facebook page with a far larger audience than Old Things. After being shared by the site's administrator on January 10, the shot went on to amass a staggering twenty-five thousand likes and nearly seven hundred comments in less than forty-eight hours.[2] The nature of the remarks varied from the satirical to the historical and the personal. Some commentators mocked the tape player's presence, while others confirmed the machine's popularity in Egyptian households and recalled how many citizens returned to Egypt from elsewhere in the Middle East with cassette devices in hand. One man's statements, however, departed from the rest. He claimed to know the people in the photo.

Joining the online conversation, a user by the name of Ashraf Bakr tried to offer some clarity to an otherwise-obscure portrait. Hours after the image turned up on Farouk of Egypt, he maintained that the digitized relic originated from Iraq, where the three men were residing at a distance from their home city of Girga in the Upper Egyptian province of Sohag. Prior to returning to their homeland, he elaborated, they purchased the cassette radio from a local shop and decided to take a picture with it. Eager to unpack this story a bit further, I reached out to Ashraf with a few questions. When, exactly, was the photo taken? Who snapped it? How much did the cassette radio cost? And why did the men exhibit the technology? In reply, he explained that the photo op unfolded in the city of Ramadi in central Iraq in 1975.[3] As for the shot's subjects, the men were construction workers and friends of Ashraf's father, who led them on a shopping expedition in the run-up to their return to Egypt. In Ishtar Electronics Shop the workers used part of their savings to purchase the cassette player for twenty Iraqi dinars, a relatively affordable sum in comparison to the product's price back in Egypt. Ashraf, then in the fourth grade, joined the group on the outing and remembered a subsequent stop at a photo studio next door. There, he saw his father's friends proudly display their "big" purchase, second only to a black-and-white television set at the time, and witnessed a basic camera with a trailing black cloth capture the picture that ended up on Facebook more than four decades later (fig. 4).

In addition to enchanting Facebook users, this photo and the recollections inspired by it introduce several key themes at the center of this chapter and Egypt's modern history. The image calls attention to migrant workers and changing material landscapes, the development of a burgeoning consumer culture that existed within and outside of Egypt's national borders, the allure surrounding certain commodities, and the intersections of leisure and media technologies. Additionally, it highlights the usefulness of photographs as historical documents, which, if read in a careful and critical manner, may reveal more than what they physically picture. The discussion to follow investigates these interconnected

لناس اللي بتصور مشكلة iPhone 6...كمان كم سنة حيشوفوا صورهم كذا

See Translation

حاجات قديمه
January 9 at 7:41am · 🌐   👍 Like Page

لناس اللي بتصور مشكلة iPhone 6...كمان كم سنة حيشوفوا صورهم كذا

See Translation

👍 Like   💬 Comment   ➤ Share

👍😢😮 25K   Top Comments ˅

1 share   483 Comments

FIGURE 4. Three Egyptians pose with a cassette radio in a photo posted on Facebook in 2017 (https://www.facebook.com/king.farouk.faroukmisr).

topics in greater detail and begins in the 1970s, when an "old" technology was "new" and when such images signaled the upward mobility of those who were photographed by visually indexing their increased purchasing power. In so doing, it sheds some light on the historical development of Egypt's cassette-tape culture and the creation of a wider culture of consumption that proved integral to the making of modern Egypt.

OIL, AUDIOTAPE TECHNOLOGY, AND TRANSNATIONAL TRAVEL

At the start of Anwar Sadat's tenure as Egypt's president in 1970, oil revenues from five leading producers in the Middle East totaled some $4.21 billion. Five years later, this sum skyrocketed to an estimated $51.98 billion, a twelvefold increase, and continued to climb.[4] Sadat's announcement of Egypt's economic opening in 1974 coincided with a dramatic rise in oil prices following the 1973 October War. The resulting profits paved the way for new plans across the Middle East. Oil-boom economies, in and outside of the Arabian Peninsula, soon required substantial foreign labor to implement sweeping national schemes, from the development of vital industries to the construction of vast infrastructure projects. With the largest population in the region, Egypt presented a major source of manpower for neighboring nations.[5] In response to an unprecedented demand for labor and in pursuit of personal gain, many Egyptians strove to secure employment abroad, if only on a temporary basis, starting in the 1970s.[6] Domestic wages in Egypt often could not compete with international salaries in oil-rich destinations and the allure of greater earnings elsewhere inspired countless citizens to cross national borders.[7] The oil-fueled movement of these individuals played a key part in the story of a second commodity: audiotape technology.

The exact number of Egyptians working abroad in the 1970s and the 1980s is difficult to determine. Most experts agree that available data are incomplete and imprecise, if not intentionally altered by local authorities to political ends.[8] Despite these limitations, some statistics may serve to broadly illustrate how migration became a popular practice under Sadat (1970–1981) and continued to be commonplace under Husni Mubarak (1981–2011). According to one estimate, approximately five hundred thousand Egyptians found employment in oil-producing Arab states by the mid-1970s, a twenty-five-fold increase from those laboring in the same countries in the 1950s.[9] By the early 1980s, it is widely reported, the total number of Egyptians living in "economic exile" had climbed to three million, or approximately one in every fifteen citizens.[10] In reality, these figures may well have been higher. Egyptians who migrated illegally rarely surfaced in official records.[11] Predominately the domain of men, Egyptian migration was otherwise diverse. Rural and urban, literate and illiterate, and lower-, middle-, and upper-class citizens all traveled abroad to perform skilled, semiskilled, and unskilled labor. Migration, in this sense, was a national phenomenon. It involved everyone from construction workers and college professors to mechanics and medical doctors, all of whom welcomed support from private parties, personal contacts, and the Egyptian government.[12] In the mid- to late twentieth century, more Egyptians were on the move than ever before.

From the 1970s to the 1990s, sociologists, anthropologists, economists, and political scientists all engaged Egyptian migrants as a subject of serious academic inquiry. Since the turn of the century, though, historians have contributed surprisingly little to this body of literature. With a few notable exceptions, retrospective investigations are relatively rare.[13] Irrespective of one's disciplinary background, a common theme across this scholarship is the money made by Egyptians abroad. This focus is understandable. Monetary gain was the primary motivation for most Egyptians to migrate in the first place, and members of this community often strove to minimize expenses outside of Egypt to enhance their standards of living back home. This strategy is no more evident than in the case of remittances, or foreign earnings returning to Egypt.

According to the Central Bank of Egypt, workers transferred $6 million to Egypt in 1971. With the oil boom well under way, this figure soared to $2.2 billion by 1979, tripling the year's earnings from the Suez Canal.[14] Only five years later, remittances climbed even higher, reportedly reaching $3.3 billion, with unofficial approximations ranging from $6 billion to $10 billion, a sum that exceeded Egypt's revenues from cotton, tourism, exported oil, and the Suez Canal combined.[15] These transnational flows of cash made many things possible for migrants in Egypt, from marrying and schooling children to building or remodeling a house and paying off a debt that made migrating viable. Additionally, migrants routinely mobilized their international earnings to acquire consumer durables back home, material evidence of success and a "modern" lifestyle.

The money made by Egyptian migrants, though, was not the only thing to traverse national borders. Teachers and doctors, engineers and bureaucrats, farmers and construction workers, along with others up and down the socio-economic ladder, purchased consumer products that made their way on wheels, wings, and waves to Egyptian soil. These purchases, in turn, visibly altered the material landscapes of cities and villages, from Alexandria to Aswan. To begin to gauge the sheer number of objects pouring into Egypt, it is useful to consider a report on the return of Egyptian migrants in *Akhir Saʿa*. In the article, Mahmud ʿUthman, the president of EgyptAir's Merchandise Sector as well as Cairo airport's freight hold, claims that 512,000 parcels, weighing approximately twelve million kilograms, passed through his transit area in the first six months of 1982 alone, an impressive increase from the 380,000 packages received by the airport in all of 1981.[16] As was the case with the quantities of cash remitted by migrants, these line items, again, were in all likelihood greater.[17] Travelers, after all, regularly carried things on their person and in suitcases that never entered cargo bays, and other actors on the move, as we will see in chapter 2, strategically wielded and openly flouted the law to smuggle a wide array of items across Egypt's borders. Among the more common objects Egyptians acquired abroad were audiocassette players.[18]

One of the easiest places to procure cassette technology beyond Egypt's borders was the Arabian Peninsula. Whether studying, vacationing, visiting relatives, performing the annual Muslim pilgrimages (Hajj and ʿUmra), or pursuing paid openings abroad, Egyptians were able to purchase the popular machines from leading international companies with local agents across the Red Sea. Both National and Toshiba, two Japanese competitors, listed locations for stores selling cassette players throughout Saudi Arabia in the mid-1970s prior to publicizing addresses in Egypt on the pages of *Ruz al-Yusuf* and *Akhir Saʿa*.[19] Similarly, the South Korean Samsung made inroads in the Gulf before identifying a licensed representative in Egypt. As early as 1980, the company directed Egyptians to their branch in Kuwait, where customers were free to browse and buy a wide array of cassette radios.[20] The attainment of cassette technology in the Gulf was so common, it seems, that such scenes even enjoy some traction in Egyptian cinema. Ahmad al-Guindi's comedy *You Fly* (*Tir Inta*, 2009), for example, opens with a flashback.[21] The year is 1985 and an Egyptian couple in Kuwait City fastens their belongings atop a sedan bound for Egypt. Among the migrant workers' prized possessions is a dual-cassette player they obtained in Kuwait. Perhaps one of the most popular theaters to acquire cassette technology, the Arabian Peninsula was not the only outlet to do so in the Middle East. By the end of the 1970s, companies like National boasted twenty-six branches blanketing the region, from Tripoli and Tehran to Aleppo and Aden.[22] Amid the electronics to fill these stores were audiocassette players of all different shapes and sizes.

Often lost in Gulf-centric discussions of the oil boom are other places that proved popular among mobile Egyptians. One such locale was Libya.[23] Near the beginning of 1985, a foreign correspondent for the *Washington Post* ventured outside of Cairo to witness how economic migrants were changing the material terrain of Egypt's countryside. In the village of Dahshour, the reporter spoke with a young man who had returned from Libya not too long ago. Courtesy of a three-year stint abroad as a farmhand, he had accrued enough money to marry, build a house, buy more land, purchase a television set, and amass some livestock back in Egypt. "He even has a cassette recorder," the journalist relayed, with an air of amusement, at the end of the vignette.[24] Whether this particular recorder came from Libya is unclear, but many Egyptians did purchase them there. As early as 1976, a writer for the *Guardian* observed how Tripoli's bustling bazaar, "where Libyans jostle with expatriate workers, mostly from Egypt and Tunisia, in what appears to be a frantic rush to spend their money," contained an entire alleyway specializing in cassette technology.[25] On the frequent flow of cassette players across Egypt's borders, a cultural critic who came of age between Cairo and Upper Egypt in the 1970s recalls in his memoir how peasants, builders, and other laborers from a small village would often return with "customary" gifts after heading not to the Gulf but to Libya. Cassette players, he explains, accompanied these travelers on such a regular basis that their transnational passage inspired a popular song.[26]

At a distance from Libya, Egyptians in Iraq, like the ones in our opening photograph, joined their compatriots in purchasing cassette players for themselves and others before returning home. Throughout much of the 1980s, Egyptians worked in Iraq with a war raging in the background. The enduring conflict between Iraq and Iran (1980–1988) resulted in severe shortages of labor.[27] Foreigners filled many of these openings, with officials in Baghdad and Cairo at one point claiming that Egyptians occupied "almost half of the jobs in Iraq."[28] By the end of the decade, this would change. Iraq's invasion of Kuwait in 1990 prompted thousands of Egyptians to flee both countries. Unlike the actors in al-Guindi's film, these workers-turned-refugees did not have the luxury of leaving of their own accord, and many departed with only what they could carry. A series of pictures capturing the arrival of a single ferry from Jordan in a Sinai port starts to reveal some of the objects that survived the arduous journey.[29] Among the valued belongings are multiple cassette radios, which Egyptians hold close in their hands. Not all cassette players, however, made it back to Egypt safe and sound. Like many other things, the technology, too, was collateral damage in the armed conflict. During the Gulf crisis, numerous Egyptians accused Iraqis in Kuwait and at the border with Jordan of seizing their electronics, cassette radios included.[30] Momentary migration and its monetary rewards were clearly not without risk. At the same time, not all Egyptians who came into contact with cassette players abroad were migrant workers.

In the midst of the oil boom and Egypt's economic opening, the Middle East experienced notable advancements in mass transportation. In the 1970s, the region was the "fastest-growing air market in the world," and by 1985, over a dozen different international airlines called it home.[31] Migrant workers populated many Middle East flights, but they were not the only passengers onboard. Transnational travelers of all sorts joined them, including Egyptians performing pilgrimage. In 1979, nearly fifty thousand Egyptians went on Hajj. Three years later, this number doubled, and it rose further still in later years.[32] As was the case with migrants, pilgrims, too, purchased consumer durables abroad. The shopping in which they engaged is the subject of one *Ruz al-Yusuf* cartoon from 1971.[33] Set in a village, the illustration introduces a mural depicting one person's pilgrimage. In addition to the phrases "God is great" (*Allahu Akbar*) and "a blessed pilgrimage" (*Hajj mabrur*), images of an electric blender, wristwatch, transistor radio, and reel-to-reel tape player, soon to be surpassed by the compact cassette recorder, appear on the home's exterior, a space traditionally occupied by pictures of the *ka'ba* and the pilgrim's journey. The sketch makes a mockery of the material gains to be made on Hajj, but its content is not as far removed from reality as one might expect. At least some Egyptians appeared alongside the cassette players they picked up as pilgrims in paintings that projected both piety and purchasing power (figs. 5–6). Thus, regardless of their reasons for traveling, no shortage of Egyptians encountered cassette technology outside of Egypt.

The advent of Egypt's cassette culture, then, was in part transnational, with Egyptian migrant workers leading the way. Traveling abroad in pursuit of oil-inspired opportunities, this highly mobile community wielded newfound purchasing power to fulfill personal desires. Some of these aspirations took the shape of consumer durables that evidenced one's success and made everyday life more enjoyable. Sadat's *infitah*, arguably, was as much a matter of the Arab world and Egyptians laboring around it as it was the West and foreign funding from it. The accompanying oil boom did more than stoke anxiety in the United States.[34] It ushered in an era of increasingly interconnected economies in the Middle East where momentary migration provided many people with a means of achieving

FIGURES 5 AND 6. Paintings of pilgrims with cassette players. Photos by Ann Parker and Avon Neal, in *Hajj Paintings: Folk Art of the Great Pilgrimage* (Cairo: American University in Cairo Press, 2009), 94–95.

upward mobility through monetary gain. Whether the resulting consumption engaged in by Egyptians was positive or negative is a subject of debate.[35] But the role played by mobile Egyptians in the historical development of the country's cassette culture is beyond any doubt. At the same time, if transnational travel made purchasing cassette technology possible for countless citizens, it was not a prerequisite for procuring the coveted commodity.

THE MAKING OF A DOMESTIC MARKET

Although traveling undoubtedly enabled many Egyptians to encounter, afford, and acquire cassette players, among other items, it was not always necessary to obtain Walkmans, cassette radios, and car stereos. Based on an ad for a business in Beirut, it appears that interested parties may have been able to order audiotape players from the comfort of their homes in Egypt. In one of the earliest notices for the technology in *Akhir Sa'a*, in the spring of 1970, the Across the East Company for Supplies (Sharikat 'abr al-Sharq lil-Turiddat) offered to ship foreign goods it collected from international factories to the seaside city of Alexandria.[36] Among the products available to Egyptian consumers at the time were washers, dryers, and ovens, radios, cassette radios, and cassette recorders. Predating the opening up of Egypt's economy by almost four years, this intermediary's announcement sheds light on the overlooked flow of everyday goods across the Mediterranean and suggests that Egyptians were able to secure cassette players from abroad without ever setting foot outside of Egypt. Having uncovered some of the outlets for audiotape technology beyond Egypt's national borders, it is important that we now turn to the medium's domestic availability. By accounting for both the local and the international scenes when it comes to the sale of cassette players, a more vibrant picture of the technology's robust commercial landscape and Egypt's wider consumer culture comes into view.

As was the case with cassette players abroad, numerous companies competed with one another for consumers in Egypt's urban centers and rural peripheries. Among the businesses that sold, marketed, and, in some cases, manufactured the technology on-site were public-sector entities. Of all these enterprises few were more integral to the production and popularization of cassette players than Philips, a Dutch electronics firm responsible for the technology's invention whose long-standing Egyptian branch was nationalized in 1961 as a result of President Gamal Abdel Nasser's July Laws.[37] Following this momentous set of measures, Philips often surfaced as a public-sector "success story" in the Egyptian press. In an article covering a meeting between the company's president and Sadat, for instance, several figures serve to evidence the apparent triumphs of Philips in the aftermath of Nasser's executive decrees. From 1961 to 1975, the report contends, the business's employees and factory space nearly quadrupled, to 20,600 square meters, and its production numbers soared.[38]

In addition to enjoying favorable local coverage in the popular press, Philips harnessed the same weekly magazines that praised the company as a tool to promote its latest electronics. Nearing the end of 1975, the president of Philips's Egypt operations announced that consumers would soon be able to acquire a new item from the public-sector giant: cassette players.[39] Starting in 1976, he declared, Philips would begin to locally produce cassette radios and car cassette stereos. In line with this pledge, Philips started to make and market cassette players in Egypt the following year and gradually expanded its audiotape arsenal to include multiple devices by the late 1970s.[40] The company, however, did not enjoy a monopoly on audiocassette technology in Egypt at this time. An increasing number of international entities with local delegates aimed to redirect customers away from Philips and toward their respective inventories.

Around the same time that Philips entered the compact cassette market, National designated the Great Nasr Company for Trading (Sharikat al-Nasr al-ʿAdthim lil-Tijara) as its sole licensed agent in Egypt and alerted prospective customers to the presence of its cassette players near and far. In a number of advertisements from 1977, the brand specified no fewer than ten different businesses, based in multiple governorates, which carried its electronics and openly welcomed wholesale distribution requests from additional parties in an effort to grow its national network.[41] Following suit, Toshiba, which similarly used to note only its presence in the Gulf in Egyptian magazines a mere few years earlier, named an official representative in Egypt by the early 1980s. According to contemporary advertisements, its agent, the ʿArabi Company (Sharikat al-ʿArabi), boasted branches in Cairo and Port Saʿid in 1983 and added a third address in the capital in 1984.[42] Perhaps taking a page out of the Philips playbook, Toshiba shortly thereafter started to advertise not only small Walkmans and sizable boom boxes from afar but also a cassette radio "built in Egypt by the hands of Egypt's workers."[43] Joining both of these Japanese rivals were still other international competitors, such as Sony and Samsung, which also strategized to establish a local foothold in Egypt.[44] Regardless of the exact shape the undertakings assumed, all of these developments collectively enhanced the commercial landscape for audiocassette players, which increasingly migrated from the factory floors of prominent companies and their partners to public- and private-sector stores across the country.

If advertisements and announcements from major manufacturers offer a window onto the commercial life of audiocassette technology in Egypt, still other sources add color to this vista. Photographs and films lend a further glimpse into the circulation of cassette players on a national scale. In a report on the "rebirth" of the Sinai in the mid-1980s, for example, readers encountered a group of men inspecting one of several cassette radios in a well-stocked shop in the coastal city of al-ʿArish on Egypt's outskirts, where stores had "transformed from ruins into boutiques with the latest equipment and appliances."[45] The machine's maker is difficult to determine, but the picture's purpose is less ambiguous. In an article praising Mubarak's role in revitalizing the peninsula following the 1973 war and the complete withdrawal of Israeli soldiers from the Sinai in 1982, the scene indexes the new "era of prosperity" ushered in by the president.

If editors selected a shot of cassette radios in a crammed shop to signal the Sinai's modernity, filmmakers wielded other images of the technology to convey the ills of the same consumer culture on display in the picture. Following its advent as an economic free zone in 1976, Port Saʿid became a mecca for conspicuous consumption in Egypt.[46] The city's consumer culture surfaces in contemporary Egyptian films critical of Sadat's *infitah* and the nouveau riche empowered by it. In *The People at the Top* (*Ahl al-Qimma*, 1981), a drama involving a respectable police officer and a pickpocket who turns suspect businessman, citizens smuggle cassette players and other imported goods through Port Saʿid; in *The Bus Driver* (*Sawwaq al-Utubis*, 1983), a drama chronicling the quest of one working-class man to raise enough money to save his father's wood shop from financial ruin, the same items line the walls of a house, within the city's limits, belonging to the hero's sister and brother-in-law, an affluent, unlikable trader who refuses to help him.[47] Regardless of these divergent takes on Egypt's burgeoning consumer culture, all these materials jointly confirm the sale, circulation, and acquisition of cassette players on a local plane.

Prevailing discussions of Egypt's economic opening in the 1970s and the 1980s tend to concentrate on sweeping developments. Plans to attract foreign investment, to boost and bolster the private sector, and to transition from a socialist system to a Western-oriented capitalism form the foundation of these grand narratives, which generally privilege policies engineered by the state and imposed from above.[48] In tracing the varied interactions of ordinary and elite Egyptians with cassette players at home and abroad, a more nuanced, micro-level picture of Egypt's changing economy emerges through the lens of a particular technology. Indeed, by scrutinizing the commercial life of audiotape technology, the significant role played by countless migrant workers in altering Egypt's material landscapes, the intense competition among private- and public-sector enterprises, and the ill-defined boundaries between Egyptian and foreign goods in the case of companies that were, in many ways, at once local and international, become clearer. At the same time, advertisements were not the only places where cassette players surfaced in the popular Egyptian press. As we will soon see, cassette technology also emerged in articles on persons of note, ranging from singers and actors to politicians and athletes, in weekly magazines. Together, these items contributed to the mass medium's increasing allure and arguably strengthened the acoustic commodity's commercial life by heightening its public profile.

ARTISTS, ATHLETES, AND THE ALLURE OF AUDIOTAPES

Accomplished Egyptians posed with cassette players on numerous occasions in print. Although they were by no means official spokesmen for the technology, as was the case with some celebrities who surfaced in select advertisements, these individuals' presence alongside cassette radios and amplifiers—at work and at home—undoubtedly enhanced the mass medium's visibility in the public eye. In so doing, these pictures not only evidenced the success of commercial ventures in selling cassette players to a mélange of middle- to upper-class citizens but also contributed to an "economy of desire" that found additional support in department store displays. Notably, in contrast to these captivating exhibits, which "pictured the desirable," in the words of the historian William Leach, photographs published in national magazines with mass readerships arguably advanced the appeal of commodities, like cassette technology, to an even greater extent. Such scenes circulated freely across Egypt's cities and villages and were not confined to any single storefront window or showroom.[49] In the spirit of unpacking the allure generated by these images, it is useful to begin with Egyptian musicians, who, unlike the vast majority of their compatriots, harnessed audiotapes for both professional proceedings and recreational purposes.

A number of Egypt's leading artists appeared alongside cassette players in the popular press. At times, the technology in these news items enabled entertainers to hone their craft. In a series of snapshots paying tribute to the late 'Abd al-Halim Hafiz (d. 1977), the singer sharpens his repertoire in the presence of a cassette radio on multiple occasions. In the first of two published photographs, the performer sits in a room, hard at work, with a poet, a distributor, and two composers. On a coffee table in the middle of the musical giants is a portable cassette player, which assists those present in perfecting 'Abd al-Halim's ballads before a live performance.[50] In a second picture, 'Abd al-Halim studiously stares at another cassette radio. This time, sitting alone, he holds a musical score in one hand and the machine's dials in the other. A recording of Muhammad 'Abd al-Wahhab's "Without Asking Why" ("Min Ghayr Layh"), a track 'Abd al-Halim scrutinized but never officially recorded, sounds from the device's speakers.[51] Joining 'Abd al-Halim were other artists who harnessed audiotapes to record their practice sessions and to reflect upon their productions. Egyptian readers, for instance, encountered 'Ali Isma'il, a composer known for his October War tunes, playing an upright piano beside a bulky cassette radio, and Ahmad Rami, a poet who penned songs for Umm Kulthum, listening intently to her voice on a smaller device in two other profiles.[52] Rounding out these images were pictures of other, iconic entertainers, like Farid al-Atrash, who simply stood by tape players in their lavish homes.[53] Together, these materials served as a form of free advertising for cassettes, which gained even greater visibility in reports on famous footballers from two of Egypt's biggest adversaries: *al-Ahly* and *al-Zamalek*.

Regardless of the colors one sported on the field, listening to cassettes off of it constituted a common pastime for a number of Egypt's star athletes. In a series of reports on the daily lives of professional footballers, writers for *Akhir Sa'a* ventured into the homes of several players. On more than one occasion, their popular hosts openly expressed a fondness of audiotapes. Mahmud al-Khatib, a center forward for *al-Ahly*, explained that tennis, billiards, and cassettes were his favorite hobbies. Among the tapes he most often played on his bedside radio were Umm Kulthum, 'Abd al-Wahhab, and the Arabic Music Troupe.[54] A rival footballer, meanwhile, 'Ali Khalil of *al-Zamalek*, similarly enjoyed tuning into tapes on a regular basis in his free time. A photograph of the striker's living room reveals an amplifier equipped with a cassette deck and an external speaker. To the machine's right, Khalil sorts through a stack of tapes, not unlike the pile that covered his opponent's nightstand.[55] In both of these cases, listening to cassettes, it seems, was mainly an individual activity. For others, however, a greater degree of sociality was involved. Khalil's teammate, Muhammad Salah, played tapes with his wife and their three-year-old son. According to the defender, his library exceeded 150 recordings and mostly consisted of Warda, 'Abd al-Halim, and Umm Kulthum.[56] Even in the event that athletes did not discuss their love of tapes at any length, cassette players still regularly surfaced in shots of them in their private homes.[57] These images, in turn, accompanied electronics advertisements that featured the likes of other famous footballers, such as Brazil's Pelé, in the Egyptian press, where they further enhanced the technology's public appeal.[58] In this regard, a third collection of pictures was no exception. Only this time, the subject was a head of state.

In the late 1970s, Faruq Ibrahim, one of Egypt's most illustrious photographers, set out to document a "day in the life" of Anwar Sadat for *Akhbar al-Yawm*, a widely read newspaper. The objective of what would become one of Ibrahim's most contentious shoots was simple: to depict the country's leader as an ordinary citizen. To this end, he snapped intimate pictures of the president swimming, shaving in his undergarments, and spending time with his grandchildren. A large cassette radio, requiring an electrical current to function, is visible in a number of the shots, including one of Sadat reading the morning paper in his pajamas in bed and another of the president with a paper and his pipe outside as "tranquil music" resonates from a nearby tape (fig. 7).[59] In a third scene, Egypt's first lady,

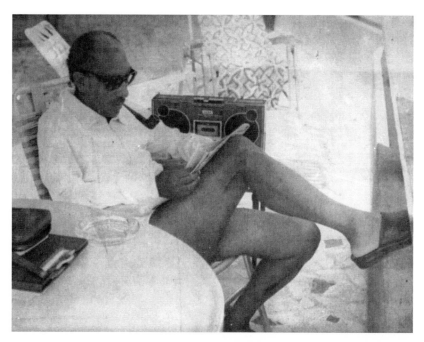

FIGURE 7. Sadat smokes, reads, and listens to "tranquil music" on a cassette player while outdoors. In Amir al-Zuhar, *Suwar wa Asrar min Hayat al-Kibar* (Cairo: Akbhar al-Yawm, 1997), 38.

Jehan, relaxes on a covered porch swing next to her husband with a smaller, battery-operated cassette radio in her hand.[60]

Applauded by some for normalizing Sadat and ridiculed by others for the very same reason, this set of images illustrates two important points. First, Faruq's film records how Egypt's president, like many other public figures, enjoyed listening to cassette recordings on a regular basis.[61] Second, the camera captures what Sadat (and his photographer) considered commonplace. After all, the president strove to momentarily shed his power and prestige and to appear as "one of the people" through Faruq's lens. In this sense, enjoying cassettes, it appears, was as ordinary as grooming or as routine as relaxing with one's family. It was an activity, in short, to which most Egyptians, from the president's predecessor to the common man, could relate.[62] In reality, of course, Sadat was no ordinary citizen, and his elite status as Egypt's ruler served only to magnify the already-hearty allure surrounding audiotape technology in the popular press.

Photographs of prominent public figures with cassette players in weekly periodicals served as a visual reminder of the technology's mass circulation across a certain collective of middle- to upper-class Egyptians in the 1970s and the 1980s. Whether used to advance one's career or, more often, to relax when one was not at work, cassette radios, recorders, and amplifiers in all these pictures converge to constitute a key appliance in the lives of prestigious people. Whether surfacing on a well-known actor's end table, a distinguished pilot's terrace, or a talented painter's bench, the medium's presence in these instances and countless others arguably maximized its allure among readers who often did not enjoy the same degree of fame, success, or financial security.[63] In an effort to capitalize on the appeal advanced by these images, while countering the idea that cassette players were solely an instrument of the elite, retailers endeavored to reach the widest consumer pool possible in Egypt. With this aim in mind, one of the strategies adopted by marketers targeted the Egyptian household and, more specifically, the "modern home," a space whose "modernity" derived not from its occupants but from its objects.

DOMESTICATING CASSETTE PLAYERS: MAKING THE HOME "MODERN"

As early as 1950, Ahmad Amin, a prominent Egyptian intellectual approaching the end of his life, observed how the physical characteristics of many homes in Egypt were changing. "Material civilization" (al-madaniyya al-maddiyya), the distraught man of letters declared in his autobiography, "has invaded the home" (ghazat al-bayt). "Electric light, radio, telephone, heating apparatuses, cooling appliances, and various sorts of furniture," Amin lamented, "were now present." While almost certainly enhancing a property's value, these additions, in the writer's eyes, did not necessarily increase a "home's happiness" (sa'adat al-bayt).[64] If the "invasion" of a select assortment of consumer goods into domestic spaces during the first half of the twentieth century disturbed Amin, there is little doubt he would have been even more unnerved with the influx of objects into homes a few decades after he had passed away. Over the course of the 1970s and the 1980s, manufacturers, marketers, and intermediaries displayed a wide array of commodities on the pages of the popular Egyptian press. One of the recurring themes in these public notices was the home, or, more precisely, the "modern home" (al-bayt al-'asri / al-bayt al-hadith), which served as an important canvas for a burgeoning consumer culture to make its mark.

Throughout the mid- to late twentieth century, material objects that many Egyptian consumers once considered indulgences increasingly came to be regarded as essentials. As one Ruz al-Yusuf reporter noted when profiling a successful import company in central Cairo at the outset of the *infitah*, several of the commodities procured by the business were "luxuries" (*kamaliyat*) that had since become "necessities" (*daruriyat*) under Sadat.[65] The owners of such enterprises found a useful ally in Egyptian magazines, where they marketed everything from electronics to kitchen appliances as being integral to the making of the "modern home." This discourse, notably, was part and parcel of broader efforts to locate consumer goods within the domestic sphere and to forge a more intimate relationship between households and a growing culture of consumption. To these ends, even advertisements that did not explicitly mention the "home" framed numerous items as "household objects." By regularly featuring cassette players in the same notices for washers, dryers, ovens, refrigerators, and vacuum cleaners, for instance, retailers depicted the technology as a domestic implement. Other announcements, meanwhile, further solidified the domestication of cassette players by presenting them as "gifts" for specific people. Such was the case with a message from the Company for Modern Fashion (Sharikat al-Azya' al-Haditha), a public-sector entity, which encouraged Egyptians to purchase fabrics, furniture, chandeliers, carpets, rugs, and cassette players for newlyweds, who, in many cases, would be furnishing a new home together.[66] At the same time, a number of advertisements did not simply allude to the home but directly cited the "modern home" as a destination for goods.

In the mid-1970s, Toshiba released a notice targeting consumers in Egypt and their compatriots in the Gulf. Colorful cassette players peppered the text, which listed what the company called "all the requirements of the modern home." Vacuum cleaners, electric heaters, meat grinders, television sets, fruit mixers, and fans were among the products available to customers through the corporation's agent in Saudi Arabia.[67] For those looking to "modernize" their private abodes from within Egypt's borders, other entities offered a solution. The same year Toshiba ran its ad, a far smaller enterprise operating in Cairo, the Rubi Organization for Trading (Mu'assasat Rubi lil-Tijara), circulated notices employing the banner "all that is required of the modern home." According to the business, these essentials included heaters, washers, refrigerators, gas cookers, children's toys, and radios. To assist readers in envisioning these objects in their residences, Rubi inserted photos of various items, including cassette players, in its announcements.[68] Not to be outdone by a local competitor, Omar Effendi, a public-sector entity with a wider reach, similarly called attention to "products necessary to the modern home" in advertisements that displayed everything from china sets to cassette radios.[69]

Based on a fourth text from Sednaoui, a family business nationalized under Nasser, the idea of the "modern home" continued to resonate with consumers for years to come. In 1988, Sednaoui showcased its furniture, clothing, carpets, dishes, cooking appliances, and electronics in a captivating notice. At the top of the publication, which featured several cassette players, the store proclaimed in big bold letters: "The happy marital home starts here. All the bride's needs and those of the modern home."[70] If material goods did not determine a home's "happiness" in Amin's eyes, they were essential to it in Sednaoui's advertisement. Thus, whether operating abroad or locally, in the public or private sector, multiple entities competed to make Egyptian homes "modern."

The exact shape of the "modern home," more often than not, was left to the imagination of citizens. This decision, on behalf of advertising teams, was almost certainly deliberate. It lent the impression that the modern home was accessible to the widest possible range of Egyptians, from those living in spacious villas who did not think twice about purchasing cassette players and other material objects to those residing in rooftop shacks who may have needed to take out a loan or accrue some savings in order to procure the very same things. What was less open to interpretation than the precise form of the modern home was what may be called the "materialization of modernity" in advertisements for items that were widely deemed as "essential" to Egyptian residences. In these announcements, modernity, like the products it accompanied, was a commodity that could be acquired with cash or credit cards in small shops or large retail outlets. As for the home, its modern nature originated not from its inhabitants but from the items contained by it.[71] In other words, what it meant to be modern in this particular historical circumstance had less to do with who one was and more with what one possessed.

Modernity, in short, was inextricably linked to consumer goods in notices distributed by major companies and minor intermediaries in the Egyptian press. In this regard, a remark made by the media studies scholar Stuart Ewen in a different historical context—American mass advertising in the 1920s—resonates with Egyptian advertising half a century later. "Only in the instance of an individual ad," Ewen states, "was consumption a question of *what to buy*." "In the broader context of a burgeoning consumer culture," he continues, "the foremost political imperative was *what to dream*."[72] For those who dreamed of being modern under Sadat and Mubarak, one way of doing so, businesses insisted, was to part with one's pounds to pick up cassette players and other objects.

While undoubtedly an important dimension of many advertisements, the modern home, of course, was not at the center of every notice for cassette technology. Commercial ventures adopted multiple strategies to sell cassette radios, recorders, and amplifiers to Egyptian consumers. At times, notices for cassette players detailed and extolled the technical attributes of specific machines, from the power of the speakers to the precision of the playback.[73] In other moments, documents framed particular devices as a "friend" or a "companion" to their owners, who could carry the machines with them wherever they went.[74] There were then attempts to situate the mass medium in a more local setting, with which most, if not all, Egyptians would be familiar. This tactic perhaps is most evident in the case of national holidays, with Ramadan, a holy month of fasting for Muslims, at the forefront.[75] National and its local Egyptian agent, for example, printed an announcement that prominently exhibited a crescent moon and encouraged prospective patrons to spend evening gatherings during Ramadan with the company's televisions and cassette radios.[76] Likewise, Telimisr, a public-sector entity, displayed a table denoting the times for praying and fasting, and instructed readers to "enjoy the magnificent month of Ramadan programs" with the same products.[77]

Despite some differences, all these advertising strategies shared a singular aim: to make cassette players desirable. But how successful were marketing campaigns when it came to audiotape technology? According to the president of Philips's Egypt operations, "the presence of cassette players and radios had become a common sight in every house" by the early 1980s.[78] Although most likely an exaggeration, the official's statement does speak to a growing desire among Egyptians to own cassette players at home, a phenomenon that other sources, such as contemporary ethnographies, appear to confirm.[79] Yet how did Egyptians use cassette players once they obtained them? This topic is addressed in much greater detail in subsequent chapters, which cover particular practices, people, and events of note, but, for the time being, photographs that have since migrated from private albums to garbage bags begin to provide some clues.

ORDINARY EGYPTIANS AND THE HIDDEN HISTORY OF LEISURE

As a number of scholars have recognized, many studies on photography in the Middle East tend to prioritize "Orientalist" pictures produced by outsiders, images Stephen Sheehi calls "'Othering' representations."[80] Recently, nuanced investigations of indigenous studios, actors, and photographic traditions across the region have begun to enrich and reorient this body of scholarship.[81] Nevertheless, historians of the Middle East continue to pay insufficient attention to vernacular photo albums, or those containing shots of daily life produced by ordinary people.[82] Drawing inspiration from the pioneering work of Lucie Ryzova on Egyptian "peer albums," which often recorded the leisure activities of single subjects, in the early to mid-twentieth century, the pages to follow consider a collection of amateur photographs from a few decades later.[83]

Unlike Ryzova's photos, the following snapshots did not surface in albums, seldom carry captions, and show men and women socializing together, lending the impression that they originated from family holdings. Like Ryzova's images, the pictures turned up at a distance from their original homes, eventually arriving at the Ezbekiya Wall (Sur al-Ezbekiya), a robust paper market above a metro stop in central Cairo. Once there, they migrated, yet again, into garbage bags, the first of which I encountered at one of the market's kiosks and the second across town at the Cairo International Book Fair, where Ezbekiya vendors temporarily relocated in 2016. In both instances, the photos circulated freely amid unrelated items, requiring me, when possible, to piece back together pages of the original albums. As we will see, these pictures are of value because they shed light on the interactions of ordinary Egyptians with audiotapes and the object's relationship to leisure, a topic that remains on the margins of Egypt's historical record.[84]

The first constellation of photos, spanning five shots in total, captures what appears to be an extended family's outing to one of Egypt's coastlines in the early to mid-1970s. The precise location of the day trip is difficult to determine, but the low-rise residential buildings bordering the beach in the background suggest that it may be Alexandria, a popular destination among Egyptians for swimming, sunbathing, and summering. Faint traces of an adhesive and a handwritten "8" on the back of the images indicate that they once belonged in an album, perhaps side by side on adjacent leaflets. In the shots, there are three distinct generations. Children relax, play in the sand, and enjoy lunch, while the adults, varying in age, mostly unwind in wooden chairs under the sun or in the shade of a parasol propped up behind them. In two of the photos, a mustachioed man, who has the air of a father figure, tans with a beverage in his hand and a cassette radio perched atop his lap (fig. 8). In a third scene, the same machine rests safely above a smaller seat intended for a young boy or girl, perhaps after being placed there by its owner to take either a group photo or a dip in the sea. Sand and the cassette player, clearly, were not to mix.

FIGURE 8. A cassette radio accompanies a man at the beach,
n.d. Photo in possession of the author.

Based on the device's design, the cassette player, in all likelihood, is a National
product and, more specifically, the RQ-435 DS, which was among the first compact
cassette radios to be advertised in the popular Egyptian press. With the end of 1971
on the horizon, the model appeared above a motorcycle saddle in an *Akhir Saʿa*
announcement, which opened with a question meant to underscore the player's
portability: "Why don't you take your friend [*nadimak*] with you wherever you
go?"[85] The vast mobility emphasized by the manufacturer—a common theme
in nationwide advertisements for audiotape technology—is confirmed in the
family's informal snapshots. The player, powered by six different batteries in lieu

of an electrical outlet, joins the anonymous group on their excursion to the shore. What remains more open to interpretation are the recorded sounds that imbued the everyday scenes preserved in the photos. From the cassette player's presence, however, it is safe to say that the seaside trip was certainly not a silent affair and that one did not need to personally own a cassette player to reap its benefits. The machines surfaced in public spaces—cafés, barber shops, beaches—and were shared among friends and family members, who enjoyed the technology in public and in private, at work and at play.

In a second cluster of photos, the varying encounters of ordinary Egyptians with cassette players in leisurely settings gain greater clarity. Two actors, a man and a woman, appear in most of the black-and-white shots, which, when read as a collage, reveal that the subjects are a young Coptic couple and likely the creators of a photo album that no longer exists. The collection of images, approaching nearly a dozen in total, document significant moments as well as daily occurrences in the duo's life together. A number of pictures, for instance, detail their wedding day. At various points during the big event, the bride gazes into a mirror in a lace, floor-length gown, watches the groom sign what seems to be a marriage certificate, slow dances with her new husband in the presence of their well-dressed guests, and looks out the rearview window of the getaway car after the ceremony draws to a close. A faded mark left behind by a red ink pen on the back of one of the photos indicates that the two became husband and wife in 1971.

There are then other images recording the pair's time with one another: the woman holding the wheel of a sleek sedan as her partner looks on in amusement, and the two embracing, perhaps on a date, in the back of a carriage driven by a man in a turban. In a final string of photos, the two make the most of a sunny afternoon with what seems to be another couple. As was the case with the beach outing, the precise setting is impossible to pinpoint, but the parties seem to be meeting on the balcony of a public establishment, such as a café, restaurant, hotel, or a combination of the three. Trees tower behind them, and cups of water, empty bottles of Coca-Cola, and handbags litter their table. A cassette radio, closely resembling the Philips 467, joins the objects in a group shot, and another image reveals that the device was not alone. A second radio, featuring a tape deck, surfaces behind the first machine. The exact purpose of having both mechanisms present is unknown, but their coexistence suggests that the couples may have been taking turns selecting the occasion's "soundtrack" or recording what the other player broadcast. In either event, cassettes added a layer of sound to what otherwise appears to be a serene gathering.

If the ability of cassette radios to both play and produce recordings was not entirely clear with regard to the balcony get-together, this capability is more on display in a final array of pictures revolving around an outdoor celebration. A few dozen photographs, likely from the late 1970s or early 1980s, cast some light on the party's details. In the colorful shots, which still bear traces of a paste that likely held them in place in a past album, a large crowd of men, women, and children enjoy an open-air buffet and sit around tables draped in decorative cloth as a musical ensemble, featuring an accordion, tambourine, bass, and electronic keyboard, plays on a stage. Although many different individuals appear at the event, a little girl in a white gown and her well-attired parents stand out above the rest. The mother holds, lifts, and escorts the child around the function, where multiple people greet her, while the father assists the youngster in cutting a three-tier cake nearly as tall as her. The family's status as important actors, however, is perhaps most evident in the case of their up-close encounters with the evening's singers, all of whom directly interact with the mom, dad, and daughter over the course of the joyous festivities.

Mahir al-ʿAttar, who starred in some films in the 1960s and frequently performed live in the 1970s, serenades and parades the girl before the band, while a young Ahmad ʿAdawiya, a popular (shaʿbi) performer whose celebrity was on the rise, and a more seasoned ʿAida al-Shaʿir, who had already collaborated with several famous composers, stand next to the family with microphones in hand. In addition to highlighting the event's guests of honor, the appearance of these artists and their supporting cast of instrumentalists shed light on a curious item atop the family's table: a cassette radio. The portable cassette player turns up in no fewer than five images. When al-ʿAttar leans in to give the little girl a kiss on her mother's lap, the camera captures the device a few feet away. When the girl's father cracks a smile in his two-piece suit, the mechanism emerges once more above the table. But why was a cassette player there in the first place? With well-known entertainers and a live band on-site, it is likely that the family utilized the tape player not to relay sounds but to record them. As the artists and guests approached their seats, the cassette radio, it seems, preserved the exchanges that ensued, creating a historical record of the celebration. Regardless of the exact content of these photographs, collectively, they serve as snapshots of cassette technology in action in Egypt, which will gain only greater clarity in the chapters to follow.

CASSETTE CULTURE AND MASS CONSUMPTION

In comparison to workers and work, consumers and consumption have traditionally received much less attention from historians of the modern Middle East. Indeed, in the case of Egypt, one need only consider any number of nuanced studies on unions, guilds, industries, and labor politics to begin to gain a sense of this scholarly imbalance.[86] Although such accounts are undoubtedly useful for unpacking questions of identity, nationalism, and class formation, among other subjects, they lend the impression that work constitutes an important area of academic inquiry while shopping does not.[87] More recently, some historians have begun to challenge this perception by critically exploring particular commodities, consumer practices, and commercial institutions in Egypt and across the greater Middle East, yet much work remains to be done.[88]

In this chapter, we placed mass consumption into direct conversation with cassette culture, elucidating their shared historical origins. Starting with a grainy photograph on Facebook, our journey took us from storeroom floors as far away as the Arabian Peninsula to recreational haunts in Egypt. By unpacking the commercial life of a single everyday technology, the advent of Egypt's cassette culture and changing economic landscape under Anwar Sadat and, later, Husni Mubarak, came into greater view. To date, historians have tended to approach this dynamic terrain, Egypt's economic opening, and its consequences through numerical outcomes, state policies, and failed programs.[89] By painting a more grounded, panoramic picture of Egyptian society through the lens of an expanding consumer culture, as it was experienced by elite and ordinary citizens, a different historical account of the *infitah* and its top-down economic and political dimensions emerges.

Indeed, as we witnessed, the manufacturing and marketing, circulation and acquisition, use and enjoyment of cassette players provided productive avenues for making sense of broader historical developments. These changes ranged from the material impact of migrant workers and the fashioning of the modern home to the allure generated by companies and celebrities around certain commodities and the recreational activities undertaken by ordinary individuals whose lives remain largely a mystery. Collectively, these interconnected topics shed valuable light on the dawn of Egypt's cassette culture and the creation of a wider culture of consumption, as well as on the making of modern Egypt in the mid- to late twentieth century. At the same time, this story of mass consumption, cassette culture, and their intertwined origins remains incomplete. To fully comprehend the advent of audiotape technology and the consumer culture of which it was a part in Egypt, we must consider both the outward appearance and the inner dynamics of Egypt's changing economic terrain, in which consumers and customs agents, thieves and travelers, marketers and manufacturers, smugglers and store owners, all played an active part.

Chapter 2

DESIRING

Theft, Smuggling, and the Limits of the Law

IN EGYPT, PORTABILITY WAS A CENTRAL DIMENSION OF CASSETTE technology's public profile. In the popular press, companies regularly spotlighted the small medium's vast mobility. Compact, lightweight, and battery operated, cassette players, they stressed, were not restricted to any single setting. Nowhere is this point more apparent than in advertisements. In one such notice from 1971, National presents one of its newest cassette radios atop a motorcycle in a grassy field. A caption accompanying the image informs prospective customers that the enterprise has "a moveable friend to introduce to everyone who relishes music."[1] Like the vehicle upon which it is perched, the cassette radio could join its owner on any journey and, with it in hand, people could enjoy their favorite music "anytime, anywhere." Multiple power sources made this possible. Six batteries ensured the device's boundless reach, and an optional cable allowed for charging it in a car. As was the case with older radios that didn't have tape decks, the cassette player also could be plugged into an electrical outlet at home, but it was not beholden to Egypt's partial power grid.[2] Perhaps one of the first entities to underline the "friendship" afforded by cassette players in Egypt, National was one among many ventures to emphasize the technology's great mobility.[3]

In this regard, manufacturers were not alone. Outside of advertisements, still other materials in Egypt underscore the ease with which cassette players traveled. On the colorful cover of one issue of *Sabah al-Khayr*, a weekly magazine, a man and a woman enjoy a picnic on the grass outdoors.[4] Judging from the sailboats in the background, the outing's likely location is somewhere along the Nile. Behind the pair stands a bright red motorcycle, and a cassette radio rests on the ground between them. Once again demonstrating the ability of cassette players to wander widely with their users, the scene recalls the advertisement from National six years earlier. In one cartoon a man known as a *misaharati* walks the streets to wake up fasting Egyptians for *suhur*, the predawn meal during Ramadan.[5] In the *Ruz al-Yusuf* drawing, however, he performs this task not with his voice, as was commonplace, but with a cassette recording of it, courtesy of the tape player in his hand. The cartoon's title, "Misaharati Modern," captures the humorous transformation of this traditional practice. In a similar vein as this sketch, a comic published in Cairo further illustrates cassette players moving with their operators wherever they went. On the item's cover, Mickey Mouse holds a blaring boom box by his head as he rocks out with Goofy on the go.[6] The exact nature of these materials aside, mobility, clearly, was a key feature of cassette players, and the medium's portability made it all the more desirable for Egyptian consumers. At the same time, though, cassette technology did not always move in the ways companies advertised, illustrators depicted, and its inventor envisioned.

In an effort to further unpack the making of Egypt's cassette culture, this chapter focuses on two central threads in the criminal biography of cassette technology in the 1970s and 1980s. Beginning with theft, I illuminate the disappearance of cassette players from cars, stores, and homes, all of which experienced notable developments in the mid- to late twentieth century. Through a counterreading of "popular crime reports," I argue that security success stories staging the falls of criminals in the press actually reveal a robust black market for cassette devices. After engaging this commercial space, which proved difficult to police and that adds a layer of complexity to the burgeoning consumer culture introduced in chapter 1, I pivot to a second practice that bolstered it and contributed to a broader economy of desire. Specifically, I explore how citizens from different walks of life wielded and flouted the law to smuggle cassette players across Egypt's borders. The suspect passage of cassette technology radically reorients drug-centric accounts of smuggling in the Middle East and calls attention to the questionable transit of many consumer goods under Anwar Sadat.[7] In the process of considering what theft and smuggling offer to the interconnected histories of cassette technology and consumer culture in Egypt, the pages to follow ultimately shed greater light on the origins of Egypt's cassette culture and elaborate on the technology's commercial life in relation to the law and its limits.

STEALING CASSETTE PLAYERS

Two of Egypt's leading weekly magazines, *Ruz al-Yusuf* and *Akhir Sa'a*, documented the theft of cassette players throughout the mid- to late twentieth century. The majority of the investigative reports to appear therein did not concern the victims of thefts but the perpetrators responsible for organizing and executing crimes. In the case of *Ruz al-Yusuf*, multiple journalists recorded the theft of coveted technologies. The stories they penned splashed across the pages of "People and Crime," "The Crime of the Week," and weekly news updates. As for *Akhir Sa'a*, a single reporter, Ra'fat Butrus, usually covered the swiping of cassette players and other movable appliances. Like the articles of his peers at *Ruz al-Yusuf*, Butrus's writings were not restricted to any single part of the competing publication. Regardless of the author, section, or magazine, these investigative pieces, or "popular crime reports," generally followed a standard template: people broke the law, security officials caught them, and those under arrest often confessed to their crimes. Popular crime reports, in this sense, were success stories for the security sector: they reveal less about how policing worked in practice than about how the police wished to be perceived by the public.

Our discussion of cassette players in the context of the law and its limits begins with a close treatment of three popular crime reports published in the "Crime of the Week" sections of *Akhir Sa'a* and *Ruz al-Yusuf* between 1979 and 1981. During this time, it was arguably all the more important to promote the competency of the police in Egypt in light of then-recent historical developments, from the 1977 bread riots, which Egypt's president notoriously referred to as a "thieves' uprising," to rising Islamic militancy, which led a matter of months later to the kidnapping and killing of a former government minister by radical Islamists posing as policemen.[8] In the course of traversing cars, stores, and homes, the case studies in this chapter offer a rich glimpse into not only the theft of cassette players but also their presence, popularity, and circulation across greater Cairo during the final years of Sadat's presidency. These examples also illuminate the ways that journalists staged the security sector's triumphs over thieves in the press, while a counterreading of the very same narratives casts light on a key dimension of cassette technology's commercial life and Egypt's consumer culture: the black market.

EGYPT'S AUTO BOOM: CARS, CASSETTE STEREOS, AND A CHICKEN VENDOR

In the midst of the oil boom, Egypt experienced another surge in the 1970s. It was during this decade that automobile ownership reached new heights.[9] Once the possession of a privileged few, private passenger cars fell within the reach of far more people.[10] According to one estimate, the number of private cars in Egypt rose from 108,222 in 1970 to 283,959 in 1979, only to soar further still to 684,187 by 1985.[11] Registered cars in Cairo, alone, reportedly tripled between 1977 and 1984.[12] As one journalist observed in the mid-1970s, black-and-white taxis competed for "every inch of roadway" with the latest foreign imports, from Mercedes to Peugeot, potent symbols of status in Cairo's streets.[13] The auto boom altered Egypt's landscape as well as its soundscape. In urban centers, traffic jams became increasingly commonplace and the noises of horns honking an inseparable part of daily life.[14] There were then the sounds generated by cassette stereos, which afforded Egyptians unprecedented control over the acoustics of their commutes. Often played at high volumes, cassette recordings either delighted or disturbed those within earshot.[15] With more people behind the wheel than ever before, the need for auto parts, too, increased, inspiring a vast market for them.[16] A coveted commodity from the perspective of motorists, cassette players in cars also drew the attention of thieves, who contributed to that marketplace.

One such thief who had the great misfortune of appearing in print was Khalaf Ahmad Husayn, a twenty-two-year old who handled poultry at his uncle's shop in Cairo's well-to-do district of Misr al-Jadida. For the services Khalaf rendered to his relative, he earned, on average, E£7 per day. To supplement his income, he allegedly followed in the less-than-legal footsteps of his eight siblings, who, with the exception of two brothers, excelled in the art of taking what was not theirs. With no parents present to guide him—Khalaf's father had passed away a few years earlier and his mother lived abroad in Kuwait—the young man began to steal cassette players from cars in northeastern Cairo. He committed his crimes at an impressive rate, an average of two thefts per week, in the areas of Misr al-Jadida, al-Zaytun, and Hada'iq al-Qubba. By the time the police apprehended him in January 1981, he had broken into forty vehicles. Were it not for the reportedly diligent efforts of Detective 'Abd al-Hayy Isma'il, Lieutenant Colonel Sa'id al-'Abbar,

Colonel Hafiz Shafiq, and Brigadier General ʿAbbas al-ʿAsi, who worked together to bring Khalaf to justice, the young man's crime spree, we are told, would likely have continued for some time.

Unlike some of his fellow car thieves, Khalaf did not steal cassette stereos for his own enjoyment. His goals were strictly monetary. He sold the devices he removed from vehicles to a man from ʿAbbasiyya who operated an electronics shop in the orbit of his thefts. In exchange for every cassette player, the vendor paid Khalaf up to E£40, nearly a week's worth of wages at his uncle's shop. Once acquiring the devices, the shop owner resold the merchandise to his customers for a profit. Ultimately, this lucrative enterprise came to an end with Khalaf's arrest, but not before the store owner managed to traffic a percentage of the stolen cassette stereos to his relatives in the northern province of Kafr al-Shaykh, more than one hundred kilometers away from Cairo. When the police arrived at the electronics shop, eleven cassette players remained on-site, all of which the officers promptly transferred to the precinct in Wayli. With the cassette devices recovered and the security sector's success all but cemented in *Ruz al-Yusuf*, Faiza Saʿd concluded her "Crime of the Week" column on a triumphant note. "The cassette thief has fallen into the hands of the police," she proclaimed, "now you can rest assured about the stereos in your cars."[17] Perhaps unsurprisingly, this conclusion would prove presumptuous. Reporters for *Ruz al-Yusuf* and *Akhir Saʿa* continued to publicize the theft of cassette players and cassette tapes from cars across Cairo throughout the 1980s and into the 1990s.[18] For the moment, however, one less thief was on the loose.

Saʿd's report on Khalaf's capture begins to reveal some of the ways journalists staged the successes of the security sector in the state-controlled Egyptian press. The column opens with an account of the young man's life and a description of his criminal activities to grab the reader's attention. After an attempt to captivate its audience, the story then shifts from Khalaf to those who put an end to his illegal undertakings. The author cites these authorities by name and their corresponding ranks reveal a clear chain of command and the importance assigned by officials to catching a lowly car thief. The efforts of all parties involved in Khalaf's arrest, Saʿd emphasizes, were tireless and resulted in a seamlessly executed operation. Accenting this thoughtfully constructed narrative was a black-and-white carica-ture. The drawing, presumably of Khalaf, shows a downtrodden boy behind bars with only a chicken and a cassette stereo to keep him company. Driving home the security sector's success, this calculated sketch was replaced by equally measured photographs in still other crime reports that similarly staged the triumph of the law over local criminals, who targeted not only private passenger cars but also public commercial spaces.

SACRIFICE AND SHOPPING: STORES, CASSETTE RADIOS, AND A GRINNING OFFICER

At the start of 1972, Egypt's newly appointed prime minister Dr. ʿAziz Sidky announced a decree prohibiting the import of several items. Among the consumer goods included in the ban were refrigerators, washing machines, television sets, and radios.[19] Such an action was necessary, Sidky maintained, to mobilize Egypt and its economy for the "total confrontation" to come with Israel, which, as a result of the 1967 war, had gained control of the Sinai, territory Egypt wished to recover. Although this declaration may seem exceptional at first glance, it was actually part and parcel of broader public appeals, in which political authorities demanded discipline, devotion, and sacrifice from citizens, calling on Egyptians to change everything from their spending habits to their values for the conflict that awaited. Contemporary slogans, like "Everything for the Battle" and "No Voice Louder Than the Battle," echoed and encapsulated these aims. In the fall of 1973, the battle arrived. Egyptian soldiers crossed the Suez Canal, breaching Israeli fortifications on the other side, and Sadat secured a political victory in a surprise attack that culminated in a stalemate. After the October War, Sadat announced the *infitah*, Egypt's economic opening, in the "October Paper," and years of imposed austerity made consumer goods all the more desirable in an Egypt no longer on the cusp of combat. Boutiques multiplied, imported commodities spread, and shopping simultaneously satisfied material longings and sparked debate on mass consumption and its discontents. Amid these developments, cassette radios surfaced in more and more stores, captivating customers as well as criminals who sought to capitalize on the new technology.

One group to appear on the pages of *Akhir Saʿa* used stolen cars to carry out a series of heists in Cairo. Led by a man called "Sukkar" (Sugar), the motley crew targeted stores to alleviate the financial woes of its members. The leader of the pack sought to secure a better life for his newly born daughter, and his assistants, "Zaqzuq" (Chirper), a full-time thug, and Ahmad, a former student, required money to marry their fiancées. The final member of the four-person team, "Naʿnaʿ" (Mint), a cab driver, needed cash to find a new home for his family following their forced eviction from a building the state had declared unsafe to inhabit. Division

of labor maximized the gang's profits. Ahmad kept watch for the authorities, Na'na'
drove the getaway car, and Zaqzuq, along with Sukkar, broke into stores under the
cover of darkness. By perfecting this system, the squad successfully ransacked
seventy-six stores over the course of twenty-five days in 1979. The estimated value
of the items they seized was in the ballpark of E£500,000 and among the more
notable goods they snatched were cassette radios. After acquiring the devices, the
men sold them directly to customers whose eagerness to purchase the increasingly
popular technology may very well have exceeded their interest in learning how
the suppliers obtained it in the first place.

The hard work of numerous officials eventually led to the arrest of Sukkar
and his men. Building on the preliminary findings of Major General Tharwat
'Atallah, who was among the first to discern a pattern underlying a string of unsolved thefts, Brigadier General 'Abd al-Hamid Mansur, Colonel 'Abbas al-'Asi, and
Lieutenant Colonel Muhammed 'Abd al-Nabi met to discuss which steps should
be taken to curtail the crime wave. By the end of their secret session, the officers
selected 'Abd al-Nabi to oversee a store theft unit. Shortly thereafter, Majors Nabil
Salih, Muhammed Anwar, and Muhammad 'Ala' increased their neighborhood
patrols. One of the contingents spotted Sukkar and his men breaking into a store in
Misr al-Jadida. After foiling the heist and detaining the group, authorities moved
the stolen goods, along with the gang, to the office of 'Abd al-Nabi. In a black-and-
white photo accompanying Ra'fat Butrus's article on the arrests, the triumphant
official grins in the midst of the somber-faced criminals. Three cassette radios
rest atop his desk while three other devices appear alongside an array of small
television sets in the right hand corner of the frame. The caption reminds the
report's audience that "this photograph is not of a big trading store" but of 'Abd
al-Nabi's workspace.[20]

The image accompanying Butrus's publication brilliantly frames the victory
of the law for all to see. In the shot, officers openly bask in the recent arrests as
thieves anxiously await their fates. The stolen objects, now recovered and deliberately placed, face the camera and fill the room. Meticulously scripted, the
picture, like the narrative supported by it, served to publicly extol the security
sector and its triumphs. In a similar fashion as Sa'd's column, Butrus's report
reads like a detective novel. It begins with a discussion of the gang's members,
motives, and activities. Building up to the group's downfall, Butrus mentions no
fewer than seven different officers and calls attention to a covert meeting. Why
this session took place in "secret" is unclear, but its clandestine nature was likely

intended to intrigue the article's audience. The plan that emerged from this assembly was swiftly implemented and quickly achieved its desired result: the capture of Sukkar's crew. This outcome, Butrus concludes, was possible only because of the tireless work of officials who effectively cooperated, skillfully communicated, and formed a potent vanguard against crime, which extended beyond Egypt's streets and commercial enterprises to private residences.

THE "MODERN HOME": APPLIANCES, CASSETTE PLAYERS, AND FUNNY FORENSICS

Throughout the 1970s and 1980s, the making of the "modern home" in Egypt enjoyed an intimate relationship with the advertisement and acquisition of durable consumer goods. Electrical appliances, in particular, were the subject of many household expenditures. Here, one need only consider contemporary ethnographies, which begin to bring the accumulation of sought-after items into bright relief, even among Egypt's less affluent members. In a bottom-up account of Cairo's poor, Unni Wikan acknowledges a noticeable increase in the purchase of "prestigious consumer goods" between 1969 and 1982.[21] By the end of this period, nine families she had followed for years owned television sets, something only three enjoyed at the start of the stretch, while eight of them possessed washing machines, seven gas stoves, and six cassette players, all objects they were without nearly a decade earlier.[22] In these regards, Wikan's subjects were not alone. In a second study of low-income families in greater Cairo, Homa Hoodfar documents similar material desires and patterns of consumption. In a perceptive survey of popular electrical goods in the mid-1980s, she records the presence of television sets in fifty-five of fifty-nine households, with washing machines in fifty-three and cassette players in forty-four.[23] In the vast majority of cases, families had acquired these coveted consumer durables only over the previous decade. Collectively, modern technologies reshaped homes across the socioeconomic spectrum in Egypt, inspiring pride, envy, and criticism along the way, and contributed to a higher level of material well-being. Enjoyed by those within the home, some of these objects also stirred the interest of outsiders.

Nearly two years after the fall of Sukkar and his men, Wafiq Fayid, a father of two, orchestrated three hundred robberies across Cairo and Giza. Born into a middle-class family, Wafiq, Ra'fat Butrus relays in another popular crime report, learned how to steal at an early age. After his mother passed away, Wafiq's father remarried and started a new life by leaving his son behind in a juvenile center. There, Wafiq acquired the tools that would allow him to later elude law enforcement for six long years, during which he single-handedly stole an estimated E£2,000,000 worth of cash, jewelry, and electronics, including quite a few cassette players. Wafiq obtained these items not from stores, as was the case with Sukkar's gang, but from the homes of foreigners and Egyptians. The only shred of evidence he left behind at the scenes of his crimes was a single fingerprint. Rather than leading investigators to the thief, this forensic clue threw them further off his trail. The print's size led experts to believe it belonged to an adolescent. To make matters worse, officials were unable to track the items Wafiq stole, objects he distributed to four merchants, one of whom ultimately played a part in bringing an end to his illustrious career.

With no suspect in sight for the crimes Wafiq committed, the police caught a break when a citizen filed a report against a man who swindled him out of E£110,000. In following up on the complaint, authorities apprehended a suspect after a lengthy pursuit beginning by the Giza Pyramids and ending in the downtown district of Doqqi. During the interrogation that ensued, officers noticed the existence of an extra digit on each of the man's hands in their custody. Intrigued by this anomaly, they crosschecked the sixth fingerprint against existing ones in their records and found a match. The middle-aged man in front of them was none other than the mistaken "young thief" behind a rash of unsolved robberies. Well aware that his additional digits were smaller than his other fingers, Wafiq had deliberately chosen which fingerprints to leave behind during his heists. In the words of Butrus, he "utilized this genetic defect to commit his crimes."[24] Ultimately, Wafiq's arrest, we are told, would not have been possible without the "around-the-clock" efforts of detectives, police officers, forensic experts, government representatives, and members of the secret police (*mukhabarat*). To celebrate this success, officials went so far as to invite journalists to a special event to learn more about the man behind the home break-ins. It is unknown whether Butrus attended this gathering, but it is beyond any doubt that the security sector scored yet another public victory with the publication of his sensational report on the six-fingered thief.

In a number of ways, Butrus's article on Wafiq's capture recalls elements of his earlier column on Sukkar's circle. The journalist invites readers to learn about the criminal's rough childhood, transformation into a thief, and the campaigns he led prior to recounting the daunting obstacles officers overcame to apprehend him. Wafiq's arrest, Butrus underscores, was due to the attentiveness of security

FIGURE 9. Wafiq poses with the things he stole. In Ra'fat Butrus, "Lughz 'al-Basma' al-Sadisa Wara' Akbar 'Amaliyat Nasb," *Akhir Sa'a*, no. 2409 (24 December 1980): 60.

officials. Agents spotted his extra fingers and only then decided to run the digits in their system. The station's well-oiled database, in turn, revealed the robber's true identity. Once in custody, Wafiq appeared in print with some of the objects he took from people's homes.

In one photograph, Wafiq juggles handfuls of jewelry and a bundle of cash (fig. 9). His smirk lends the impression that officials caught him in the middle of a theft, but a pair of handcuffs, dangling from one of his wrists, tells another story. Upon closer inspection, officials likely fastened and then unlocked Wafiq's restraints to allow him to pose with the items in hand in the attention-grabbing shot, which would not have been possible with the shackles secured. In a second, equally curated image, Wafiq points to the electronics he stole in what appears to be a warehouse. Several cassette radios sit atop television sets while others rest haphazardly on a shelf below. On the basis of this arrangement, authorities, it seems, sought to showcase some of the appliances they found. Wafiq's "candid" pose, meanwhile, assumes that of a guide, but was likely in response to an officer's command. Much like their subject, who choreographed his robberies by leaving behind a single print, both pictures rely on staging to convey the success of the security sector in bringing a criminal to justice. Butrus's report, accordingly, reduces a master framer to a mere prop.

STAGING SUCCESS: FROM POPULAR CRIME REPORTS TO POLICE EXHIBITIONS

The idea of staging was central to popular crime reports. The authors behind these investigative pieces, unlike the officers responsible for police dispatches, wrote with the masses in mind. The resulting publications were not intended for the eyes of a few or destined to collect dust in the file cabinets of police precincts. Sensational entries in *Ruz al-Yusuf, Akhir Sa'a*, and other leading magazines regularly reached thousands of Egyptians on a weekly basis and endeavored to accomplish two objectives. On the one hand, they informed citizens of the demise of "dangerous" thieves, which served to evidence the success of the government's war on crime. On the other hand, the reports also entertained those who perused them by framing the triumphs of law enforcement in a way that showered state authorities with praise and made for enjoyable reading.

The criminals profiled by journalists did not subscribe to a single mold of which Egyptian readers could grow tired. Bakers and barbers, businessmen and cab drivers, the unemployed and lackluster students, all broke the law in the popular press. No matter one's standing as a "home-grown son" (*ibn al-balad*), a "son of the aristocracy" (*ibn al-dhawat*), or anywhere in between, all sorts of offenders ended up in police custody, behind bars, and on the pages of state-controlled magazines.[25] The stories of criminals to appear in print were engaging. A state employee who robbed homes with his mistress, youths who transported stolen electronics under loaves of bread atop their bicycles, and a young girl who lured drivers off the road and into ambushes with her feminine wiles, all made headlines. Rhetorical flourishes drew readers in further to already gripping narratives. Writers, for instance, often cited the comical nicknames of criminals. "The Senator" led a crew of white-collar thieves; Muhammad "Peugeot" stole French cars by the same name on interprovincial highways; and Hassan "Mazika" (Hassan Music) enjoyed spending time at discotheques when he was not targeting Mercedes, known as *al-zalamukat*, or the behinds of ducks, due to their shape.[26] Together, all of these narrative elements played a part in producing reports that simultaneously educated and entertained those who came into contact with them.

Regardless of the differences among thieves and the crimes they committed, the law always prevailed in popular crime reports. To dramatize the successes of the security sector, writers employed several strategies. For one, they stressed that the task of catching criminals was not an easy one by citing officials who openly voiced their frustrations with cases. One of the more common hurdles identified by authorities in the press was the lack of leads for tracing electronics that vanished from cars, stores, and homes. Far from highlighting the inadequacies of those in charge of upholding the law, the tactical acknowledgment of such obstacles made eventual arrests appear all the more impressive. At the foundation of every security operation in print was excellent communication. On paper, investigators, beat cops, forensic experts, the secret police, and senior government officials labored together as a close-knit team. Far from miraculous, this flawless cooperation was commonplace. The hard work of individuals underwrote the teamwork. Reporters stressed the diligence of particular actors and noted the names of those who deserved the public's praise. Staged photographs accompanying articles further solidified the achievements of industrious agents and the state they served. Images illustrated not only what thieves stole but also the scope of what officials recovered and, when possible, returned to the rightful owners. At times, the careful staging of popular crime reports translated to other arenas off the printed page.

On an annual basis, the Central Police Headquarters in Cairo organized events to showcase the items officers seized from thieves. The estimated value of the objects at the 1987 exhibition exceeded E£3,000,000 and originated from the caches of fifteen criminal networks. Among the more abundant devices on display were electrical appliances. Visitors were free to browse these items in a hall housing no less than thirty television sets, thirty videocassette players, and fifty cassette stereos. In an effort to publicize this event, President Mubarak's interior minister, General Zaki Badr, encouraged all Egyptians to stop by the exhibition in one of Butrus's columns in *Akhir Sa'a*.[27] No less surprising than the reporter's coverage of this occasion was the minister's call to attend it. There were few better ways to showcase the government's triumphs over thieves than a public spectacle highlighting the missteps of criminals and the brilliance of those who caught them. On many fronts, popular crime reports served as more powerful reminders of the security sector's successes than the annual expositions at Cairo police headquarters. On a weekly basis, articles detailing the falls of thieves circulated throughout Egypt, where citizens learned of the latest arrests without ever setting foot in a police precinct. The very same records that glorify law enforcement, however, also illuminate another aspect of Egypt's cassette culture that proved difficult to police.

THE MAKING OF A BLACK MARKET

While exposés on failed criminals in the popular Egyptian press aimed to publi-cize the successes of the security sector, they also reveal the presence of a thriv-ing black market for cassette technology. One of the phenomena that sustained this arena was theft. When it came to the unlawful movement of cassette players in Egypt thieves played a prominent part, and the passage of pocketed machines became apparent only with their sensational demises in print. The circulation of stolen cassette players, as we have seen, assumed different forms. Khalaf, the poultry vendor, sold cassette stereos he stripped from cars to the owner of a local electronics shop, while Sukkar and his crew supplied customers direct-ly with the cassette radios they seized from stores and Wafīq distributed the devices he snatched from people's homes to multiple merchants. Joining these offenders were still other Egyptians. Muhammad Hasanayn, who hailed from an upper-class background, followed in the footsteps of Sukkar's gang and swiped cassette radios from shops, while a "Muʿalim ʿArabi," the owner of a bakery, sold stolen electronics, procured by his employees, at unbeatable prices.[28] When wo-ven together, these seemingly disparate incidents begin to reveal a more vivid mosaic of a coveted technology in motion. At the center of this arrangement is a commercial landscape whose existence demonstrates not the triumph of the law but its limits.

The black market for cassette players in Egypt was neither limited to a single location nor did it necessarily take the shape of outwardly illegal enterprises. Customers at the ʿAbbasiyya electronics shop, for instance, may very well have been unable to differentiate the cassette stereos Khalaf stole from nearby cars from those that store owners imported from Sony, Toshiba, and other international companies. Likewise, the patrons of Wafīq's merchants may not have known the cassette radios on display came not directly from factory floors as far away as Ja-pan but from people's homes across Cairo. Even in the cases of Sukkar, Muhammad Hasanayn, and Muʿalim ʿArabi, consumers may have been under the impression that they were purchasing cassette players from official vendors. The quantity of stolen merchandise in each man's possession, as photographs in magazines made clear, rivaled, and maybe even exceeded, that on the shelves of licensed shops. Then again, perhaps, consumers cared more about the price of a cassette player than its origins. Black market retailers did not mind discounting devices they acquired for free or purchased for a fraction of the going cost. If prices influenced where individuals shopped, they also played a role in prompting people to steal cassette players in Egypt to sell in the first place.

The cost of cassette players, at least initially, exceeded that of their predecessor, transistor radios. In the months following Nasser's death in 1970, Sadat's administration lowered the prices on "essential" goods.[29] Along with the costs of tea, kerosene, batteries, shoes, sugar, compact refrigerators, and winter clothing, the price of another item, which seemed noticeably less "essential," also fell. Four companies reduced the cost of transistor radios.[30] Discounts ranged from 12 percent to 22 percent and multiple models became available for between E£7 and E£11, sums cassette players would soon surpass.[31] At the end of 1975, Philips announced an exciting new line of products in Egypt. Shortly, it proclaimed, consumers would be able to purchase a portable cassette radio for approximately E£60 and a car cassette stereo for E£65.[32] Accompanying these items was a pocket transistor radio for E£4.5.[33] Cassette players were clearly more expensive than transistor radios early on. This relatively higher price tag, however, did not necessarily diminish the new technology's demand. The longevity of cassette players, a durable good that lasted for years, often made them a more justifiable, onetime expense, while the cost of cassette tapes was minimal. Various mechanisms, meanwhile, from stores selling goods on credit to savings clubs pooling resources, enabled even the less fortunate to fulfill material desires.[34] In these regards, the price and popularity of cassette players contributed to their theft and fueled a dynamic black market.

During the 1970s and 1980s, black markets were far from a rarity in Egypt. Reports on the illegal sale of cigarettes, cement, and basic foodstuffs, to consider only a few commodities, frequently graced the pages of the popular press, where "black market traders" surfaced in no shortage of illustrations critical of their undertakings.[35] At the same time, thieves were not the only ones who contributed to black markets and the suspect circulation of cassette players and other consumer goods. Smugglers, too, took advantage of portable cassette technology, and their activities, which proved all the more difficult to police, add another important dimension to the development of Egypt's cassette culture and the broader culture of consumption surrounding it.

TRAVELERS, CUSTOMS, AND CONTRABAND

In the summer of 1985, a student by the name of Samia 'Ali completed her doctoral degree in the United States and returned home to Egypt, eager to serve her country. Upon arriving in the airport in Cairo on a flight from New York City, 'Ali was instructed by customs agents to empty her three suitcases. She complied, and officials proceeded to meticulously examine the contents of her bags, paying particular attention to every article of clothing, which they inspected "piece by piece." To the traveler's horror, state employees paraded her belongings in front of their colleagues, who mocked, gossiped, and laughed about 'Ali's personal effects. If these "inhumane inspections" do not cease, she warned in a letter to the editors of *Ruz al-Yusuf*, citizens may very well consider immigrating to another country that places a higher premium on people's dignity.[36]

Unsurprisingly, a response from the letter's addressee, Salah Hamid, Egypt's minister of finance, was not forthcoming. However, the president of the customs department, Ahmad Bassyuni, did reply, albeit belatedly, to the recent returnee. Seven weeks after 'Ali penned her pointed complaint, Bassyuni maintained that customs officers inspected her luggage in "a peaceful manner" that lasted only a "few minutes" and was accompanied by "friendly dialogue."[37] Following this routine examination, he reports, 'Ali willingly paid the fees she incurred and that the agents kindly reduced for her sake. Customs employees, in short, were innocent of any wrongdoing, and 'Ali, the high-ranking official concluded, needed to revisit the ins and outs of traveling.

'Ali was neither the first nor the last to censure customs officials in Egypt. As early as the summer of 1971, Muhga 'Uthman had leveled a similar critique on the pages of the same periodical. Travelers, she decried, "suffer from complicated charges and an archaic system that doesn't suit the spirit of the time" (*tabi'at al-'asr*).[38] At the center of this system were customs officers, who searched more bags than national regulations stipulated and assessed charges on everything from refrigerators to pet canaries. The outdated system berated by 'Uthman at the beginning of the 1970s continued to be the target of ridicule two decades later. On the eve of Iraq's invasion of Kuwait in 1990, journalists continued to call attention to the poor experiences of their compatriots with customs. The Egyptian returning to his homeland, 'Isam 'Abd al-'Aziz and 'Isam Abu Haram exclaimed, "feels his bags have turned into a 'disaster' that drains his money."[39] As was the case with 'Ali and 'Uthman, both writers urged customs officers to welcome travelers with open arms.

The image of the overbearing customs agent found fertile ground in cartoons throughout the 1970s and 1980s. It was during those two decades that traveling abroad became less of a luxury for a select few and more of a viable undertaking for an increasing number of Egyptians. Hundreds of thousands of citizens ventured to Libya and, later, to Iraq, Jordan, and the Gulf in search of work, while others boarded buses, ships, and planes to vacation, study abroad, visit relatives, and perform the annual Muslim pilgrimage to Saudi Arabia. In many illustrations, circulating widely in the popular press and adopting colloquial Egyptian Arabic for satirical ends, customs officials brazenly invade the personal space of Egyptians in transit.

One such sketch, for instance, shows an older man standing nervously in his briefs, arms spread to his sides, as an officer rummages through his two-piece suit. "I need to confirm," the inspector explains, "you don't have any refrigerators with you."[40] The fact the official is looking not for one but multiple refrigerators on the traveler's person makes the scene all the more absurd. In a second drawing, a middle-aged man appears at his father's doorstep completely naked. Tears cascade down his cheeks as he wails: "They customed me [gamrakuni] at the airport, Dad!"[41] To fully convey the man's agony, an entirely new Arabic verb is needed. In both cases, authorities strip commuters to ensure they are not attempting to smuggle anything into Egypt.

While customs agents often forced men to shed their clothes in cartoons, they demanded to know what women were hiding underneath them. On more than one occasion, officials interrogate pregnant travelers about the nature of their protruding bellies.[42] The rigor with which these authorities allegedly performed their jobs takes on an added degree of intensity in still other illustrations. Agents accuse an obese man of smuggling food, confiscate the head of another due to his "imported ideas," and order a third to produce an import permit for his foreign wife.[43] In one sketch, an off-duty officer even commands his beloved to open her handbag.[44] Together, all of these writings and drawings cultivate the image of the "all-seeing" customs official. Nothing, these materials lead us to believe, made it past overeager men and women stationed in major points of transit like Cairo's airport, Port Sa'id's free zone, and Alexandria's harbor. As we will soon see, however, the reported thoroughness of customs agents did not prevent people from smuggling a wide array of objects, including cassette players, across Egypt's borders in the mid- to late twentieth century.

SMUGGLING IN SADAT'S EGYPT

Despite the attentiveness of customs agents and the establishment of anti-smuggling offices, local authorities struggled to stem the illicit passage of consumer goods into Egypt during Sadat's presidency. Throughout the 1970s, movies, clothing, birth control, kitchenware, car parts, and currency crossed Egypt's borders alongside cement, blenders, sewing machines, transistor radios, television sets, and cassette players. Those responsible for the transnational movement of these everyday items did not subscribe to a single mold. Men and women, young and old, urban and rural, wealthy and working class—all traveled with material things that turned up in homes, businesses, and on the black market. Notably, the entrance of these goods was not always illegal.

A number of Egyptians creatively employed the law to import foreign products. Others, meanwhile, simply did not declare the things they transported. A critical reading of the state-controlled press offers a window onto these activities. Weekly magazines with mass readerships regularly reported on smuggling in articles spanning multiple pages. At times, editorials assumed the form of success stories that resembled "popular crime reports." Customs agents, in these triumphant narratives, caught criminals red-handed. The heroics of officials, however, received no more attention than the complex dynamic between imports and the law. Loopholes, writers routinely lamented, enabled Egyptians from all walks of life to legally smuggle countless goods.

On the day of Nasser's death, 28 September 1970, one Egyptian journalist went so far as to declare that "the game of smuggling has become a popular sport."[45] One of the major players in this game was the "suitcase trader" (*tajir al-shanta*), who took advantage of looser restrictions on imports, as a result of the *infitah*, to cross into Egypt with large quantities of consumer goods. In August 1974, the minister of foreign trade, Fathi al-Matbuli, issued a resolution known as "number 286." The decree permitted any Egyptian citizen to import up to E£5,000 worth of foreign goods. One of the unforeseen consequences of this measure, which was intended to satisfy the needs of local consumers, was the growth of suitcase smuggling, a practice that did not begin with the economic opening but certainly benefited from one of its policies. Suitcase traders, ranging from students to street sellers, outwitted customs officials in a number of ways. Some chose to mail items to Egypt, capitalizing on the lower fees for objects arriving by post than for those transported in person.[46] Others, favoring a more hands on approach, ventured abroad and returned with things to sell in cities and villages.[47] Still others, once becoming established, employed men and women to travel on their behalf. In return for all-expenses-paid trips to ports around the Mediterranean and the Red Sea, "suitcase carriers" (*himal al-shanta*) retrieved crates, boxes, and bags from cargo-laden piers.[48] Upon arriving in Egypt by boat, car, and plane, they surrendered their "personal items" to handlers, who sold them for a small fortune. Regardless of one's approach, suitcase smugglers legally imported a wide variety of consumer goods.

Joining suitcase traders and carriers were other smugglers who utilized the law to outmaneuver authorities. Egyptians working in the tourism industry played an important part in the suspect movement of materials during Sadat's tenure. Starting in 1973, a new regulation enabled parties to avoid customs fees on supplies destined for the tourism sector.[49] The main objective of the decree was to generate (foreign) investment in one of the mainstays of the national economy. As was the case with al-Matbuli's resolution, Law No. 1 inadvertently provided Egyptians with a second avenue to smuggle goods. Hotel owners, in adherence with the law, applied for import permits from the Ministry of Tourism. As a part of their application, they submitted lists of objects, including everything from furniture to flatware, to be used in their establishments. Not every item requested by applicants ended up where they proposed. Once clearing customs, a percentage of goods entered the marketplace. Here, the case of cement is particularly telling. Cement, a central component of any construction project, reportedly fetched E£60 per ton on the black market in the spring of 1977, four times its official value at the time.[50] This significant discrepancy was due, in part, to businessmen selling the cement intended for hotels. Although it is impossible to gauge the exact number of people exploiting the tourism law to smuggle goods, one task force reported twenty-five violators across eighty projects in the final months of 1980 alone.[51] Those caught by officials paid double the customs fees on what they requested, while others who illegally retailed what they legally imported made a sizable profit.

Of course, not every smuggler utilized the law to import consumer goods. In fact, many simply broke it by concealing what they carried over national borders. Egyptians from across the socioeconomic spectrum masked electronics, clothing, and food, among many other things, to use, sell, and distribute as gifts in Egypt. The failures of citizens to transport objects occasionally resulted in headlines, while the missteps of officials in blocking the illicit passage of consumer goods did not surface in print. As was the case with popular crime reports documenting the falls of thieves for all to see, stories in weekly magazines publicly showcased the triumphs of law enforcement over smugglers. Lists of what authorities confiscated evidenced not only the number of items that people tried to smuggle but also the ability of customs officers to protect national industries from the perceived "onslaught" of foreign products. With the aim of gaining a glimpse into this third form of smuggling, let's shift to the illegal movement of cassette players in a city synonymous with smuggling, foreign imports, and mass consumption in Egypt: Port Saʿid.

PORT SAʿID, CASSETTE PLAYERS, AND THE *INFITAH*

After a decade of discussions, delayed by three wars (1967, 1969–1970, 1973), Port Saʿid officially became a free trade zone under Sadat's watch in 1976. In the years to follow, the city and its free zone came to embody a successful emblem of *infitah* economics at work and a glaring example of consumption gone awry. The paradoxical position occupied by Port Saʿid in national discourse played out in the popular Egyptian press, where politicians, journalists, illustrators, and ordinary citizens contemplated a common question: was the "free city" a success?

One article appearing in *Ruz al-Yusuf* two months prior to Sadat's assassination on 6 October 1981 captures some facets of this debate. In the piece, Asma Rashid interviews Ismaʿil Ghanim, a financial official who firmly believes Port Saʿid succeeded in becoming a "free city." According to Ghanim, jobs abounded, opportunities to profit were plentiful, and residents enjoyed a higher standard of living as a result of the free zone. In light of these advancements, discussions, Ghanim declares, were under way for establishing other such free zones along the Suez Canal. After acknowledging these alleged improvements, Rashid proceeds to discredit the official's claims "from the inside." She travels to the free zone, interviews ordinary people, and visits businesses. The voices of a housewife who lives in a home without carpets, a bus driver who bemoans the transformation of every shop into a boutique, and a factory owner who employs few workers all support the reporter's rebuttal: Port Saʿid's free zone failed to deliver on its promise and was not a model to be exported to Alexandria, Ismaʿiliyya, or anywhere else in Egypt.[52] Whether lauding the free zone as a success or censuring its meager contributions to the national economy, parties still found common ground on one issue: smuggling was a serious problem in Port Saʿid.

The Egyptian press rarely published an article on Port Saʿid without mentioning smuggling. One journalist, ʿAbd al-Sattar al-Tawila, went so far as to argue that the city's free zone failed to benefit Egypt in any way but succeeded in producing new forms of smuggling. Traders, he maintained, doctored receipts to defy import restrictions, lied about the origins of products to pay lower fees, employed young boys to transport goods beyond city limits, and bypassed customs altogether by moving merchandise from boats to cars under the cover of darkness.[53] The link being made between smuggling and Port Saʿid, to be certain, was not limited to print media. The same year al-Tawila published his exposé, ʿAli Badrakhan produced *The People at the Top* (*Ahl al-Qimma*, 1981; see chapter 1).[54] The film, based on a Naguib Mahfouz story, revolves around four characters. A former thief, Zaʿtar al-Nuri, works as a smuggler for Zaghlul Rafit, the manager of a fraudulent import-export firm. He retrieves foreign goods from the docks in Port Saʿid and sets up a shop near the Citadel in Cairo. No longer struggling to make a living, Zaʿtar pursues Siham, the niece of Muhammad Fawzi, a policeman who does not approve of their relationship. On one occasion, Muhammad decides to pay Zaʿtar a visit. He passes by tables covered with clothes and cassette players in *Suq al-Libya* until he finds the right boutique. Color televisions, electric fans, and cassette radios line the shop's walls. When Muhammad asks Zaʿtar if smuggling played a part in his newfound fortune, the store owner accredits his affluence to Egypt's economic opening.

Unlike the cassette radios gracing the shelves of Zaʿtar's store in Cairo, a number of cassette players did not make it past customs in Port Saʿid. According to Major ʿArafa ʿAli ʿAmr, a high-ranking administrator in the city's security sector, electronics, and especially cassette players, were at the center of "most smuggling cases."[55] Although it is impossible to determine the precise number of cassette players that were passing through Port Saʿid illegally at any given time, crime reports published over the course of nine months begin to elucidate the technology's secret circulation during Sadat's rule. Starting in July 1978, customs officials made two big busts. At the center of the first was the driver of a tractor trailer who struck a deal with smugglers to transport E£50,000 worth of goods. With the help of a young boy, agents retrieved a sewing machine, thirteen cassette radios, and hundreds of articles of clothing from spare tires inside of the truck's storage tank. Around the same time, officials discovered thirty-three cassette radios, two mixers, and numerous pieces of fabric in a second vehicle. The items came to light after the car's owner tried to bribe an officer with E£600.[56] Less than a year later, in February 1979, agents confiscated even more cassette players. Operating on a child's advice, they found forty cassette devices and dinnerware sets buried under produce in the back of a lorry. Then, in the course of inspecting multiple cars, they seized six hundred cassette players and four hundred gowns worth an estimated E£200,000.[57] According to the incident report, smugglers carefully concealed the consumer goods in customized gas tanks, but inspectors still discovered them with ease.

Articles calling attention to smuggling in Port Saʿid often served a greater purpose. Crime reports showcased the triumphs of the city's customs officers. Honest, diligent, and approachable, the agents appearing in print rejected considerable bribes, conducted meticulous searches, and acted on the advice of good Samaritans. The challenges faced by authorities, we are told, were immense. To convey the gravity of smuggling, journalists regularly cited the number of things officials confiscated. "Numbers alone," one writer claimed in September 1978, "can give you a correct picture of Port Saʿid." On these grounds, he lists what authorities impounded: twenty tons of fabric, eighteen thousand articles of clothing, and three hundred forty cassette players.[58] The time frame for the seizures is neither clear nor relevant; the figures are intended to shock.

Despite the ambiguity surrounding this data and the overt agenda of crime reporters, the mention of cassette players evidences the technology's presence, popularity, and movement at the hands of smugglers. At the same time, if the popular press illuminated the successes of officials in stemming the illegal passage of cassette technology, it also alluded to, albeit unintentionally, the machines that made it past customs. Here, one need only remember the case of the child informant. If the boy had not reached out to customs agents, dozens of cassette players would have entered Egypt. In the grand scheme of smuggling, this number may seem insignificant, but it takes on far greater weight if one considers all the times when trucks carrying contraband cleared customs or when travelers concealed cassette radios inside of their suitcases that went undetected. But where did cassette players and other consumer goods end up once eluding officers on Egypt's borders? To begin to consider one destination, we'll make our way from Port Saʿid to Cairo.

SMUGGLERS, SHOPPERS, AND SHAWARBI STREET

In *L'Égypte aujourd'hui* (1977), the prolific travel writer Jean Hureau describes a typical day in the life of Cairenes. He observes couples holding hands, friends hanging out, and locals taking little notice of foreigners on the capital's crowded streets. Downtown, he records how "department stores and beautiful boutiques filled with treasures from overseas" draw crowds. Many Egyptians browse the latest imports, and others purchase things after rounds of bargaining. Much of this activity, the guidebook informs its audience, takes place "between Tahrir Square, Ramses Street, and Opera Square" where "the windows are bursting with goods."[59]

At the center of this retail geography was a street Hureau never mentions by name, Shari'a al-Shawarbi, one of the most popular destinations for smuggled items in modern Egypt.[60] Strategically located in the heart of Cairo's commercial district, Shawarbi connected two major thoroughfares for downtown shoppers: Qasr al-Nil and 'Abd al-Khaliq Tharwat. Dozens of banks, airlines, and travel agencies surrounded it. Restaurants, cafés, and bars similarly abounded nearby. L'Américaine, Estoril, and Excelsior on Tal'at Harb; Grillon, Groppi, and Lappas on Qasr al-Nil; and Liban, Chez Riche, and Sofar on Shari'a 'Adly were all within walking distance of the road.[61] Shawarbi's proximity to these places, in addition to its short distance from the Bab al-Luq railway station, the American University in Cairo, the Central Post Office, the Ezbekiya Gardens, and several different cinemas, yielded no shortage of foot traffic.[62] Like al-Muski, Khan al-Khalili, and other commercial nodes in Egypt's capital, Shawarbi was well known for what it carried. On any given day, Egyptian consumers could expect to find imported blouses, nightgowns, shirts, shoes, and suit jackets, irons, kitchenware, cigarettes, cologne, and cassette radios in windows overlooking opposite sidewalks. What set Shawarbi Street apart from other local and national markets, however, was not only what it offered but how things ended up there.

As was the case with Port Sa'id, Shawarbi routinely surfaced in discussions concerning consumer culture and its perceived ills in Egypt. The street, local commentators repeatedly avowed, was a haven for smuggled goods, illegal dealings, and deceitful businessmen. In these regards, an article from none other than Ra'fat Butrus, the author of numerous crime reports in *Akhir Sa'a*, is representative of Shawarbi's standard portrayal in the popular press. Butrus introduces the street as a "bustling market for all that is forbidden, prohibited, and illegal."[63] How well known was the road? Its fame, he contended in February 1976, surpassed the Champs-Élysées in Paris and Piccadilly Market in London. The recent success of Shawarbi's boutiques was due in no small part to smuggling. Not too long ago, Shawarbi, we are told, housed only a few vendors specializing in old furniture. As time passed, however, shops on the once "abandoned" street began to stock and display imported wares. Like the products smuggled by its store owners, the journalist maintains, the attire, speech, and behavior of Shawarbi's traders were foreign.

According to Butrus, the street's merchants spoke immodestly, sported long hair, and blasted "obscene" music, most likely from tapes, which continued to sound and sell on Shawarbi for decades to come.[64] To import as many goods as possible, these individuals reportedly traveled abroad as suitcase traders, employed suitcase carriers, and struck deals with everyone from flight attendants to foreign embassy employees, who used their privileged positions to illegally transport goods behind the backs of customs officers. Writing in the aftermath of a politician's beating in one of Shawarbi's shops, Butrus may have overstated the breadth of the street's criminal network to stir support for a future campaign against its retailers. It is unlikely diplomats, for instance, would have jeopardized their careers by shuttling contraband to Egyptian merchants. What is beyond any doubt, though, is the close relationship between Shawarbi and smuggling.

Reporters, like Butrus, did not enjoy a monopoly on Shawarbi's maladies. Illustrators, fashionistas, and foreign diplomats, to name only a few actors, also contributed to the road's shady biography.[65] Cartoonists ridiculed the market's products, vendors, and clientele. In a two-page spread from 1976, a husband accuses his pregnant wife of buying birth control on the street and a woman claims she became acquainted with a muscle-bound man in order to visit its shops. A third drawing compares the dynamic between Shawarbi's merchants and customers to that of a cart driver whipping his blindfolded mule.[66] Still other sketches focus on the topic of smuggling.

One cartoon, from 1977, highlights the suspect movement of consumer goods from Cairo's airport to Shawarbi's boutiques. Set in a duty-free market, it shows a crowd of commuters listening to a loudspeaker. The announcement alerts "distinguished smugglers" of the imminent departure of "trip #2560" to Shawarbi street.[67] Following suit, Madiha, a well-known fashion columnist in Egypt, illuminated Shawarbi's dark side in her weekly articles. She exposed the street's deceitful dealers, counterfeit clothes, and smuggled wares, and she demanded to know why the Egyptian government allowed the market's "mafia" to operate.[68] A source of comic relief and calls to action in the Egyptian press, Shawarbi's connection with smuggling was so well established that even foreign service officers acknowledged it in their reports. In the course of covering the first major demonstration in Cairo following Sadat's announcement of the *infitah*, a David Gladstone in the British embassy recorded the damage done to downtown shops on 1 January 1975. Particularly hard hit was Shawarbi, "whose trendy boutiques," the official explained to his counterparts in England, "sell expensive imported (mainly smuggled) clothes to Cairo's rich."[69] Shawarbi's smuggled goods, in short, were a matter of both public knowledge and private record.

CONSUMER CULTURE AND CASSETTE ENCOUNTERS

On 9 April 1973, the battle between lawbreakers and those who desired to suppress them in Egypt took center stage on the front cover of *Ruz al-Yusuf* (fig. 10).[70] In a colorful drawing, Ahmad Higazi, a well-known illustrator, stages soldiers, peasants, workers, intellectuals, and the Egyptians masses on one side of the weekly magazine, and positions smugglers, exploiters, bribe-takers, and black market traders on the other.[71] President Sadat, representing "the new ministry," stands in a suit between both groups. He menaces the wrongdoers with his cane, speaks in the name of the Egyptian people, and succeeds in separating the relatively small number of villains from the vast majority of upstanding citizens, who flock behind him and form a powerful alliance.

Outside of the Egyptian press, the ability of local authorities to easily identify lawbreakers and isolate them from the larger populace was less straightforward than this *Ruz al-Yusuf* cover suggests. As we saw in the case of cassette players, theft and smuggling posed significant challenges to the security sector and contributed to a vibrant black market that proved difficult to police, while numerous citizens smuggled consumer goods across Egypt's national borders and purchased sought-after items from black market merchants. At the center of these everyday occurrences, which energized a broader economy of desire, was cassette technology, whose criminal biography calls attention not only to the triumphs of the law but also to its limits.

Prized for its portability, cassette players did not always move in expected ways. By further unpacking the social life of cassette technology in this chapter, a more nuanced picture of the medium's presence and popularity, as well as the expanding culture of consumption of which it was a part, takes shape. Theft and smuggling redirect our attention from those engaged in the manufacturing and marketing of cassette players to those involved in their acquisition and circulation. The result is a more panoramic account of cassette players specifically and consumer goods more generally, and of those who came into contact with them, whether in cars, commercial ventures, private residences, or anywhere in between. In venturing beyond advertisements and showroom floors to major points of motion, from Cairo's streets to Port Sa'id's free zone to Alexandria's coastline, cassette players in action also gain greater clarity. This change of scenery inspires no shortage of questions for future explorations of consumer culture, the law, and its limits. Perhaps most important, though, in unpacking the making of Egypt's

FIGURE 10. Sadat stands between wrongdoers and upstanding Egyptians. In Ahmad Higazi, "Hadhihi al-Harb al-Qadhira!," *Ruz al-Yusuf*, no. 2339 (9 April 1973): 1.

cassette culture in greater detail, two of the many collisions between cassette users and local authorities come into view.

With the origins of Egypt's cassette culture firmly established, the four chapters to follow navigate a series of encounters between cassette operators and public figures. As we will see, these interactions were by no means limited to theft and smuggling. Egyptian gatekeepers collided with cassette tapes, cassette players, and their diverse users in multiple contexts. Singers and listeners, for instance, piqued the interest and the ire of their fellow compatriots, who attributed the perceived "pollution" of public taste to select cassette recordings and endeavored to prevent the "illegal" replication of audio content, which traveled easily from tape to tape. Although the exact nature of these exchanges varies, they share a single foundation. Audiotape technology and its operators decentralized state-controlled Egyptian media well before the dawn of satellite television and the internet. In so doing, cassette users generated significant debates over class, politics, and cultural production. In the interest of unpacking another chapter in Egypt's recent past and the complex dynamic between public figures and cassette technology, let's turn to the creation of Egyptian culture and the making of Egypt's "vulgar soundscape."

Part II

MAKING SENSE OF A MEDIUM

The Social Life of Audiocassette Technology

Chapter 3

CENSURING

Tapes, Taste, and the Creation of Egyptian Culture

ON 16 FEBRUARY 2020, THE MUSICIANS SYNDICATE, AN ENTITY RE-sponsible for licensing artists in Egypt, outlawed the public performance of *mahraganat*. A do-it-yourself musical genre, *mahraganat*, or "festivals" in Arabic, emerged from urban, working-class neighborhoods to resound in taxis, cafés, clubs, and hotels across Egypt after the Arab Spring. Its artists sing about everyday issues in colloquial Egyptian Arabic, the language of daily life, and utilize the internet to reach a wider audience beyond local weddings, where many first made a name for themselves in the streets. The *mahraganat* ban followed a Valentine's Day concert in Cairo Stadium featuring Hassan Shakosh, a popular singer, who performed his hit song "The Neighbor's Daughter" ("Bint al-Giran"), which includes a line about drinking alcohol and smoking hashish in the event of a heartbreak. Subsequent attacks on the genre, however, were not limited to Shakosh or this track. Hany Shaker, the head of the Musicians Syndicate, censured *mahraganat* as a whole, contending it "threatened public taste"; Mohamed 'Atiyya, the undersecretary of the Ministry of Education, prohibited it in schools on the grounds of combating vulgarity; and Salah Hasballah, a member of the Egyptian parliament, claimed that *mahraganat* posed a greater danger than coronavirus to Egyptian society.[1] Although certainly striking, the nature of these critiques is by no means new.

During the 1970s and the 1980s, commentaries abounded in the Egyptian press on the downfall of music, the end of high culture, and the death of taste. Writers cited select developments in the cultural arena to support consistently dire assessments. State-controlled radio, once the major producer of "refined" songs, was releasing fewer and fewer musical numbers, while a number of state-sanctioned performers passed away.[2] To make matters worse, Egypt lost one of its premier sites for creating and consuming high national culture. The Cairo Opera House, built by Khedive Isma'il in 1869, was reduced to embers in a matter of hours in 1971. The venue's doors did not open again, elsewhere in Cairo, until 1988.[3] Finally, the very style of songs was evolving. Long ballads, once in vogue, increasingly lost ground to shorter tunes. Egypt's soundscape, in short, was changing and many writers did not approve of the new direction in which it was heading. It was in this transitory climate that audiotapes carrying content cultural gatekeepers considered questionable, most notably *sha'bi* (popular) music, became public enemy number one for a wide range of critics who held the everyday technology accountable for poisoning public taste.[4]

Artists, scholars, and censors, journalists, politicians, and physicians, all attacked cassette recordings in Egypt, where the mass medium, they maintained, played an integral role in molding the taste of countless citizens. At first glance, audiotapes deemed to be "trivial" (*tafih*), "absurd" (*sakhif*), or, most often, "vulgar" (*habit*), on account of their "unrefined" material, troubled critics on several fronts, starting with the technology's immense circulation. Cassettes carrying "cheap words" easily spread from Siwa to the Sinai. Moreover, like its reach, the audience of audiotapes was enormous. The sounds transmitted by cassettes were intelligible to millions of citizens, regardless of their educational background.[5] Last, the technology's affordability expanded its already-sizable influence. The low cost of cassettes enabled many listeners to purchase them with ease. At the same time, all of these concerns were overshadowed by two, more central anxieties.

First, from the perspective of many local observers, audiotapes empowered anyone to become an artist, resulting in the diffusion of suspect voices that degraded the ears, the morals, and the taste of Egyptians. The individuals popularized by cassettes, critics maintained, did not deserve to be heard. Rather than enriching listeners, their presence polluted Egypt's soundscape and led to complete disarray in the domain of cultural production. Second, cassettes permitted an unprecedented number of ordinary Egyptians, empowered by Anwar Sadat's economic opening, to become cultural producers. Blue-collar workers, among others with little to no background in the arts, opened cassette labels that allegedly inundated listeners with "crass" recordings. Driven to profit at all costs, these "unqualified" individuals, the narrative goes, commercialized Egyptian culture and corrupted their compatriots' aesthetic judgment. In the process of unpacking these debates and developments in this chapter, we will consider how a cultural history of Egypt's economic opening may shed new light on the crossroads of class, culture, and politics.

Our discussion opens with the intriguing dynamic between cassette technology and noise pollution in the final decades of the twentieth century, when Egyptian critics faulted "vulgar" audiotapes exclusively for contaminating Egypt's soundscape. After covering the clamor that only certain cassette recordings reportedly unleashed, I turn to the commotion generated by "vulgar" tapes in public forums, where local commentators blamed working-class Egyptians for destroying public taste. Next, I shift to the greater cultural context in which these debates unfolded by scrutinizing how state officials strove to fashion "cultured" citizens at a time when cassette technology and its users complicated their control over cultural production. In the second half of the chapter, I survey some of the content on cassettes. Starting with a popular *sha'bi* singer synonymous with "tasteless" tapes, I explore the career of Ahmad 'Adawiya before analyzing the efforts of Sawt al-Qahira, a state-controlled label, to elevate the taste of all Egyptians through "refined" cassettes. I conclude by addressing the fluidity of vulgarity as a historical concept. In elucidating Egypt's "vulgar soundscape," I show how the anxiety inspired by cassettes and their operators did not simply concern aesthetic sensibilities but entailed nothing less than a struggle over what constituted Egyptian culture and who had the right to create it.

NOISE, CASSETTE RECORDINGS, AND THE POLITICS OF POLLUTION

Approaching the end of his rule, Anwar Sadat issued a series of decrees intended to curtail traffic and to combat noise pollution in Cairo. The ordinances, which officially went into effect on 8 November 1980 and remained a topic of conversation for weeks to come, outlawed the use of car horns and criminalized "blaring loudspeakers, televisions at high volumes and impromptu tape cassette sidewalk concerts."[6] Courtesy of the president's executive actions, audiocassettes, enjoyed loudly by many Egyptians in public spaces, were no longer simply a nuisance.

Noisy cassette recordings were now illegal. Sadat, to be certain, was not the only citizen to stress the part played by tapes in the alleged contamination of Egypt's soundscape. The unwanted clamor generated by cassettes is readily evident in Egyptian magazines from the 1970s and the 1980s.

On the pages of the popular Egyptian press, we see a bandaged and beaten-down beggar praising a cassette's capacity to record his street calls.[7] No longer was it necessary for him to accost passersby for cash: the customized recording did it for him. In another scene, we witness a man smoking a water pipe in a working-class café where a cassette tape, most likely playing the latest *sha'bi* singer, blasts behind him.[8] In between puffs and in search of peace, he demands that the strident recording be replaced with a cassette containing nothing from his hand. There is then a drawing of two pedestrians passing by a cassette shop where "vulgar songs" ring out from a curbside counter (fig. 11).[9] The cartoon's caption, "Singers, Our Heads Are Killing Us," is a line from a poem penned by Bayram al-Tunsi some four decades earlier.[10] Originally directed at overly sentimental singers, the phrase, in this later instance, addresses inferior "artists" whose "meaningless" words make listeners ill. Significantly, in all these cases, only certain audiotapes pollute Egypt's soundscape. Cassettes carrying "vulgar" content make a racket, while those relaying "refined" material never seem to be too loud.[11] If "tasteful" tapes quietly captivated listeners, "trivial" cassettes appeared to penetrate, invade, and damage the ears of Egyptians.

The noise unleashed by "vulgar" cassettes alone piqued the interest of not only illustrators, who mocked and mirrored prevailing discussions, but also researchers, artists, politicians, doctors, and security officials, who ostensibly strove to protect the hearing of their compatriots by pushing for certain sounds to be silenced. As early as 1978, one writer, a Ragab al-Sayyid, highlighted the dangers posed by particular cassettes to Egypt's acoustic environment and those who inhabited it. Drawing on his background as an expert at the Institute of Seas and Fisheries in Alexandria, he argued that Egypt's soundscape, like its waters, could be polluted. To support this claim, he cited a 1977 book by R. Murray Schafer, *The Tuning of the World*, a seminal text in the field of sound studies that treated noise pollution as a cause for public concern.[12]

Although al-Sayyid touches upon several sources of noise in his treatise, he arguably reserves his harshest words for *sha'bi* cassette ballads and those who blasted them. On the final pages of his booklet, he singles out two types of working-class Egyptians—the "manual laborer" and the "modest seller"—who used

FIGURE 11. "Singers, our heads are killing us." In "Ziyadat Intishar al-Aghani al-Habita." *Ruz al-Yusuf*, no. 2860 (4 April 1983): 61.

cassette players to blare their "favorite *sha'bi* singers at the highest possible volume" around the clock. To make matters worse, the extensive mobility of audiotapes, al-Sayyid points out, permitted this "clamorous music," widely ridiculed for
its "vulgar" nature, to travel from stores and street corners to crowded buses and
private residences.[13] The reach of these cassette tapes was seemingly infinite and
the damage they caused to Egypt's soundscape, the author concludes, demanded
everyone's immediate attention.

The connection drawn by al-Sayyid between noise pollution and particular cassettes was both deliberate and commonplace. At times, the subject even
ascended to the highest corridors of power. In 1988, for example, Egypt's Upper
House of Parliament convened to address the problem of pollution. During the
session, one of the council's members inquired about the steps they could take to

"purify Egypt of the pollution in the world of singing."[14] In response to this question, which no doubt alluded to cassettes carrying *sha'bi* music, Muhammad 'Abd al-Wahhab, a fellow delegate, promised to take immediate action. Shortly after the gathering concluded, the elite artist reached out to other licensed musicians to attend to the pressing issue. At other times, the tumult induced by certain tapes caught the attention of medical professionals and security personnel. In one column published in 1986, an ear and nose doctor compared *sha'bi* cassette songs blasting in taxis to "military marches" and alerted readers to the "slow death" of people's ears in Cairo, while the director of security in the neighboring city of Giza claimed that "the chaos of voices and the chaos of tools with which to disturb" harmed both the hearing and the taste of Egyptian citizens.[15]

Whether broached in parliament or in print, the need to protect Egypt's environment and the ears of its residents offered many actors what may have seemed to be a valid reason for cracking down on noisy cassette recordings. In reality, however, those engaged in these discussions were arguably less concerned with the pollution of Egypt's soundscape than they were with the perceived contamination of Egyptian culture. Having addressed the noise reportedly produced by "vulgar" cassette tapes in practice, let's consider the commotion they caused in public forums, where no shortage of critics faulted ordinary Egyptians for poisoning public taste.

IMPOSTER ARTISTS, UNQUALIFIED PRODUCERS, AND THE COMMERCIALIZATION OF CULTURE

In the summer of 1980, *Akhir Sa'a*, an illustrated magazine, published a letter purportedly from a citizen residing in the northeastern province of Isma'ili-yya. The author of the angry missive, Ibrahim Ahmad 'Ali, directed readers to a disturbing phenomenon he witnessed on a regular basis. Audiotapes carrying "meaningless words" were assailing the ears, minds, and taste of listeners around the clock. The vulgar recordings, 'Ali asserted, offended all Egyptians, and those behind them were nothing more than "art imposter clowns" whose productions should be silenced and who "pocketed a pretty penny" from leaving listeners in a state of "unconsciousness."[16] Although it is difficult to determine whether ordinary people felt compelled to pen letters like 'Ali's message, or if those working for state-controlled periodicals assumed false identities to level their critiques, it is clear that cassettes Egyptians found to be "vulgar" elicited strong reactions. At the center of these critiques were two important figures—the "imposter artist" and the "unqualified producer"—both of whom profited from the alleged corruption of public taste and commercialized Egyptian culture.

Audiocassettes, in the opinion of many critics, facilitated the spread of "vulgar" sounds by making it possible for anyone to be an "artist" regardless of his or her training. In enabling any citizen to become a cultural producer, as opposed to a mere cultural consumer, cassettes, they claimed, lowered artistic standards and tarnished public taste. Consider, for instance, one writer's journey into the world of "trivial" recordings. During the summer of 1981, Osama al-Mansi, a cultural critic, recounts how a village girl strolled into a cassette store in downtown Cairo. There, he reports, she swayed and sang "naïve" (sadhij) words as the young man accompanying her strummed a few harsh chords on the oud. Although the performance was horrendous, the singer nevertheless received a five-year contract. Soon, her crass cassettes, like those of countless other unknown "artists," would be available to the masses, whose "artistic standards and taste," the journalist warns, would inevitably suffer from the terrible tapes.[17]

The anonymous voice ridiculed by the reporter was not extraordinary. In fact, she was one among many Egyptians who joined the ranks of artists courtesy of cassettes. As one Arab singer confessed in the 1980s: "I expected to hear refined songs in Egypt but I found something else entirely. I was struck by the astonishing number of singers and songs that constantly arose." "Everyone who enjoys his voice sings," she elaborated, "and issues a collection of new songs every two months."[18] By empowering "everyone" to become a performer, cassette technology, critics repeatedly claimed, bred only "chaos" and elevated voices that did not deserve to be broadcast.

In the Egyptian press, commentators went to considerable lengths to distinguish between cassette stars and past entertainers. Artists predating audiotapes appeared to be masters of their craft, "refined" musicians who carefully rehearsed lyrics that conveyed an important message. The voices popularized by many cassettes, in contrast, were mere pretenders, "uncultured" amateurs who created countless tracks without meaning. Whereas one enriched and enraptured Egyptians, the other inspired migraines and harmed public taste. As one citizen, who may well have been an editor, explained in a letter to Akhir Sa'a, prior to the proliferation of cassette recorders, artists meticulously chose the words to their songs and the scores to which they were set. As a result of this diligence, their works penetrated listeners "like an X-ray" and left a lingering impression. In the age of audiotapes, conversely, singers acted "like traders who [sold] undesirable goods alongside indispensable ones."[19] Cassette "artists," in short, were not artists at all.

The belief that the voices appearing on audiotapes were unfit to be broadcast is perhaps no more evident than in a sketch accompanying an editorial on cassettes and the alleged demise of taste in Egypt. In the drawing, a professional female mourner approaches a representative of "Fatsophone," a recording label based in a kiosk. The employee asks her if she would like "to record a cassette." Mistaking the word "cassette" (*kasit*) for "as a woman" (*ka-sit*), the confused client asks, "Or as a man?"[20] For its contemporary audience, the drawing's meaning would have been immediately intelligible. The crass, lower-class customer, who makes a living by making noise, stands for all of the cassette "artists" branded and berated as "vulgar" by critics. At the same time, the illustration reminds readers that the voices relayed on tapes were not solely responsible for the perceived deterioration of taste in Egypt. "Culturally illiterate" cassette producers, like the cartoon's Fatso-phone delegate, ensured that content considered suspect by cultural gatekeepers reached Egyptian ears.[21]

As audiotapes gained ground in Egypt, the number of cassette companies rose at an astonishing rate. According to one estimate, there existed twenty well-known labels prior to 1975. By 1987, that number had skyrocketed to 365 ventures, only to climb again three years later to around 500 businesses. Egyptians with little to no experience in the recording industry or in creating cultural productions of any kind ran a large number of these entities. To begin to grasp the vast number of amateur enterprises operating in Egypt, which likely even exceeded the aforementioned figures, one need only consider how by 1990 thirty cassette companies reportedly blanketed a single square in Cairo alone.[22] But who exactly founded and managed these labels? According to critics, working-class citizens, ranging from electricians to carpenters, used the money they earned from Sadat's economic opening to become cassette producers. Often based in a single apartment or a sidewalk kiosk, these ordinary Egyptians, commentators charged, pursued profits at the cost of public taste and recklessly bombarded listeners with cassette recordings that led to the death of singing, the commodification of Egyptian culture, and the contamination of Egypt's soundscape.

Discussions of suspect tapes in the press often censured lower- to middle-class citizens for fancying themselves as cultural producers. One journalist, for instance, attributed the proliferation of cassettes that corrupted taste to "street peddlers," "repeat offenders," and skilled workers who launched recording labels with the cash they acquired from the *infitah*.[23] A fellow reporter singled out plumbers, butchers, and cigarette sellers for creating works of art that were highly profitable and "incompatible with public taste," and that posed a greater danger to citizens than cocaine.²⁴ Still others occasionally faulted their nonelite compatriots for wielding their newfound financial influence to corrupt established artists. A professor of psychiatry and neurology at a leading medical school in Cairo argued that "trivial" tapes resulted from sweeping social changes in the 1970s and the 1980s that empowered a new parasitical class of "uneducated" Egyptians. "Seduced by money," the doctor bewailed, "famous writers and composers drifted, and took to writing and composing for a class intruding on art without any study or mere familiarity."²⁵ In the course of attacking working-class Egyptians for producing cassettes, local critics portrayed themselves as "educated" and "refined" in relation to their "ignorant" and "crass" compatriots. At the same time, those driving these discussions did not simply differentiate themselves from those they condemned. More importantly, they argued that ordinary people had no business making Egyptian culture.

But what motivated "imposter artists" and "unqualified producers" to create cassettes in the first place? According to commentators, Egyptians who corrupted the taste of others were blindly guided by money. In his 1993 history of Egyptian music, Kamal al-Nigmi, for example, writes that "singers riding on the vulgar wave make a living from corrupting the tastes of millions of people in an age severed from the heritage of Arab singing."²⁶ More recently, in a text published in 2015 through Egypt's Ministry of Culture, the late critic continues to berate money-minded cassette artists from beyond the grave. In a section titled "The Calamity of Arabic Singing," he states that in the mid- to late twentieth century, when cassettes came to be a dominant medium, Egypt "became a breeding ground for discordant voices and there remained nothing left except nightclub crows." These substandard—indeed, inhuman—artists, al-Nigmi declares, "caw day and night and make a living by corrupting the tastes" of listeners.²⁷ In a similar vein as al-Nigmi, Muhammad Qabil, an Egyptian artist and broadcaster, has criticized the profit-driven producers upon whom cassette artists relied. "It became familiar," he notes in his 2006 music encyclopedia, "to find a butcher's shop converted into a cassette production company." The skilled workers behind these "successful fraudulent commercial ventures," Qabil explains, cared little about safeguarding public taste. Instead, "they searched for financial gain at any cost, even at the cost of taste, which led to vulgar culture and its base currency driving out refined culture and proper singing from the markets."²⁸ Thus, whether subsisting on or striking it rich off "inferior" art, "unqualified" cassette artists and producers, commentators often contended, were behind the decline of taste in Egypt.[29]

To be certain, commentaries on cassette tapes in the popular Egyptian press did not simply concern public taste, popular music, and the reported dangers posed by it. Class, culture, and politics proved central to these debates, which reflected broader criticisms of the *infitah* and contributed to the anxieties it inspired. On the one hand, attacks on cassette recordings considered dubious by critics clearly channel contemporary critiques directed at Egypt's expanding culture of consumption, the proliferation of private companies, and the rise of newly empowered citizens who profited from Sadat's capitalist policies and strove to strengthen their financial standing. These historical developments have been well documented by Tarek Osman, Kirk Beattie, and Mohamed Hassanein Heikal, among others, who have detailed the economic and social impact of the *infitah*.[30] The cultural politics of the *infitah*, however, extend beyond the scope of these studies.

These politics are on full display in debates over audiotapes, which begin to illuminate the cultural history of Egypt's economic opening by presenting the connections critics forged between the *infitah*, its alleged ills, and cultural production. At the same time, these materials not only reflect the concerns sparked by the *infitah* but also fuel them. Egyptian culture, much like Egyptian society, is undergoing a major crisis in these texts, which place no shortage of the blame on those who benefited from Sadat's economic initiative. Those who prospered from the *infitah*, however, are not solely responsible for this "crisis." Critics also condemned ordinary citizens, who did not necessarily profit from the *infitah* but nevertheless played a pivotal part in the perceived pollution of both public taste and Egyptian culture by harnessing cassettes to become cultural producers.

The cultural arena introduced in discussions of audiotapes noticeably departs from its counterparts in several histories of Egyptian culture. In Ali Jihad Racy's analysis of records, Joel Gordon's work on films, and Virginia Danielson's account of Umm Kulthum, for example, revered artists and leading institutions dominate the creation of Egyptian culture.[31] Critically, in the sources presented so far in this chapter, both elite and ordinary Egyptians, based in small apartments, in prominent recording labels, and everywhere in between, engage in the making of Egyptian culture by way of cassette technology, which enabled an unprecedented number of people to become cultural producers. This shift, no doubt, disturbed many public figures, who strove to police an increasingly robust acoustic culture. Here, the work performed by "vulgarity" gains greater clarity.

By branding a cassette as "vulgar," critics were arguably condemning the "un-refined" nature of its creators as much as, if not more so than, its content. Thus, while a tape's lyrics may well have been "obscene," "crass," or "of the masses," all meanings entailed in the word "vulgar," commentators wielded the adjective, first and foremost, to reassert their authority over cultural production. After all, what was at stake was not only what comprised Egyptian culture but also who had the right to create it. To better understand this struggle over Egyptian culture, let's turn to the greater cultural milieu cassettes and their users inhabited and the state-controlled channels of cultural production they challenged.

"VULGAR" AUDIOTAPES IN THE AGE OF STATE CULTURE

Egypt's minister of culture from 1985 to 1987, Dr. Ahmad Haykal, once ex-claimed, "Art without obligation is like a river without banks; in the end it leads to drowning." According to him, those responsible for submerging Egyptians with purposeless, "vulgar" art committed two sins. They shirked their obligation to protect the values, morals, and taste of their compatriots, and they preyed upon Egypt's "climate of freedom" and Sadat's economic opening "to introduce cheap laughter they called art." For Haykal, "vulgar" plays, films, and cassettes were appalling because they failed to fulfill one of culture's primary objectives: crafting model citizens. Indeed, such works ran counter to the very definition of "culture" he espoused. "Culture is not an amusement," Haykal once asserted, "culture is not an empty diversion. Culture is not a mockery. Culture is not only art. Culture, rather, is *refined* art."[32] To be certain, Haykal was one among many Egyptians who censured select artworks. To better understand why some cas-settes provoked the scorn of many observers, it is necessary to situate audiotapes in relation to the wider cultural terrain they occupied. Only by documenting the state's efforts to fashion "cultured" citizens will the attacks on, and significance of, "vulgar" cassette recordings gain greater clarity.

Throughout the mid- to late twentieth century, public culture (*al-thaqafa al-ja-mahiriyya*) was more than an idea in modern Egypt; it was a state-engineered pro-gram charged with erasing "cultural illiteracy." The initiative Public Culture came into existence in 1966 at the hands of Tharwat 'Ukasha, a skilled politician who established several new sites linking culture and the state during his eight-year tenure as minister of culture (1958–1962, 1966–1970).[33] Officially one of 'Ukasha's creations, Public Culture drew inspiration from earlier programs connecting cul-ture, the state, and subject formation, including the Peoples University (founded in

1945), Culture Centers (founded in 1948), and Culture Palaces (founded in 1960).[34] The first director of Public Culture, Sa'd Kamil, was a prominent intellectual of the Egyptian Left. Once appointed, he wasted little time in selecting elite men and women to relocate from Cairo to direct culture palaces, to set up culture houses and clubs, and to oversee culture caravans across Egypt.[35] The objectives of these apparatuses were essentially twofold: to educate and elevate the taste of ordinary Egyptians and to build stronger ties between the capital and its peripheries. The foundation of both aims was a shared national culture, manufactured, distributed, and sanctioned by the government.

The success of the Public Culture program is subject to debate, but what cannot be disputed is the centrality of music to its mission.[36] State officials working for the venture established numerous ensembles, while musical plays, recitals, and competitions took place in government establishments where guests encountered select records and cassettes in "listening clubs." According to one publication, Public Culture held more than six thousand musical events between 1971 and 1980 that catered to an estimated three million people.[37] Published by a state entity, these statistics should be viewed with a grain of salt. But it is beyond any doubt that music was an indispensable instrument in the state's attempts to fashion "enlightened" Egyptians. Not all music, however, contributed to these efforts. Songs considered "tasteless" by those on the government's payroll had no role to play in creating "cultured" citizens. Refined art exclusively advanced this task, which "vulgar" audiotapes only jeopardized. In its mission to forge "cultured" Egyptians, Public Culture was not alone. A second mechanism lent welcomed support.

State-controlled Egyptian radio placed a premium on molding model citizens. To ensure that only the "right" sounds reached the public's ears, radio officials relied on a system of checks and balances. Two screening committees formed the foundation of this infrastructure. The first, known as the Text Committee (Lajnat al-Nusus), decided whether the radio should record numbers still being developed. If its members approved of a tune, the song entered production. A second panel, the Listening Committee (Lajnat al-Istima'), determined whether recorded songs should be broadcast. If the body's artists, broadcasters, and sound engineers endorsed a ballad, it was left to the discretion of stations to play it. Channels did not promote everything that came their way.

During the period under investigation, the selectivity of some leading channels was public knowledge. In 1975, delegates from four different stations openly admitted to classifying singers and allotting them airtime in accordance with their rank. Al-Sharq al-Awsat, for instance, considered Umm Kulthum, Muhammad 'Abd al-Wahhab, and 'Abd al-Halim Hafiz to be "first-tier" musicians and played their songs once a day, whereas "second-tier" artists like Farid al-Atrash, Nagat, Faiza Ahmad, Warda, and Shadia surfaced four times a week, and "third-tier" performers, such as Sabah, Su'ad Muhammad, and Maha Sabri, appeared on the air every now and again.[38] Singers branded as "vulgar" by radio employees generally fell outside of these ranks entirely. Unlike tapes, which sounded countless voices, radio popularized a smaller pool of elite artists.

Radio administrators took pride in the selectivity their system inspired and the high artistic standards it allegedly upheld. And when the medium's criteria for choosing tracks became too loose, representatives vowed to tighten them. In 1983, for example, the Listening Committee revisited its rules for approving songs. Going forward, one magazine noted, its members would only permit numbers they hailed as a "contribution" to "the world of singing."[39] From the perspective of officials, those capable of making such a "contribution" were limited.

According to Ibrahim al-Musbah, who oversaw musical works for the Radio and Television Union in the early 1980s, only ten poets out of five thousand writers could create proper songs.[40] Those not fortunate enough to earn the approval of al-Musbah and other cultural elites, like 'Abd al-Wahhab, who assisted the radio in determining who deserved to be aired, were forced to find other ways to be heard.[41] The radio's exclusivity was essential, its gatekeepers claimed, because the technology was responsible for refining the taste of all listeners across the country.[42] In this sense, officials viewed the medium as "a school without walls for all people" and pledged not to harm "public morals and dignity" or to broadcast "vulgar" words.[43] "Crass" audiotapes obstructed the efforts of radio personnel to fashion "cultured" Egyptians, and the platform's guardians did not hesitate to censure "vulgar songs that spread in brisk cassette markets" in the press.[44] Nevertheless, radio employees could not always keep "vulgar" cassette recordings off the airwaves.

With the proliferation of cassette companies, state-controlled Egyptian radio produced less music and, at times, acted as a "showcase" for cassette labels, which sent the radio tapes as "gifts" in the hope of gaining greater publicity for their productions.[45] These free cassettes, commentators regularly alleged, contained material that polluted public taste.[46] In its campaign to counter "vulgar" cassette recordings, to elevate the taste of all citizens, and, most important, to dictate who created Egyptian culture, radio found an ally in a third state entity: the censor.

Censorship was both a private and a public affair in Egypt. While decisions on what movies to cut, songs to amend, or plays to trim may have been made behind closed doors, the outcomes of backroom deliberations often surfaced on the pages of the popular press. Weekly magazines frequently noted works of art that state censors deemed unfit for public consumption because of their title, plot line, or political content, or the danger they purportedly posed to public morals. The power exhibited by censors on paper, however, belied the difficulties they faced in practice in silencing certain cultural products. Years before the advent of satellite television and the World Wide Web, audiotapes and their users posed the single greatest obstacle to those tasked with securing the perimeters of public culture. A rare look inside the Office of Art Censorship (Jihaz al-Raqaba ʿala al-Musanifat al-Fanniyya) on Qasr al-ʿAyni Street in downtown Cairo offers a useful starting point for addressing the challenges cassettes presented to officials charged with "purifying" public taste.

In an insightful interview in *Ruz al-Yusuf,* one of the most vocal critics of "vulgar" cassettes, the director of the Office of Art Censorship, ʿAbd al-Fatah Rashid, illuminated the inner workings of his office in the late 1970s. The objectives of Rashid's unit were threefold. It strove to make sure artistic works were tasteful, complied with public morals, and adhered to political, social, and religious norms. The enforcement of these guidelines, however, was not always possible, especially in the case of cassettes. When asked about "vulgar" tapes, Rashid blamed "private sector" producers who deceived censors by submitting one text for review only to record another upon receiving their approval. Unlike the first set of lyrics, the second included additional phrases the producer believed would "serve him financially."[47] If censors discovered the revised recording, Rashid claimed, they seized it and imposed a E£50 fine on its creator. Perhaps sensing this response was inadequate, the director elaborated that he was working to implement a stricter protocol whereby censors would examine every work twice—before and after it was recorded—prior to issuing a ruling. Certain impediments, though, hindered this plan. Rashid's team consisted of a mere fifteen censors who toiled away over seven tape recorders. To make matters worse, his office was inundated with audiotapes. In addition to reviewing commercial cassettes, his staff was responsible for screening every personal tape that crossed Egypt's national borders.

If the director of art censorship sounded defensive in his conversation with *Ruz al-Yusuf,* it is likely because several Egyptian critics attributed the proliferation of cassettes carrying "suspect" content to the shortcomings of state censors like Rashid. At times, the voices behind these attacks opted for anonymity. One commentator, going simply by the name of "an artist," repeatedly chastised censors in *Ruz al-Yusuf*. In January 1979, the mystery writer, who may well have been a state-sanctioned musician suffering from waning sales, slammed censors for partaking in the pollution of public taste by permitting companies to produce "vulgar" cassettes.[48] Six months later, he harangued state censors, once again, for signing off on tapes with sexually suggestive lyrics.[49] Judging by a third rebuke from the same alias nearly a year later, censors, it would seem, continued to struggle with cassettes. "Cassette tapes brimming with triviality," the "artist" railed, in familiar fashion, "are increasing and are being sold brazenly in commercial shops and on the sidewalk."[50]

Others, meanwhile, elected to waive their anonymity when slamming censors. In a letter to the editors of *Akhir Sa'a*, a certain Fathi Mansur questioned the absence of censorship at a time when "singing and art had become a job for those without one" and "vulgar" songs continued to spread on cassettes at an alarming rate. No tape, he asserted, should circulate without the approval of censors, who needed to punish those behind "foul tapes" that facilitated the "decline of public taste."[51] The origin of Fathi's message, a small village in the northern province of Daqahliyya, suggests that suspect cassettes extended well beyond Egypt's urban centers; "tasteless" tapes, it would seem, were a nationwide problem that demanded the attention and the action of Egyptian gatekeepers. In conversation with these writers and in an effort to reign in certain tapes, a wide array of Egyptians proposed different ways to strengthen censorship and to save public taste.

For some politicians, the answer to "vulgar" cassettes rested upon amending existing laws. In February 1980, the first undersecretary for the Ministry of Culture, Sa'd al-Din Wahba, instructed officials to revise censorship legislation.[52] He argued that it was necessary to revisit the then-antiquated legal measures because significant changes had since transpired in the domain of technology. Among the more momentous developments cited by Wahba were audiotapes. For others, the solution to "vulgar" cassettes lay in altering the very infrastructure of state censorship.

The same month Wahba formed his committee, Muharram Fu'ad, a well-known singer, posited that stricter censorship could improve Egyptian music. To aid the efforts of censors in cracking down on "often illegal" cassette companies and the "vulgar" recordings they released, Fu'ad proposed the establishment of a "cassette room."[53] According to the artist's vision, the Office of Art Censorship, the Musicians Syndicate, and the Ministry of Industry would work together to create the room, while a music adviser would accompany artists in the space.[54] As a result of this plan, which notably stood to benefit Fu'ad and his state-controlled label (Sawt al-Qahira) by reducing the stiff competition they faced in attracting listeners, cassette production would fall more squarely within the purview of the state and elite cultural brokers.

As the number of cassette companies continued to skyrocket in Egypt, state entities, like the Specialized National Councils (al-Majalis al-Qawmiyya al-Mutakhasissa), joined artists and politicians in the battle against "vulgar" tapes. In April 1983, following a detailed study on the danger particular cassettes posed to public taste, the councils called for a novel unit within the Ministry of Culture to assess the "purity" of cassette productions before they reached the public.[55] Two months later, the councils declared an all-out "war on the cassette." In an article covering the bombastic announcement, a familiar voice compared "vulgar" cassette recordings to the Mongol ruler Hulagu Khan. What did the two have in common? In the opinion of al-Mansi, both shared a longing for "the obliteration of civilization's signposts."[56] According to the critic, there existed two types of people: those who listened to cassettes unaware of their danger, a group he likened to "drug addicts," and cultured listeners, who were aware of cassettes' harm and tried to warn others. Unsurprisingly, the Egyptians interviewed in al-Mansi's article fell firmly in the second camp.

In the years to come, the worries commentators expressed regarding the ability of censors to silence cassettes they considered "vulgar" proved to have been well founded. By the end of the 1980s, plans to eradicate "trivial" tapes in Egypt were faltering. Cassette labels continued to amend recordings before they reached consumers and after censors sanctioned them.[57] Likewise, censors failed to report the names of cassette singers to the Musicians Syndicate for its members to confirm whether or not they belonged to the body—a prerequisite for performing on tapes.[58] Sensing the weakness of state monitors, several Egyptians defied the rejections issued by censors. At times, these stands were highly public. Husayn Imam, for instance, vowed to release an audiotape partly based on the soundtrack of his popular film *Crabs*, despite censors ruling that the cassette endangered public taste on two separate occasions.[59] In other cases, citizens exercised greater caution. The owner of a clothes shop, for example, reportedly rereleased a confiscated tape once censors signed off on a revised version of the same work. Intent on duping authorities, the merchant selected identical covers for both editions of the cassette.[60] As one journalist tellingly pleaded at the start of 1990, censors were in trouble in Egypt and desperately needed support in patrolling "floods of cassettes in thousands of kiosks and stores," lest "the security wall collapse between [Egyptians] and the deluge of vulgar art and moral decline."[61] In the opinion of many critics, by the time these remarks made their way to newsstands, the wall had already crumbled.

In covering the efforts of state officials to fashion "cultured" citizens, attacks on select cassettes come into greater view. Tapes carrying *sha'bi* music and other content condemned by critics easily circulated outside of state establishments, from the Radio and Television Union to the Office of Art Censorship. By offering any citizen a means to record their voice and to reach a mass audience, cassette technology enabled an unprecedented number of people to create Egyptian culture at a time when public figures strove to dictate the shape it assumed.

To be certain, cultural gatekeepers did not simply surrender to "tasteless" tapes. On the contrary, they suggested no shortage of solutions. In addition to plans to enhance censorship, some individuals called for the formation of competitions and committees to counter the "decline" of Egyptian music. Contests offering financial rewards, they hoped, would deter lyricists from writing "vulgar" songs that they knew would sell well on cassettes, while assemblies of leading artists would combat contentious tapes by popularizing voices deemed valuable by highbrow musicians.[62] Other critics, meanwhile, looked to elite performers to personally oppose cassettes they considered "crass." 'Abd al-Wahhab assumed this responsibility in numerous cartoons in which he nursed sick songs back to health and prevented the spread of inferior music in military fatigues.[63] Of all these responses, however, none was more visible than that of Sawt al-Qahira, a state-controlled label that strove to elevate the taste of all Egyptians. But prior to exploring this entity's efforts to forge "cultured" listeners, it is first necessary to examine the career of one artist who embodied "vulgar" cassettes: Ahmad 'Adawiya. As we will see, a side-by-side exploration of 'Adawiya and Sawt al-Qahira makes clear that audiotapes actually transmitted a vast variety of voices in Egypt.

THE "LOW" AND THE "HIGH": AHMAD 'ADAWIYA AND SAWT AL-QAHIRA

In 1978, an Egyptian student by the name of Siyanat Hamdi wrote a doctoral dissertation on the decline of Egyptian music. To evaluate the dissertation, Hamdi's university invited external musicians to lead its review. Among the artists asked to discuss the findings was Muhammad 'Abd al-Wahhab, who, if he read it, would have likely enjoyed the lengthy tome, which included an entire chapter on his mastery of Arabic. The scope of Hamdi's project was panoramic in nature, covering singing in Egypt from its inception to the present day. Part and parcel of this history were "vulgar" songs, such as Ahmad 'Adawiya's "Everything on Everything" ("Kullu 'ala Kullu"), and what permitted such "inferior" numbers to spread and the "weak" voices behind them to become well known. In an article covering the student's research in *Ruz al-Yusuf*, one writer asked readers how Egyptians could "escape from 'Adawiya's school" prior to directing them to Hamdi's work.[64] If 'Abd al-Halim was "the nightingale," and Umm Kulthum was "the voice of Egypt," 'Adawiya was nothing more than "noise" that Hamdi, the reporter, and many other commentators could do without.

Few figures in Egypt's modern history are more synonymous with "vulgar cassettes" than Ahmad 'Adawiya, one of the pioneers of *sha'bi* music, a contentious genre regularly disparaged by critics. Born Ahmad Muhammad Mursi on 26 June 1945, 'Adawiya grew up listening to al-Atrash, 'Abd al-Wahhab, and 'Abd al-Halim.[65] Little is known about his early life, but according to one account, 'Adawiya's father traded livestock for a living and relocated his family to Cairo when the entertainer was still an adolescent.[66] It was in Egypt's capital where a young 'Adawiya, began to pursue music seriously. Unlike some of his peers, who enrolled in prestigious conservatories to perfect their skills, he honed his craft on Muhammad 'Ali Street, a historic avenue renowned for its musicians.[67] There, he played both the *nay* (reed flute) and the *riqq* (tambourine) with a musical troupe and followed in the footsteps of several other artists who learned how to become performers on the street. Fame and fortune, however, would have to wait until he met Sharifa Fadil, a singer and actress of some acclaim, who facilitated his introduction to Ma'mun al-Shinawi, a leading lyricist.[68] In 1973, 'Adawiya recorded his first major hit, "al-Sah al-Dah Ambu," on a cassette for Sawt al-Hubb, where al-Shinawi served as an artistic adviser.[69] The tape was an unprecedented success, selling an estimated million copies.[70] The first of many hits that 'Adawiya would release on cassettes, the recording transformed him into a household name and placed him at the center of debates on audiotapes and the "death" of taste.

From the beginning of his career, 'Adawiya attracted the ire of critics. Respected musicians ridiculed him and those belonging to his "backward" generation. Muhammad 'Abd al-Mutalab, a pioneer of the "popular song," attacked 'Adawiya on multiple occasions. When asked about the quality of songs in the mid-1970s, a time when 'Adawiya and audiotapes were gaining momentum, he

once responded bitterly, "They are machinations! A cheap trade whose manufacturers try to outdo one another in proving their ability and their superiority in
corrupting the taste of the next generation."[71] Other artists, meanwhile, denounced
'Adawiya outside of the press. In one incident, Muharram Fu'ad entered a casino
known for playing 'Adawiya's tapes in Alexandria and, upon hearing his numbers, demanded that "foreign music" be broadcast instead. The building's owner
proceeded to play one of Fu'ad's songs and, when it did not please those present,
forced him to leave the premises.[72] There is then the case of 'Abd al-Hamid Kishk,
a popular preacher who slammed 'Adawiya in one of his sermons. According to
Kishk, 'Adawiya's "al-Sah al-Dah Ambu" was as "tasteless" as it was "meaningless."[73]
Distancing himself from the singer's "vulgar" tracks and his use of colloquial Arabic, the shaykh implored Egyptian youth in classical Arabic to study high poetry.
Combined with attacks on 'Adawiya as a foul side effect of Egypt's defeat in the
1967 war and Sadat's economic opening that reportedly empowered the "culturally
illiterate," all of these commentaries cast the singer, his success, and his cassettes
in a resolutely negative light.

　　Not all Egyptian public figures, however, embraced a black-and-white view
when it came to the cassette star. Naguib Mahfouz was among those who adopted
a more nuanced stance. At times, the Nobel laureate criticized 'Adawiya's music
for its "triviality" and "crudeness," two qualities, he claimed, that resulted in his
productions being the "furthest thing from elegance," but in other moments the
author recognized his "strong, sorrow-infused voice" and recalled several of 'Adawiya's songs with ease, only to wish their lyrics were more meaningful.[74] 'Abd
al-Wahhab, similarly, did not despise 'Adawiya, but he did insist that his music
would lose its resonance. In an interview with *Akhir Sa'a* in 1976, he stated that
'Adawiya's popularity was of little concern to him "because in every country in
the world there are all sorts of artistic colors and forms." What bothered 'Abd
al-Wahhab at the time in Egypt was not 'Adawiya's presence but the absence of
"noble beautiful art," which, he believed, was "what remains in the end."[75] Unlike
the permanence enjoyed by refined music, 'Adawiya's songs, he implied, were
a passing phenomenon. Despite the reportedly "fleeting" and "crass" nature of
'Adawiya's tracks, some of Egypt's leading artists nevertheless gravitated toward
him. Among these figures was none other than 'Abd al-Wahhab.

　　The same year 'Abd al-Wahhab refrained from castigating 'Adawiya in *Akhir
Sa'a*, he tried to poach the entertainer as the co-owner of Sawt al-Fann, a major
recording label. 'Abd al-Wahhab's partner, 'Abd al-Halim, approached 'Adawiya in

London, where he was performing at the Omar Khayyam Hotel. There, he offered 'Adawiya a five-year recording deal. Shortly thereafter, 'Adawiya's label, eager to retain him, countered 'Abd al-Halim's terms by raising its star's salary to E£500 per song in addition to a cut of the price of his recordings.[76] Less than two weeks after news of Sawt al-Fann's proposal broke, *Ruz al-Yusuf* printed a picture of 'Abd al-Halim gleefully singing "al-Sah al-Dah Ambu" alongside 'Adawiya at a party.[77] The photo caused a stir (fig. 12). Arabic periodicals reprinted it and writers claimed the scene evidenced 'Abd al-Halim's approval of 'Adawiya's "vulgar" art. In response to this charge, 'Abd al-Halim reportedly denied the incident ever took place.[78] Whereas the Sawt al-Fann kingpins may have preferred to keep their dealings with 'Adawiya out of the public eye, other artists did not mind supporting the singer in a more open manner. 'Adawiya's tapes, after all, were wildly popular.

Throughout 'Adawiya's career, some of the biggest names in Egyptian music wrote compositions for him, a reality that undermines any clear-cut division drawn by critics between "cassette stars" and "esteemed artists." In the 1970s, Mahmud al-Sharif, Muhammad al-Mugi, Kamal al-Tawil, Munir Murad, and Sayyid Mikkawi, all worked with the *sha'bi* sensation.[79] Egyptian lyricists, likewise, were well aware of 'Adawiya's selling power. One need only consider how one writer penned a song for Muharram Fu'ad only to give the same text to 'Adawiya before Fu'ad could perform it because any tape 'Adawiya released sold "40,000 copies."[80] Even Egyptian celebrities who did not work directly with 'Adawiya appreciated his music. The actor, writer, and singer Is'ad Yunis stated that his songs neither could nor should be censored. Not only was it "impossible to pull a sorry tape from a taxi to put a Beethoven tape in its place," she claimed; songs like 'Adawiya's provided a useful brain break for scholars and others who could not be expected to tune into artists like French Pianist Richard Clayderman "around the clock."[81] At the same time, commentators did not accept every defense of 'Adawiya. When 'Adil Imam, an Egyptian actor who appeared in multiple films critics found to be "vulgar," claimed that local intellectuals did not approve of 'Adawiya's songs because they were "withdrawn from the people," one reporter sharply reprimanded him.[82] Being one with the people, the writer rebuked, "does not mean smoking hookah or swaying to the melody of 'Get Well Soon Umm Hassan,'" one of 'Adawiya's popular tracks.[83] Regardless of the divergent opinions that Egyptians expressed toward 'Adawiya, there was one thing everyone agreed on: audiocassettes were integral to his career.

"عبدالحليم حافظ" يغنى السح الدح أُمبو !!

FIGURE 12. "'Abd al-Halim Hafiz sings *al-Sah al-Dah Ambu*!!" In
"'Abd al-Halim Hafiz Yughanni al-Sah al-Dah Ambu!!," *Ruz al-Yusuf,*
no. 2488 (16 February 1976): 47.

Throughout the mid- to late twentieth century, Egyptians encountered 'Adawiya's tapes in several different settings, from cafés to taxis to hair salons. As
one writer observed early on, 'Adawiya's voice emerged from "Cairo's side streets
and alleyways to take the ears of the middle class by storm and to impose its
songs upon it by way of cassette tapes for no apparent reason!"[84] Notably, one

place where ʿAdawiya's tracks did not resonate was state-controlled radio. Contrary to the claims of some scholars, ʿAdawiya and other up-and-coming artists did not simply turn to cassettes in the 1970s "as a practical solution for low-cost distribution and promotion."[85] Although the affordability of both processes was a plus, ʿAdawiya and his peers harnessed audiotapes, first and foremost, because Egyptian radio refused to broadcast what its officials deemed "vulgar" material. Forced to find another way to be heard, ʿAdawiya used tapes as a tool to reach a mass audience and to make his name known outside of weddings and Cairo's backstreets.[86] In overcoming the radio's ban by way of tapes, ʿAdawiya confirmed what one writer called "the success of the illegitimate" and contributed to the perceived demise of taste.[87]

Two of ʿAdawiya's most popular songs, both of which surfaced at the start of the *infitah* in the mid-1970s, shed further light on his cassettes and the attacks inspired by them. The first track, "A Little Bit Up, a Little Bit Down" ("Haba Fuq wa-Haba Taht"), revolves around a man and a woman who resides above him (see the appendix). ʿAdawiya plays the part of the man, who glances up at the "gorgeous" girl only to have his flirtatious gestures go unrequited. "Oh, people upstairs," the singer pleads, "go on and look at who is below, or is the up not aware of who is down anymore?" The emotional refrain, which clearly captures the man's frustrations with the beauty above him, also signals a key divide between the duo's respective classes, a rift many listeners would have readily identified with the *infitah*. This division, reportedly, was not lost on ʿAdawiya.

According to one article, the singer confirmed that "A Little Bit Up, a Little Bit Down" was a "sincere" commentary on class disparities resulting from Egypt's economic opening.[88] This theme, to be certain, appears in more than one of ʿAdawiya's early hits. In "Everything on Everything" ("Kullu ʿala Kullu"), a second song, ʿAdawiya again engages someone who is better off than himself (see the appendix). Whether this wealthier individual is a man or a woman is open to interpretation, but what is beyond any doubt is the singer's exasperation in a chaotic world.[89] "What does he think we are," ʿAdawiya asks throughout the tune, "are we not good enough for him?" While both of the aforementioned songs may be read in relation to the *infitah*, they arguably proved popular not for their potential political import but for their embrace of familiar scenes, common obstacles, and colloquial Egyptian Arabic. How popular were these songs? The titles of each turned into contemporary catch phrases, cited by many citizens aware of ʿAdawiya's tapes.

Critics, of course, did not accept 'Adawiya's interpretation of his art or that of those who endorsed it. On the contrary, commentators regularly rebuked those who found "meaning" in 'Adawiya's reportedly "meaningless" songs. One article on audiotapes and the decline of taste, for instance, acknowledged those "who confirm that Ahmad 'Adawiya is the new Sayyid Darwish," one of Egypt's most revered musicians, and publish such errant viewpoints in the press. Other individuals, the same editorial elaborates, insist that 'Adawiya's recordings are insightful and contend that "Haba Fuq wa-Haba Taht" is "a revolutionary song, progressive, and socialist, demanding the rich 'who are up' to bring about social justice and 'to look at who is below.'" Among those to allegedly promote these opinions were some of the biggest composers and lyricists in Egypt, and as a result of their declarations, the reporters rail, "Ahmad 'Adawiya has become a political leader more famous than Ahmad 'Urabi," an iconic revolutionary from a century prior.[90] At a time when singing in Egypt was "crazy," the journalists implored public figures to be "intelligent" when writing about 'Adawiya and his "vulgar" tracks. In this regard, the article's authors were not alone. From the perspective of many critics, 'Adawiya was a foul outcome of the *infitah*, not one of the phenomenon's most astute observers. Notwithstanding the attacks, which reduced 'Adawiya's songs to "nonsense," his voice continued to circulate widely on tapes that entertained and enraged.

Statistics recording the sales of 'Adawiya's tapes are exceedingly difficult to locate, but it appears that the singer outpaced many of his compatriots who benefited from state-controlled radio broadcasts and access to national stages. Annual figures published for 1976 accredit the performer with the top-selling cassette in all of Egypt. Throughout the year, one of his tapes, *'Adawiya in London* (*'Adawiya fi Lundun*), reportedly sold thirty-six thousand units, not to mention countless more pirated copies, while 'Abd al-Halim's final recording, "The Coffee Cup Fortune Teller" ("Qari'at al-Fangan"), came in a distant second with its eighteen thousand sales. In addition to upstaging his fellow artists, 'Adawiya also surpassed Egypt's leading Qur'an reciter, Muhammad Mahmoud al-Tablawi, who sold twenty thousand cassettes, by a significant margin.[91] But why were 'Adawiya's tapes so popular in the first place?

According to contemporary commentators, the proliferation of 'Adawiya's cassettes was a matter of timing, audience, and content. The performer, they maintained, emerged with a "strange new voice" when several of Egypt's most beloved artists passed away. Stepping into the immense void these stars left behind,

'Adawiya, the story goes, gained traction with a "new class" of Egyptians consisting mainly of skilled workers and merchants (the same group of citizens whom critics accused of profiting from Sadat's *infitah* and contributing to the "decline" of public taste). For these individuals, 'Adawiya epitomized "their long lost wish" by singing about daily problems, to which they could relate, in the vernacular they understood.[92] Cassette technology, in turn, permitted this class to play songs that were banned from state-controlled Egyptian radio. One of the figures this group flocked to was 'Adawiya, whose lyrics, one writer explains in similarly classist terms, were "strange to the ears of cultured, educated, and bourgeois listeners."[93]

To see these observations in action, one need only consider a scene from a contemporary Egyptian film we have already encountered, *The People at the Top* (*Ahl al-Qimma*, 1981). At one point in the picture, a petty thief turned dishonest businessman, Za'tar, picks up his love interest, Siham, and her coworker Fathiyya from a bank in Cairo after their shifts. Once the three set off, Za'tar slides a cassette tape into his stereo and one of 'Adawiya's major hits, "Oh, Crowded World!" ("Zahma ya Dunya Zahma"), washes over the car's occupants. Fathiyya, riding shotgun, disapproves of the "annoying" song along with 'Adawiya's other numbers because of their "vulgar" words, while Za'tar praises the recording for its "witty" and "unassuming" lyrics. Siham, meanwhile, finds most songs "tasteless" but believes 'Adawiya's tracks are nonetheless "amusing."[94] Notably, Za'tar, the only character who applauds 'Adawiya unabashedly in the brief exchange, embodies the ills of Egypt's economic opening and belongs to the same class of citizens condemned by critics on a regular basis for corrupting public taste in the popular Egyptian press.

Ultimately, by utilizing cassettes, 'Adawiya blazed a new course for anyone aspiring to be an artist outside of state-controlled Egyptian radio and provided no shortage of material for irate listeners. Yet audiotapes, contrary to the arguments of many voices in the popular press, did not simply transmit content critics found to be "trivial." Cassettes also carried sounds that many people deemed to be "refined" and believed were central to the production of "cultured" citizens.

If critics held private-sector companies, run by "unqualified" individuals, responsible for the production of "vulgar" tapes and the corruption of public taste, they lauded Sawt al-Qahira as a means to elevate the taste of all citizens through "refined" cassettes. In one emblematic narrative of the company's history, the Egyptian Ministry of Information warmly introduces Sawt al-Qahira as "a civilizational beacon radiating the finest forms of art and creative media." Chief among the enterprise's objectives, we are told, was to "refine public taste, to elevate one's being, and to alleviate one's existence." To these ends, the label's representatives endeavored to expose Egyptians to a select range of state-sanctioned voices in order to "counter their wallowing in waves of triviality, to enrich their sense of being, to refine their sense of art, and to elevate their level of music," all things writers censuring select cassette recordings regularly demanded.[95] In line with the missions of other state-controlled entities, Sawt al-Qahira, in short, aspired to fashion a more "cultured" listener that spurned the reportedly "tasteless" noises generated by its competitors.

To guarantee the high quality of its productions, Sawt al-Qahira employed artistic committees to evaluate the material on its albums, which, for at least three decades, found a home, first and foremost, on audiocassettes. Beginning in 1973, the state-controlled enterprise manufactured its first set of cassettes, numbering 7,561 tapes in total. The relatively small assortment accompanied its far larger record releases for the year, which exceeded 655,000 discs. The company's cassettes originated from a factory in Alexandria. Four years into the plant's operations, a decree from the Ministry of Information altered the label's name from Sawt al-Qahira Record Company to Sawt al-Qahira for Audio and Visuals. The new name signaled a changing expertise. In 1981, citing a waning demand on behalf of consumers, Sawt al-Qahira ceased to manufacture records. The very next year, in 1982, the label increased its production of cassettes from slightly over 737,000 to more than one million for the first time in its history.[96] Throughout the 1980s and the 1990s, Sawt al-Qahira's production of cassettes fell below seven figures on only two occasions and exceeded two million tapes annually a dozen separate years.

Glossy photographs, accompanying the Ministry of Information's history of Sawt al-Qahira, show Egyptian employees working diligently in the company's state-of-the-art facilities in Alexandria. Women manage master recordings, while men handle packaging, the creation of cassette cases, and the printing of cassette sleeves and posters.[97] If examined together, these images convey a clear message. Sawt al-Qahira's cassette division shared nothing in common with the so-called "companies" blasted by critics for producing "vulgar" tapes. For one, the label was not limited to a single room or a sidewalk kiosk. It operated out of not one, but two, well-lit, technologically advanced factories. Furthermore, its professional, uniformed staff sharply departed from portrayals of "untrained" cassette creators, ranging from butchers to cigarette vendors, in scathing accounts of more dubious tapes. Far from simple shots of two places of work, the illustrations, accordingly, advanced the image of Sawt al-Qahira as both a response and an answer to "vulgar" cassettes and those behind them. But exactly which sounds ended up on the hundreds of blank tapes in these carefully curated pictures in the mid- to late twentieth century? Which types of recordings, that is to say, did the state-controlled company produce, circulate, and sell in an effort to popularize and preserve high culture, to counter ʿAdawiya and other cassette stars who purportedly "endangered" public taste, and to profit in a competitive marketplace? And how might these acoustic offerings complicate accounts of cassettes with only controversial content?

Cassette catalogs from Sawt al-Qahira shed light on the company's productions and the wide range of recordings available to Egyptians. Inside the commercial documents, the label's inventory shows that cassettes did not simply challenge high, state-sanctioned culture but also were integral to its circulation. One such text, a small orange booklet titled "Musical Evenings," begins to bring these points into relief.[98] Over the course of forty-five pages, Sawt al-Qahira advertises recordings it created between 1975 and 1988. In perusing the offerings, one is immediately struck by the presence of certain sounds and the absence of others. Classical music (e.g., symphonies), traditional Arab culture (e.g., folk dance), state-sanctioned stars (e.g., Muhammad ʿAbd al-Wahhab), and past greats (e.g., Sayyid Darwish) occupy the majority of the entries, while *shaʿbi* singers fail to grace a single page despite their tremendous popularity at the time. Notably, nearly one out of every five albums for sale showcases the Ministry of Culture's Arabic Music Troupe, a professional ensemble led by ʿAbd al-Halim Nawira, a trained composer and instrumentalist who also assisted state-controlled Egyptian radio as a musical inspector. The cassettes on display, it is safe to say, would have elated those who loudly attacked other tapes.

In a second, more comprehensive catalog, published in 2004, Sawt al-Qahira's efforts to create and cater to "cultured" listeners gain even greater clarity. The detailed volume introduces more than one thousand recordings from the 1970s through the 1990s.[99] One of the paragons of permissible music in Egypt, Umm Kulthum, eclipses the first twenty pages of the text. In the sections that follow, the company's belief in cassettes as a formative medium becomes even more apparent. Some tapes introduce listeners to new languages, while others assist them in "correctly" remembering historic events, such as Nasser's nationalization of the Suez Canal in 1956, Egypt's "victory" in the October War of 1973, and Sadat's trip to Israel in 1977, by relaying the speeches of past presidents. Still other cassettes target particular demographics. One tape from 1993, for example, aims to shape even the youngest of listeners through musical numbers tackling specific topics. In addition to teaching basic vocabulary—"dog," "zoo," "tree"—the recording covers significant notions, including God, order, and admiration for the father, and essential values such as generosity, cleanliness, and cooperation.[100] Given all of these acoustic offerings, cassettes, from the perspective of Sawt al-Qahira and its supporters, clearly had a crucial role to play in enlightening and elevating the taste of all Egyptians, from day laborers to those still in diapers.

A third and final catalog introduces one other facet of the company's cassette division and its attempts to craft sound citizens that bear mentioning. Beginning in the mid-1970s, Sawt al-Qahira started to produce cassettes carrying religious content. One company booklet, which I acquired at a Cairene outlet, reveals the presence of twenty-six different shaykhs on tapes between 1975 and 1989.[101] During this time frame, Egyptians could choose among no fewer than eight hundred different Islamic recordings, ranging from recitation (*tilawa*) to interpretation (*tafsir*), from the company's collections. In the catalog, the label classifies its religious productions by the Qur'anic chapter(s) they contain and the numbers of verses they cover. The majority of the entries are "master" editions, but a select number are "from the mosque," a phrase likely indicating a live recording of a scholar reciting or remarking on the Qur'an before an audience. As was the case with its other cassettes, the company's Islamic recordings similarly enabled select voices—in this case, those sanctioned by religious and political gatekeepers—to reach a wider audience and, occasionally, to profit from their work. Equally important, the resulting tapes boosted the company's efforts to combat cassettes critics found to be "vulgar" by bolstering Egypt's "ethical soundscape."[102]

While Sawt al-Qahira was undoubtedly at the forefront of harnessing cassettes in an attempt to fashion "cultured" citizens, the company was not the only state entity to pursue this aim through audiotapes. Other enterprises followed suit. To consider only a few examples, the High Committee for Music in Cairo released a cassette alongside a booklet in 1983 to showcase Egypt's refined music and to assist readers in elevating their taste.[103] The president of the General Egyptian Book Organization publicized his plans in 1989 to issue a tape that would combine the best of colloquial and classical Arabic poetry by incorporating the works of 'Abd al-Rahman al-Abnudi and Muhammad Abu Duma on a single recording.[104] Even the Egyptian Armed Forces bought into the idea that cassettes could be used to school Egyptian citizens. In 1980, the military introduced tapes for learning Hebrew. At once educational and in line with national security interests, the recordings featured a broadcaster for al-Sharq al-Awsat, Aynas Gawher, who was fluent in the foreign language.[105] Not to be outdone by any of these initiatives, Egypt's Ministry of Culture mobilized cassettes to extol the actions of ruling regimes and to preserve and promote selected aspects of the country's musical heritage. Less than a week after Sadat signed a peace treaty with Israel in 1979, the ministry was fast at work on manufacturing a tape celebrating the historic development, while in the years to follow the ministry turned to cassettes on more than one occasion to record local folkloric ballads, Egyptian musicians playing traditional instruments such as the *nay* and the oud, and audiobooks honoring state-sanctioned stars like Umm Kulthum and Muhammad 'Abd al-Wahhab.[106] Mobile, durable, and affordable, audiotapes presented the state and its constituent bodies with a powerful technology for shaping Egypt's acoustic culture.

Contrary to the claims of many Egyptian observers, cassettes clearly channeled more than contentious sounds in the mid- to late twentieth century. Audiotapes, in fact, were vital to the material and social life of all voices from the 1970s to the 1990s and beyond. At times challenging the commercial and cultural dominance of state-sanctioned icons, tapes also solidified the stardom of the very same artists. That is to say, cassettes simultaneously broadcast Umm Kulthum and Ahmad 'Adawiya, 'Abd al-Halim Hafiz and Michael Jackson, Anwar Sadat and Shaykh Kishk, and anyone with access to a tape recorder. As one writer observed during a few months' sojourn to Egypt in the mid-1980s, car stereos, portable Walkmans, and boom boxes played everything—classical music, Qur'anic recitation, Western pop, leading Egyptian singers—in private vehicles, public buses, shops, hotels, and social clubs from Alexandria to Aswan.[107] This wide array of sounds is no more evident than in the case of one cassette I came across in Cairo. The tape features Beethoven on one side and Hassan al-Asmar on the other (fig. 13). What was once a recording of an esteemed European composer, then, became a platform for a popular Egyptian *sha'bi* singer, who, like 'Adawiya, was berated by public figures for his allegedly "vulgar" lyrics. Thus, although cassettes certainly infuriated many individuals who strove to dictate who created Egyptian culture and the shape that culture assumed, they were far from the exclusive property of provocative voices.

FIGURE 13. Beethoven and Hassan al-Asmar surface on a single tape. Photo by the author.

CONCLUSION: EGYPT'S VULGAR SOUNDSCAPE

Audiotapes were part and parcel of broader historical debates on "vulgar" media in modern Egypt in the mid- to late twentieth century, and although cassette technology dominated many of these discussions, it was not, as Walter Armbrust has shown, at the center of every critique.[108] Records, radio, and television also attracted the ire of commentators, albeit to a lesser extent because of their greater centralization.[109] Writers, likewise, faulted actors for "using expressions and movements that tear public taste to pieces" in theatrical productions and voiced their disgust with both "vulgar" movies that bombarded viewers with gratuitous sex scenes in the cinema and "dangerous" videotapes that corrupted citizens' morals further afield.[110] Together, all of these diverse, yet equally undesirable noises contributed to the vitality of Egypt's vulgar soundscape.

Although multiple media technologies played a part in generating passionate debates over the perceived demise of public taste and the alleged end of high culture in Egypt, cassette recordings arguably inflamed these discussions to a greater degree. In addition to the small technology's immense mobility, mass audience, and low price point, cassettes permitted citizens from all different backgrounds to play a part in the making of Egyptian culture in ways that other devices simply did not. By enabling essentially anyone to become a cultural producer, regardless of age, gender, education, class, location, or financial standing, audiocassettes radically expanded the perimeters of cultural production and infinitely enriched Egypt's soundscape.

In the process of elucidating the impact of audiocassettes and their users on the creation of Egyptian culture, this chapter has raised a number of broader questions: What was the impact of other "forgotten" media technologies, and how might these untold stories invite us to reenvision the making of modern nations? How did the transition from cultural consumers to cultural producers play out in other historical contexts, and what new insights might these cases offer into the intersections of class, culture, and politics? And what might cultural histories of phenomena perceived to be primarily economic, political, or social in nature, such as the *infitah*, add to our understanding of the modern Middle East? All of these inquiries, no doubt, merit further research.

Having elucidated one untold episode in the history of modern Egypt and Egyptian culture over the preceding pages, let's conclude by addressing the fluidity of vulgarity as a historical concept. Cultural categories, like "high" and "low," "crass" and "refined," are not immune to change. The adjectives assigned to any given art form at one point in time may very well not apply to it at another. The ability of objects to travel between labels reminds us of the permeability of these concepts and the fact that they, like the items they describe, are products of a particular moment. With respect to Egypt, the fluidity of vulgarity is no more evident than in the case of one voice at the center of this chapter, Ahmad 'Adawiya, who, in recent years, has begun to emerge in a new light. In this regard, two episodes prove particularly instructive.

The first occurrence revolves around a self-described "boutique bookstore" in one of Cairo's more upscale neighborhoods. Located on a crowded thoroughfare in Zamalek, al-Diwan caters primarily to expatriates and middle- to upper-class Egyptians. To meet the needs of its clientele, the shop offers a rich selection of English- and Arabic-language texts, in addition to an assortment of Egyptian music. Among the artists available on CD in December 2011 were 'Amr Diab, Khalid, Latifa, and Ramy Sabry, who fell under the banner of "Arabic Remix," and Sayyid Darwish, Umm Kulthum, Farid al-Atrash, and 'Abd al-Halim Hafiz, under "Arabic Legends." Notably, 'Adawiya and his fellow *sha'bi* singers, who achieved stardom through cassettes, appeared under neither header and failed to surface on the shop's shelves altogether. When I inquired about 'Adawiya's conspicuous absence, one employee informed me, in no uncertain terms, that al-Diwan "did not sell *that* kind of music." Nevertheless, upon a return visit to the store in January 2016, I came across 'Adawiya in a different location.

At a distance from the music department and across from the cash registers, 'Adawiya's face graced the cover of what appeared to be an audiotape released by Sawt al-Hubb. Upon closer inspection, however, the *Adawiyat 4* cassette turned out to be a trendy notebook. One of several new notepads modeled on older audio and videocassette tapes, the item transformed a cultural production condemned by many critics into a voiceless object. Still unwilling to sell 'Adawiya's actual recordings, al-Diwan, it appears, did not mind profiting off the artist's silent "tape." What was once a "tasteless" cassette, in the eyes of many Egyptian commentators, had become a cool gift.

'Adawiya's music appeared only on paper in al-Diwan, but the performer's numbers simultaneously surfaced on genuine audiocassettes at another unexpected venue across Cairo. During an outing at the start of 2016 on al-Bursa al-Gadida Street, I came across several of 'Adawiya's cassette recordings behind sliding glass doors shielding the voices of religious authorities and state-sanctioned artists who embodied "high" Egyptian culture. The place I found these audiotapes was none other than a Sawt al-Qahira outlet. In the case of the recordings on display, a second Egyptian label, Good News 4 Music, reissued 'Adawiya's tapes at the turn of the century after acquiring the rights to reproduce Sawt al-Hubb's catalog. Sawt al-Qahira, in turn, showcased the rereleased cassettes in its downtown branch. What was once an example of "vulgar" noise par excellence, in the opinion of many local critics, now lined the shelves of a company whose stakeholders strove decades earlier to elevate the taste of all Egyptians and to counter the very tapes it now sold. What could explain this puzzling occurrence?

One of the reasons behind this development was evident for all to hear around the corner from Sawt al-Qahira. On Shawarbi Street, a small kiosk, not unlike the ones that sold 'Adawiya's cassettes during the road's heyday as a bustling black market, supplied passersby with the latest hits of a new musical genre on their flash drives. Less than a decade in the making, *mahraganat*, which we first encountered at the very start of this chapter, draws inspiration from the *sha'bi* music 'Adawiya pioneered. Building on this earlier musical tradition and blending electronic beats and hip-hop, its performers similarly address everyday subjects, sing in colloquial Egyptian Arabic, and, as was the case with 'Adawiya, have garnered their fair share of criticism for creating what cultural gatekeepers deem to be "trivial" art.[111] Even before the 2020 ban, radio stations, including the Sawt al-Qahira–supervised Nagham FM, marginalized *mahraganat* productions to protect "public taste," while the Musicians Syndicate refused to grant its artists licenses on account of their "vulgar" lyrics.[112] The alleged "tastelessness" of this new genre, combined with a generational shift when it comes to local critics, has arguably prompted a number of Egyptians to rethink 'Adawiya's cassettes.

However, as in the case of al-Diwan, which sold 'Adawiya's tape-turned-notebook but not his actual audio recordings, this reappraisal remains fraught with complexity. While the *mahraganat* music blaring in places like Shawarbi may well have paved the way for one of Sawt al-Qahira's branches to stock 'Adawiya's tapes, it did not stir the company to market his cassettes at a second, more visible venue. 'Adawiya was nowhere to be found in Sawt al-Qahira's tent at the 2016 Cairo International Book Fair, where visitors were free to buy and browse thousands of its cassette recordings. Among the artists available in the label's booth were the same state-sanctioned icons whose voices 'Adawiya accompanied at a distance from the fairgrounds in the venture's more central shop. Though certainly a part of Egypt's history, 'Adawiya's tapes, it seems, were still too "vulgar" for some settings where Egyptian culture was staged, celebrated, and consumed.

At the end of an interview in 2014 with Mufīd Fawzi, an Egyptian broad-caster for Dream TV, 'Adawiya was asked to choose a title to describe himself. Fawzi presented his guest with three possibilities: "Singer of the Egyptian Street" (*mughani al-hara al-misriyya*), "'Adawiya is A-OK" ('*Adawiya zay al-ful*), and "I Am History" (*ana tarikh*). Without a second's hesitation, the entertainer selected the final option.[113] In reality, 'Adawiya and countless other Egyptians who have been accused of producing and performing "vulgar" art remain to be written into Egypt's historical record. In offering an alternative history of Egypt's soundscape, economic opening, and cultural production in the mid- to late twentieth century, this chapter has taken a step in this direction. For the significance of so-called "meaningless" sounds, though, to be truly understood, much work remains to be done.

At the same time, cassette technology and its users did not only have an impact on the creation of Egyptian culture; they also altered the circulation of content. For the first time in Egypt's history, cassettes enabled anyone to become a cultural distributor. No longer limited to well-established channels of cultural production, recorded material began to move in a wide variety of ways that proved difficult to police. At the foundation of these sonorous circuits was an increasingly common activity: piracy. As we will see in chapter 4, piracy, as a popular practice, is nothing new. It began not with digital files online, but with magnetic tape reels decades earlier, when cassettes and their operators altered the very movement of cultural content at a time when Egyptian radio was state controlled, major recording labels exercised great authority, and elite artists wielded immense power.

Chapter 4

COPYING

Piracy, Cultural Content, and Sonorous Circuits

SHARIF ʿARAFAʾS BIOPIC *HALIM* (2006) TRACES THE MOMENTOUS journey of one of Egypt's most beloved artists—ʿAbd al-Halim Hafiz—from a struggling crooner to a revolutionary icon to a household name.[1] One of the more prominent players in this transformation is Muhammad ʿAbd al-Wahhab, a contemporary composer, singer, and kingmaker. Following a disastrous performance early on in the film at the National Theater in Alexandria, where ʿAbd al-Halim is booed off the stage and asked to perform ʿAbd al-Wahhab's songs, the young singer seeks out the advice of the "musician of the century." In Cairo, a comical exchange unfolds between the two artists in ʿAbd al-Wahhab's lavish living room. There, ʿAbd al-Halim introduces his host to Magdi al-ʿAmrusi, who joined him on the visit, as a "lawyer" and a "friend." The remark prompts the icon to ask his guests if he is being sued. Al-ʿAmrusi reassures him this is not the case, and ʿAbd al-Wahhab lets out a long, exaggerated laugh.

Unlike the actors in ʿArafa's picture, ʿAbd al-Halim and ʿAbd al-Wahhab did not laugh about lawsuits outside of the movies. In fact, both artists tried, and failed, to wield the law to protect the rights of their musical productions as well as those of the artists they represented as the cofounders of Sawt al-Fann, a major recording company, in the age of the audiocassette. One of their most formidable adversaries on this front was Sayyid Ismaʿil, a singer and a composer from the northeastern province of al-Sharqiyya. Born in the 1920s, Ismaʿil graduated from the Arab Music Institute in Cairo. Later, he earned a degree from the prestigious High Institute for Theatrical Arts, completing his studies alongside ʿAbd al-Halim in 1951.[2] Like ʿAbd al-Wahhab, Ismaʿil went on to sing, compose, and establish a prominent recording label, Randa Phone, named after his daughter, Randa, whose mother, ʿAida al-Shaʿir, was an Egyptian singer of some acclaim. Unlike, ʿAbd al-Halim and ʿAbd al-Wahhab, Ismaʿil has long since been forgotten by scholars of Egypt, even though his questionable use of audiocassette tapes altered the passage of Egyptian culture.

Building on our discussion of cultural production in chapter 3 and the suspect movement of audiotape technology in chapter 2, the pages to follow are not limited to any one segment of Egyptian society. Companies and consumers, politicians and police officers, artists and enthusiasts, all play a part in this chapter, which further elucidates the intersections of cassettes, culture, and contemporary politics by unpacking the contentious circulation of audiocassette recordings and the efforts to limit their mobility. Our history of cassettes and the things carried by them begins with a legal battle pitting ʿAbd al-Halim and ʿAbd al-Wahhab, two of Egypt's leading artists, against Ismaʿil, a third performer who succeeded in "stealing" their recordings. After introducing this fascinating standoff, I scrutinize the steps taken by public figures to eliminate counterfeit cassettes, before demonstrating how multiple forms of piracy hindered all of these efforts. As we will see, copying sounds, in the case of Egypt, was not simply a matter of replicating recordings. Audiotape technology empowered an unprecedented number of people to become cultural distributors, changing the very circulation of cultural content.

PIRACY: CASSETTES AND THE ILLUSION OF COPYRIGHTS

In the late 1970s, Sawt al-Fann, Randa Phone, and their respective representatives collided over cassette recordings in Cairo's courts. Sawt al-Fann fired the first shot. According to reports published in the popular press in December 1976, ʿAbd al-Wahhab, the venture's visionary, demanded E£200,000 in damages from companies that recorded his songs on audiotapes.[3] One of the parties responsible for reproducing ʿAbd al-Wahhab's tracks without his permission was Ismaʿil, whose label, Randa Phone, also released cassettes for several other leading artists affiliated with Sawt al-Fann, including ʿAbd al-Halim, Asmahan, and Farid al-Atrash.[4] To make the artist pay for his serious transgressions, the co-owners of Sawt al-Fann sued Isma'il for E£100,000.

The lawsuit, however, was dismissed by the North Cairo Court in January 1977. Ironically, during the trial, it came to light that the Society for Authors and Composers (Jam'iya al-Mu'alifin wa al-Mulahinin), an international entity with a local branch over which 'Abd al-Wahhab presided in Egypt's capital, permitted Isma'il to produce the cassettes in question. Victorious, the owner of Randa Phone publicly vowed to continue to manufacture similar audiotapes for the benefit of listeners.[5] Two months after the court's verdict, 'Abd al-Halim passed away from liver failure in England, leaving 'Abd al-Wahhab to deal with the defeat in Egypt.

After mourning the death of his friend, co-owner, and fellow musician, 'Abd al-Wahhab renewed his legal battle against Isma'il before the end of the calendar year.[6] The plaintiff's background in music and management enabled him to level the same lawsuit from a different angle. This time around, he sued Isma'il not as the co-owner of Sawt al-Fann but as a singer (*mutrib*) who had failed to financially benefit from the agreement struck by the accused with the society.[7] Not surprisingly, the gravity of the renewed legal battle carried well beyond the confines of the courtroom to the association overseen by 'Abd al-Wahhab. In the aftermath of a lengthy discussion concerning Isma'il's cassettes and his potential dismissal from the society, 'Abd al-Wahhab resigned as the entity's president in May 1978. Prior to storming out of the meeting, the artist informed his colleagues that he was "unable to preside over a society where one of its members assails the rights of others."[8] Ultimately, the resignation was short-lived, but the spirited discussions concerning cassette piracy continued for years to come in Egypt. But before engaging with these debates, let's first consider the final chapter in the Isma'il–'Abd al-Wahhab saga.

In the fall of 1979, Isma'il went on the offensive. Already entangled in more than one legal battle, the owner of Randa Phone countersued 'Abd al-Wahhab, 'Abd al-Halim's heirs, and Sawt al-Fann for E£100,000. The grounds for the lawsuit was a cassette tape created by Sawt al-Fann with the same 'Abd al-Halim hits that Isma'il had then recently produced. Remarkably, 'Abd al-Wahhab, Isma'il contended, did not obtain the necessary approval from the Society for Authors and Composers to manufacture the tape.[9] In October 1980, further details regarding 'Abd al-Wahhab's lawsuit and Isma'il's counterattack surfaced in the popular press. According to one report, 'Abd al-Wahhab and 'Abd al-Halim's heirs then sought E£500,000 in compensation, while Isma'il also upped the ante, requesting

FIGURE 14. Randa Phone cassettes (from left to right): 'Abd al-Halim Hafiz, Muhammad 'Abd al-Wahhab, Farid al-Atrash, Nagat, and Sayyid Isma'il. Photo by the author.

E£505,000 in damages. These astonishing figures exceeded the original amounts that either party demanded five times over.[10] More than two years later, in the spring of 1983, lawsuits between 'Abd al-Wahhab and Isma'il remained open and ongoing in Egypt's courts.[11]

Throughout these legal battles, and until 'Abd al-Wahhab's death in 1991, Isma'il continued to produce, distribute, and profit from the songs of Sawt al-Fann artists. 'Abd al-Halim, 'Abd al-Wahhab, al-Atrash, and Nagat all appeared on cassettes carrying the Randa Phone insignia and Isma'il's name (fig. 14). Joining these musicians were several other stars, including Fairuz, Shadia, Layla Murad, Nagat 'Ali, Sa'd 'Abd al-Wahhab, Ahmad Fu'ad Hassan, Umm Kulthum, and even Isma'il, who released his own music, along with that of his wife, through the label. A survey of these tapes reveals that Randa Phone, unlike the vast majority of its competitors in Egypt, rarely printed copyright disclaimers on its tapes. Isma'il may have vigorously defended his right to reproduce music in court, but he felt little need to stake his claim on audio content outside of it.

The long-forgotten clashes between 'Abd al-Halim, 'Abd al-Wahhab, and Isma'il offer an instructive starting point for a historical exploration of cassette-tape piracy in Egypt. First, the court cases unsettle and enrich prevailing accounts of state-sanctioned musicians being in complete control of their careers by revealing the unauthorized reproduction, circulation, and sale of their music on audiotapes.[12] Second, these conflicts illuminate how people tried, and failed, to restrict what they deemed to be pirated content. Third, Isma'il's reproduction of songs from a period predating the invention of the audiotape calls attention to the connections between cassettes and other media, including records, radio, films, and television, which provided everyone from individual listeners to commercial ventures with a wealth of material to replicate on tapes. Taking these themes into account, let's consider how piracy played out in practice in Egypt, where audiocassettes empowered anyone with a tape recorder to become a cultural distributor.

POLICING PIRATES: FROM WORDS TO ACTION

Beginning in the early 1980s, cassette companies started to gain greater traction in Egypt. According to statistics published in the press, the number of cassette ventures doubled from twenty to forty in less than a month at the start of 1981.[13] By the end of the decade, one estimate placed the number of cassette operations at more than five hundred.[14] In reality, these figures were likely far greater. Many enterprises involved in the production, distribution, and sale of cassettes remained under the state's radar and off the pages of official reports. With the expansion of the cassette market, the increasing availability of cassette players, and the growing demand for audiotapes in an era of mass consumption, piracy became an ever-more-pressing problem for local gatekeepers.

The steps taken by Egyptian artists and authorities to crack down on the "illegal" circulation of cassette content widely varied, ranging from the establishment of a special police force to the drafting of new laws to the placement of a stamp on cassette covers. The objective of these diverse measures, however, was one and the same: to bring order to an increasingly decentralized cassette culture. At the forefront of antipiracy efforts was a familiar face, 'Abd al-Wahhab, who was both the owner of a major cassette company and a victim of cassette piracy.

In the spring of 1979, the Society for Authors and Composers convened in Cairo under 'Abd al-Wahhab's leadership to discuss a disturbing new report published by the organization's counterpart in Paris. According to the document, the number of pirated cassettes circulating worldwide had reached 850 million per year, with Egypt contributing 300,000 tapes, annually, to the staggering total.[15] To play its part in cracking down on piracy globally, the society outlined multiple initiatives to be implemented locally. For starters, 'Abd al-Wahhab and his fellow members proposed that a stamp be placed on the sleeves of cassettes. The visible marker, issued by the society, would aid a novel security unit—"the cassette police" (*shurtat al-kasit*)—in differentiating legitimate from counterfeit recordings. As for those responsible for producing pirated tapes, that is, those without the society's stamp, the association advocated for criminal trials in accordance with article 47 of Law No. 354, which protected the rights of authors.

In response to pressure from ʿAbd al-Wahhab, Egypt's then president Anwar Sadat instructed his interior minister Nabwa Ismaʿil to establish a special police force to combat cassette counterfeiting shortly after the society's meeting in April.[16] The executive decision came on the heels of Egypt's entrance into the Geneva Convention (1971), an international agreement whose signatories swore to restrict the illegal reproduction and distribution of phonograms, or recorded sounds. Those apprehended by the police unit and convicted of practicing piracy in Egypt would be required to pay a fine. Second-time offenders would face more severe punishment, namely short-term prison sentences, lasting no more than six months, in addition to the confiscation of their recording equipment and the closure of their operations. To facilitate the force's crackdown on piracy, within months of the security unit's creation the Society for Authors and Composers distributed a million stamps to be placed on cassette jackets.[17] Together, all of these developments worked to criminalize cassette piracy, which, in the words of ʿAbd al-Wahhab, had become "a profession for the unemployed" whose products distorted artistic works and endangered public taste.[18]

Within a year of launching those measures, the society met again to discuss the effectiveness of antipiracy programs. The timing of the session was of the essence since "the number of counterfeit cassettes was *continuously* rising despite police campaigns."[19] The growth of piracy in Egypt prompted some local actors to propose new solutions. One such initiative was introduced by Mahmud Lutfi, the legal adviser for the society, who drew on his knowledge of copyright regulations abroad to aid artists at home. In the winter of 1980, Lutfi, following a meeting in Senegal for the Union of Authors and Composers, presented a new way to ensure the payment of copyright royalties. The plan focused on blank tapes and, more specifically, the companies that produced them. According to the proposal, a percentage of the companies' sales would go to artists. Thus, even if piracy could not be eradicated, authors and composers would at least profit from the purchase of blank cassettes.[20] Other actors, less keen on suggesting new ideas, criticized existing mechanisms. Nasir Husayn publicly attacked the cassette police on the pages of *Ruz al-Yusuf.* In a biting editorial in April 1981, the writer pointed to "gangs that kidnap and loot artistic works without any deterrent or protection." The freedom with which these groups operated in Egypt prompted Husayn to pose a simple question at the end of his article: "Where are the cassette police . . . and why are they not performing their work until now?"[21]

The journalist's critical remarks in the popular press piqued the attention of General Muhammad 'Abd al-Halim, the director of the cassette police and an assistant to the interior minister. Eager to defend his position and the officers overseen by him, 'Abd al-Halim responded to Nasir's sharply worded article in the following issue of *Ruz al-Yusuf.* The cassette police, he explained, were working closely with cassette companies to bring an end to piracy in Egypt. Starting from the ground up, the police looked into the legal standing of cassette ventures. Once verifying that the proper paperwork was in place, the special task force instructed businesses to apply a distinctive marker on all of their cassette recordings. These symbols, in turn, would enable 'Abd al-Halim and his officers to easily spot counterfeit audiotapes during raids.

The campaigns conducted by 'Abd al-Halim and his men relied, in part, on tips from the same commercial enterprises they monitored and protected. Businesses, after all, had a vested interest in reporting people who detracted from their profits. In the first two years of its existence, the cassette police conducted six operations, resulting in the confiscation of both pirated audiocassettes and videotapes. Despite the successes of these campaigns, however, Nasir took care to remind readers in the very same column that more needed to be done by 'Abd al-Halim's unit. Words and "the language of warnings," the writer concluded, "are of little use with this *breed* of people."[22] To assist the police in targeting pirates—criminals who, in the eyes of Nasir, constituted another type of people entirely—some cassette companies offered much-needed support.

CONSUMERS, COMPANIES, AND CASSETTE JACKETS

In a sharply worded article on cassette piracy in advance of the First Festival for the Arabic Song, Jan al-Kisan, a Syrian author and cultural commentator, acknowledged the difficulty of protecting copyrighted content in the age of the audiocassette. With the proliferation of tape recorders in the Middle East, authorities could do little to prevent people from recording songs off the radio or from other tapes. Far worse than those who created tapes for personal use, however, were cassette dealers. Unlike the average listener, companies produced poor recordings for profit. The cassettes released by them, al-Kisan maintained, grossly degraded original artworks and brazenly defied copyright regulations. Authors, composers, and singers "gain[ed] nothing from this work except false fame, horrible distortion, financial setback, and the loss of morale." Cassette merchants, meanwhile, freely dictated public taste, determined the prices for cultural productions, and "treat[ed] the song as a cheap commodity."²³ Global copyright laws held little purchase locally, where songs once heard on the radio were now sold on the sidewalk.

Al-Kisan's editorial, penned in Damascus in 1977 and published in the Cairo-based periodical *al-Majalla al-Musiqiyya* (Music Magazine), reads as a call to arms. In the piece, pirated recordings seemingly inundate Middle Eastern markets to such an extent that audiocassettes abiding by copyright laws do not even surface a single time in the discussion. This notable omission lends the impression that all cassettes, irrespective of their content, are illegal. On the difficulty of policing piracy, al-Kisan urges authorities to crack down on cassette companies, which, he claims, are single-handedly destroying Arabic music and corrupting the taste of the masses. To be certain, al-Kisan was not alone in this regard. Similar accusations echoed elsewhere.

Other articles also held companies accountable for pirated cassettes, which, at times, included songs from multiple labels and artists. Known as "cocktails," these unauthorized tapes, critics claimed, assaulted the rights of numerous parties, from singers to writers to recording labels.²⁴ Together, the reports framed cassette enterprises as the perpetrators of piracy par excellence. In reality, however, the picture was far more complicated. Cassette companies were also the victims of piracy, and their representatives strove to eliminate the alarming practice.

Piracy meant that legal cassette ventures lost out on large sums of cash. According to one estimate, losses amounted to more than E£100 million per year by the late 1990s, when pirated tapes drastically undercut the cost of original recordings and, consequently, enjoyed the lion's share of sales in Egypt. At the turn of the century, counterfeit cassettes were available for as little as E£2.50, while their legitimate counterparts cost upward of E£7–E£10.²⁵ To ensure that the content they released was not copied, businessmen adopted different strategies. Some officials pushed for only legitimate recording labels to be able to acquire blank tapes from factory floors, while others went so far as to offer to purchase new cars for the cassette police so they could better perform their duties.²⁶ Still other company executives turned their attention to cassette jackets, which grew more and more detailed over time and, therefore, less easy to replicate, at least in theory.

The standard cassette sleeve initially consisted of two and a half panels. The artist's name and photograph, along with the album's title and the label's trademark, appeared on the cover of the cassette, and the names of songs, authors, and composers, in addition to the company's address, adorned the remaining space.

More intricate cassette jackets were double sided. Artist, album, and company details continued to occupy one plane, while a photo of the musician extended across a second surface, which resembled a miniature poster.[27] Building on this more elaborate layout, many cassette sleeves later expanded to five or seven panels. With more space to operate, companies placed song lyrics and several pictures of the artist at the buyer's fingertips.[28] These flashier designs served two purposes. On the one hand, they deterred potential pirates. On the other hand, they attracted prospective consumers. To accomplish the first objective, which proved far more difficult to realize than the second one, some companies utilized cassette jackets to address piracy directly, targeting both would-be criminals and ordinary listeners.

Three of the companies to take an active stand against piracy on the packaging of their products were Muhsin Gabir's 'Alam al-Fann (The World of Art), Tariq 'Abdullah's High Quality, and Ahmad 'Abdu and Khaled 'Abdullah's al-Nur (Sharikat al-Nur lil-Intaj al-I'lami wa al-Tawzi'). The cassette sleeve for Nadia Mustafa's *Don't Fear for Me* (*Ma Takhafsh 'Alaya*), for instance, includes a message from 'Alam al-Fann to "the listener."[29] The subject of the note is a troubling phenomenon on the rise in Egypt. Piracy, the disclaimer warns below the album's tracks, was no longer limited to audio recordings; people also forged trademarks. To differentiate legitimate from counterfeit cassettes, the notification instructs consumers to confirm the position of the company's name on the tape as well as the case, in addition to verifying the enterprise's watermark on the back of the cover. If the visual or audio quality of the product seemed suspect, the label encouraged customers to alert either the company or the police. To motivate people to pick up the phone, 'Alam al-Fann provided the numbers for both entities and offered Egyptians a financial reward for any information on the whereabouts of pirates. The back of Mustafa's cassette-tape cover clarified the amount of this handsome prize—E£5,000—and declared that criminal penalties and civil damages awaited those responsible for any reproduction of the text at hand.[30]

Following suit, Tariq 'Abdullah's company, High Quality, similarly enticed consumers to become informants by offering to purchase information on the activities, places, and associates of pirates. As was the case with its competitor, the company provided people with the phone number of the cassette police and aided them in identifying counterfeit copies of their tapes. The packaging of one recording starring twelve different artists, for example, clarified the locations of the company's slogan on the cassette and its plastic packaging, as well as the color of the tape and its jacket.[31] Other High Quality cassette sleeves, adopting another approach to piracy, went so far as to cite specific pieces of legislation violated by pirates. Such was the case with the packaging for Ihab's *Sweetheart* (*Habib al-ʾAlb*) and Hamada Hilal's *The House of Time* (*Dar al-Zaman*), which threatened legal action against those responsible for its unsanctioned reproduction.[32]

There were then cassette companies that invoked neither the law nor the police but enlisted a higher power altogether in an effort to combat cassette piracy and dissuade its potential supporters. On the sleeve of one cassette recording featuring a popular Islamic preacher, ʿAmr Khalid, discussing "devotion," al-Nur issued an "important warning."[33] In bold, blue font, the label explained how another cassette venture produced some of Khalid's work without obtaining either his or its permission, prompting the company to take action against the parties behind the unauthorized tapes. The conduct of those responsible for the counterfeit cassettes, al-Nur asserted, was "unacceptable to any God-fearing Muslim." The company, accordingly, implored consumers to refrain from purchasing the "poor quality" tapes and their "stolen" content, lest they, too, end up "participating in the sin" of piracy. In the event that this religious appeal fell flat, al-Nur went on to note not once, but twice, on the same cassette's packaging that part of the tape's proceeds would go toward aiding orphans at a local charity. Pirates and their supporters, in short, stood to harm not only al-Nur's profits but also some of Egypt's most vulnerable children. Whether buying leads, referencing laws, disclosing ways to distinguish fraudulent tapes from original ones, or addressing proper Islamic conduct, cassette jackets, it is clear, presented companies with a public platform to discuss piracy directly with consumers, who may or may not have been listening.

A LOSING BATTLE

Antipiracy efforts, regardless of the exact form they assumed in Egypt, failed to bring an end to the reproduction of audio content on cassette tapes. Globally, pirated cassettes skyrocketed to an astonishing six billion tapes per year by 1981, a sevenfold increase from 1979.[34] Nationally, cassette piracy was a thriving industry run by what one Egyptian writer called a well-organized "mafia" in 1990.[35] Steps to eradicate the production, circulation, and sale of counterfeit cassettes in Egypt inspired only creativity. In response to the establishment of the cassette police, for example, Egyptians engaging in piracy adopted a variety of new techniques to avoid detection.

Some individuals, in direct defiance of company warnings, duplicated the sleeves of legitimate cassettes. After printing the forgeries in bulk, they sold the jackets to vendors who fitted them to cases containing pirated recordings. Others, meanwhile, utilized special printers to professionally brand cassettes with the names of labels, songs, and artists. The resulting replicas were so precise that even the companies responsible for manufacturing the authentic tapes struggled to distinguish the originals from the imitations. Still others disguised fraudulent cassettes within the covers of accredited recordings. Copies of the latest songs, for example, were marketed as Qur'anic recitation.[36] Vendors informed customers of this ruse while authorities remained in the dark. To make matters worse for cultural and political gatekeepers, pirated tapes were available to consumers often within hours of the authorized product's debut, leaving little or no time for officials to prevent people from purchasing the very items they aimed to confiscate. For all of these reasons, pirated audiotapes were a nightmare to police and impossible to eliminate from the public sphere, where their users altered the very movement of cultural content.

In the absence of concrete statistics on the number of counterfeit cassettes circulating in Egypt in the mid- to late twentieth century, the sheer quantity of tapes seized by the police begin to shed light on the pervasiveness of piracy well into President Husni Mubarak's rule. According to a statement from General Husayn 'Abd al-Rahman, the police force he directed confiscated around six hundred thousand cassettes per year by the start of the 1990s. During a single campaign targeting two popular quarters in Cairo—'Attaba and Ahmad Hilmi—the police seized fifteen thousand pirated tapes.[37] A week after *Ruz al-Yusuf* published these alarming figures, members of the Society for Authors and Composers publicly criticized the organization to which they belonged. On the pages of the same periodical, artists censured the regular absence of board members at meetings, the entity's inability to wield any real power, and the conflicts of interest that arose between cassette companies and select members, such as 'Abd al-Wahhab and Muhammad al-Mugi, who managed cassette labels. The composer Muhammad 'Ali Sulayman, taking the attacks one step further, accused the society of "encouraging cassette producers not to pay the fees of authors and composers" through its lack of authority. The stamp designed by the society and distributed to prevent the theft of audio content, he lamented, "was not on a single tape in the market."[38] A leading voice in the war on cassette piracy, the society appears as nothing more than a weak, dysfunctional organization in the editorial, incapable of regulating the circulation of audiocassettes near and far.

Even Mahmud Lutfi, a senior member of the society and one of Egypt's most vocal critics of cassette piracy, eventually acknowledged the failure of the measures he championed. In 1999, the legal consultant begrudgingly recognized the inability of the police to restrict counterfeit recordings. The force's struggles, he explained, were compounded by the unwillingness of other actors to enforce regulations that were already in place, which imposed a E£5,000 fine or short-term prison sentence for cassette pirates. Since officials amended the laws in 1992 to make them more stringent, not a single person had been sentenced in court for breaking them.[39] To better understand the losing battle waged by Lutfi, the Society for Authors and Composers, and the police against cassette piracy, we need to further explore how piracy played out in practice in Egypt. To gain a stronger grasp on the inner mechanics of this popular practice, let's turn to three forms of piracy—personal, state, and international—that highlight the significant obstacles authorities confronted when trying to control the circulation of recorded voices.

REPRODUCING EGYPTIAN RECORDINGS

Authorities striving to eliminate cassette piracy in Egypt grappled, first and foremost, with private citizens. Anyone with access to a tape recorder was capable of copying audio content from cassettes, movies, radio broadcasts, television shows, records, and live performances. The exteriors of audiotapes begin to evidence instances of personal piracy that proved difficult, if not impossible, for cultural and political gatekeepers to police. In the spirit of unpacking this form of piracy, a rich assortment of audiotapes originating from a single building in downtown Cairo offers a small window onto the wider production of counterfeit cassettes by ordinary Egyptians in the mid- to late twentieth century.[40] The collection includes forty-six tapes, in total, spanning multiple voices, genres, and decades. Twenty-six of the recordings are original tapes, released by licensed companies, while the remaining twenty recordings are pirated tapes, created by individual listeners. The unauthorized cassettes fall into two general categories.

The first group of cassettes consists of content over which people recorded. Tapes that were once home to the tracks of Midhat Salih, Georgette Sayegh, and Western disco artists, have been converted to feature the songs of Yusri al-Hamuli, Ahmad 'Adawiya, and Khalid 'Agag. The only visible clue of the unauthorized transfers is a few words fixed to the top of each tape. On pieces of paper, listeners scribbled the names of the Egyptian artists in pen. Two other musicians who suffered the same fate as Salih and Sayegh in the collection are Umm Kulthum and Beethoven, whom users replaced with Nadia Mustafa and Hassan al-Asmar. The erasure of both icons, even more so than the disappearance of their fellow performers, brilliantly confirms that no one, regardless of high standing in the Arab or Western musical canons, was immune to being supplanted on tapes.

Not all cases of personal piracy involved the substitution of one voice for another. Blank tapes also facilitated the unauthorized reproduction of acoustic content at a distance from the eyes and ears of Egyptian authorities. Returning to our collection, we encounter several such tapes that were filled with music. Angham, Simsim Shihab, and Ahmad 'Adawiya are a few of the Egyptian artists to surface on once-empty cassettes, which begs this question: From where did all these voices originate? In the case of our informal archive, Egyptians turned to both the radio and other cassettes to produce pirated tapes. It was necessary to harness each mass medium since certain singers, like Angham and Mustafa, were readily available on national airwaves, while other artists, like 'Adawiya and al-Asmar, circulated only on audiotapes because of their alleged vulgarity, which, as we saw in chapter 3, gatekeepers condemned for endangering public taste.

Looking beyond our cassette collection, it is impossible to know how many Egyptians profited from the sounds they personally copied, but it is beyond any doubt that the recordings they reproduced on tapes detracted from company coffers and artist earnings. Because of its scale and scope, personal piracy posed perhaps the single greatest challenge to Egyptian authorities who were eager to control the circulation of cultural content, but it was certainly not the only obstacle they struggled to overcome and eliminate.

State employees also produced pirated cassette tapes. Workers at the Egyptian Radio and Television Union, located in the Maspero building along the Nile in downtown Cairo, contributed to cassette piracy in more ways than one. Perhaps the most visible players in the reproduction of audio material were broadcasters, who provided people with a national stage to disseminate content they stole from the cassettes of their fellow compatriots.[41] There were then the activities of other Maspero employees, whose actions were less evident but by no means less important. Sound engineers, working behind the scenes, transferred radio programs from the building's audio archive to cassette tapes, which were then sold to radio stations abroad or presented as gifts from powerful people in exchange for unknown favors. According to 'Abd al-Qadir Shuhayb, a journalist for *Ruz al-Yusuf*, such was the case with *The Hallowed Ka'ba (al-Ka'ba al-Sharifa)*, a thirty-part series placed on cassettes for a group of Arab princes. Those responsible for the unlicensed reproduction, as well as that of other recordings, the writer observes, may well have been acting on the orders of their superiors at the union.[42]

A letter to the editors of *Akhir Sa'a* suggests that state employees at Maspero may well have been retailing unauthorized cassettes for some time. Published in the fall of 1980, four years after Shuhayb's exposé surfaced in *Ruz al-Yusuf*, the message opens on a provocative note: "They whispered in my ear, if you want any copy of a rare recording of Umm Kulthum, Shaykh Rifa'at, 'Abd al-Halim, or anyone else . . . you can obtain it from the radio for a certain price."[43] The author of the text, a Tariq Hamdi, proceeds to criticize the unacceptable transfer of priceless recordings, "a national treasure," to audiotapes. From these materials, cassette piracy, it would seem, pervaded even governmental entities charged with shaping and safeguarding Egyptian culture.

A close reading of the above snapshots implicates state employees in the production, circulation, and sale of counterfeit cassettes. Consequently, it further illustrates the limitations of antipiracy measures and forces us to recognize the institutionalization of cassette piracy. Police campaigns and Society for Authors and Composers initiatives stood little chance of succeeding in Egypt if they could not even prevent a governmental entity, yet alone anyone with a tape recorder, from engaging in acts of piracy. This is not to say, though, that local gatekeepers simply turned a blind eye to what was transpiring at Maspero. After radio officials reissued Umm Kulthum's songs on another medium, videocassettes, in 1986, Lutfi and 'Abd al-Wahhab threatened to file a lawsuit against the union unless the artists behind the tracks were paid for the novel product. A new financial agreement was necessary, both men argued, because the videotape did not yet exist when Umm Kulthum signed her broadcasting contract. Two years after 'Abd al-Wahhab initially expressed his concerns to the Radio and Television Union's president, however, his letter had yet to receive a response.[44]

By playing, manufacturing, and selling counterfeit cassette tapes, broadcasters, sound engineers, and their superiors at Maspero all engaged in state piracy, a practice that state-controlled companies, such as Sawt al-Qahira, further exacerbated by creating, distributing, and retailing cassettes without the permission of artists. Here, one need only consider an incident unfolding in the fall of 1979, when Muhammad al-Kahlawi, a popular (*sha'bi*) singer, demanded that a prosecutor meet at once with Sawt al-Qahira officials. The cause of al-Kahlawi's grievance was a cassette recording containing several of his songs, which he never granted the label the rights to reproduce.[45] Notably, in response to al-Kahlawi's accusation,

Sawt al-Qahira administrators admitted no wrongdoing. Thus, whether taking place behind closed doors in Maspero or in the studios of a major recording label, state piracy further contributed to the alarming growth of counterfeit cassettes, which circulated widely within Egypt's borders and well beyond them.

The voices of Egyptians at times resonated on pirated cassettes at a distance from their point of origin. A trip by one of the country's leading shaykhs to the United States offers a glimpse into the sonorous circuits supporting international piracy. In the late 1970s, Mahmud Khalil al-Husari embarked on a tour of Islamic centers in America, where he was the first shaykh to recite the Qur'an in Congress. During his sojourn, he met with the recently elected American president, Jimmy Carter, who would be in office from 1977 to 1981, and who received al-Husari as part of an Egyptian delegation, which included 'Abd al-Halim Mahmud, the Shaykh of al-Azhar, and Ashraf Ghorbal, Egypt's ambassador to the United States, in the Oval Office.[46] A black-and-white Kodak contact sheet chronicling the occasion captures Carter smiling widely as he shakes al-Husari's hand.[47] The president reportedly admired the shaykh's voice, and al-Husari offered to send Carter a sampling of his audio recordings from Egypt. Shortly after this brief encounter drew to a close, though, the shaykh learned that his work was already available across the Atlantic. It was an unwelcomed epiphany.

En route to Illinois, al-Husari stumbled upon a surprising advertisement in the *Chicago Tribune*. There, a company called the Islamic Recording Service marketed his Qur'anic recitations alongside those of several other shaykhs. Significantly, no agreement existed between al-Husari, his Egyptian partners, and the foreign entity, which illegally transferred his voice from Sawt al-Qahira records to blank tapes that subsequently garnered sizable profits in the States.[48] The advertisement no doubt came as a major shock to the shaykh, who was already a victim of counterfeit cassettes back in Egypt, where a number of Qur'an readers, in 1984, established a syndicate to demand payment for their recordings.[49] Unlike the fraudulent tapes in al-Husari's homeland, however, those in the United States clearly reveal that piracy crossed continents through transnational channels over which Egyptian gatekeepers enjoyed little to no control.

To be certain, not all Egyptians needed to travel abroad to discover their voices, or those of their compatriots, on pirated cassette tapes. Occasionally, fraudulent cassette recordings, circulating elsewhere, found their way back to Egypt. Around the time of al-Husari's visit to America, an Italian company piqued the attention of authorities in Cairo. Songs from several major stars, including Umm Kulthum,

'Abd al-Halim, al-Atrash, and 'Abd al-Wahhab, appeared on a series of pirated tapes carrying the foreign entity's trademark.[50] To ensure that the company was held accountable for the unauthorized products, the Society for Authors and Composers contacted its counterpart in Italy to discuss the blatant act of piracy. Other times, only word of pirated tapes reached artists in Egypt.

In the winter of 1990, 'Abd al-Wahhab received a letter from the Tunisian government congratulating him on the release of his recent song "Without Asking Why" ("Min Ghayr Layh"). The message arrived after the musician accused the Society for Authors and Composers in Tunisia of promoting cassette piracy. Despite the entity's claims to the contrary at the time, the congratulatory letter from President Ben Ali's government confirmed 'Abd al-Wahhab's earlier suspicions. In a second correspondence, the iconic performer asked his Tunisian colleagues how his song was available on tapes in a country where his label, Sawt al-Fann, had not distributed it. In light of this violation, 'Abd al-Wahhab, along with some other artists in Egypt, proceeded to accuse the Tunisian society of endorsing counterfeit cassettes by providing pirates with business licenses.[51] Much to 'Abd al-Wahhab's likely dismay, an answer from the foreign body was not forthcoming.

In short, as cassette piracy played out, the reproduction of Egyptian recordings assumed many different forms. At home, in Egypt, private citizens harnessed cassette tapes as a tabula rasa to record and rerecord what their hearts desired, while state employees, working for entities intent on shaping Egyptian culture, copied select sounds to audiocassettes for particular parties and mass audiences. Outside of Egypt, commercial ventures in the United States, Europe, the Middle East, and farther afield, contributed to the making and movement of unauthorized tapes. The actions of these international entities broadened cassette piracy and posed yet another obstacle to authorities who were already fighting a losing battle back in Egypt. Ultimately, by enabling people to reproduce sounds from records, radio broadcasts, and other cassettes, to consider only a few acoustic items, audiotape technology and its users radically expanded the circulation of cultural content at a time when Egyptian gatekeepers strove in vain to control the shape it assumed.

CASSETTES, CIRCULATION, AND CULTURAL CONTENT

Near the start of 1984, the Egyptian Ministry of Culture publicized its plans to glorify selected artistic giants in audiobooks that comprised cassette-tape recordings. The first icon to receive this honor would be a familiar face: Muhammad 'Abd al-Wahhab.[52] The following year, *Ruz al-Yusuf* reported that

'Abd al-Wahhab's audiobook would consist of ten cassettes covering his illustrious career. The tapes would include his most prominent songs, along with a "scientific analysis" of them, while the resulting audiobook would be sent to Egyptian embassies and cultural centers around the world.[53] In the summer of 2019, I came across one of these books, not abroad, but in Cairo.[54] Inside a faux snakeskin binder, the Ministry of Culture, the Radio and Television Union, and Sawt al-Qahira proudly present 'Abd al-Wahhab's "artistic history" in fading gold font. As promised, ten cassette recordings showcase the performer's momentous journey.

Colorful cassette sleeves display the names of two record labels in the audiobook. On paper, Sawt al-Qahira is responsible for most of the recordings, which surface under a single title: "Art History of Mohamed Abdel Wahhab." Sawt al-Fann, meanwhile, headlines two of the ten tapes, which respectively feature songs from 'Abd al-Wahhab and his longtime friend and Sawt al-Fann cofounder, 'Abd al-Halim Hafiz. Time has altered the original audiobook. Upon closer inspection, I discovered that the Sawt al-Fann tapes were likely added to the binder, perhaps by its owner. The Sawt al-Qahira cases are numbered and tapes 3 and 5 are missing. Moreover, only half of the plastic cases contained actual audiotapes. Of the five remaining cassettes, four were released by Sawt al-Fann, while the fifth and final tape originated from a surprising place. In the upper left corner of the audiobook, a Sawt al-Qahira case shielded a Randa Phone recording of 'Abd al-Wahhab's music. How the cassette tape ended up there is unclear, but it is beyond any doubt that Sayyid Isma'il's presence in a state-sanctioned project celebrating 'Abd al-Wahhab's legacy would have infuriated the honoree to no end.

In many ways, this history of cassette-tape piracy adds much-needed context to the above recording's appearance. If 'Abd al-Wahhab's clashes with Isma'il in the popular press and Cairo's courts opened this chapter, the convergence of the two entertainers in an audiobook, decades later, brings this exploration full circle. At the same time, the mere existence of the Randa Phone cassette underscores an important reality. Whether or not powerful individuals like 'Abd al-Wahhab or 'Abd al-Halim approved, Isma'il and countless other Egyptians regularly harnessed audiocassette technology to copy a wide range of sounds. In this regard, the presence of Isma'il's tape in 'Abd al-Wahhab's audiobook is oddly fitting. No matter the steps taken by contemporary authorities to police "unauthorized" audiotapes, cassette piracy prevailed in Egypt, where an everyday technology and its many users altered the very movement of cultural content.

If piracy is one key thread in the history of Egypt's cassette culture, then audiotapes are but one chapter in the history of piracy. In the case of Egypt, this narrative opens not with cassettes but with records. As early as the turn of the twentieth century, officials working for the Gramophone Company, a major player in the world of recorded sound, discussed and debated the dubbing of records in the Middle East. Letters between the label's headquarters in England and one of its branches in Egypt confirm the unauthorized reproduction of the venture's recordings in Turkey and in Syria, and outline a number of potential solutions.[55] These recommendations include utilizing connections in Beirut, bringing a lawsuit against those responsible for the counterfeit goods, and emblazoning a copyright disclaimer in Turkish and in French on all "Oriental records" before they left the company's factory floor in Germany.[56] The impact of these proposals is difficult to determine, but decades after these conversations transpired, the end of unauthorized records in the Middle East appeared nowhere in sight. As *Ruz al-Yusuf* reports, Egyptian recordings continued to surface on pirated records well into the rule of Gamal Abdel Nasser (1954–1970), outlasting the local British Occupation, the Ottoman Empire, and the Egyptian monarchy.[57]

Piracy, then, did not begin with audiotape technology. But as we have seen in this chapter, piracy became a popular practice, for the first time, courtesy of cassette tapes. The process of pressing records was an expensive, specialized, and time-consuming affair. For all of these reasons, the production of unauthorized records on a large scale was limited to a small number of well-equipped enterprises. The reproduction of sounds on audiotapes, conversely, was simpler, faster, and far more affordable. Indeed, the only tools required were a tape and a tape player. With the push of a button, anyone was capable of transferring countless sounds, from a wide array of sources, to audiocassettes. The possibilities were endless. And with a dual-cassette deck, material could be copied from one tape to another with ease and little expertise. In light of these differences, piracy, once within the purview of a few, became an activity of the many.

Audiocassette technology, accordingly, empowered anyone, regardless of age, location, gender, education, class, or economic standing, to become a cultural distributor. No longer restricted to the traditional role of cultural consumers, elite and ordinary Egyptians alike played an unprecedented part in the creation and circulation of cultural productions. As a result of these actions, audiotape technology and its diverse users drastically expanded the movement of cultural content at a point when major recording labels reigned, mass media was state controlled, and elite artists exercised immense power.

To be certain, cultural and political gatekeepers in Egypt did not simply surrender to cassette piracy. On the contrary, they strove to crack down on the making and movement of unauthorized audiotapes by going to court, writing and amending national laws, joining international conventions, establishing a novel police unit, and communicating with consumers on cassette jackets. Regardless of the forms these multifaceted measures took, artists, pundits, police officers, and company executives similarly failed to eliminate the unsanctioned reproduction of audio recordings by state employees, international companies, and anyone in possession of a tape recorder. The theft of audio content was far harder to police than the theft of cassette players.

In the end, cassettes not only recorded new sounds. They replicated existing ones. The reproduction of audio recordings on cassette tapes radically transformed the circulation of cultural content long before the dawn of satellite television and social media. At the same time, the ease with which many Egyptians copied any number of sounds troubled more than just artists, company executives, and law enforcement agents. Cassettes, recorded, copied, and circulated by individuals, challenged ruling regimes and their hold on history. As we will see in the next chapter, which places a sonorous spectacle into conversation with a subversive anthem, the creative possibilities and circulatory potential of cassettes powerfully converged in the case of one Egyptian artist who criticized political authorities and countered the very stories told by them through informal audiotapes.

Chapter 5

SUBVERTING

Shaykh Imam, Official Stories, and Counterhistories

ON THE MORNING OF 8 JUNE 1995, *AL-AHRAM*, EGYPT'S LEADING
newspaper, announced the passing of an iconic performer. The obituary, spanning
only four lines and surfacing on the thirtieth page of the state-controlled periodical, was remarkably unremarkable. Buried among advertisements for American
air conditioners, Korean television sets, and Swiss timepieces, the publication did
little more than confirm the death of Shaykh Imam. It recorded the artist's age,
claimed he was suffering from diabetes, and stated that Imam "became famous
after the setback of 1967," when he performed a number of "critical songs" penned
by Ahmad Fu'ad Nigm. The text concluded by citing one of Imam's awards from
an international association.[1]

This shallow portrayal of the artist of note deeply incensed many of his compatriots, who considered the superficial text irreverent, if not insulting. To mend
Imam's maligned legacy, a number of Egyptians went so far as to submit a second
obituary to *al-Ahram*, which the paper published the following day on the thir-
ty-first page. Unlike the earlier write-up, which merely marked Imam's departure,
the second actually mourned his death. It addressed Imam as "the artist of the
people," declared when his funeral would take place, and presented a black-and-
white photo of the deceased donning dark-rimmed sunglasses. After recording

Imam's birth in the village of Abu al-Numrus and his passing in the Cairo quarter of Hush Qadam, the column concluded by listing the names of more than 170 signatories, which included the likes of filmmaker Youssef Chahine, actor ʿAdil Imam, and writer Sonallah Ibrahim. The staggering number of names cascaded down the page and served as a visible reminder of the late singer's significance.[2]

Although it may seem odd to begin a discussion of Imam with notices of his death, these competing obituaries in *al-Ahram* provide a useful starting point for an exploration of official stories, counterhistories, and cassette technology. As we will see, the ideas of writing and rewriting were central not only to Imam's demise but also to his life's work. These two concepts are no more apparent than in the case of one event and the song inspired by it, which take center stage in this chapter and call attention to the crossroads of history, mass media, and popular culture. Building on our discussion of the creative power and circulatory potential of audiotapes in chapters 3 and 4, the pages to follow examine how these two technical attributes enabled Imam to challenge the Egyptian government's hold on history, a fact *al-Ahram* conveniently left out of his obituary.

In what is widely regarded as one of the warmest receptions an American president ever received overseas, Richard Nixon landed in Cairo on 12 June 1974. This chapter explores the writing and reframing of that event. I begin with a close reading in the state-controlled Egyptian press of Nixon's stay. Once unpacking what I call a "sonorous spectacle," I explore how one contemporary song, "Father Nixon" ("Nixon Baba"), directly challenged the Egyptian government's "official story" of the visit. To make sense of this unofficial soundtrack, I start with its singer, an "ordinary icon" whose voice spread on noncommercial cassettes created and circulated by individual listeners. After elucidating Imam's historical trajectory and the centrality of tapes to his career, I illuminate the movement of "Nixon Baba" in and outside of Egypt, before charting the track's lasting resonance, which witnessed a resurgence during the Arab Spring. As this chapter shows, cassette technology served as a powerful tool not only to criticize ruling regimes but also to counter the very narratives crafted by their advocates. By wielding audiotapes as a weapon, Imam did nothing less than narrate Egypt's history anew before a mass audience.

WELCOMING NIXON: OFFICIAL STORIES AND INFORMAL CASSETTES

The first of five stops on a weeklong "tour for peace" in the Middle East, Egypt presented an embattled Richard Nixon with a momentary reprieve from the throes of Watergate and a valuable opportunity to bolster his image abroad. In many ways, the journey was historic.[3] It was the first to be undertaken by a US head of state to Egypt in more than thirty years and succeeded a number of watershed moments, including Anwar Sadat's expulsion of Soviet advisers in July 1972, the first public announcement of Nixon's secret recordings in July 1973, the October War of 1973, and the resumption of full diplomatic relations between Egypt and the United States in April 1974.[4]

The stated objectives of the sojourn were twofold. Both Nixon and Sadat sought to strengthen US-Egypt relations and to promote peace in the Middle East. From the minute Nixon landed to the moment he departed, state-controlled Egyptian media closely followed his stay. Television and radio programs broadcast his arrival, periodicals published his speeches, and reporters publicized everything from a phone call he placed to the color of the mosquito net covering his bed.[5] Despite the brevity of the three-day trip, Nixon and Sadat managed to cover great ground. They paraded around Cairo, Alexandria, and the greater Nile Delta amid cheering Egyptians before they signed a statement confirming a mutual desire for closer economic, political, and cultural relations between the two countries.[6] On the eve of flying to Saudi Arabia, where a far-quieter reception awaited Nixon, Egypt's "great guest" invited his "heroic host" to come to the White House.[7] Less than two months later, before Sadat ever had a chance to set foot stateside, Nixon announced his resignation from the Oval Office on 8 August 1974.

At first glance, Nixon's tour of Egypt resonates with discussions of national celebrations and state-engineered stories across the Middle East. Elie Podeh, for instance, has examined iconic moments and their public legacy in the Arab world.[8] One of the five states to fall within his purview is Egypt, in which case he discusses the commemoration of King Farouk's coronation, the Free Officers' ascension to power, and the October War, among other twentieth-century moments. The celebrations detailed by Podeh are part and parcel of larger national narratives, the subject of a second volume by Laurie Brand.[9] Undertaking a comparative study of state rhetoric, Brand explores what she calls the "official stories" told by political regimes intent on securing their legitimacy and longevity. Drawing on government textbooks and the writings of elites, Brand scrutinizes a series of historical events and the work performed by them in Algeria and Egypt.

Notably, both Podeh and Brand similarly preface their groundbreaking analyses with methodological limitations. Podeh explains that he will be approaching festivities from the perspectives of those who orchestrated them, since historians, allegedly, are unable to uncover how ordinary people made sense of the things they witnessed.[10] Brand, meanwhile, admits that her work does not account for the role played by popular culture in the making—and, I would add, unmaking—of the stories told by states.[11] This chapter expands on both of these studies by unpacking the fanfare surrounding Nixon's visit, a national event, and the circulation of an incendiary composition on informal audiocassettes that unsettled the state's official story of his welcome. In so doing, it casts new light on both Egypt's history and the production of it.

THE SIGHTS AND SOUNDS OF A SONOROUS SPECTACLE

What Nixon's trip to Egypt lacked in time it made up for in spectacular moments. In this regard, the president's arrival in Cairo is particularly instructive. Before Nixon even landed, the Egyptian government took several steps to ensure that his first encounter with Sadat was properly staged. Authorities shut down the airport, adorned the runway with a red carpet, and assembled a robust honor guard prior to the descent of Nixon's plane. Shortly after receiving his guest, who was honored with a twenty-one-gun salute, Sadat escorted Nixon to a jet-black Cadillac.[12] The convertible, a security nightmare, served as a platform for the two men to stand side by side as a caravan of nearly two hundred vehicles left the airport for Qubba Palace.[13] The motorcade moved slowly, taking an hour to traverse only slightly more than ten kilometers, in the scorching sun.[14]

The leisurely pace at which the convoy coasted guaranteed that the presidents and the seas of Egyptians lining the streets around them greeted one another for more than a few seconds. How large were the crowds? The exact number of people bearing witness to Nixon's arrival is difficult to determine, but the masses prompted at least one Egyptian observer to compare Nixon's welcome to Gamal Abdel Nasser's funeral four years earlier, when millions of Egyptians flooded Cairo's thoroughfares to publicly express their anguish.[15] As was the case with the speed of the Cadillac carrying Nixon and Sadat, the car's course was deliberate. The presidents traveled down highways recently straightened by workers with bulldozers and passed under archways erected especially for the occasion.[16] The procession was far from a silent affair. Onlookers shouted in Arabic, "We believe in Nixon!," "Welcome to a man of peace!," and "We will not forget Palestine!" while sound trucks supported other chants in English, including "Long live Sadat" and "Long live Nixon."[17] Men played wooden flutes, a band of children performed curbside, and horns greeted the dignitaries at their final destination (fig. 15).[18] In

FIGURE 15. A roadside ensemble of children welcomes Sadat and Nixon. From Memory of Modern Egypt.

the words of one *Newsweek* reporter, the commotion surrounding Nixon in Cairo "made *Aïda* look like an off-Broadway revue."[19]

Nixon's arrival in Egypt begins to capture some of the key aspects of his welcome. First and foremost, the public procession illustrates the importance placed by the Egyptian government on planning his greeting, which extended far beyond the airport to the production of signs, the presentation of awards, the renovation of parade routes, and the establishment of an official office to coordinate the president's "popular reception" (*istiqbal sha'bi*) in Cairo.[20] Notably, the significant preparation that went into these undertakings reveals the great value assigned by Sadat's administration to both sights and sounds. The active role played by the government in celebrating Nixon's visit on a visual level is no more evident than in the placards directed at the guest of honor. The Ministry of Social Affairs, the Ministry of Information, and the Arab Socialist Union all welcomed Nixon on billboards, lampposts, and archways.[21] Mass-produced posters featuring the faces of Nixon and Sadat joined these displays and added to both men's respective visibility.[22] At the same time, Nixon's welcome, the visuals accompanying it, and the sounds attending it were not limited to Cairo. Egyptians residing elsewhere played an active part in the sonorous spectacle.

At a distance from the capital, Nixon's welcome was no less awesome. On the morning of 13 June, the presidents embarked on a second procession that came to constitute another important chapter in the "official story" of the historic visit. Leaving behind roads for rails, Sadat and Nixon boarded a train bound for Alexandria. Standing once more at Sadat's side, Nixon rode in a special open-air coach that provided its passengers and nearby crowds with unhindered views of one another. At times, no more than a few feet separated the world leaders from enthusiastic Egyptians who flooded adjacent platforms.[23] Like the airport motorcade, the train was in no rush. It slowed at stations in Benha, Quesna, Tanta, Kaft al-Zayyat, Itay al-Barud, Damhour, Abu Hummus, and Kafr al-Dawwar, where crowds awaited it with signs, banners, and flocks of doves.[24] Photographs of the train's journey evidence Nixon's extravagant reception across the greater Nile Delta.

In one image, Nixon smiles as a series of soldiers prevent cheering onlookers from coming too close to the tracks.[25] In another shot, Nixon joyously leans over the car's railing, pointing to a man waving with both hands, arms high above his head, as Sadat strikes a pose, staring directly into the lens of a nearby camera capturing the moment.[26] In a third photo, a banner proclaiming "We Trust Nixon" in English hangs atop a makeshift stand in the foreground, while a "welcome" sign in Arabic and English, along with a number of black-and-white posters featuring Sadat and his guest of honor, adorn a building in the background.[27] Notably, the point of origin for all three photographs is none other than the train car carrying Nixon and Sadat, whose administration went to great lengths to transform Nixon's welcome into a nationwide event. Documenting what Nixon saw and heard was part and parcel of this process. Staging and scripting went hand in hand.

Joining the presidents on their journey from Cairo to Alexandria were no fewer than a hundred newsmen, who served as witnesses to Nixon's booming reception. According to one reporter for the *Chicago Tribune*, the American president said he was "overwhelmed" by the cheering masses, whose chants of "Nixon!" occasionally "drowned out the clatter of the train."[28] Public-address systems, along the lines of those outfitted to sound trucks in Cairo, facilitated the cheers. According to Wilton Wynn, a *Times* correspondent on-site in Kafr al-Zayyat, speakers instructed spectators how to shout "Wel-come Nixon, wel-come Nixon, Sadat, Sadat." This exercise seems to have enjoyed a great degree of success. By the time the train appeared, Wynn reports, an ensemble "began to play with fury, and the chant 'Wel-come Nixon!' split the air."[29] The noises accompanying Nixon's appearance en route to Alexandria did not die down in the coastal city. A musical troupe greeted the presidents with national songs upon their arrival, while cheering and clapping joined the sounds of woodwinds and women ululating in the streets.[30] Outside of the Sidi Gaber train station, newly paved roads, triumphant archways, and a third parade awaited the two politicians.[31] For both men, the scene had surely become a familiar one.

At a distance from the eyes and ears of Egyptian crowds, the state organized still other spectacles. Nixon received Egypt's highest honor, the Collar of the Nile, in addition to the keys to cities, a gold medal, and flowers from children during various ceremonies.[32] Two of Egypt's leading newspapers, the state-controlled *al-Ahram* and *al-Jumhuriyya*, closely documented these honors and served as public platforms for multiple parties to personally welcome the American president. On their pages, everyone from an oil company and a shoe factory to a national ministry and "the people of Alexandria" greeted the foreign leader.[33] These notices were not without precedent. In fact, they closely mirrored other texts that centered solely on Sadat. In the same month that Nixon visited Egypt, "the people of Port Saʿid" and "the people of Ismaʿiliyya" welcomed Sadat, the "heroic" president responsible for their liberation during the war in 1973.[34] As we will soon see, all of this fanfare would inspire "Nixon Baba," an informal response to Nixon's official welcome. But prior to exploring this subversive song, let's first turn to the voice behind it: Shaykh Imam.

SHAYKH IMAM: THE MAKING OF AN ORDINARY ICON

Much like the editors of *al-Ahram*, commentators have yet to afford Shaykh Imam the same attention as state-sponsored artists, who enjoy lengthy literary afterlives, or even his partner Ahmad Fu'ad Nigm, whose poetry is the subject of detailed studies.[35] Those who have addressed Imam often rush to unite him with Nigm in print and, consequently, neglect major aspects of his trajectory.[36] In the spirit of enhancing current accounts of Imam and also unpacking the voice behind cassette recordings of "Nixon Baba," it is useful to begin with Imam's life before Nigm. Here, the musician's memoir, which was recorded in 1993 by Ayman al-Hakim, a writer for *al-Kawakib*, an Egyptian weekly, offers a unique window onto Imam's evolution.

Born Imam Ahmad Muhammad 'Isa on 2 July 1918 in a small village outside of central Cairo, Imam was the only one of eight boys to survive more than a few days past birth.[37] Shortly thereafter, he lost his sight to a rural medicine administered by his mother to cure an eye infection.[38] Like the other children in Abu al-Numrus, Imam attended a local *kuttab*, or primary school, where he learned to recite the Qur'an, which he memorized at the age of twelve. Sometime later, Imam left Abu al-Numrus for Cairo on the recommendation of a Shaykh Mahmud Sulayman, who, after hearing the boy sing at a local wedding, encouraged Imam to continue his religious studies in the capital.[39] Imam's Islamic education in Cairo, however, was not to last.

Outside of his classes, Imam frequented cafés to listen to Shaykh Muhammad Rifa'at recite the Qur'an over the radio. This hobby ultimately led to his dismissal from the Islamic institute.[40] Homeless, Imam ventured to the working-class neighborhood of al-Ghuriyya. There, he scraped out a living by singing at weddings and religious festivals, and by reciting the Qur'an in houses and stores. During one of his performances, he piqued the attention of Shaykh Darwish al-Hariri, who invited him to be his student.[41] After learning the fundamentals of "Eastern music" from one of its masters, who instructed well-known artists like Zakariyya Ahmad and Muhammad 'Abd al-Wahhab, Imam added the oud to his musical arsenal and dedicated himself to his art on a full-time basis by 1945.[42] In the years to come, he continued to sing at local events and even enjoyed a brief stint with Ahmad's troupe.[43] In 1962, Imam met Nigm and began to set his poetry to music.

If Imam honed his craft prior to joining forces with Nigm, his voice spread by way of informal cassette recordings that carried the poet's colloquial verses. In the absence of state-controlled Egyptian media, which refused to broadcast Nigm and Imam's critical collaborations, noncommercial cassette tapes enabled the duo to reach a wider audience.[44] Throughout Sadat's rule, Imam's tapes were not available in stores, kiosks, or on the streets. Instead, listeners manufactured them at a distance from soundproof professional studios. Egyptian universities, political demonstrations, social clubs, the artists' apartment, and the homes of friends all served as spots to record Imam singing. The resulting cassettes, which

FIGURE 16. Shaykh Imam smiles alongside Nur al-Din al-ʿAqqad's children, ʿAsim and ʿAfaf, in the Cairo suburb of Maadi, where a cassette radio records his in-house performance, 1976. Source: Sayyid ʿInaba.

enthusiasts copied and distributed among one another, afforded the singer's live performances a degree of permanence.[45]

In his recent treatment of Imam, the Egyptian writer Amir al-ʿUmri recalls how he replicated and traded the artist's audiotapes with friends. He remembers how they "placed two recording devices together" to duplicate cassettes "recorded during sessions hosted by Shaykh Imam in the houses of his friends and followers." Over time, al-ʿUmri's collection of Imam's amateur tapes gradually grew.[46] In some cases, individuals with a large number of the singer's cassettes shared them with interested parties. The family of Nur al-Din al-ʿAqqad, an Egyptian politician, possessed most of Imam's tracks and enjoyed a close relationship with the performer, who personally directed people to their informal audio archive (fig. 16). Once establishing a rapport with the family, fans of Imam were free to copy cassettes in their home in Maadi.[47] As one may expect, the quality of Imam's tapes was not always high.[48] Nevertheless, they managed to evade state censors, bypass cultural gatekeepers, and freely circulate within Egypt and well beyond the nation's borders. In all of these regards, cassette recordings of "Nixon Baba" were no exception.

"NIXON BABA": AN UNOFFICIAL SOUNDTRACK

On the eve of Nixon's departure from Egypt, Henry Tanner, a correspondent for the *New York Times*, reflected on the president's warm reception. "So far there has not been an incident in the entire extraordinary spectacle," he observed. "Not a single jarring note, not a single dissenting voice has been heard."[49] The silence described by Tanner was not a lasting one. Nigm and Imam were fast at work on a new collaboration, "Nixon Baba," which directly challenged the "official story" of the foreign dignitary's welcome. The song's account of Nixon's visit notably departed in more ways than one from the coverage offered by state-controlled Egyptian media (see the appendix).

First and foremost, "Nixon Baba" bound Nixon to a crisis that irreparably damaged his image: Watergate. After opening with "Welcome Father Nixon, O you of Watergate," the lyrics cleverly allude to the leader's national woes on multiple occasions. Imam, for instance, points to Nixon's then "frail" state and comments on the possibility of him being "no longer around." Unlike the crowds who shouted "welcome," the singer, well aware of Nixon's shattered credibility, refuses to greet him out of ignorance. In addition to spotlighting the president's political troubles across the Atlantic, the composition offers a jarring counternarrative of his local reception in Egypt.

In one verse, the song compares Nixon's arrival to a *zar*, or a ceremony for excising spirits, in which the parade's officials appear as spiders alongside convulsing whores.[50] Sadat, the devil, possesses the woman responsible for vanquishing him and leads the theatrical show. Meanwhile, in a second verse, Nixon's welcome assumes the form of a wedding procession, or *zaffa*. The American president plays the part of a groom one married as a last resort, a pathetic figure on which Imam audibly spits. Both scenes are part and parcel of a "never-ending *mulid*," a chaotic celebration usually held in honor of Prophet Muhammad's birthday or the nativity of other religious figures, not a politician's visit.[51] All of this rich imagery, which evokes the types of events in which Imam performed prior to meeting Nigm, was immediately intelligible to Egyptian listeners, many of whom encountered the verses on informal cassette recordings.

A passing exchange in Ahdaf Soueif's 2000 novel *In the Eye of the Sun* offers a small window onto the social life of such recordings. In the book, Asya, an Egyptian studying abroad in England, struggles to translate Nigm and Imam's "Nixon Baba." In the company of friends and family, she listens to the track on a cassette smuggled by her sister, Deena, out of Egypt. The recording begins with "crackling," "whispers," and "applause," acoustic evidence of its amateur production at a Cairo University concert four months earlier in March 1976.[52] The performance, Deena recounts, almost did not occur. When Nigm and Imam arrived on campus, at the request of "the Cultural Society," students found the doors to the lecture halls locked. The dean, in possession of the keys, refused to meet with Imam's admirers and his secretary offered little support. In search of a space for Imam to sing, Deena and her classmates looked for an auditorium that had been forgotten by the administration. In the "Insects Department," located apart from the school's main building, they found an open hall where Imam performed. The dean, Deena reports, was less than thrilled, and dissolved the Cultural Society for "endangering order in the college."[53]

Once making its way from Egypt to England on a cassette, "Nixon Baba" captivated a new audience in Soueif's story. After every few lines of the song, the group present pauses Imam's tape, allowing Asya ample time to explain each phrase, at length. Starting with the song's opening couplet, she attempts to elucidate why Imam refers to Nixon as "father" (*baba*), the singer's wry use of the verb "honored" (*sharaft*), and the grammatical construction binding the president to the event that plagued him back home: Watergate. Barely into the song and already eager to relinquish her role as interpreter, Asya forges on to the next two lines at the behest of her companions. Following a "deep breath," she proceeds to unpack the meanings of two words denoting "worth" and "appearance," before breaking down another lyric that refers to both "bowls" of beans and oil and the Arab "rulers" welcoming Nixon on his tour of the Middle East.[54] Ultimately, Asya finishes the first stanza of "Nixon Baba" before the phone rings, sparing her from translating any further. On the call, she confesses that the composition requires a "page of footnotes for every line."[55] For Egyptian listeners, however, the verses were far from a mystery and the "footnotes" readily known. Spanning only five pages in Soueif's lengthy tome, this fictional account of Imam's cassette draws inspiration from the material life of his actual tapes. Fans of Imam recorded "Nixon Baba" and other songs at a distance from professional studios during public and private events, like the Cairo University concert. Copies of the recordings subsequently evaded authorities on audiotapes.

Grainy home videos of these acoustic affairs confirm the presence of cassette recorders in Imam's vicinity as late as the 1990s.[56] At times, the informal recordings yielded by concerts resulted in official productions. Following Nixon's visit to Egypt, a sound engineer from Tunisia by the name of Al-Hashimi Bin Faraj traveled to Cairo.[57] Once in the capital, he sought out Imam. Like many others to visit the artist in Hush Qadam, Bin Faraj recorded Imam performing several songs, including "Nixon Baba." Two years later, in 1976, Le Chant du Monde released an album in Paris titled *Le Cheikh Imam chante Negm* (Shaykh Imam sings Nigm).[58] The LP, which included "Nixon Baba," was based on Bin Faraj's earlier recording.[59] The making of this record, one of a few albums released in France to feature Imam, clearly captures the movement of "Nixon Baba" at a distance from Egypt.[60] More often than not, though, the song traveled, near and far, not on vinyl records but on cassette tapes, like the one in Soueif's novel.[61] Listeners recorded, distributed, and duplicated the anthem well beyond the reach of Egyptian gatekeepers. And despite the best efforts of Sadat's regime to control the "official story" of Nixon's visit, it could not prevent Nigm and Imam's "Nixon Baba" from becoming the sonorous spectacle's unofficial soundtrack.

As a result of noncommercial cassette recordings, "Nixon Baba" appears to have made quite a splash. According to its artists, the song "spread at the speed of lightning" and surpassed their earlier collaborations.[62] Faith Petric, an American folk artist who traveled to Egypt and profiled Imam in 1980, lends weight to the tune's initial popularity. "Nixon Baba," she maintains, "became such a hit that people were singing it in the streets."[63] Although it is difficult to confirm these claims, perhaps the most telling indication that the informal anthem may have been heard widely on audiocassettes was the Egyptian government's decision to arrest Nigm and Imam shortly after Nixon's visit. In a letter to the Foreign and Commonwealth Office at the end of September 1974, a British embassy official noted that Nigm and Imam, along with their friend and fellow artist, Muhammad 'Ali, were apprehended for "smoking hashish." This charge, however, was certainly spurious. As the diplomat observes, "Everyone assumes (and is probably intended to) that the real offence lay in their lampooning not just of the regime but of the US connexion, Uncle Henry and all." The "lampooning" the attaché mentions, no doubt, refers to "Nixon Baba," which continued to wander on copied cassettes to such an extent that both the Egyptian government and foreign envoys, it appears, were well aware of the audio recording and its "famous blind singer."[64]

While it is challenging to completely elucidate the immediate impact of "Nixon Baba," the song's lasting resonance is beyond any doubt. Video recordings on YouTube verify its longevity. In one clip from 1984, the first year Imam was free to travel abroad, the singer performs "Nixon Baba" before a boisterous audience in Algeria.[65] There, Imam's cassettes, one local journalist explains, preceded the musician's physical arrival.[66] Still other uploads on YouTube illustrate the record-ing's more recent afterlife. A four-year old boy with a Levantine accent recites the song in a grainy home video, a full orchestra performs it with a choir at a cultural center in Alexandria, and Maryam Salih, an independent Egyptian artist who grew up with Imam's music, sings an electro-rock version of it in downtown Cairo.[67] There is then the case of a 2020 Facebook post, appearing on a popular Middle Eastern page, where the first line of "Nixon Baba" serves as the caption to a formal photograph of Sadat and Nixon waving as their motorcade passes below a "We Trust Nixon" banner in Egypt's streets.[68] Here, the lyric's mere presence, "Welcome Father Nixon, O you of Watergate!," forcefully reframes state-controlled Egyptian media coverage of Nixon's stay some four decades earlier. Once a coun-terhistory circulating on noncommercial cassettes, Imam's song enjoys new life online, where it continues to shape people's perceptions of Nixon's welcome. In all of these instances, the reappearance of "Nixon Baba" is part and parcel of Imam's wider resurgence, which has witnessed the founding of Facebook groups in his memory, the creation of associations to celebrate his legacy, and the revival of his music on- and off-line, including by protesters in Tahrir Square in the days leading up to Husni Mubarak's historic fall.[69]

Perhaps most tellingly, even those who disliked "Nixon Baba" could not help but to remember the song long after Nixon's official welcome faded from memory. In this regard, an article surfacing in *Ruz al-Yusuf* further underscores the musical number's enduring resonance. In the editorial, two artists take center stage, Sayyid Mikkawi and Shaykh Imam. Early on, both performers, we are told, embarked on similar tracks. They enrolled in *kuttabs*, memorized the Qur'an, and went on to recite it. Later, however, their trajectories diverged. According to Imam, he chose "the path of revolution and poverty," whereas Mikkawi chose "the path of pageantry and power." Consequently, Imam elaborates, one became an "artist of the people" and the other an "artist of the aristocrats."[70] In response to these remarks, Mikkawi ridiculed two of Imam's songs. First, he attacked "Guevara Is Dead" ("Jifara Mat"), questioning why "an artist of the people" in Egypt would mourn a revolutionary a world away. "Has Egypt," Mikkawi retorts, "abandoned its heroes to the point where one sings to Guevara?"[71] Not wasting any time and neglecting the fact that Imam does indeed mention one such hero, Salah al-Din, in the same song, Mikkawi proceeds to criticize "Nixon Baba." In familiar fashion, he attacks Imam by posing a question. "Does committed nationalist singing," he asks, "mean that one sings a song in which he says to Nixon (come close to be spat on)"?[72] The fact that Mikkawi so easily recalls this line, if only to condemn it, is significant. "Nixon Baba" had surfaced fourteen years earlier. Thus, regardless of one's opinion of the subversive anthem, it is clear that Imam's performance of it continued to endure in the ears of listeners, supporters and critics alike, well after the curtain fell on Nixon's official reception.[73]

Three days prior to Nixon's arrival in Cairo on 12 June 1974, a reporter for the *Washington Post* relayed a conversation between two Egyptians. One, a working professional, bemoaned the horrendous state of his country's roads and the absence of tires available for purchase in the local markets. "But Mr. Nixon is coming," the man concluded, "so we won't have to put up with this much longer."[74] Jim Hoagland, a Pulitzer Prize–winning journalist, takes this statement seriously and cites it as evidence of the inflated expectations held by Egyptians with regard to Nixon's visit. Three other readings, however, are possible. First, the man's final remark may illustrate the extent to which state-controlled Egyptian media succeeded in exaggerating the significance of Nixon's sojourn. At the same time, this comment may allude to the Egyptian government finally taking action to address domestic problems prior to Nixon's historic stay. Or, perhaps, the statement was made in jest, a wry critique of regime rhetoric. In the case of Hoagland's report, it is impossible to know the exact meaning behind the anonymous man's words. But, on the basis of "Nixon Baba," it is clear that not all Egyptians celebrated Nixon's visit alongside Sadat and his administration.

Both *Time* and *Newsweek* characterized Nixon's trip to the Middle East as a "hegira," drawing a direct comparison between the American president's fleeing from the turmoil of Watergate and Prophet Muhammad's escaping persecution in Mecca.[75] Despite reports to the contrary, the informal production, circulation, and performance of "Nixon Baba" on cassettes confirm that Nixon was not immune to criticism in Egypt. A matter of days after the foreign leader's resignation, *Ruz al-Yusuf* announced an important victory. The same magazine whose reporters publicly declared to "see through" Watergate now boasted that it alerted readers to Nixon's departure before other news outlets.[76] To substantiate this claim, editors republished an article from 5 August that announced that Nixon had secretly agreed to vacate the presidency if both Republicans and Democrats accepted certain conditions.[77] This text, the editors argued, served as evidence that *Ruz al-Yusuf* "does not lie" and is "more truthful" than the *New York Times* and its competitors. The delicious irony of this proud proclamation would not have been lost on Imam, Nigm, or anyone else listening to cassette recordings of "Nixon Baba" in Egypt and well beyond its borders.

SHAYKH IMAM AND COMPOSING HISTORY

In Sonallah Ibrahim's novel *Dhat*, the book's namesake, an ordinary Egyptian woman, works for a local newspaper in Cairo. Stationed in one of the periodical's more meaningless departments, a unit responsible for identifying errors and compiling reports that never make any difference, Dhat, one day, encounters a photographer carrying a tape recorder. Not in any rush to actually work, the man plays a cassette relaying "something far more radical and subversive" than either "'Adawiya" or "Shaykh Imam."[78] The recording features the voice of a Sa'd Idris Halawa, a hardworking peasant striving to make an honest living in the Nile Delta. Addressing the "people of Aghour," a small village and perhaps his home, Halawa condemns a recent action taken by Anwar Sadat, namely his decision to open an embassy for Israel on 26 February 1980. Furious and frustrated, Halawa calls upon Sadat to expel the Israeli ambassador from Cairo at once, and he threatens to kill himself and two hostages, "members of the weary and oppressed people," if the president, or, in his words, the "Khedive," an Ottoman title hearkening back to an era when other individuals ruled with absolute authority, does not comply with his demand.[79] While the content of this fictional recording is certainly fiery, the narrator's opening observation concerning the cassette's subversiveness easily overshadowing that of Imam's tapes misses a central point.

Audiotape technology enabled individuals, like Imam, not to simply criticize ruling regimes but to vocally deconstruct the very stories told by them. Whether praising politically active youth in "Raja'u al-Talamidha" ("Return of the Students"), holding the military and Gamal Abdel Nasser accountable for Egypt's devastating defeat to Israel in the 1967 war in "Baqara Haha" ("Haha's Cow") and "al-Hamdulillah" ("Praise Be to God"), or mocking the promises of French president Valéry Giscard d'Estaing, who visited Egypt shortly after Nixon, in "d'Estaing" (see the appendix), Imam harnessed audiotape technology to compose Egypt's history anew before a mass audience, undermining the state's dominant narratives of contemporary events on more than one occasion. This power, I contend, is far more subversive than attacking any one person. By challenging a ruling regime's hold on history, its production, performance, and remembrance, Imam's informal cassettes, created and circulated by individual listeners, compel one to reexamine

Egypt's historical record and the power dynamics at play in its construction. Notably, this challenge, posed by Imam through audiotapes made of little more than magnetic reels, plastic cases, and a few metal screws, arrived long before satellite television and social media sites empowered people to reorient state-engineered accounts through far more advanced technologies.

Ultimately, Imam embodied, expressed, and emboldened oppositional politics. By lending a voice to ordinary people, ridiculing foreign leaders, and taking Egypt's rulers to task, he confronted political authorities and the tales spun by them. In so doing, Imam found an especially attentive audience in the Egyptian Left and the Arab Left more broadly, whose intertwined histories are only beginning to be reimagined.[80] At a point in time when Islamism was gaining ground, Imam played a key part in keeping the flame of resistance alive among leftists. This feat was all the more impressive in light of the fact that he did not have access to the same national platforms as his peers. Unlike Umm Kulthum, Imam never had the luxury of requesting that a song be played less often on Egyptian radio.[81] Imam, accordingly, may not have reached a truly national audience, but he broke new ground in reshaping national narratives. The singer's life, lyrics, and informal cassettes evidence political dissent in a time of authoritarian rule, calling attention not to the consolidation of power but to its contestation, highlighting contention in an age of imposed consensus. By mobilizing the creative power and circulatory potential of audiotapes, Imam subverted one of the most powerful tools in the arsenal of Egypt's ruling regimes: their stories.

In navigating Imam's audiotapes, the productive power of popular culture becomes readily apparent. Cultural products, that is to say, do not merely reflect historical developments. They play an active part in the fashioning of history. In this regard, another point must be made. Too often, scholars marshal cultural productions, whether in the form of films, novels, cartoons, poems, or countless other creative objects, only to illustrate what we already know about the Middle East and the region's rich past. Here, one need only consider how the lyrics of several Egyptian songs audibly advance Nasser's pan-Arab agenda. In the case of Imam, conversely, we see how informal cassette recordings challenge what we think we know, or, in this instance, the Egyptian government's "official story" of Nixon's visit. As a result, "Nixon Baba" raises several broader questions. First and foremost, how might other cultural products, from North Africa to the Arabian Gulf, reorient Middle East history and our understanding of it? Likewise, how might historically rigorous accounts of popular culture reimagine the making of modern nations? And what is the future of popular culture, as an avenue of academic inquiry, in Middle East studies? The answers to these questions promise to enhance both the writing and rewriting of Middle East history.

Anwar Sadat was by no means a stranger to the scripting and rescripting of Egypt's past. As one Egyptian historian observes in passing, Sadat penned two different iterations of his autobiography.[82] The first version, *Unknown Pages* (*Safahat Majhula*), ceased production after he became president in 1970.[83] The second version, *In Search of Identity* (*Al-Bahth 'an al-Dhat*), presented then president Sadat in a more heroic light.[84] These competing autobiographies, much like Imam's dueling obituaries, brilliantly underscore Sadat's attempts to not only secure but also rethink his place in Egyptian history. Consequently, they capture the dynamic nature of the historiographical enterprise. Unlike Sadat's *In Search of Identity*, however, it is safe to say that Nigm and Imam's "Nixon Baba" was not a revisionist history of which Sadat would approve. The construction of Egypt's past, from the perspective of its ruling regimes, was not an activity to be undertaken by just anyone. As we will see in the next chapter, the writing and rewriting of Egypt's history are not limited to Sadat and Imam. Audiotapes that continue to linger in Egypt raise key questions for present-day historians.

Chapter 6

ARCHIVING

Microhistory and Material Traces of Tapes Past

ON THE UNPAVED STREETS SOUTH OF THE CITADEL IN CAIRO'S FRI-
day Market (Suq al-Jumʿa), cassettes collect dust as crowds of Egyptians make their
weekly purchases. One of the recordings, cushioned by a blanket, commemorates
Egypt's second president, Gamal Abdel Nasser (1954–1970), promoting two of the
iconic leader's national addresses, while another tape, tossed on the ground, pays
tribute to Bakhita Khalifa Barih (d. 1966), a Coptic woman who was the subject
of a mass on the fortieth anniversary of her passing.[1] Across the capital, in Khan
al-Khalili, a second market catering to foreigners and locals alike, Abu Hamza rests
in the shadow of two major landmarks, the storied El Fishawy Café and the historic
al-Husayn Mosque. Thousands of cassettes, carrying everything from comedy acts
to sermons and popular music, surface alongside videotapes and compact discs on
the recording label's wooden shelves. Meanwhile, at a distance from the shop, in
Zamalek, a more upscale part of the metropolis, a third cassette collection emerges
in the back of a trailer brimming with antiques, only to vanish a week later when
the chief executive officer of a bank allegedly bought the entire lot to launch an
audio library. There are then other cassette venues of which I heard but never saw,
such as a kiosk in the Cairo suburb of Maadi where the owner's daughters, more
than one cab driver alleged, sold few tapes but socialized with potential suitors.

Whether discarded or displayed, audiotapes, in all of these settings, evidence a once-robust cassette culture of which only material traces remain in Egypt.

This chapter incorporates the voices of a library director, an electronics dealer, and a religious scholar, among others, to offer a microhistory of audiotape technology in Egypt.[2] Taking place in Cairo in the summers of 2015 and 2019, the conversations through which these voices emerge provide a more intimate picture of cultural production under Husni Mubarak (1981–2011) and raise important questions with respect to the preservation of Egypt's cultural heritage after his downfall. The sounding of some voices and the silencing of others, the use of audiotapes as historical records, and the fashioning of alternative archives are among the topics that gain greater clarity in the pages to follow, which pave the way for future ethnographies of sound that are historically rigorous and attuned to the daily lives of ordinary people. Drawing inspiration from innovative studies of Fado, Maftirim, and Salsa in places as disparate as Lisbon, Istanbul, and Cali, this chapter does not navigate a type of music making but instead traces the social life of audiocassettes in Cairo.[3] In so doing, it similarly traverses multiple sites, from a public library and a private collection to an electronics outlet and online platforms, which collectively provide a productive window onto a wider cassette culture and Egypt's recent past.

As Donald Reid has deftly demonstrated in his scholarship on museums and Cairo University, institutional histories need not lose sight of individuals and may yield valuable insights into larger historical matters.[4] With both of these points in mind, each of the sections in this chapter open with an establishment's present-day setting before diving into its past development. By relying on oral interviews, in addition to textual materials, such as cassette sleeves, and visual sources, like photographs, we will spotlight places whose histories remain unwritten and redress "the relative absence of micro-narratives" in modern Middle East historiography.[5] As will become clear, the conversations that form the foundation of this investigation add color to a number of the issues covered throughout this book, from the passage of cassette technology across Egypt's borders to the circulation of audiotapes at home. More importantly, they enhance and complicate prevailing historical narratives in and outside of the state-controlled Egyptian press. In this regard, memories in particular perform multiple tasks here, connecting the past to the present, linking the momentous and the mundane, and conveying information that other historical actors felt did not merit documentation.

By drawing on all these resources, we will directly contribute to the study of cultural production and cultural conservation in modern Egypt. More specifically, we will elucidate how ordinary citizens participated in the making of Egyptian culture and unpack the politics of preservation when it comes to audio recordings.[6] Accordingly, the subject of archives is central to this discussion, which looks beyond the familiar topics of missing documents, restrictive research clearances, and an ever-watchful security sector to the making of multimedia libraries and the fate of informal cassette collections that continue to linger in kiosks, stores, and warehouses. To begin to make sense of these interconnected themes, our journey starts at the Cairo Opera House.

AUDIOCASSETTES AND THE STAGING OF CULTURAL HERITAGE

In the shadow of Saʿd Zaghlul's statue, a towering monument depicting the iconic Egyptian nationalist saluting toward the Qasr al-Nil Bridge connecting Zamalek to Tahrir Square and downtown Cairo, the Music Library rests at the eastern entrance of the Opera House complex. Part and parcel of the National Cultural Center (al-Markaz al-Thaqafi al-Qawmi), an umbrella organization belonging to the Ministry of Culture that oversees all on-site activities, the library is but one of many buildings located within the gated grounds, which contain nearly a dozen different structures for creating, preserving, staging, and debating cultural productions. A publication from one of these entities, the Cultural Development Fund (Sunduq al-Tanmiyya al-Thaqafiyya), is one of the few documents to introduce the Music Library's mission and materials.

According to a short, one-page entry, the establishment's purpose is twofold. On the one hand, it assembles and archives "musical heritage" (al-turath al-musiqi). On the other hand, it provides "integral cultural services" (al-khidamat al-thaqafiyya mutakamila). In the spirit of realizing both of these objectives, the library welcomes researchers as well as members of the general public to make use of its audio, visual, and textual resources. At the time of the passage's printing in 1997, these holdings consisted of 4,483 audiotapes, 1,020 records, 1,008 videocassettes, and 310 compact discs, in addition to 3,580 musical scores, 2,197 Arabic books, 2,015 foreign-language texts, and 246 reference items in Arabic and English.[7] Whether originating from the old Opera House, the Cairo Symphony Orchestra Library, or the new Opera House, all these historical sources eventually made their way to the Music Library following its opening at the hands of former first lady Suzanne Mubarak on 24 December 1994.

The inauguration of the Music Library in the mid-1990s marks one of several milestones in a broader campaign undertaken by the Ministry of Culture and Mubarak's administration to establish libraries in Cairo in particular and across Egypt more generally. Within a few weeks of the Music Library's opening, Suzanne Mubarak attended a similar event a few miles away on Muhammad Mazhar Street. This time appearing at the former palace of Princess Samiha Kamil, the eldest daughter of Sultan Husayn Kamil (r. 1914–1917), she celebrated the mansion's conversion into the Greater Cairo Library on 24 January 1995. Less than two months later, the Mubarak Public Library, named after the president (only to be renamed the Egypt Public Library following his ousting), opened its doors down the Nile in Giza on 21 March 1995. Once the private residence of ʿAbd al-Hakim ʿAmr, a founder of the Free Officers who held several different political posts under Nasser, the library, like its predecessors, boasted not only books but also audio materials, including cassette tapes. Rounding out these new institutions in Cairo, a library named after Talʿat Harb, a vocal advocate for Egypt's economic independence who founded Bank Misr in 1920, later debuted in the working-class neighborhood of Sayyida Zaynab on 25 November 1995. At the same time, the building of libraries under Mubarak was not limited to Egypt's capital.

The Village Libraries initiative (Maktabat al-Qura), a state-engineered program overseen by Suzanne Mubarak, simultaneously strove to enlighten "poor villages" up and down the Nile. Following a competition held by the Cultural Development Fund, selected engineers and architects worked together to construct libraries at a distance from Cairo in Buheira, to the north, and in al-Minya, to the south, in September 1994, and later in Aswan in March 1996. Whether taking place in or outside of Cairo, the ceremonies celebrating the beginnings of many of these libraries did not simply announce the starts of new enterprises. They provided public figures, like the former first lady, with a stage to publicize their investment in education and in Egyptian culture.

A handful of color photographs preserved in a paper folder within the Music Library shed light on the venture's grand opening. Starting outside, a sharply dressed Suzanne Mubarak cuts a blue-and-white ribbon in one of the shots. To make this task as easy possible, a stocky man in a suit, perhaps one of her bodyguards, stretches out the strip of paper before the first lady as she snips it in the presence of a small crowd. Among those in attendance are Faruq Husni, Egypt's Minister of Culture from 1987 to 2011, and Nasir al-Ansary, the director of the

Cairo Opera House from 1991 to 1997, two officials who never appear to be too far from the occasion's action.

In another photo, Suzanne, now indoors, looks over a miniature violin in the company of the same men. The instrument likely originated from a nearby ensemble, led by a third man in a tuxedo and entirely comprising children in matching attire. From the group's presence, it appears that the young artists performed for the Music Library's guests of honor. In still other pictures, the first lady holds the faces of a young boy and girl belonging to the group and playfully points at the children with the Minister of Culture as the Opera House director smiles. Overall, the photo shoot lends the impression that political authorities care about the arts, education, and the Music Library, a sentiment that was again on display only a few weeks later. On 17 January 1995, Husni and al-Ansary escorted 'Atif Sidqi, Egypt's prime minister from 1986 to 1996, around the premises. Notably, the Music Library's director 'Abbas Muhammad Salama, who remained on-site long after photographers departed and public figures like Mubarak and Sidqi disappeared, surfaces in only one of the images documenting both visits. Standing in the foreground, off to the side, he is the only person sporting a badge, perhaps justifying his presence.

If state publications and official photo ops reveal only a fraction of the Music Library's development, then conversations with 'Abbas, who has overseen the institution since its inception, yield additional insights into both the enterprise's past and its present.[8] Before embarking on a career at the Music Library, 'Abbas received a bachelor's degree in library and archival studies in 1987. Shortly after graduating, he made his way to *Ruz al-Yusuf*, a leading Egyptian magazine based in Cairo. At the popular periodical, 'Abbas aspired to create a "modern" record-keeping system, but he soon ended up serving a rotation at the al-Ahram Foundation (Mu'assasat al-Ahram), which he left, shortly thereafter, in search of work more in line with his professional skill set. Sometime later, 'Abbas found a position in the bibliography department at the Egyptian National Library (Dar al-Kutub). There, he cataloged a significant number of texts over the course of a year until Dr. Ratiba al-Hefny, the first director of the new Opera House (1988–1990), offered to employ him. Two to three months later, Tariq al-Hassan succeeded al-Hefny as director (1990–1991) and instructed the newly hired 'Abbas to reenvision the Opera House's library.

Before al-Hassan's arrival, the library had been limited to a single room developed by Dr. Husayn Fawzi, a prominent scholar of music, history, and geography.

Five employees managed its collections, which consisted solely of books. At al-Hassan's command, the library migrated to a larger room in the main opera building. As the library's holdings continued to gradually expand, thanks in large part to 'Abbas, al-Hassan suggested that the venture move yet again to a more spacious environment. Ultimately, this recommendation came to fruition under al-Hassan's successor, Nasir al-Ansary, who personally worked with 'Abbas to identify the Music Library's present-day setting in 1993. By the end of the following year, in December 1994, al-Ansary celebrated the repository's new home alongside Suzanne Mubarak and Faruq Husni.

The Music Library enjoys the distinction of being the first "multimedia" library in Egypt. But how did its audiotapes, videocassettes, and records end up on its shelves? According to 'Abbas, the earliest audiocassettes came from a series of boxes. Around the time of the library's first move within the Opera House, 'Abbas made a startling discovery. He found five hundred cassettes in a single storeroom. The tapes lacked any information concerning their contents and had been deposited by sound engineers who documented Opera House occasions but cared little about the recordings after they created them. To make the tapes more accessible, 'Abbas began to listen to the neglected reels, one by one. He then recorded the actors involved on the cassettes' jackets in pen and compiled the dates and locations of the events in a spreadsheet.

The library's first videotapes surfaced in a similarly surprising manner. Early in his career, 'Abbas ran into the director of a second storage area in the opera complex. The employee informed him that a government inspector was coming to perform a routine check and that he needed to send off four hundred videotapes, lest the official ask why the items remained in his care. 'Abbas replied that the recordings, which documented Opera House events, belonged in the library, much to the wonder of the worker who thought that the library contained only books. As for the initial records, LPs arrived from multiple locations. Several came from the personal estate of Dr. Fawzi, while others emerged from the private collections of fellow Egyptians. Ultimately, all of these items, along with written works, formed the foundation of the Music Library's multimedia archive.

Within the Music Library, visual, textual, and audio sources surface in different rooms. For the audiocassette collection, several metal cases with sliding glass doors contain thousands of tapes that at one time occupied wooden shelves in the same space. The recordings fall under several categories. A digital index compiled by 'Abbas reveals thirteen different classifications with further subdivisions.

These groupings are wide ranging, including "religious works," "ballet and modern dance," "folk art, acrobats, and circus," "cultural activities," "recitals," and "chamber music." Listeners, accordingly, could encounter an academic discussion of Muhammad 'Abd al-Wahhab's contributions to Arabic music, an evening gathering honoring prominent poets writing in colloquial Arabic, or any number of concerts showcasing professional ensembles on the library's cassettes. One common thread uniting these seemingly disparate acoustic events is the place in which they unfolded. Nearly all of the affairs on the tapes occurred at the Cairo Opera House complex, where sound engineers recorded them and 'Abbas archived the resulting productions. The few cassettes that did not originate at the Opera House came from recording labels, such as Sawt al-Qahira, and carried singers like Umm Kulthum, Faiza Ahmad, and a handful of other artists whose repertoires nicely complemented the audio library's "high" cultural content. Together, these tapes contributed to the Opera House's broader aims.

As a pamphlet published by the Cairo Opera Press explains, the Music Library advances the Opera House's efforts in "enriching cultural life and anchoring the value of knowledge and the spirit of enlightenment to build the creative Egyptian subject" (al-insan al-misri al-mubdi').[9] To these ends, the Music Library offers visitors access to what administrators working for the National Cultural Center deem to be materials worthy of preservation and public consumption. Thus, the cultural heritage presented at the Music Library is by no means comprehensive. Indeed, the cassette tapes on display elevate certain sounds and entirely exclude others. In this regard, the remarks of 'Abbas on cassettes, vulgarity, and the study of Egyptian culture are noteworthy.

On the impact of audiotapes and their users on Egyptian music, the Music Library director claimed that some entities, such as Sawt al-Hubb, Sawt al-Fann, and Sawt al-Qahira, three major recording labels in Egypt, released cassettes carrying "high culture," while other actors harnessed the technology to spread "low culture." Audiotapes, 'Abbas elaborated, empowered everyone from elite musicians to garbage collectors to create and circulate cultural works that shared little in common with one another other than the platform on which they appeared. From the librarian's point of view, the immense usability of audiotapes posed certain problems. 'Abbas claimed that illiterate microbus drivers from the countryside, for instance, blasted "vulgar songs" (aghani habta) with "meaningless" lyrics, which he and other passengers were then forced to hear during their daily commutes. Such audiotapes significantly diverged from other cassettes broadcasting the likes of

Umm Kulthum and Muhammad ʿAbd al-Wahhab, two emblems of high Egyptian culture who crafted what ʿAbbas considered "refined" melodies.

To be certain, ʿAbbas did not believe that only particular kinds of performers deserved to be studied. He admitted that *shaʿbi* singers like Ahmad ʿAdawiya and Shaʿban ʿAbd al-Rahim, who cultural critics repeatedly slammed for being "vulgar" and whose music traveled widely on cassette recordings, were an undeniable part of Egypt's cultural history. Nonetheless, he argued that these figures should be examined in specific contexts, such as the "weakening of public taste" or the rise of "vulgar music." As for the lack of books on ʿAdawiya and ʿAbd al-Rahim, ʿAbbas pointed to an imbalance in sources. The legacies of artists like Umm Kulthum and ʿAbd al-Wahhab were more accessible to writers than those of entertainers like ʿAdawiya and ʿAbd al-Rahim. This fact, perhaps, is no more apparent than in the Music Library and its collections.

The Music Library's holdings, in large part, are shaped by its close relationship with the Opera House, for which it serves as a major repository. Nevertheless, the library has arguably made few attempts to expand the material horizons of its cassette archive. Such endeavors would require financial support and additional personnel that the entity simply does not enjoy. As of July 2015, only one other employee assisted ʿAbbas at the Music Library. Even from the establishment's start, ʿAbbas exclaimed, the little support received by the library amounted to E£8,000 from the late Dr. Fawzi's estate, a selection of CDs from various embassies, and some recording equipment from the Opera House. Thus, cassette recordings carrying ballet recitals and opera performances that relatively few Egyptians witnessed, and likely even fewer would return to hear, are easily available to researchers, while audiotapes containing sounds consumed by far more citizens continue to collect dust in kiosks and shops, warehouses and homes, across Egypt.

As Mark Katz has convincingly argued in a panoramic history of recording technology, records, cassettes, CDs, and MP3 files do not merely preserve art; they transform it.[10] In the case of Cairo's Music Library, audiotapes, much like books, musical scores, and other published works, function as historical records. They materialize past acoustic events and make fleeting moments available to listeners for years, even decades, after they transpired. In so doing, the recordings offer a window onto Egypt's cassette-tape culture, albeit a carefully curated one, and call attention to the politics of staging and preserving cultural heritage. In the interest of further unpacking the social life of cassettes and their users, as well as the ideas of inclusion and exclusion when it comes to the historical study of Egyptian culture and the nation's soundscape, let's step outside of the Music Library and travel across town to a second cassette venture that has since ceased to exist.

AUDIOTAPES AS ENTERPRISE PAST: THE HISTORY OF A FORMER LABEL

Massara, the first of multiple subway stations in the working-class neighborhood of Shubra, is just five metro stops from the Opera House, to the east and north. A few blocks south of the Massara entrance on Shubra Street, a major thoroughfare, a second avenue, by the name of Ahmad Badawi, appears. Home to a series of cafés, pharmacies, and restaurants, and in the vicinity of mosques as well as churches, the road runs past a small electronics outlet. Rather unremarkable from the outside, the one-room store contains thousands of audiocassettes. Stacked in colorful columns from floor to ceiling, the recordings engulf an entire wall, which, with the exception of a few miscellaneous items, appears to be composed of audiotapes entirely (fig. 17). How did these countless cassette recordings, spanning so many voices, genres, and recording labels, and likely even surpassing the Music Library's official cassette collection in terms of sheer numbers, end up in a shop known for television sets, remote controls, and electrical cable?

Mansur 'Abd al-'Al, the venue's proprietor, first developed an interest in cassette tapes not in Egypt but across the Red Sea in Saudi Arabia.[11] Like many Egyptian citizens, Mansur traveled abroad to the Gulf during Anwar Sadat's rule in an effort to improve his financial standing. In Riyadh, he worked in aluminum production. On the factory floor, he met employees from as far away as India and communicated with his fellow economic migrants in English in the event that Arabic was not a common language. Outside of work, Mansur crossed paths with cassette stores that crept up in the capital. At the time, in the late 1970s, the audiotapes he encountered sold for a single Saudi riyal, or approximately sixteen Egyptian piastres, a fee that undercut the cost of cassettes back in Egypt by no small amount. Sometime after visiting Riyadh's cassette vendors, Mansur decided to change career paths. He packed up his belongings, purchased a thousand audiotapes, and traveled back to Egypt. At least some Egyptian migrants, it seems, returned home with not only cassette players, as we saw in chapter 1, but also cassette recordings, enabling them to disseminate new and established voices from the Gulf and well beyond the peninsula's borders.

Upon arriving in Egypt, Mansur explained to an astonished customs agent that he aspired to open a cassette store after having worked in Saudi Arabia for

FIGURE 17. A wall of cassettes in Mansur's electronics shop, 2015. Photo by the author.

the past few years. The officer, he recalls, was a respectable man who understood Mansur's ambitions and assessed a reasonable fee on the recordings, which filled two whole shipping cartons and carried the voices of Michael Jackson, Abba, Boney M., and the Dolly Dots, a popular Dutch girl band, not to mention Bollywood singers. In Shubra, Mansur began to sell the cassettes he acquired abroad and gradually learned which sounds local listeners desired. This increasing awareness led Mansur to expand his commercial activities from cassette distribution to production. In the mid-1980s, the newly emboldened entrepreneur launched the Egyptphone Company (Sharikat Egyptphone) in his present-day shop.

Unlike other cassette labels, which employed numerous workers to scout artists, circulate tapes, handle customers, and keep track of finances, Egyptphone was very much a one-man operation. Mansur fulfilled the roles of multiple employees he could not afford to hire, and rather than working with prominent singers who demanded large sums of money, he set his sights on smaller musical troupes that performed at weddings, birthday parties, and other celebrations. To produce what he called "simple things" (*hagat basita*) and "oriental music," Mansur rented studio space, with a standard recording session involving five or six instrumentalists and lasting between three and five hours. To keep his overhead as low as possible, he relied on word of mouth when it came to marketing his productions. In this regard, the trajectory of one of Mansur's earlier cassettes, *An Evening with Abbas & Hindia* (*Sahra ma' 'Abbas wa Hindiyya*), is particularly emblematic.

After manufacturing a thousand copies of the recording, which Mansur described as "oriental dance" (*raqs sharqi*), the producer deliberated how to best distribute the latest addition to his inventory. Television commercials were out of the question. A single minute of airtime, Mansur claims, ran as much as E£8,000. A more cost-effective means of promotion was to let the tapes "market themselves" on public transport. With a couple hundred cassettes in hand, Mansur went to bus stations across Cairo that serviced commuters traveling to the rest of the country. He passed out several tapes, free of charge, and *Abbas & Hindia* soon began to boom on buses. Passengers apparently enjoyed the recording and purchased copies of the tape from Mansur for around E£1.50 before embarking on their journeys. The album, it would appear, sold relatively well. Mansur went on to produce at least two other tapes starring the same duo. The director of the Music Library, no doubt, would have disdained this form of advertising and the kinds of tapes popularized by it. But in the case of Mansur's label, it was a necessity. As the business owner recounts, the cost of the Ministry of Culture's "art license" alone, which permitted people like himself to legally sell cassettes, ran nearly E£1,000, a considerable sum. This fee, in fact, was so great for Mansur that he penned a complaint to Egypt's president. Needless to say, his letter failed to elicit a response.

In many ways, the history of Egyptphone endures only in the memories of its founder. The cassette label eventually closed and failed to produce any renowned artists. The voices it did manage to elevate, if only momentarily, left behind little in the way of a paper trail and many of the label's recordings are no longer accessible. Mansur, for instance, could not produce a single Egyptphone cassette from the veritable wall of audiotapes in his shop when I met with him in 2015. Indeed, the first time I ever encountered any Egyptphone offering was on the shelves of another company four years later, when I stumbled upon a few Egyptphone recordings at Abu Hamza in Khan al-Khalili. Among the lingering tapes, traces of a label no longer, was a copy of *An Evening with Abbas & Hindia, Part 2*. On the cassette's cover, the two forgotten performers come into view. A smiling young man, stylishly dressed, appears in the background, fingers poised atop the bass buttons of a red and white accordion strapped to his shoulders, while a smirking young woman stands in the foreground in sheer sleeves and a blue sequin brassiere with mesh below covering the remainder of her torso. A pair of finger cymbals rest high above her head. From the half-wound reel, it seems the Egyptphone recording had been played, if not purchased.

For all of these reasons, a number of Egyptians with whom I spoke about cassette culture instructed me to focus on "prestigious" companies, such as Sawt al-Qahira, as opposed to "amateur" enterprises, like Mansur's venture. This general sentiment applied not only to the study of recording labels but also to the study of artists. Upon hearing my interest in *sha'bi* performers, like Ahmad 'Adawiya, and subversive singers, like Shaykh Imam, a prominent professor of media studies at Cairo University recommended that I instead follow in the footsteps of other researchers, who began with Sayyid Darwish, a pioneer of "modern" Egyptian music, before moving onto Umm Kulthum and Muhammad 'Abd al-Wahhab. A security officer in Shubra shared this opinion. Initially determined to uncover my "ulterior motives" for speaking with Egyptphone's founder, whose electronics shop was around the corner from a police precinct, he eventually suggested that I head to Sawt al-Qahira rather than wasting my time on a "nobody" like Mansur.[12] In both of these cases, certain places and people merit careful analysis, while other settings and individuals are unworthy of exploration. Insofar as Egypt's cassette culture is concerned, this belief is by no means new. Indeed, one need only consider the odd occasion when Mansur and Egyptphone graced the pages of the popular Egyptian press over thirty years ago.

On 30 March 1988, *Akhir Sa'a* published an investigative report that strove to illuminate what the weekly magazine deemed to be a "dangerous phenomenon." In the interest of rescuing "Egyptian taste from destruction at the hands of cheap art traders who strive for nothing except exorbitant wealth at the cost of Egyptian society's morals and values," the periodical assigned one of its reporters to dive deep into the world of "vulgar tapes" (*al-shara'it al-habita*) to assess how the "acoustic toxins" (*al-sumum al-sawtiyya*) on such cassettes reached listeners.[13] To solve this mystery, the writer speaks with several different actors, including an unskilled laborer who became a cassette singer, a customs employee who became a cassette composer, and various state officials in charge of policing cassette content. Among the individuals interviewed by the journalist is a former "scrap metal" worker who turns out to be none other than Mansur.

At the start, the *Akhir Sa'a* article frames Mansur as a cassette company owner and producer who defends the "vulgar cassette songs" he created and distributed to his compatriots. Mansur begins by saying that there is a market in Egypt for his "light" tunes, a number of which targeted specific members of the working class, such as bus drivers and microbus drivers, and which he refuses to recognize as "vulgar." One of the melodies he produced, for example, catered to construction workers. "Give it a bit of a weld," the number went, "the love market has a hole in it."[14] After permitting Mansur to briefly mention these numbers, which clearly evidence the very "problem" *Akhir Sa'a* sought to solve, the journalist asks Mansur to discuss his "beginning" with cassettes. What may appear to be an innocent question, at first glance, was arguably posed to highlight the cultural producer's lack of training in the arena of cultural production.

In response, Mansur explains that earlier in life he aspired to strike it rich and traveled to Saudi Arabia, where he worked in "scrap metal" production. Following a three-year stint abroad, we are told, he returned to Egypt and opened a store for electrical appliances. The business, however, was not successful, leading him to turn to cassette tapes in light of their great popularity. This transition, Mansur insists, was commonplace in Egypt. After a period of time selling tapes, Mansur launched a cassette production company. Notably, the name of this venture surfaces nowhere in the article, lest the state-controlled *Akhir Sa'a* inadvertently elevate the very cassette labels its writers and editors aimed to eradicate. Mansur goes on gradually to explain how he observed the "inclinations" of some

Egyptians and proceeded to produce several recordings. At the time of the article's publication, he was in the middle of manufacturing three cassette tapes. After acknowledging these current endeavors, Mansur reportedly made an important confession.

According to the *Akhir Sa'a* journalist, Mansur admitted that he was dissatisfied with the cassette recordings released by his label. "I am not content with all of the cassettes I have introduced," he allegedly declared, "but I am compelled to produce them because I consider the material returns that will come from this production." Elaborating on this claim, Mansur reportedly avowed that "all of the voices" on his tapes were "the farthest thing possible from singing." In fact, many of the artists with whom he worked, Mansur is cited as saying, could neither read nor write. To perform, they memorized lyrics in advance of recording them. With the cassette producer's apparent "guilt" established, Mansur's brief appearance in print concluded with one final disclosure. The cassette entrepreneur, we are told, attempted to create "refined art" and desired to record a song along the lines of Farid al-Atrash's "Night Stars" ("Nujum al-Layl"), a respected ballad, but the demand for such productions, Mansur maintained, simply did not exist.

Notably, Mansur was not the only one to be interviewed in the *Akhir Sa'a* article who expressed doubts about cassette recordings. Sha'ban 'Abd al-Rahim, a *sha'bi* singer hailing from a long line of ironers in Shubra, Mansur's stomping grounds, states that he wanted to present "purposeful songs" (*aghani hadifa*) but was "forced" to perform what his label demanded. The cassette celebrity, in short, was a "victim" of a newspaper salesman who became a cassette-tape producer who exploited his "ignorance" and made him sing "vulgar words."[15] Whether Mansur or Sha'ban made any of these "confessions," or merely said what they believed the *Akhir Sa'a* writer wanted to hear, is open to interpretation. What is less ambiguous is the article's agenda.

A colorful sketch accompanying the *Akhir Sa'a* report on "suspect" cassettes cleverly captures a number of the piece's themes. In the illustration, a well-dressed couple passes by a small cassette shop, not unlike Mansur's store, carved out of a brick wall. The entity's name, "Vulgarphone" (Habitphone), surfaces atop its entrance for all to see in bold red letters. Out front, a man with a sizable mustache, who appears to be the owner, smirks and smokes *shisha*. Sitting barely above the sidewalk, he dons a scarf, sandals, and traditional white turban. Despite the looseness of his robe, he seems to be as wide as he is tall. The pedestrians, meanwhile, look nothing like the merchant. The woman stands alongside her male companion in black heels, a knee-high red dress, and a stylish hat. A fashionable black necklace and matching handbag complete her ensemble. Not to be out-dressed, her partner sports a pair of shiny dress shoes, a tie, and a two-piece navy suit. A cigarette rests between his lips. In sharp contrast to the smiling vendor, the couple expresses no signs of contentment. The man raises his chin high in the air, refusing to even make eye contact with the retailer, while the woman stares sorrowfully at the salesman, her eyes hollow.[16] The image, needless to say, is rife with dichotomies. The cassette dealer is working class, more rural than urban, and fills his bulging belly by making and selling "vulgar" art, which he proudly advertises as such. The duo, conversely, is urban, upper class, and "refined."

From the article joining the drawing, we are led to believe that Mansur more closely resembles the cassette merchant, responsible for the perceived pollution of public taste in Egypt, than he does the "cultured" onlookers, who correctly lament or rightly ignore what the writer deems to be "vulgar" tapes and those behind them. Rather than trying to discover the origins of a "dangerous phenomenon" or the inner mechanics of a "cassette mafia," this discussion has explored the history of Egyptphone on its own terms. In the absence of hardly any extant sources, Mansur's recollections shed light on the company's past and another side of Egypt's broader cassette culture, traces of which endure in his small shop. Tapes that once circulated near and far now sit silently on the electronic store's shelves. The individuals elevated by many of these albums, from ʿAmr Diab to Hassan al-Asmar, remain household names, even though their cassettes no longer play.

What is the fate of this forgotten cassette collection? According to the onetime cassette producer, the holdings have piqued the attention of few local parties. Cairo University and the American University in Cairo are committed to archiving Egyptian culture, Mansur contended, but not the kind of cultural productions popularized by his cassettes. "High culture" alone, Mansur clarified, was what concerned both educational outlets. Whether this alleged lack of interest will change awaits to be seen. For the time being, however, the store's audiotapes, which constitute another alternative archive, continue to function as wallpaper. In this regard, Mansur's cassettes are not alone. Other audiotapes that have since fallen out of favor similarly evidence a once-dynamic soundscape whose physical traces spark additional questions concerning the production and preservation of Egypt's past. In the spirit of further exploring the insights these items may offer, let's leave behind Shubra for a final institution that strove to control Islamic discourse at a time when audiotapes enabled an unprecedented number of people to speak in the name of Islam.

AUDIBLE ISLAM: FROM AL-AZHAR TO SHAYKH ʿANTAR

On one end of Ahmad Badawi Street, an elevated highway, commemorating the start of the 1973 war, weaves its way around Egypt's capital. Beginning across the Nile in Duqqi, the 6th of October Bridge passes by Shubra before eventually arriving in Nasr City. At a distance from Mansur's shop, the popular thoroughfare ultimately links up with al-Nasr Road, connecting commuters to two major landmarks, al-Azhar University and the Monument to the Unknown Soldier, a memorial that serves as Sadat's final resting place and pays tribute to Egyptians who fell in the October War. In the immediate orbit of both of these destinations, a side street, named after ʿAbd al-ʿAziz Muhammad al-Shinawi, an Egyptian historian who taught at al-Azhar and wrote on everything from Europe to the Ottoman Empire, houses a rectangular building that towers above its neighbors: the Islamic Research Academy (Majmaʿ al-Buhuth al-Islamiyya).

The academy's sleek exterior belies its older origins, which can be traced back to a legal edict from nearly sixty years ago. Issued in the summer of 1961, Law No. 103 was part and parcel of a broader push by Nasser's regime to modernize and monopolize al-Azhar, Egypt's premier site of Islamic learning. The reorganization of the religious institution played out on two different fronts. First, al-Azhar's curriculum expanded. New subjects, like mathematics and geography, were introduced and new faculties, like medicine and engineering, were established. Second, the law reshaped al-Azhar's administration and resituated it more firmly within the purview of the state.[17] One of the outcomes of this top-down restructuring was the academy.

Among the academy's central roles was to serve as a censor for cultural productions, including audiocassette tapes. In *The Ethical Soundscape*, Charles Hirschkind alludes to this task in passing. He mentions how the academy was responsible for approving all "Islamic texts and recordings" intended for commercial consumption in Egypt.[18] How this process played out in practice, however, is not entirely clear. What kinds of audiotapes did the academy review? Who was responsible for assessing them? What did this process entail? And in what ways did the academy and al-Azhar harness cassette-tape technology to project their authority and police Islamic sounds? With these questions in mind, I visited the academy in the summer of 2019.

Dr. Hany Shams al-Din, the director of general relations and media, welcomed me in Nasr City. In the academy's front foyer, he explained to me that an internal unit called the General Department for Research, Writing, and Translation (al-Idara al-ʿAmma lil-Buhuth wa al-Taʾlif wa al-Tarjama) was responsible for reviewing all cultural works concerning religion.[19] In the case of audiocassettes, he claimed, these items included sermons, songs, exegeses, and "everything related to the Islamic calling" (al-daʿwa al-Islamiyya). These acoustic materials, in turn, were scrutinized by experts in a "special room" for audiotapes. This process encompassed multiple steps. First, a cassette producer presented a recording to the academy for inspection, which then distributed it to two committees. One delegation, composed of Azhari authorities who specialized in the recording's religious content, listened to the cassette to determine whether it was "in agreement with the Qurʾan and the Sunna" and "in accordance with the opinion of the scholars." A second committee, meanwhile, assessed the tape on political grounds. One of the questions it routinely asked, for example, was whether cassette recordings rejected violence. Tapes that abided by both religious guidelines and political mandates received the academy's approval and could be sold in Egypt. But exactly how effective was this system? In the absence of the academy's archive, which remains off-limits to researchers, a collection of cassette-tape recordings, covered in dust at a distance from the religious establishment and its onetime owner, begins to offer some answers.

On the second floor of an aging mall in Zamalek, Egypt's acoustic culture is available for purchase at Mazzika Zaman (Past Music). The shop's origins date back four decades, when Samir Fuʾad, a talented musician born in Cairo, embarked on a new career path. According to Ahmad Muhammad Ibrahim, the store's current owner, Samir began to study the lifestyles of the elite Egyptians for whom he frequently performed as part of a band.[20] He developed an appreciation for what they desired in their homes and in 1979 launched a commercial enterprise to cater to their needs. Initially only an idea, Gallery Samir Fuʾad became a physical shop in 1981. Based in the working-class neighborhood of al-Warraq in Giza, the establishment supplied shoppers with everything from artwork and furniture to radios and record players. Over time, Samir's name became well known and a man approached him with an opportunity to grow his burgeoning business. In 1991, Samir started to market his wares in Zamalek. He rented a stall in the Marriott hotel. The space's dimensions dictated what he could display. Drawing on his vast inventory in al-Warraq, Samir exhibited smaller items, like records, record players, and musical instruments, across the Nile. As a result of these selections, Ahmad recalls, Samir's shop became known as the "music place." This popular perception prompted the owner to rebrand his business. In 1996, when Samir relocated to the present-day mall, he opened two new stores under the banner Mazzika Samir Fu'ad (Samir Fu'ad Music). In 2000, Ahmad began to manage one of these entities, which had expanded to nine different shops by the time Samir retired in 2013. With Samir's departure, Ahmad took over one of the stores and Mazzika Samir Fu'ad became Mazzika Zaman.

Mazzika Zaman is first and foremost a record store, but its catalog is not limited to discs. Behind a sliding glass door, columns of cassette tapes greet prospective customers. Some of these recordings trickled into the shop, a few tapes at a time, from here and there. Other cassettes, meanwhile, arrived en masse, near-complete libraries no longer of use. One such assortment, totaling 160 tapes, came from an apartment building in Zamalek where the wife of Mubarak's younger son, Gamal, reportedly resided. The collection's curator, Ahmad explained, was eager to find a new home for the cassettes since he was able to listen to many things online, not to mention the fact that a single flash drive took up far less space and could house the content of countless tapes. With the exception of a few "foreign cassettes," which belonged to the owner's daughter and were not for sale, Ahmad purchased the entire collection in April 2019. Shortly thereafter, what was once a private library became a public commodity at Mazzika Zaman.

Excluding a handful of audiotapes, featuring voices like Hassan al-Asmar, Gamal Abdel Nasser, Evelyn King, and 'Abd al-Halim Hafiz, the vast majority of the collection's cassettes, nearly 91 percent of them, contain Islamic sounds. Sermons, Qur'anic recitation (*tilawa*), religious lessons (*durus diniyya*), Qur'anic exegesis (*tafsir*), religious songs (*anashid diniyya*) and records of Prophet Muhammad's words and actions (*hadith*) all contribute to the diverse assortment. Some of the individuals who animate these Islamic genres are renowned orators. 'Abd al-Basit 'Abd al-Samad, Muhammad Sadiq al-Minshawi, and Muhammad Mahmoud al-Tablawi, for example, surface on more than one occasion. Household names, however, by no means monopolize the collection. No fewer than forty-seven different voices materialize on the magnetic reels in various states of repair.

Much like the genres and people they relay, the cassettes in the collection span multiple decades and sites of production. The oldest tape is from 1974, and the most recent is from 2006. Some of the recordings come from nearby neighborhoods, like Muhandasin, 'Attaba, and Duqqi, whereas others are from further afield in Jedda, Mecca, and Riyadh. Significantly, slightly more than a third of the Islamic tapes are amateur productions, created by individual listeners, while the remaining two-thirds are professional products, manufactured by companies. Of the ninety-seven Islamic cassettes released by commercial enterprises, fifty different entities are responsible for their assembly. Together, the audiocassette recordings reveal a robust acoustic arena in which an unprecedented number of people performed Islam before a mass audience. The resultant productions piqued the attention of both the general public and religious gatekeepers intent on policing Islamic sounds in Egypt.

Evidence of al-Azhar's efforts to monitor Islamic recordings through the academy is present on the sleeves and cases of the collection's enduring cassettes. Consider one audiotape from Abu Hamza. The recording showcases Shaykh Muhammad Mahmoud al-Tablawi reciting the Qur'an. On the cassette's front cover, al-Tablawi sports a distinctively Azhari cap and solemnly holds what is presumably a copy of the holy book. A superimposed image of the shaykh, smiling, extends to the back side of the cassette's jacket. On this second plane, Abu Hamza confirms the cassette's content and the tape's law-abiding status. The venture notes the Qur'anic passages covered on each side of the recording, parts of chapters 53 and 54 on the first side and chapter 56 in its entirety on the second side, and it identifies two stamps of approval. The first permission code is from al-Azhar (96/619), and the second authorization is from the state censor (96/165). Turning to the audiotape, both endorsements appear once more. The state censor's code graces side 1 of the cassette, and the phrase "permitted by al-Azhar" adorns side 2. Below both acknowledgments, Abu Hamza declares that it, alone, owns the recording's rights. From this tape alone, al-Azhar and the academy, it would seem, enjoyed a firm grip on Islamic recordings in Egypt. This cassette, however, is the exception, not the norm, in the collection.

Although religious gatekeepers may have aspired to review every Islamic recording in Egypt, the vast majority of the collection's cassettes do not display a permission code from al-Azhar. In fact, fewer than one in five of the cassettes exhibit any indication of al-Azhar's approval. Instead, the collection's contents underscore the creative power and circulatory potential of audiotapes. In these regards, the highly participatory nature of cassette-tape technology was both a blessing and a curse. As we saw in chapters 3 and 4, the mass medium empowered an unprecedented number of people to become cultural producers and cultural distributors, as opposed to mere cultural consumers. In so doing, the technology and its users posed an unparalleled challenge to religious gatekeepers eager to centralize Islamic discourse in Egypt. A couple of cassette recordings in the collection begin to bring the contours of the resulting confrontation into greater relief.

The ability of individuals, yet alone commercial enterprises, to record anyone, anywhere, anytime, left little to no room for those in the employ of al-Azhar to review and, if need be, revise Islamic content before it reached a wider audience. This practice and the "problems" inspired by it are readily evident in the case of one amateur recording. The live production features ʿAbd al-Hamid Kishk, an infamous preacher whose handwritten name surfaces on the cassette's jacket. Throughout his career, Shaykh Kishk regularly grounded his passionate sermons in current affairs and did not shy away from publicly criticizing people in positions of power. In the 1970s and 1980s, cassette recorders routinely accompanied the talented orator at his pulpit in Cairo. The technology was such a familiar sight at Masjid al-Malak that its administrators provided prayer-goers with more electrical outlets than most other mosques.[21] Much like the masjid's leadership, Kishk, it appears, was well aware of the cassette players in his presence. On at least one occasion, he told those in attendance that "police agents were seated among them, taping his remarks while pretending to pray."[22] If Kishk's cassette and countless other like it outside of the collection confirm the productive power of audiotapes, still other recordings illustrate the technology's circulatory reach, which, from the perspective of religious gatekeepers, was no less concerning.

Cassette-tape technology served as a tool for creating and circulating acoustic content. In a world where al-Azhar and its academy aspired to authorize every Islamic recording in Egypt, the immense mobility of religious material on audiotapes constituted a significant hurdle. Whether a blank tape or a professional production, every cassette was capable of becoming something else. With the push of a button, users recorded, rerecorded, and distributed what they desired with minimal effort. The ease with which Islamic content traveled on audiotapes at a distance from the eyes and ears of religious gatekeepers is no more apparent than in the case of a second cassette in the collection. Manufactured in Japan, the audiotape originally relayed the sounds of *Sangam*, a hit Indian film from 1964 about two men who fall in love with the same childhood friend. The picture's songs, however, no longer surface on the cassette. What was once the soundtrack of a Bollywood drama became a vessel for Islam's most sacred text. Evidence of this transformation is visible on the cassette's eroding exterior. At some point in time, the audiotape's owner penned "Qurʾan Karim" on both sides of the tape.

The informal label likely served as a useful reminder of the item's new content: Qur'anic recitation. Unauthorized tapes, like this one in the collection, moved freely alongside their licensed counterparts and further illustrate the inability of religious gatekeepers to control not only the production but also the circulation of Islamic sounds in Egypt.

In sharp contrast to Dr. Shams al-Din's account of the academy and its seamless regulation of Islamic sounds, our cassette collection tells a different, more decentralized story. Countless individuals perform Islam before a mass audience with little to no oversight. Indeed, the presence of these recordings highlights the shortcomings, not the strengths, of Egypt's religious gatekeepers when it came to controlling audiotapes. This is not to say, though, that al-Azhar and the academy accepted this reality. On the contrary, religious officials still strove to dictate who expressed Islam regardless of the obstacles in their way. To gain a better sense of how production, circulation, and the question of control collided in the case of Islamic cassettes in Egypt, let's consider one final voice in the collection, whose audiotape recordings continue to stir controversy today (fig. 18).

Shaykh 'Antar Sa'id Mussallam was born in the village of 'Ima in the northern Egyptian governorate of al-Gharbiyya on 17 November 1936. Little is known about his early life, but according to one account, Shaykh 'Antar lost his sight to a primitive medicine administered by his grandmother to treat a routine eye infection when he was a year old.[23] Like many other children in Egypt's countryside, Shaykh 'Antar enrolled in a *kuttab* and went on to attend an Azhari institute for elementary school. By the time he was eight, he had memorized the Qur'an. Four years later, he started to recite the holy book at local events, like funeral ceremonies, in surrounding villages in the Nile Delta. It was around this time that Shaykh 'Antar's education took an important turn.

Still a young boy, Shaykh 'Antar came into contact with multiple instruments, including the oud and the *kaman* (violin), and began to master the melodic modes (*maqamat*) underlying Arab music. Whether or not the shaykh was self-taught when it came to music and recitation is a point of contention, but the ease with which he fused both art forms set him apart from his peers. In merging *tarab* and *tilawa*, Shaykh 'Antar developed a large following, which often encountered his voice on audiotapes. Sawt al-Gharbiyya (The Voice of al-Gharbiyya), a recording label based in Tanta, produced some of these cassettes, while others, like the one in our collection, originated from individual listeners, who personally recorded

FIGURE 18. A cassette recording of Shaykh 'Antar. Photo by the author.

his unique recitations.[24] The resulting tapes, bolstered by cassette piracy, proved to be both tremendously popular and provocative.

From the viewpoint of Egypt's religious gatekeepers, Shaykh 'Antar's ability to recite the Qur'an in a manner that departed from well-established norms was not something to be celebrated but condemned. His "originality" when it came to performing the sacred text was an unwelcomed innovation. At the peak of the reciter's popularity in the 1980s, when sales of his cassettes reportedly rivaled Ahmad 'Adawiya and Hassan al-Asmar in Egypt's countryside and its working class communities, al-Azhar banned Shaykh 'Antar from reciting the Qur'an.[25] The exact details of this ban are difficult to determine. The official record of the ruling remains sealed somewhere inside the academy's archive, well beyond the reach of researchers. But it is clear that at least some Egyptians backed al-Azhar in its clash with Shaykh 'Antar. Among those to support the religious institution was the first writer to share Shaykh 'Antar's story with a wider audience.

In *Alhan al-Sama'* (*Celestial Melodies*), Mahmud al-Sa'adni, a prominent Egyptian journalist, introduces Shaykh 'Antar as a self-taught reciter, with an "extremely beautiful voice," whose lack of formal study led to his downfall.[26] Qur'anic recitation, he explains early on, is a science whose practitioners must adhere to certain guidelines. In an effort to illustrate where Shaykh 'Antar went "wrong," al-Saʿadni recounts one of the times he heard him perform. He details the shaykh's recitation of a single Qurʾanic passage involving Ibrahim and God.[27] According to the author, Shaykh ʿAntar "pronounced Ibrahim one time correctly, 'Ibrahim,' then repeated it 'Ibraham,' then repeated it 'Barahim,' then repeated it 'Birhum.'"[28] Such errors in speech, al-Saʿadni argues, were unacceptable and grounds for an embargo. Although the writer wishes al-Azhar would have reeducated Shaykh ʿAntar, instead of silencing him outright, he nevertheless confirms that the religious institution was "right" to act the way it did.[29] If al-Saʿadni was among the first to weigh in on the subject, he was not the last. Two decades later, the clash between al-Azhar and Shaykh ʿAntar surfaced once again as a topic of discussion, this time online.

In a post published on a popular Facebook page dedicated to Qurʾanic recitation on 26 December 2016, Hisham Faruq, the president of Alexandria's Court of Appeals and an honorary member of the Qurʾan Reciters Syndicate (Niqabat al-Qurraʾ), reflected on the controversy surrounding Shaykh ʿAntar.[30] From the start, Hisham identifies the shaykh as a point of contention, par excellence, and sets out to provide a neutral account of the divisive reciter. He takes care to clarify that he neither knew the shaykh personally nor witnessed him perform, but he did listen to his audiotapes. The first time Hisham encountered one of these recordings was at his grandfather's house in the 1970s. He was nine or ten years old and remembers the shaykh's handwritten name on the cassette's exterior. He enjoyed the informal production and recalls how Shaykh ʿAntar's audience raised their voices during breaks, or even at times in the middle of a recitation, to express their adoration. It was only when he grew up, Hisham confesses, that he became aware of the shaykh's "mistakes."

According to the Facebook post, Shaykh ʿAntar succeeded in memorizing the Qurʾan, but failed to properly recite it, at least at the start of his career. In the 1970s, Hisham elaborates, Shaykh ʿAntar recited the Qurʾan how he wished, defying the ten accepted schools of Qurʾanic recitation and the four exceptions to their respective guidelines. The resulting infractions compelled religious gatekeepers to act. And although some of Shaykh ʿAntar's supporters thought al-Azhar's ban was a ruse, a plot engineered by rival reciters on Egyptian radio weary of the shaykh's celebrity status courtesy of cassette tapes, Hisham believes this was not the case. He heard the shaykh commit "horrible" mistakes on audiotapes.[31] But what happened to Shaykh ʿAntar after al-Azhar's ruling?

Unlike al-Saʿadni, who alleges that the shaykh disappeared, Hisham contends that the reciter's journey did not end with al-Azhar's decision.[32] In the mid-1980s, he claims, Shaykh ʿAntar penned a letter of repentance in the Egyptian press. Following this admission of guilt, the story goes, al-Azhar permitted him to record once more with cassette companies, and the new recitations, by then subject to al-Azhar's oversight, were free of any mistakes. In light of these developments, Hisham concludes that attacks on Shaykh ʿAntar, after he repented, are unmerited, while his "errant" recordings, before he expressed his remorse, should be silenced. To achieve this aim, Hisham enlists the help of Facebook users. He instructs them to stop circulating Shaykh ʿAntar's earlier cassette recordings, or, better yet, to set them ablaze and destroy them. He marshals Shaykh ʿAntar's letter from thirty years ago, which he is unable to reproduce but reportedly read, as evidence for these actions. According to Hisham, in the text Shaykh ʿAntar announced his "absolution from old recordings with mistakes in recitation and demanded those who possess them to burn and destroy them." On these grounds, he leads his audience to believe that erasing any traces of Shaykh ʿAntar's legacy, before al-Azhar's ban, was in line with the reciter's wishes.

Hisham's post generated no shortage of responses. One Facebook user, a self-identified supporter of Shaykh ʿAntar, applauded the contributor for his "faultless" account, while another commentator called attention to the shaykh's popularity outside of Egypt, where his voice traveled to places as far away as Algeria despite its absence on Egyptian radio. A third reader posed a question. After thanking Hisham for his efforts nearly two years earlier, Samy Ahmed, a resident of Cairo, sought to "clarify something very important." The matter at hand concerned a cassette recording of Shaykh ʿAntar reciting at a funeral ceremony in his hometown. Samy confesses that he quite enjoyed the recitation and often repeated it in the same manner as the shaykh. But after reading Hisham's entry, he was having doubts about this practice. "Is this recitation," Samy asks, "included in the recitations that the shaykh wills to be burned?"[33] The question did not elicit a response, but its existence likely infuriated another commenter, who did not mince words when it came to Hisham's thoughts on Shaykh ʿAntar and his audiotapes.

According to Mohamed Ezzat, who grew up in the same governorate as Shaykh ʿAntar, "most" of what Hisham had written was "wrong." In an effort to set the record straight on Facebook, he posted a video addressed to "every critic of Shaykh

'Antar Sa'id Mussallam." Upon clicking "Play," the video's link redirects Facebook users away from Hisham's post to a YouTube channel bearing Mohamed's name. In September 2019, the channel boasted more than seven thousand subscribers and fifty-nine videos. The subject of every video is a familiar face, Shaykh 'Antar, whose recitations constitute the vast majority of the channel's content. The titles of the videos vary. Some pinpoint particular parts of the Qur'an covered by the shaykh, while others showcase "rare" and "old" recitations. One of the clips, a recording of Shaykh 'Antar reciting chapter 75 of the Qur'an, has been viewed more than 353,000 times, while a second recording of chapters 59 and 79, from the shaykh's "youth," has received over 816,000 views since it was first made available to visitors in December 2016, the same month Hisham's post was published on Facebook.[34] If Mohamed likely found Hisham's call to destroy some of Shaykh 'Antar's cassettes appalling, it is safe to say that Hisham equally abhorred Mohamed's efforts to preserve and promote some of the very same recordings. Once limited to audiotapes, Shaykh 'Antar's recitations now resonate in cyberspace.

In the absence of key historical sources, including the academy's record of al-Azhar's ruling and Shaykh 'Antar's "letter of repentance" in the Egyptian press, the exact details of this overlooked clash remain murky. But remnants of Shaykh 'Antar's cassettes, along with those of countless other people who performed Islam, begin to reveal a dynamic acoustic culture that proved impossible for religious gatekeepers to ever completely control. In so doing, they provide a starting point for writing a more nuanced history of the academy and its cultural politics in the absence of the institution's official archive. At the same time, these traces invite us to think more broadly beyond the academy. By opening up an analytical space between extremism and ethical labor, two frames of reference that tend to dominate discussions of Islamic sounds, lingering cassette recordings call attention to the power dynamics underlying the public production of Islam. Accordingly, they raise a central question: who has the right to express Islam? This inquiry, critically, played out not only in the press and political arena in Egypt but also on cassettes consisting of little more than magnetic reels, plastic cases, and metal screws. Ultimately, enduring audiotapes, on the ground and online, invite us to further reimagine "the archive" in Middle East studies and to consider what other histories of Islam and Egypt such an endeavor may make possible.

IMAGINING AUDIOTAPES AND THE ARCHIVE ANEW

On Everyday Egypt, a popular Instagram account dedicated to displaying scenes of daily life in cities and in villages across the country, a black-and-white snapshot suggests that cassette tapes continued to circulate, at a distance from Cairo, long after the dawn of compact discs and flash drives. In the picture, captured in August 2014 and uploaded online three months later, a beaming young man sits in what appears to be a small kiosk.[35] Behind him, row upon row of audiotapes line the narrow store's walls, from which two fluorescent bulbs leap forward, perhaps to light the way for nighttime shoppers intent on exploring the crammed shelves. According to the photographer, the man in the image's foreground is a "regular customer" at "the only audio cassette tapes shop" in Dishna, a Nile-side city known for its sugarcane in the Upper Egyptian province of Qina. Beyond the little information provided in this one-line caption, nothing else is known about the patron, the business, or its proprietor. Likewise, the content on the vast array of audiocassette recordings remains a complete mystery, and any audible clues exceed the camera's technical capabilities. What stories may this anonymous consumer tell? What insights might be gleaned from the historical trajectory of this intriguing commercial venture? How might the blurry tapes, stacked in the background, contribute to our understanding of Dishna's soundscape, Egypt's broader cassette culture, and the production and preservation of Egyptian culture?

Material remnants of a once-robust cassette-tape culture endure in contemporary Egypt, in shadows and in broad daylight, in remote warehouses and in central libraries, on storeroom shelves and atop the streets of crowded weekend markets. Throughout this chapter, we have navigated some of these spaces, but many more settings remain unexplored. Among these places are institutions such as the Library of Sacred Music at the St. Andrews Church in downtown Cairo. According to a guidebook from 1975, the religious repository contained an unparalleled and "rapidly" expanding assortment of records and cassettes, which were available to rent for "a small weekly fee."[36] The mention of this site in a text for tourists leads one to wonder who made use of these tapes, while the very existence of the recordings, at least at one point in time, prompts one to ponder how cassettes may have shaped religiosity, more generally, in Egypt beyond Islam.

Outside of establishments, private citizens also possess cassettes that merit mention. One such assortment of audiotapes briefly surfaces in a 2011 documentary on Scheherazade, a well-known Egyptian singer who, throughout the 1970s, exchanged cassettes in the mail with her husband Mahmoud Ramzi, a skilled cello player who performed abroad in Oman.[37] On the transnational tapes, the lovers discuss their days, hardships, and feelings, topics they could not always cover over unreliable phone lines.[38] This exercise, to be certain, was not limited to elites.[39] As Farha Ghannam and Soraya Duval de Dampierre reveal, ordinary Egyptian migrants and their family members back home also mailed cassettes, or entrusted travelers with them, to remain connected across great distances.[40] Joining these international tapes were other recordings that never exited Egypt. In a recent video from *Mada Masr*, an aging Egyptian man warmly recalls the cassettes he traded with loved ones after he left Aswan as a child and settled in Cairo.[41] The tapes, still in his possession, bring tears to his eyes. Collectively, cassettes like these enabled Egyptians to communicate regardless of their ability to read or write, activities that eluded many in the mid- to late twentieth century.[42] Although a more detailed exploration of personal messages extends beyond the scope of this study, such recordings stand to shed further light on Egypt's recent past and the inner lives of its citizens.[43] At the same time, audiotapes in public and private collections are not immune to the passage of time. Physical traces of Egypt's cassette culture continue to disappear.

The changing landscape of audiotape technology in Egypt is readily visible at one location in downtown Cairo. On al-Bursa al-Gadida Street, the contents of Sawt al-Qahira's branch have significantly shifted since the start of my fieldwork for this book. When I first visited the label's shop in 2016, I discovered a wide array of cassette recordings covering multiple genres, decades, and voices. Three years later, when I returned to the store in 2019, that scene no longer existed. The number of tapes available to visitors had dramatically diminished and cassettes containing music were almost entirely gone. Where audiotapes starring Umm Kulthum once appeared there were now DVDs featuring Shaykh Muhammad Mutawalli al-Sha'rawi. Where Ahmad 'Adawiya's cassettes once caught me off guard, CDs carrying everyone from Layla Murad to Mahir al-'Attar lined the shelves. Indeed, the vast majority of cassettes still on display in the showroom paralleled the dusty holdings in the branch's back room. A large collection of Islamic cassettes, encompassing hundreds of recordings, greeted customers at the front entrance. From the shop's latest inventory, Islamic sounds, it would (errantly) seem, dominated Egypt's cassette-tape culture.

If lingering audiotapes inspire key questions with regard to the production and preservation of Egypt's past, their physical disappearance from the public sphere prompts us to briefly consider one other place where cassette recordings continue to circulate: cyberspace. As we already saw in the case of Shaykh 'Antar, the internet serves as a powerful tool for exploring the acoustic legacies of iconic artists and long-forgotten performers. Videos, like the ones on Mohamed's channel, make insightful recordings, which are increasingly difficult to find offline, available for mass consumption. At the same time, they are also valuable for more than what they directly relay. YouTube comments, for example, reveal how non–state actors praise, condemn, and remember past voices. The promise of digital platforms, however, is not without peril.

Contrary to popular belief, online collections are no more permanent than their off-line counterparts. A YouTube channel can disappear. A Facebook page can cease to exist. A SoundCloud station can go dark. The precarity of digital platforms is no more evident than in the case of one online radio station. In 2013, Dr. Esmat al-Nimr, a surgeon, and 'Alaa al-Mislimani, a web developer, launched Misrfone in Egypt. In many ways, the online radio station embodies a private collection gone public. It broadcasts MP3 files based on wax cylinders, vinyl records, and audiotapes from Dr. al-Nimr's personal library.[44] The result is more than five hundred hours of recorded music, covering nearly a century, with the majority of the audio content coinciding with the Nahda, or Arab renaissance. The aims of Misrfone are at once archival and educational. The station strives to safeguard Egypt's cultural heritage, making it available to the general public free of charge, and to broaden what is played on Egyptian radio, highlighting the historical depth and breadth of Egyptian culture. In pursuing these objectives, the station's cofounders have encountered their fair share of obstacles. In 2014, Misrfone applied for a grant from the German government to restore, secure, and share its recordings, only to run into issues with an Egyptian administration increasingly weary of foreign funding. Then, in 2019, the station led an Indiegogo crowdfunding campaign that fell well short of its $500 goal to cover website-related expenses.[45] Although Misrfone continues to broadcast, its future, as an educational outlet and alternative archive, remains deeply uncertain.

There are then websites whose unstable holdings are not a cause for concern but an asset, where the arrival and departure of Egyptian culture poses even greater challenges to researchers. On a daily basis, commerce and culture collide online. One digital economy at the center of this crossroads is Discogs. A self-described "music database and marketplace," Discogs and its users regularly catalog and commodify millions of recordings.[46] Initially launched in 2000 as a music directory, Discogs made recordings available to purchase in 2005.[47] Today, the site features entries for several Egyptian voices, some of whose records, CDs, and audiotapes can be purchased but cannot be heard prior to payment. Unlike Misrfone, Discogs does not stream what it showcases. Joining Discogs are no shortage of rival marketplaces, with eBay perhaps being its biggest competitor. Established in 1995, eBay stages countless auctions for creative labors. Among the goods available on the site are Egyptian recordings, including audiocassettes that have since traveled well beyond Egypt's borders.[48] Significantly, the cultural productions sold on both of these platforms regularly end up in private collections, never to be seen or heard again by a wider audience. What insights might these cultural works and now collector's items offer into Egypt's cultural heritage, in particular, and the creation and conservation of Middle Eastern culture more broadly? And what new horizons might the treatment of online communities as alternative archives open to scholars of the Middle East?

For the time being, these questions remain open, but oral interviews will undoubtedly prove central to many future interdisciplinary inquiries into the histories of mass media and their users in Egypt and the greater Middle East. "Memory," Doreen Lee rightly observes in her ethnography of student activists in Indonesia, "is productive. It produces archives, spatial practices, bodies of writing, ways of talking and remembrance."[49] In the case of Egypt's cassette culture, personal recollections also critically enhanced historical accounts that had little use for them. Working from a limited set of documents, 'Abbas Muhammad Salama managed the Music Library's materials, and Mansur 'Abd al-'Al produced tapes that "polluted" public taste. Detailed conversations with both men greatly enriched these one-dimensional narratives and enabled the writing of micro-histories in the absence of extensive paper trails. As physical evidence of Egypt's cassette-tape culture continues to fade, and online platforms begin to provide some historical insights, oral interviews will prove all the more valuable in uncovering Egypt's cultural past, broadening its academic study, and complicating its public preservation.

In the end, by following traces of cassette-tape technology and mobilizing the memories of its users, we were able to elucidate the production of Egyptian culture from the bottom up and call into question the politics of its top-down preservation. Although 'Abbas, alone, oversees a "formal" audio library, the cassettes currently collecting dust in the care of Mansur, Ahmad, and countless other Egyptians similarly constitute valuable collections, whose contents significantly expand the cultural heritage on display at the Music Library and other state-sponsored venues. Likewise, the very same objects invite us to rethink "the archive" in Middle East studies and to explore the novel vistas such an undertaking may make viable. Having opened with the physical fragments of a once thriving cassette culture in Cairo, this history of modern Egypt through the window of audiotape technology now concludes by placing these material remnants into conversation with the historical study of mass media and the Middle East. Our point of departure is a familiar place: a sidewalk kiosk in a Cairo suburb whose cassettes have now nearly vanished.

CONCLUSION

IN THE SUMMER OF 2019, I RETURNED TO THE CAIRO NEIGHBORHOOD of Maadi where I had resided four years earlier. In my absence, some of the commodities at the kiosk across the street from my former apartment had changed. Previously home to hundreds, even thousands, of audiotapes, the shop's towering display case no longer contained a single cassette recording (fig. 19). Instead, cartons of Lipton tea, containers of Nescafé, and a wide assortment of smoking paraphernalia lined the shelves. How did the shop's vast collection of cassettes disappear in the first place, and in such a short time? According to Nasir, the stand's proprietor, this vanishing act was a recent development.

Within a year of my departure, an official from the Interior Ministry paid Nasir a visit. The objective of the outing was to ensure that his kiosk was permitted to sell the audiotapes in its showcase. Much to business owner's dismay, the only license on the premises had expired years earlier. Taped to the top of the stand, the easily overlooked document, which authorized Nasir's father to sell cassettes at the shop, was last renewed for E£1,003.10 on 25 July 2010 and had expired on 29 December 2011. Permits like that one needed to be updated every year in Egypt, and failure to do so could result in significant fines or, worse yet, arrests. This top-down system, it seems, was not always in place. Licenses, Nasir maintained, gained traction only in the late 1990s or the early 2000s, and although he was well aware of the potential punishments awaiting those without them, Nasir decided

FIGURE 19. A cassette collection no longer, 2019. Photo by the author.

not to renew the permit because the handful of tapes he was selling did not justify the added expense for him. The choice was a costly one. The official imposed a E£5,000 fine on Nasir, who, in addition to incurring the sizable fee, lost possession of all his cassettes. At times responsible for the conservation of culture, the state, in this case, was behind its confiscation.

Eager to reclaim the recordings, Nasir accompanied the government employee to a police precinct, where he paid the substantial sanction but failed to receive all of his belongings in return. In fact, Nasir never saw most of the audiotapes again. According to the vendor, no more than a third of the commandeered cassettes made their way back to Maadi and only a fraction of the tapes appeared at the kiosk by the time I returned in July 2019. A rectangular frame fixed to the stand's door highlighted what remained. Among the lingering tapes was one featuring ʿAli al-Higar, an Egyptian artist who sang in celebration of the January 25 Revolution, and another starring Tamer Hosny, a fellow Egyptian citizen whose celebrity standing suffered early on in the mass uprising when he pleaded with protesters to go home and warmly referred to then president Husni Mubarak as "our father" on national television. Notwithstanding the threat of future fines, Nasir refrained from relegating these final tapes to a different place. The cassettes served as a fond reminder of another time. In sharing the story of this other time in Egypt's past through cassette technology, the media of the masses, this book has tried to enhance prevailing conversations in Middle East studies and to spark others yet to take place.

MAKING SENSE OF THE MODERN MIDDLE EAST

In 2011, Ramy Essam, an unknown singer from the city of Mansoura, made a name for himself in Tahrir Square by setting the chants of protesters to song. One year later, he released a record titled *Political Flyers (Manshurat)*. The album's opening number, "Leave" ("Irhal"), is composed of contemporary slogans from the January 25 Revolution. In the professional recording, Ramy relays the demands of countless demonstrators.[1] The content of the song is clear, but its historical context is less evident. In the days leading up to Mubarak's downfall, Egyptians from all walks of life openly expressed their discontent with the present as well as their desires for the future. By shouting "leave" in the streets, citizens laid claim to public spaces and loudly defied local authorities intent on silencing them. In amplifying these words, Ramy sustained protesters, who partook in his performances. Unlike the studio recording of "Irhal," which features

Ramy singing alone, initial renditions of the radical track involved the artist as well as his audience. Demonstrators echoed every verse, collectively rendering the revolutionary anthem.[2] Together, all of these historical factors are central to understanding the song's origins, social life, and significance to those hearing it firsthand in downtown Cairo during a time of immense unrest.

Media of the Masses has made a case for the historically rigorous study of both the content and the context of sounds. Audiotapes released by Randa Phone revealed lively clashes over pirated recordings, which altered the circulation of cultural content. Cassettes carrying Ahmad 'Adawiya and other artists, condemned by critics as "vulgar," illuminated a contest over the creation of culture and who had the right to produce it. Shaykh 'Antar's recitations challenged religious conventions, calling into question who is allowed to express Islam, while Shaykh Imam's songs undermined the Egyptian government's grasp on history by countering the official stories told by its advocates. Through historicizing these sounds, the objective has not been to re-create a soundscape we can personally experience. As the historian Mark Smith has opined, sensory history should not strive to revive the past for present consumption but investigate what transpired on its own terms.[3] With this in mind, I set out to explore the social life of sounds, from their creation and circulation to their policing and preservation, to elucidate what they meant to various actors at particular points in time and, consequently, our understanding of it. By adopting such an approach, it is possible to gain a greater appreciation of the centrality of sound to daily life and the making of modern nations.

In the process of navigating Egypt's soundscape, this book has invited us to reconsider the sorts of sounds we explore in Middle East studies. Listening inherently involves a choice. It is an act that prioritizes certain sounds over others. In this regard, the practice has much in common with academic publications. Scholars of the modern Middle East have predominately paid attention to Islamic sounds and state-sanctioned performers. The resulting investigations offer valuable insights into the crossroads of culture, politics, and religion, but they are not without their shortcomings. In the spirit of building on that body of work and redressing its limited breadth, this study has taken both spiritual and secular sounds into account, acknowledging the role played by religion in shaping Egypt's soundscape while making room for its nonreligious elements in the nation's historical record. Likewise, this exploration has introduced individuals who were not routinely praised by contemporary gatekeepers but were nevertheless popular among local listeners, placing subversive and state-sanctioned voices into conversation. The result is a more complex picture of Egypt's soundscape, one that neither reduces acoustic culture to religion nor restricts it to artists endorsed by ruling regimes. Moving forward, we must continue to critically contemplate the voices we sound and silence in Middle East studies.

Sound constitutes one of many threads in the broader mosaic of sensory scholarship. In the arenas of Middle East history, in particular, and Middle East studies, more generally, conversations concerning sound and the senses still have much ground to cover. What may multisensory histories, for example, offer to the field of Middle East studies? What insights may scholars of the Middle East glean from their counterparts working on the senses in other geographical contexts? How may our five basic faculties afford new opportunities for bridging disciplinary boundaries? And in what ways may the human sensorium assist us in rethinking conventional categories of analysis and aid us in identifying novel intellectual horizons? Historians undoubtedly will have a key part to play in addressing and, ultimately, answering these questions, as people in the past, much like we do now, made sense of the world around them through all of the tools at their disposal. On this front, one particularly promising point of departure is everyday technologies.

EVERYDAY TECHNOLOGIES IN ACTION

Erika Iris, a self-taught Chicago-based artist, regularly works with nonconventional materials. Among the more imaginative objects in her unorthodox toolkit are audiotapes, whose recycled ribbons act as ink. Drawing inspiration from the idea of "the ghost in the machine," a popular concept originally coined by the British philosopher Gilbert Ryle in his critique of Cartesian dualism, which posits a distinction between the intangible mind and the physical body, Iris carefully unravels reels of magnetic tape to visually reconstruct the voices on them. The resulting illustrations of iconic performers, pieced back together with scissors, glue, and X-Acto knives, take anywhere between a few days and a few weeks to complete. A wide range of celebrities surface on Iris's captivating canvases.[4] Keith Richards, Jimi Hendrix, the Notorious B.I.G., Madonna, Michael Jackson, and Aretha Franklin—all rise from audiotapes. In this regard, *Media of the Masses* shares something with Iris's artwork. But in lieu of extracting a single individual from a cassette, it has tried to re-create a nation's recent past. In so doing, Egypt, much like the subjects of Iris's artistry, emerges through audiotape technology.

Throughout this monograph, I have explored how the historical study of one everyday technology "in action," as opposed to an "invention-centric" account of the very same object, may enhance our understanding of modern Egypt. This approach to cassette tapes and players was not part and parcel of a predetermined plan but an unexpected outcome of my early research. Turning through the pages of popular Egyptian periodicals, I frequently came across cassette technology in surprising places, from cartoons to crime reports to court cases. These serendipitous discoveries reshaped what I expected this study to be, the story of a single mass medium, and what it became, a history of modern Egypt. In this sense, the book's trajectory mirrors that of the technology at its foundation. Originally exhibited as a dictation device in the West, audiotapes empowered countless people to become active participants in the creation of culture and circulation of content a world away. Only by looking beyond the invention of the compact cassette, an event involving a rather limited set of individuals, places, and historical circumstances, was it possible to elucidate one of the many paths taken by the technology once it left the walls of its workshop in Europe and traveled to Egypt. This shift in perspective, critically, raises a key question. What may the biographies of other everyday technologies in action offer to the study of Middle East history?

Recently, a growing number of Middle East historians have begun to explore human experiences through the lens of nonhuman actors, such as animals, diseases, food, and natural disasters. This exciting scholarship has shed new light on several fields of inquiry, including empire, identity, and the environment.[5] At the same time, much more work remains to be done on everyday technologies, not as historical actors in their own right but as tools infused with agency by people, items whose lives, much like those of their users, may reveal a great deal about the past. At the forefront of these ordinary objects are mass media. By exploring the social life of one mass medium whose history in Egypt was yet to be written, this study uncovered how cassette technology and its users subverted state-controlled Egyptian media well before the advent of satellite television and the internet. In the course of chronicling this development, this book presents a new approach to mass media in Middle East studies. Bridging close readings of specific cultural products performed by anthropologists and broader accounts of particular technologies penned by historians, it reveals how media technologies can serve as insightful windows onto dynamic societies. Consequently, several questions come to mind that merit our consideration.

How might a history of records compel us to rethink life and leisure in the shadow of empires? What might a history of radio add to our understanding of political rivalries and quotidian affairs across the Middle East? How might a historically rigorous account of videocassettes reframe treatments of cinema and subject formation from North Africa to the Arabian Peninsula? How will we write these histories? Will libraries, academic centers, and state archives, in and outside of the Middle East, provide answers? Or, will attics, street markets, and online platforms supply us with clues that supplement and escape conventional collections? Finally, what are the disciplinary divides to be traversed, and how might the intersections of social history, cultural anthropology, and sensory studies prove especially productive for reevaluating the Middle East? Regardless of the findings inspired by these inquiries, which collectively present an opportunity to further question the "newness" of new media, like the internet, and to bring to light the connections between media technologies that did not exist in isolation of one another, one thing is certain. Future scholarship on mass media and other everyday technologies in action must critically examine things we take for granted, placing ordinary objects into direct conversation with broader historical matters. To accomplish this task, we will likely need to reimagine the archive in Middle East studies.

NATIONS WITHOUT NATIONAL ARCHIVES

Around the corner from the "First Mall" in Giza, a city well known for its ancient wonders, an easily overlooked storage facility overflows with historical artifacts. The objects within the structure's walls are decidedly more modern than the monuments some seven kilometers away. Books, newspapers, and magazines rest atop one another in stacks that defy both order and gravity, and photographs of private and public affairs fill cardboard boxes that enjoy no catalog. Some of the images surface on the pages of family albums that have since ceased to exist in their entirety; other amateur shots endure in isolation, relying upon their inheritors to reassemble what they picture: a wedding, a graduation, a trip to the beach. The origins of these things vary, but the majority of the materials arrived from estate sales farther afield or courtesy of street dealers specializing in possessions no longer of use to their onetime owners. Together, these items form the foundation of an informal collection that not only sheds welcomed light on Egypt's recent past but also empowers one to write the nation's history anew. Part of a wider network of warehouses, this site is but one of many nodes in Egypt's "shadow archive."

Over the course of this study, I have harnessed a wide array of sources to illuminate the making of modern Egypt and to expand the methodological horizons of Middle East scholarship. Films, Facebook pages, foreign newspapers, guidebooks, photographs, and oral interviews, audiotape recordings, sleeves, and collections have all played a part in this book. At the center of these sources is the state-controlled Egyptian press. Reading popular periodicals against the grain has yielded valuable insights into cultural, political, economic, and social developments. Police reports inadvertently revealed a thriving black market, criticisms of cassette content perceived to be "vulgar" exposed a struggle over who had the right to create culture, and advertisements showcasing cassette players illustrated the making of the "modern home." At the same time, a sustained treatment of weekly magazines is not without its challenges. Popular periodicals, like *Ruz al-Yusuf*, routinely ended up in the trash. Rather than archiving these materials, historical actors more often than not read and then discarded them. Consequently, single issues are far more commonplace than continuous runs, and no digital archives yet exist for most Egyptian magazines. Together, these trying circumstances require researchers to piece periodicals back together.

Other historical materials, meanwhile, have made it online. The internet, as we have seen, constitutes a valuable, if underutilized, repository for researchers. Much information can be mined from a single YouTube video. Outside of the actual footage, "views," "comments," and "shares" all can be interpreted in a critical manner. Not everything online, however, is easy to decipher. Facebook photos routinely lack the most basic of facts, including the names of their creators, points of origin, or even whom they depict. And unless someone is willing and able to fill in the blanks, as was the case with the curious studio portrait that opened chapter 1, this important information is difficult, if not impossible, to ascertain otherwise. There is then the matter of the medium itself.

Today, one is hard-pressed to find a cassette player to listen to the tapes cited in this book. Will items online at the moment be available fifty years from now? Or will things as mundane as software updates and as momentous as technological breakthroughs render present primary sources inaccessible in the future? In short, how will we not only write the histories of unstable media but also write history with the very same decentered platforms, beginning with audiotapes and moving up to the internet? And how much of our lives will continue to be preserved on paper? Such questions are worth asking because they will compel us to reconsider how we archive things presently for writing history later. Notwithstanding how all of this plays out, one thing is without a doubt: between promise and precarity, inevitable obstacles will inspire new opportunities.

Ultimately, archives are neither objective nor comprehensive. They elide certain pasts and render others visible. In this regard, national archives across the Middle East present two major challenges. Local gatekeepers, from librarians to state security agents, regularly restrict access to their holdings, and the contents of their collections offer a curated view of a more chaotic past. In the absence of the Egyptian National Archives, I strove to write a history of Egypt from elsewhere in this book, drawing upon diverse materials that exist in the establishment's "shadow." Shadow archives, like the one I harnessed, have no single address. They consist of a constellation of sites whose sources supply historians with a broader idea of the past and its remains, as opposed to what a select number of people found worthy of preservation and continue to police. Shadow archives, accordingly, not only enable us to write the histories of nations in the absence of their national archives, in the Middle East or well beyond its borders, but also permit us to construct new kinds of histories altogether. As official documents prove increasingly difficult to access and historical research and national security grow even more intertwined in countries like Egypt, historians will need to continually rethink what constitutes an "archive" and counter the efforts of prevailing authorities all too eager to monopolize the past in the present. Looking ahead, shadow archives have the potential to play a critical role in this intellectual labor. Indeed, they may very well become the archives to which we turn to make sense of the past in the future.

ORDINARY THINGS AND THE STORIES THEY TELL

For one week in October 2016, a commercial space once belonging to Kodak in downtown Cairo transformed, momentarily, into a museum exhibit. Limited to a single room, the articles on display evoked Egypt's modern, not ancient, past. Among the products to appear on a rectangular table in the center of the gallery were a chess set, a hand broom, a cigarette box, and a glass milk bottle. Two sewing machines (Nefertiti and Singer), a pair of radios (Telimisr and Banha), and a telephone switch box accompanied these ordinary objects, which were joined by a taximeter, a family portrait, and a talcum powder canister, along with a few other things (fig. 20). Near the table, a Coca-Cola cooler stood against a wall, a sequin dress cascaded down a mannequin, and an Ar-

FIGURE 20. The Modern Egypt Project in downtown Cairo. From "Modern Egypt Project: The British Museum in Cairo," at https://www.youtube.com/watch?v=9XRaQFTFqKo.

abic-letter typewriter sat atop a pedestal a few feet away from an eye chart mounted on a metal stand. On the room's white walls, selected texts, including pages from national newspapers like *al-Jumhuriyya*, were displayed in frames, while a colorful poster, titled "Industry" ("al-Sana'a"), hung from a piece of string and depicted Egyptians hard at work. Together, all these materials bolstered a larger initiative, the Modern Egypt Project, a recent undertaking led by the British Museum in London to display the history of Egypt over the past century through its everyday artifacts.

The goals of the Modern Egypt Project are essentially twofold. On the one hand, it aims to demonstrate how Egypt's modern history can be collected, embodied, and presented to a global audience. On the other hand, the project attempts to radically reenvision traditional representations of Egypt with which onlookers are already familiar. In these regards, *Media of the Masses* shares much with the Modern Egypt Project. By showing how Egypt's recent past can be elucidated through the lens of an everyday item, the cassette tape, this book makes a case for placing audiotapes and cassette players "on the table" at the Cairo showcase. Equally important, this study invites us to think in more panoramic terms that exceed any one museum initiative, mass medium, or nation insofar as it poses a simple question. What might other everyday technologies teach us about the history of not only Egypt and the greater Middle East but also any number of places around the world? The answers to this question will undoubtedly assume many different forms. The starting point of each response, however, is one and the same. To reimagine the past, we need only begin by reconsidering the ordinary things that surround us.

Appendix

A LITTLE BIT UP, A LITTLE BIT DOWN (*HABA FUQ WA-HABA TAHT*), 1974[1]

Gorgeous lives upstairs and I live down below
I looked up with longing, my heart swayed, and I was wounded

Oh people upstairs, go on and look at who is below
Or is the up not aware of who is down anymore?

A little bit up, a little bit down
A look up, a look down
Oh you up there

Her window is curtained and a grapevine adorns it
And in a cage there is bird, bewildered
It reminds me of a story

A story of a heart, in love, and longing ruling over it
A glance of an eye, I fell in love, and no one feels for me

Oh, people upstairs, go on and look at who is below
Or is the up not aware of who is down anymore?

A little bit up, a little bit down
A look up, a look down
Oh, you up there

EVERYTHING ON EVERYTHING (*KULLU ʿALA KULLU*)

Everything on everything
When you see him tell him

What does he think we are?
Are we not good enough for him?

Go and tell him
What has happened
Everything on everything

Outside, who is outside?
That's us, us, the bosses

If the door knocks
We know who's outside

What does he think we are?
Are we not good enough for him?

Go and tell him
What has happened
Everything on everything

Tell him if you were hard to get
And you had no match

My heart is not a stage
For the hobby of acting

What does he think we are?
Are we not good enough for him?

Go and tell him
What has happened
Tell him everything

Everything on everything
When you see him tell him
Tell him everything
When you see him tell him

What does he think we are?
Are we not good enough for him?

Go and tell him
What has happened
Tell him everything

FATHER NIXON (*NIXON BABA*), 1974

Welcome Father Nixon, O you of Watergate
They have honored your arrival, the sultans [*salatin*, also means "bowls"] of beans and oil
They rolled out the red carpet for you from Ras al-Tin to Mecca
And from there you will pass through Acre ["do the impossible"] and they'll say you
made the pilgrimage
Round and round the never-ending *mulid* goes
O family of the Prophet, give us your blessings

The day your spies welcomed you, they put on a great big show
In which the whores convulse and Shaykh Shamhuwrash [the devil; an allusion to
Sadat] possesses the leader of the *zar*
As the parade continues an entourage of spiders creeps in order of their standing
Round and round the never-ending *mulid* goes
O family of the Prophet, give us your blessings

They invited you and said, "Come, eat bonbons and harissa"
And because you are now frail [*mahayif*, also describes someone taken "lightly," a
target of mockery], you believed we were easy prey
You dropped by and they welcomed you with a wedding procession
(To no merit of your own, you joke of a groom)
Turn your face and we will spit on you. *Shubash* [a call performers shout at wed-
dings], O family of the groom

Round and round the never-ending *mulid* goes
O family of the Prophet, give us your blessings

Heed my words for they will remain with you, even if you are no longer around
I will not shout "welcome" (or "ignorance") or tell you, "come" or "don't come"
They say Egyptian meat, wherever it goes, burns
And that is from the effect of *kosheri*, beans, and bug-infested oil
Round and round the never-ending *mulid* goes
O family of the Prophet, give us your blessings

D'ESTAING, 1975[2]

Valéry Giscard d'Estaing
And his lady love, too
Will grab the wolf by its tail ["do the impossible"]
And feed every hungry mouth in town

Oh, man, you guys
Check out all the *gentleman* people walking around
We're going to be spoiled rotten
And life will just be fabulous
We'll have color TV
And new service clubs galore
And rather than running on gas, cars will run on *parfan* ["perfume," in French]

Behold, a great cultural renaissance awaits
We'll make it big
On the stage and screen
Or, even, at the zoo
Life will be sweet like *zalabiyya* [a fried dough ball soaked in syrup]
Who needs Syria or Libya?
We'll make an *Arab* Union[3]
With London and the Vatican

The poor will eat sweet potatoes
And strut down the street with swagger

And instead of calling their kids Shalata [a common Egyptian name with lower-class connotations]
They'll name them *Jean.*

All of this is courtesy of my magnanimous friend
d'Estaing, the *Romantiki* [the "Romantic," in Arabic]
And not one of you will be able to keep up
with me, my neighborhood, and my crowd

Notes

INTRODUCTION

1. Timeline, Philips Museum, Eindhoven, the Netherlands. One key factor in Philips's establishing of this "global standard" for cassette-tape technology was Ottens's push for the company to freely license his invention, which would serve as a model for the Dutch company's competitors in Japan and elsewhere around the world. See Neil Genzlinger, "Lou Ottens, Father of Countless Mixtapes, Is Dead at 94," *New York Times* (11 March 2021).

2. Notably, Ottens's vision for what would become the compact cassette was inspired by his frustration with the reel-to-reel tape recorder and his hours-long struggle one day to operate the existing technology. See Zack Taylor, "Cassette: A Documentary Mixtape," 87 (2016).

3. "Philips Operating Instructions: EL-3300," 3.

4. Igor Kopytoff, "The Cultural Biography of Things: Commoditization as Process," in *The Social Life of Things: Commodities in Cultural Perspective*, ed. Arjun Appadurai (New York: Cambridge University Press, 1986), 67.

5. Carl Ipsen, *Fumo: Italy's Love Affair with the Cigarette* (Stanford, CA: Stanford University Press, 2016); Kerry Ross, *Photography for Everyone: The Cultural Lives of Cameras and Consumers in Early Twentieth-Century Japan* (Stanford, CA: Stanford University Press, 2015); Marie Sarita Gaytán, *¡Tequila! Distilling the Spirit of Mexico* (Stanford, CA: Stanford University Press, 2014).

6. Beshara Doumani, *Rediscovering Palestine: Merchants and Peasants in Jabal*

Nablus, 1700–1900 (Berkeley: University of California Press, 1995), 131–81; Elliott Colla, *Conflicted Antiquities: Egyptology, Egyptomania, Egyptian Modernity* (Durham, NC: Duke University Press, 2007), 24–66; Arash Khazeni, *Sky Blue Stone: The Turquoise Trade in World History* (Berkeley: University of California Press, 2014).

7. David Nye, *Technology Matters: Questions to Live With* (Cambridge, MA: MIT Press, 2006), 56–61.

8. David Edgerton, *The Shock of the Old: Technology and Global History since 1900* (New York: Oxford University Press, 2007), xi–iii.

9. For histories of technologies in action, see, e.g., Stephen Sheehi, *The Arab Imago: A Social History of Portrait Photography, 1860–1910* (Princeton, NJ: Princeton University Press, 2016); Daniel Stolz, "Positioning the Watch Hand: 'Ulama' and the Practice of Mechanical Timekeeping in Cairo, 1737–1874," *International Journal of Middle East Studies* 47, no. 3 (2015): 489–510; Mostafa Minawi, *The Ottoman Scramble for Africa: Empire and Diplomacy in the Sahara and the Hijaz* (Stanford, CA: Stanford University Press, 2016), 99–139; Nancy Reynolds, "Building the Past: Rockscapes and the Aswan High Dam in Egypt," in *Water on Sand: Environmental Histories of the Middle East and North Africa*, ed. Alan Mikhail (New York: Oxford University Press, 2013), 181–205; Nile Green, "Journeymen, Middlemen: Travel, Transculture, and Technology in the Origins of Muslim Printing," *International Journal of Middle East Studies* 41, no. 2 (2009): 203–24; Eric Tagliacozzo, "Hajj in the Time of Cholera: Pilgrim Ships and Contagion from Southeast Asia to the Red Sea," in *Global Muslims in the Age of Steam and Print*, ed. James Gelvin and Nile Green (Berkeley: University of California Press, 2013), 103–20. See also On Barak, *On Time: Technology and Temporality in Modern Egypt* (Berkeley: University of California Press, 2013); Toby Jones, *Desert Kingdom: How Oil and Water Forged Modern Saudi Arabia* (Cambridge, MA: Harvard University Press, 2010); Avner Wishnitzer, "Into the Dark: Power, Light, and Nocturnal Life in 18th-Century Istanbul," *International Journal of Middle East Studies* 46, no. 3 (2014): 513–31.

10. On social media and the Middle East uprisings, see Mohamed Zayani, *Networked Publics and Digital Contention: The Politics of Everyday Life in Tunisia* (Oxford: Oxford University Press, 2015); Linda Herrera, *Revolution in the Age of Social Media: The Egyptian Popular Insurrection and the Internet* (New York: Verso, 2014); David Faris, *Dissent and Revolution in a Digital Age: Social Media, Blogging and Activism in Egypt* (New York: I. B. Tauris, 2013); Philip Howard and Muzammil Hussain, *Democracy's Fourth Wave? Digital Media and the Arab Spring* (New York: Oxford University Press, 2013). On al-Jazeera, see Marc Lynch, *Voices of the New Arab Public: Iraq, Al-Jazeera, and Middle East Politics Today* (New York: Columbia University Press, 2006); Mohamed

Zayani, ed., *The Al Jazeera Phenomenon: Critical Perspectives on New Arab Media* (Boulder, CO: Paradigm Publishers, 2005); Hugh Miles, *Al-Jazeera: The Inside Story of the Arab News Channel that is Challenging the West* (New York: Grove Press, 2005). For a study connecting al-Jazeera and the Arab Spring, see Sam Cherribi, *Fridays of Rage: Al-Jazeera, the Arab Spring, and Political Islam* (New York: Oxford University Press, 2017).

11. On social media and the World Wide Web, see Adi Kuntsman and Rebecca Stein, *Digital Militarism: Israel's Occupation in the Social Media Age* (Stanford, CA: Stanford University Press, 2015); Negar Mottahedeh, *#iranelection: Hashtag Solidarity and the Transformation of Online Life* (Stanford, CA: Stanford University Press, 2015); Gary R. Bunt, *iMuslims: Rewiring the House of Islam* (Chapel Hill: University of North Carolina Press, 2009). On television, see Marwan Kraidy, *Reality Television and Arab Politics: Contention in Public Life* (New York: Cambridge University Press, 2010); Susanne Olsson, *Preaching Islamic Revival: 'Amr Khaled, Mass Media and Social Change in Egypt* (New York: I. B. Tauris, 2015); Walter Armbrust, "The Riddle of Ramadan: Media, Consumer Culture, and the 'Christmasization' of a Muslim Holiday," in *Everyday Life in the Muslim Middle East*, ed. Donna Lee Bowen and Evelyn A. Early (Bloomington: Indiana University Press, 2002), 335–48.

12. For ethnographies, see Lila Abu-Lughod, *Dramas of Nationhood: The Politics of Television in Egypt* (Chicago: University of Chicago Press, 2005); Christa Salamandra, "Moustache Hairs Lost: Ramadan Television Serials and the Construction of Identity in Damascus, Syria," *Visual Anthropology* 10, nos. 2–4 (1998): 226–46; Walter Armbrust, *Mass Culture and Modernism in Egypt* (New York: Cambridge University Press, 1996). For historical works, see Andrea Stanton, *"This Is Jerusalem Calling": State Radio in Mandate Palestine* (Austin: University of Texas Press, 2013); Rebecca Scales, "Subversive Sound: Transnational Radio, Arabic Recordings, and the Dangers of Listening in French Colonial Algeria, 1934–1939," *Comparative Studies in Society and History* 52, no. 2 (2010): 384–417; Ziad Fahmy, "Media-Capitalism: Colloquial Mass Culture and Nationalism in Egypt, 1908–18," *International Journal of Middle East Studies* 42, no. 1 (2010): 83–103; Ali Jihad Racy, "Musical Change and Commercial Recording in Egypt, 1904–1932," (PhD diss., University of Illinois at Urbana-Champaign, 1977). For two studies that strike a middle ground, see Joel Gordon, *Revolutionary Melodrama: Popular Film and Civic Identity in Nasser's Egypt* (Chicago: Middle East Documentation Center, 2002); Jonathan Smolin, *Moroccan Noir: Police, Crime, and Politics in Popular Culture* (Bloomington: Indiana University Press, 2013).

13. Lila Abu-Lughod, "Bedouins, Cassettes and Technologies of Public Culture," *Middle East Report*, no. 159 (1989): 9–10; Farha Ghannam, *Remaking the Modern: Space,*

Relocation, and the Politics of Identity in a Global Cairo (Los Angeles: University of California Press, 2002), 142–44, 146, 148–51, 155; Ted Swedenburg, "Saida Sultan/Danna International: Transgender Pop and the Polysemiotics of Sex, Nation, and Ethnicity on the Israeli-Egyptian Border," *Musical Quarterly* 81, no. 1 (1997): 89, 91. See also Ted Swedenburg, "Nubian Music in Cairo," in *The Garland Encyclopedia of World Music*, vol. 6, *The Middle East*, ed. Virginia Danielson, Dwight Reynolds, and Scott Marcus (New York: Routledge, 2002), 642.

14. El-Shawan Castelo-Branco S., "Some Aspects of the Cassette Industry in Egypt," *World of Music* 29, no. 2 (1987): 36.

15. According to one Egyptian commentator, cassette companies produced 8,960 songs from 1990 to 1998. See Muhammad Qabil, *Mawsu'at al-Ghina' fi Misr* (Cairo: Dar al-Shuruq, 2006), 13; Joel Gordon, "Singing the Pulse of the Egyptian-Arab Street: Shaaban Abd Al-Rahim and the Geo-Pop-Politics of Fast Food," *Popular Music* 22, no. 1 (2003): 75.

16. Charles Hirschkind, *The Ethical Soundscape: Cassette Sermons and Islamic Counterpublics* (New York: Columbia University Press, 2006), 39. For a second study addressing cassette sermons, see Aaron Rock-Singer, "Censoring the Kishkophone: Religion and State Power in Mubarak's Egypt," *International Journal of Middle East Studies* 49, no. 3 (2017): 437–56.

17. An EMI catalog, for instance, clearly underscores the breadth of Egypt's cassette-tape culture. Arabic nursery rhymes, belly-dance tracks, Bollywood songs, Qur'anic recitation, and the Beatles, to name only a few items, all appear on cassette recordings. See *Kataluj 'Umumi Kamil li-Kafat al-Tasjilat al-'Arabiyya 1977* (Athens: EMI Greece, 1977).

18. Peter Manuel, *Cassette Culture: Popular Music and Technology in North India* (Chicago: University of Chicago Press, 1993). See also Negar Mottahedeh, *Whisper Tapes: Kate Millet in Iran* (Stanford, CA: Stanford University Press, 2019); Flagg Miller, *The Audacious Ascetic: What Osama Bin Laden's Sound Archive Reveals About Al-Qa'ida* (New York: Oxford University Press, 2015); Flagg Miller, *The Moral Resonance of Arab Media: Audiocassette Poetry and Culture in Yemen* (Cambridge, MA: Harvard Center for Middle Eastern Studies, 2007); Annabelle Sreberny and Ali Mohammadi, *Small Media, Big Revolution: Communication, Culture, and the Iranian Revolution* (Minneapolis: University of Minnesota, 1994).

19. Chandra Mukerji, "Entangled in Questions of Cultural Analysis," *History and Technology* 30, no. 5 (2014): 255.

20. George H. Roeder Jr., "Coming to Our Senses," *Journal of American History* 81, no. 3 (1994): 1112.

21. Mark M. Smith, "Still Coming to 'Our' Senses: An Introduction," *Journal of American History* 95, no. 2 (2008): 380. See also Mark M. Smith, *Sensing the Past: Seeing, Hearing, Smelling, Tasting, and Touching in History* (Berkeley: University of California Press, 2007); Mark M. Smith, *Listening to Nineteenth-Century America* (Chapel Hill: University of North Carolina Press, 2001).

22. David Howes, "Charting the Sensorial Revolution," *Senses & Society* 1, no. 1 (2006): 115.

23. R. Murray Schafer, *The Tuning of the World* (New York: Knopf, 1977), 7. This seminal text was later reprinted in the 1990s. See R. Murray Schafer, *The Soundscape: Our Sonic Environment and the Tuning of the World* (Rochester, NY: Destiny Books, 1994).

24. Jonathan Sterne, *The Audible Past: Cultural Origins of Sound Reproduction* (Durham, NC: Duke University Press, 2003), 26. For some seminal histories, see Karin Bijsterveld, *Mechanical Sound: Technology, Culture, and Public Problems of Noise in the Twentieth Century* (Cambridge, MA: MIT Press, 2008); Lisa Gitelman, *Always Already New: Media, History, and the Data of Culture* (Cambridge, MA: MIT Press, 2006); Richard Cullen Rath, *How Early America Sounded* (Ithaca, NY: Cornell University Press, 2005); Emily Thompson, *The Soundscape of Modernity: Architectural Acoustics and the Culture of Listening in America, 1900–1933* (Cambridge, MA: MIT Press, 2002).

25. Sophia Rosenfeld, "On Being Heard: A Case for Paying Attention to the Historical Ear," *American Historical Review*, no. 116 (2011): 317.

26. See, e.g., Trevor Pinch and Karin Bijsterveld, eds., *The Oxford Handbook of Sound Studies* (New York: Oxford University Press, 2012); Mark M. Smith, ed., *Hearing History: A Reader* (Athens: University of Georgia Press, 2004); Michael Bull and Les Back, eds., *The Auditory Culture Reader* (Oxford, UK: Berg, 2003). It is worth noting that one reader, which does manage to address sound in the Middle East, albeit sparingly, includes two entries from an anthropologist and a philosopher/activist, as opposed to historians, see Jonathan Sterne, ed., *The Sound Studies Reader* (New York: Routledge, 2012), 54–69, 329–35.

27. Ziad Fahmy, "Coming to Our Senses: Historicizing Sound and Noise in the Middle East," *History Compass* 11, no. 4 (2013): 306; Andrea Stanton and Carole Woodall, "Roundtable: Bringing Sound into Middle East Studies: Introduction," *International Journal of Middle East Studies* 48, no. 1 (2016): 113–14. Elaborating on these critiques, Jonathan Shannon has observed that "even the majority of ethnographic texts on the

region depict Middle Easterners as living in near silence." See Jonathan H. Shannon, "Roundtable: Sounding North Africa and the Middle East: Introduction," *International Journal of Middle East Studies* 44, no. 4 (2012): 775.

28. Paul Starkey, "Modern Egyptian Culture in the Arab World," in *The Cambridge History of Egypt*, ed. M. W. Daly (New York: Cambridge University Press, 1998), 394–426.

29. Steven Connor, "Edison's Teeth: Touching Hearing," in *Hearing Cultures: Essays on Sound, Listening, and Modernity*, ed. Veit Erlmann (Oxford, UK: Berg Press, 2004), 153.

30. For recent histories attuned to sound in Middle East studies, see Ziad Fahmy, *Street Sounds: Listening to Everyday Life in Modern Egypt* (Stanford, CA: Stanford University Press, 2020); Maria Malmström, *The Streets Are Talking to Me: Affective Fragments in Sisi's Egypt* (Berkeley: University of California Press, 2019); Mottahedeh, *Whisper Tapes*; Nahid Siamdoust, *Soundtrack of the Revolution: The Politics of Music in Iran* (Stanford, CA: Stanford University Press, 2017); J. Martin Daughtry, *Listening to War: Sound, Music, Trauma, and Survival in Wartime Iraq* (New York: Oxford University Press, 2015); Stanton, *"This Is Jerusalem Calling"*; Ziad Fahmy, *Ordinary Egyptians: Creating the Modern Nation through Popular Culture* (Stanford, CA: Stanford University Press, 2011); Carole Woodall, "Sensing the City: Sound, Movement, and the Night in 1920s Istanbul" (PhD diss., New York University, 2008).

31. Jeanette Jouili and Annelies Moors, "Introduction: Islamic Sounds and the Politics of Listening," *Anthropological Quarterly* 87, no. 4 (2014): 977.

32. For early sound-sensitive studies, see Kristina Nelson, *The Art of Reciting the Qur'an* (Austin: University of Texas Press, 1985); Richard Antoun, *Muslim Preacher in the Modern World: A Jordanian Case Study in Comparative Perspective* (Princeton, NJ: Princeton University Press, 1989); Patrick Gaffney, *The Prophet's Pulpit: Islamic Preaching in Contemporary Egypt* (Berkeley: University of California Press, 1994). On the call to prayer, see Scott Marcus, *Music in Egypt: Experiencing Music, Expressing Culture* (New York: Oxford University Press, 2007), 1–15; Isaac A. Weiner, "Calling Everyone to Pray: Pluralism, Secularism, and the Adhān in Hamtramck, Michigan," *Anthropological Quarterly* 87, no. 4 (2014): 1049–77. On Qur'anic recitation, see Lauren E. Osborne, "From Text to Sound to Perception: Modes and Relationships of Meaning in the Recited Qur'an" (PhD diss., University of Chicago, 2014); Anne K. Rasmussen, *Women, the Recited Qur'an, and Islamic Music in Indonesia* (Berkeley: University of California Press, 2010); Michael Frishkopf, "Mediated Qur'anic Recitation and the Contestation of Islam in Contemporary Egypt," in *Music and the Play of Power in the Middle East*, ed. Laudan Nosshin (Farnham, UK: Ashgate, 2009), 75–114; Anna M. Gade,

Perfection Makes Practice: Learning, Emotion, and the Recited Qur'an in Indonesia (Honolulu: University of Hawai'i Press, 2004). On Sufi rituals, see Hager El Hadidi, *Zar: Spirit Possession, Music, and Healing Rituals in Egypt* (New York: American University in Cairo Press, 2016); Emilio Spadola, *The Calls of Islam: Sufis, Islamists, and Mass Mediation in Urban Morocco* (Bloomington: Indiana University Press, 2014); Samuli Schielke, *The Perils of Joy: Contesting Mulid Festivals in Contemporary Egypt* (Syracuse, NY: Syracuse University Press, 2013); Michael Frishkopf, "Tarab ('Enchantment') in the Mystic Sufi Chant of Egypt," in *Colors of Enchantment: Theater, Dance, Music, and the Visual Arts of the Middle East*, ed. Sherifa Zuhur (Cairo: American University in Cairo Press, 2001), 239–76.

   33. On responses to music and new technologies, see Jonas Otterbeck and Anders Ackfeldt, "Music and Islam," *Contemporary Islam* 6, no. 3 (2012): 227–33; Göran Larsson, *Muslims and the New Media: Historical and Contemporary Debates* (Burlington, VT: Ashgate, 2011). For the use of media by Muslim authorities, see Jacquelene Brinton, *Preaching Islamic Renewal: Religious Authority and Media in Contemporary Egypt* (Oakland: University of California Press, 2016); Charles Hirschkind, "Experiments in Devotion Online: The YouTube Khutba," *International Journal of Middle East Studies* 44, no. 1 (2012): 5–21; Yasmin Moll, "Islamic Televangelism: Religion, Media and Visuality," *Arab Media & Society*, no. 10 (2010): 1–27; Hirschkind, *The Ethical Soundscape*; Lindsay Wise, "'Words from the Heart': New Forms of Islamic Preaching in Egypt" (MPhil thesis, Oxford University, 2003); Brinkley Messick, "Media Muftis: Radio Fatwas in Yemen," in *Islamic Legal Interpretation: Muftis and Their Fatwas*, ed. Khalid Muhammad Masud, Brinkley Messick, and David S. Powers (Cambridge, MA: Harvard University Press, 1996), 310–23. For a study of mass media in Egypt that focuses on religion but privileges Christianity, see Febe Armanios and Andrew Amstutz, "Emerging Christian Media in Egypt: Clerical Authority and the Visualization of Women in Coptic Video Films," *International Journal of Middle East Studies* 45, no. 3 (2013): 513–33.

   34. Dale Eickelman and Jon Anderson, "Redefining Muslim Publics," in *New Media in the Muslim World: The Emerging Public Sphere*, ed. Dale Eickelman and Jon Anderson (Bloomington: Indiana University Press, 1999), 1; Hirschkind, *The Ethical Soundscape*, 108; Karin van Nieuwkerk, "Artistic Developments in the Muslim Cultural Sphere: Ethics, Aesthetics, and the Performing Arts," in *Muslim Rap, Halal Soaps, and Revolutionary Theater*, ed. Karin van Nieuwkerk (Austin: University of Texas Press, 2011), 2–4. For three edited volumes that address the relationship between sound and Islam, see Michael Frishkopf and Federico Spinetti, eds., *Music, Sound, and Architecture in Islam* (Austin: University of Texas Press, 2017); Karin van Nieuwkerk, Mark LeVine,

and Martin Stokes, eds., *Islam and Popular Culture* (Austin: University of Texas Press, 2016); Khaled Hroub, ed., *Religious Broadcasting in the Middle East* (New York: Columbia University Press, 2012).

35. Virginia Danielson, *The Voice of Egypt: Umm Kulthum, Arabic Song, and Egyptian Society in the Twentieth Century* (Chicago: University of Chicago Press, 1997), 9.

36. See, e.g., Danielson, *The Voice of Egypt*; Laura Lohman, *Umm Kulthum: Artistic Agency and the Shaping of an Arab Legend* (Middletown, CT: Wesleyan University Press, 2010); Sa'd Ramadan, ed., *Umm Kulthum: Sawt fi Tarikh al-Umma* (Tunis: Ma'had al-Musiqa al-'Arabiyya, 2000); Martin Stokes, "'Abd Al-Halim's Microphone," in *Music and the Play of Power in the Middle East, North Africa and Central Asia*, ed. Laudan Nooshin (Burlington, VT: Ashgate, 2009), 55–74; Joel Gordon, "The Nightingale and the Ra'is: 'Abd Al-Halim Hafiz and Nasserist Longings," in *Rethinking Nasserism: Revolution and Historical Memory in Modern Egypt*, ed. Elie Podeh and Onn Winckler (Gainesville: University Press of Florida, 2004), 307–23; Armbrust, *Mass Culture and Modernism in Egypt*, 63–94; Mahmud 'Awad, *Muhammad 'Abd al-Wahhab alladhi la Ya'rifuhu Ahad* (Cairo: Dar al-Ma'arif, 1991); Christopher Stone, *Popular Culture and Nationalism in Lebanon: The Fairouz and Rahbani Nation* (New York: Routledge, 2008).

37. For a few treatments of "suspect" entertainers in Egypt, see Daniel Gilman, *Cairo Pop: Youth Music in Contemporary Egypt* (Minneapolis: University of Minnesota Press, 2014); Mark LeVine, *Heavy Metal Islam: Rock, Resistance, and the Struggle for the Soul of Islam* (New York: Three Rivers Press, 2008), 60–105; Armbrust, *Mass Culture and Modernism in Egypt*, 165–220; Karin van Nieuwkerk, *"A Trade Like Any Other": Female Singers and Dancers in Egypt* (Austin: University of Texas Press, 1995).

38. Ziad Fahmy, "Early Egyptian Radio: From Media-Capitalism to Media-Etatism, 1925–1934," *Middle East Journal of Culture and Communication* [Forthcoming].

39. Hilmi Ahmad Shalabi, *Tarikh al-Idha'a al-Misriyya: Dirasa Tarikhiyya (1934–1952)* (Cairo: Al-Hay'a al-'Amma al-Misriyya lil-Kitab, 1995), 27.

40. Station owners, for example, broadcast pleas for public support and made their case to remain alongside a government station in the press. Shalabi, 30.

41. The Free Officers consisted mainly of junior officers intent on bringing an end to the monarchy's corruption and British influence in Egypt. Egypt's first three presidents, Muhammad Naguib, Gamal Abdel Nasser, and Anwar Sadat would all emerge from their ranks. For more on the Free Officers and this period in Egypt's past, see

Joel Gordon, *Nasser's Blessed Movement: Egypt's Free Officers and the July Revolution* (New York: Oxford University Press, 1992).

42. On Nasser's investment in, and use of, the radio, see Adeed Dawisha, *Arab Nationalism in the Twentieth Century: From Triumph to Despair* (Princeton, NJ: Princeton University Press, 2003), 147–48.

43. Another state-controlled medium, introduced in Egypt in 1960, was television. See, e.g., Elizabeth Seymour, "Imagining Modernity: Consuming Identities and Constructing the Ideal Nation on Egyptian Television" (PhD diss., SUNY Binghamton University, 1999), 24–30.

44. Alain Corbin, *Village Bells: Sound and Meaning in the 19th-Century French Countryside*, trans. Martin Thom (New York: Columbia University Press, 1998), ix. For the original monograph, see Alain Corbin, *Les cloches de la terre: Paysage sonore et culture sensible dans les campagnes au XIXe siècle* (Paris: A. Michel, 1994).

45. For histories of recording technologies in America alone, see Susan Schmidt Horning, *Chasing Sound: Technology, Culture, and the Art of Studio Recording from Edison to the LP* (Baltimore: Johns Hopkins University Press, 2013); David Suisman, *Selling Sounds: The Commercial Revolution in American Music* (Cambridge, MA: Harvard University Press, 2012); Tim Anderson, *Making Easy Listening: Material Culture and Postwar American Recording* (Minneapolis: University of Minnesota, 2006); William Kenney, *Recorded Music in American Life: The Phonograph and Popular Memory, 1890–1945* (New York: Oxford University Press, 2003); David Morton, *Off the Record: The Technology and Culture of Sound Recording in America* (New Brunswick, NJ: Rutgers University Press, 1999).

46. Ann Laura Stoler, *Along the Archival Grain: Epistemic Anxieties and Colonial Common Sense* (Princeton, NJ: Princeton University Press, 2009), 44. For detailed discussions of "archives" outside of the Middle East, see, e.g., Doreen Lee, *Activist Archives: Youth Culture and the Political Past in Indonesia* (Durham, NC: Duke University Press, 2016); Kathryn Burns, *Into the Archive: Writing and Power in Colonial Peru* (Durham, NC: Duke University Press, 2010); Natalie Zemon Davis, *Fiction in the Archives: Pardon Tales and Their Tellers in Sixteenth-Century France* (Stanford, CA: Stanford University Press, 1987). For a few Middle East exceptions, see Rosie Bsheer, *Archive Wars: The Politics of History in Saudi Arabia* (Stanford, CA: Stanford University Press, 2020); Sherene Seikaly, "Gaza as Archive," in *Gaza as Metaphor*, ed. Helga Tawil-Souri and Dina Matar (London: Hurst & Co., 2016), 225–31; Lucie Ryzova, "Mourning the Archive: Middle Eastern Photographic Heritage between Neoliberalism and Digital Reproduction," *Comparative Studies in Society and History* 56, no. 4 (2014): 1027–61; Yoav Di-Capua,

Gatekeepers of the Arab Past: Historians and History Writing in Twentieth-Century Egypt (Berkeley: University of California Press, 2009); Marilyn Booth, "Fiction's Imaginative Archive and the Newspaper's Local Scandals: The Case of Nineteenth-Century Egypt," in *Archive Stories: Facts, Fictions, and the Writing of History*, ed. Antoinette Burton (Durham, NC: Duke University Press, 2005), 274–95.

47. Kirsten Weld, *Paper Cadavers: The Archives of Dictatorship in Guatemala* (Durham, NC: Duke University Press, 2014), 13.

48. Ibrahim ʿAbduh, *Tarikh bila Wathaʾiq* (Cairo: Muʿassasat Sajil al-ʿArab, 1975), 11.

49. Anthony Gorman, *Historians, State, and Politics in Twentieth Century Egypt: Contesting the Nation* (New York: Routledge, 2003), 76; Khaled Fahmy, "How Do We Write Our Military History?," *Ahram Online* (2013); Omnia El Shakry, "'History without Documents': The Vexed Archives of Decolonization in the Middle East," *American Historical Review* 120, no. 3 (2015): 924. On a related note, also see Dina Ezzat, "65 Years Later: The 'Cairo Fire' of 1952 Revisited," *Ahram Online* (2017), https://english.ahram.org.eg/NewsContent/1/64/257110/Egypt/Politics-/-years-later-The-'Cairo-Fire'-of--revisited.aspx.

50. Jean Allman, "Phantoms of the Archive: Kwame Nkrumah, a Nazi Pilot Named Hanna, and the Contingencies of Postcolonial History-Writing," *American Historical Review* 118, no. 1 (2013): 120.

51. Beth Baron, *The Women's Awakening in Egypt: Culture, Society, and the Press* (New Haven, CT: Yale University Press, 1994); Hanan Kholoussy, *For Better, for Worse: The Marriage Crisis That Made Modern Egypt* (Stanford, CA: Stanford University Press, 2010); Fahmy, *Ordinary Egyptians*; Michael Ezekiel Gasper, *The Power of Representation: Publics, Peasants, and Islam in Egypt* (Stanford, CA: Stanford University Press, 2009). See also Wilson C. Jacob, *Working Out Egypt: Effendi Masculinity and Subject Formation in Colonial Modernity, 1870–1940* (Durham, NC: Duke University Press, 2011).

52. In this regard, this study joins a limited number of other histories to use the press post-1952. See Laura Bier, *Revolutionary Womanhood: Feminisms, Modernity, and the State in Nasser's Egypt* (Stanford, CA: Stanford University Press, 2011); Aaron Rock-Singer, *Practicing Islam in Egypt: Print Media and the Islamic Revival* (New York: Cambridge University Press, 2019).

53. Born Fatima al-Yusuf, the actress came to fame as Ruz al-Yusuf. On the magazine's founding, see Fatima al-Yusuf, *Dhikrayat*, 2nd ed. (Cairo: Muʿassasat Ruz al-Yusuf, 1976), 115–18.

54. On the start of *Akhir Saʿa*, see Huda al-Tabiʿi, "Taqdim," in *Muhammad al-*

Tabi'i, by Sabri Abu al-Majd (Cairo: Mu'assasat Dar al-Ta'awun lil-Tiba'a wa al-Nashr, 1993), 28–29.

55. Law No. 156 transferred the ownership of four publishing houses—al-Ahram, Dar al-Hilal, Ruz al-Yusuf, and Akhbar al-Yawm (which printed *Akhir Sa'a*)—to the National Union, which was later replaced by the Arab Socialist Union. The law required all papers and journalists to obtain licenses from the union to operate. See William Rugh, *The Arab Press: News Media and Political Process in the Arab World*, 2nd ed. (Syracuse, NY: Syracuse University Press, 1987), 37–8; Fouad Fahmy Shafik, "The Press and Politics of Modern Egypt, 1798–1970: A Comparative Analysis of Casual Relationships" (PhD diss., New York University, 1981), 402–3.

56. Gorman, *Historians, State, and Politics in Twentieth Century Egypt*, 77.

57. This remark applies to multiple postcolonial presses in the Middle East. See Ami Ayalon, *The Press in the Arab Middle East: A History* (New York: Oxford University Press, 1995), 245.

58. Salah Mutawalli, "Idha'a 'ala al-Futat," *Akhir Sa'a*, no. 2795 (18 May 1988): 62.

59. *Tarab* literally means "to be moved" in Arabic. In the context of Salah's letter, it refers to performers who enraptured listeners, generating an emotional response with their songs. For more on the meanings of *tarab* in the context of music, see Ali Jihad Racy, *Making Music in the Arab World: The Culture and Artistry of Tarab* (New York: Cambridge University Press, 2004), 5–6.

60. Muhammad Higazi, "Idha'a..Mustahlika," *Ruz al-Yusuf*, no. 3134 (4 July 1988): 45.

61. Lucie Ryzova, *The Age of the Efendiyya: Passages to Modernity in National-Colonial Egypt* (New York: Oxford University Press, 2014), 30.

62. Bier, *Revolutionary Womanhood*; Jesse Ferris, *Nasser's Gamble: How Intervention in Yemen Caused the Six-Day War and the Decline of Egyptian Power* (Princeton, NJ: Princeton University Press, 2013); Fawaz Gerges, *Making the Arab World: Nasser, Qutb, and the Clash That Shaped the Middle East* (Princeton, NJ: Princeton University Press, 2018). See also Reem Abou-El-Fadl, *Foreign Policy as Nation Making: Turkey and Egypt in the Cold War* (New York: Cambridge University Press, 2019); Mériam Belli, *An Incurable Past: Nasser's Egypt Then and Now* (Gainesville: University Press of Florida, 2013).

63. For a few recent treatments of some of these respective developments, see Rock-Singer, *Practicing Islam in Egypt*; Relli Shechter, *The Rise of the Egyptian Middle Class: Socio-Economic Mobility and Public Discontent from Nasser to Sadat* (New York: Cambridge University Press, 2019); Zeinab Abul-Magd, *Militarizing the Nation: The Army, Business, and Revolution in Egypt* (New York: Columbia University Press, 2018).

1. SELLING

1. Hagat 'Adima, "Al-Nas illi Bittisawur Masika iPhone 6.... Kaman Kam Sana Hayashufu Suwarhum Kida," Facebook, January 9, 2017, https://www.facebook.com/7agatAdeema/.

2. Faruq Misr, "Al-Nas illi Bittisawur Masika iPhone 6.... Kaman Kam Sana Hayashufu Suwarhum Kida," Facebook, January 10, 2017, https://www.facebook.com/king.farouk.faroukmisr.

3. Ashraf Bakr, Facebook messages to author, 11 January 2017 and 9 April 2017.

4. These five countries are Saudi Arabia, Kuwait, Iraq, the United Arab Emirates, and Libya. See Saad Eddin Ibrahim, "Oil, Migration and the New Arab Social Order," in *Rich and Poor States in the Middle East: Egypt and the New Arab Order*, ed. Malcolm Kerr and El Sayed Yassin (Boulder, CO: Westview Press, 1982), 22.

5. According to one oft-cited report, in 1975 Egypt's population was 37,364,900 and its workforce 12,522,200, while the combined population and workforce of Saudi Arabia, Libya, and Kuwait, three major oil-producing destinations for Egyptian migrant workers, was 7,288,300 and 1,567,500, respectively. J. S. Birks and C. A. Sinclair, *International Migration and Development in the Arab Region* (Geneva: International Labour Office, 1980), 131–32.

6. Although selected Egyptians secured employment abroad before the 1970s, momentary migration became a mass phenomenon only under Anwar Sadat. For a recent discussion of migration earlier on, under Gamal Abdel Nasser, see Gerasimos Tsourapas, "Nasser's Educators and Agitators across *al-Watan al-Arabi*: Tracing the Foreign Policy Importance of Egyptian Regional Migration, 1952–1967," *British Journal of Middle Eastern Studies* 43, no. 3 (2016): 324–41.

7. Exactly how much more Egyptian workers stood to make in oil-producing Arab countries depended on profession, destination, and time of departure, but experts consistently agree that Egyptian nationals earned more abroad than they would at home. See, e.g., Nazli Choucri, "The New Migration in the Middle East: A Problem for Whom?," *International Migration Review* 11, no. 4 (1977): 434; Nazih Ayubi, "Implementation Capability and Political Feasibility of the Open Door Policy in Egypt," in *Rich and Poor States in the Middle East: Egypt and the New Arab Order*, ed. Malcolm Kerr and El Sayed Yassin (Boulder, CO: Westview Press, 1982), 398; Richard Adams Jr., "Worker Remittances and Inequality in Rural Egypt," *Economic Development and Cultural Change* 38, no. 1 (1989): 47.

8. On the difficulties of this data, see Abdelmegid Farrag, "Migration between Arab Countries," in *Manpower and Employment in Arab Countries Some Critical Issues*

(Geneva: International Labour Office, 1976), 85; Fred Halliday, "Migration and the Labour Force in the Oil Producing States of the Middle East," *Development and Change* 8, no. 3 (1977): 246; Robert LaTowsky, "Egyptian Labor Abroad: Mass Participation and Modest Returns," *MERIP Reports*, no. 123 (1984): 12; Petra Weyland, *Inside the Third World Village* (New York: Routledge, 1993), 5.

9. Gil Feiler, "Scope and Some Effects of Remittances of Egyptian Migrant Workers in the Arab Oil-Producing Countries, 1973–1984," *Asian and African Studies* 21 (1987): 305.

10. David Lamb, "Egyptians Flee Ailing Economy: Millions of Workers Go Into Exile; Mubarak Offers 'No Magic Wand,'" *Los Angeles Times* (27 August 1982): C6. Notably, the same year this article was published, Egypt's Ministry for Foreign Affairs arrived at a similar figure. Based on consulate statistics, it placed the number of Egyptians working in oil-rich Arab countries at 2.9 million. See Ralph Sell, "Egyptian International Labor Migration and Social Processes: Toward Regional Integration," *International Migration Review* 22, no. 3 (1988): 91.

11. Instances of illegal migration assumed multiple forms, from clandestine border crossings to Egyptians remaining past their sanctioned stays either as pilgrims in Saudi Arabia or as guests of relatives across the Middle East. See J. S. Birks and C. A. Sinclair, "Egypt: A Frustrated Labor Exporter?," *Middle East Journal* 33, no. 3 (1979): 292; Fatma Khafagy, "Women and Labor Migration: One Village in Egypt," *MERIP Reports*, no. 124 (1984): 18.

12. Various entities aided Egyptians intent on working abroad. In 1971, migration became a constitutional right in Egypt, but it was not until a few years later, during the oil boom, that this privilege became more practical for many people. Whether abolishing exit visas, decentralizing passports, or ending the mandatory transfer of a percentage of one's foreign earnings to Egypt, the state-led liberalization of emigration went hand in hand with the opening up of Egypt's economy. In 1981, these top-down measures culminated in the establishment of the Ministry of State for Emigration Affairs. Outside of the Egyptian government, travel agencies, professional contractors, and personal connections within families, neighborhoods, and informal networks lent prospective migrants further assistance still. For more on these developments, see Ali Dessouki, "The Shift in Egypt's Migration Policy: 1952–1978," *Middle Eastern Studies* 18, no. 1 (1982): 58–63; LaTowsky, "Egyptian Labor Abroad," 12; Delwin Roy, "Egyptian Emigrant Labor: Domestic Consequences," *Middle Eastern Studies* 27, no. 4 (1991): 560.

13. For two such exceptions, see Gerasimos Tsourapas, *The Politics of Migration in Modern Egypt: Strategies for Regime Survival in Autocracies* (New York: Cambridge

University Press, 2019); Relli Shechter, *The Rise of the Egyptian Middle Class: Socio-Economic Mobility and Public Discontent from Nasser to Sadat* (New York: Cambridge University Press, 2019).

14. Henry Bruton, "Egypt's Development in the Seventies," *Economic Development and Cultural Change* 31, no. 4 (1983): 687.

15. Judith Miller, "Wave of Arab Migration Ending with Oil Boom," *New York Times* (6 October 1985): 16. The difference between these two estimates is due to the fact that not all remittances passed through formal channels. In lieu of using banks, many Egyptian migrants moved cash across national borders through friends, relatives, and currency dealers, often to the ire of the Egyptian government, circumventing the state's accounting procedures altogether and rendering any official data on remittances incomplete. As one political scientist has pointed out, the unrecorded remittances of Egyptian migrant workers were so immense that they contributed to the creation of a "hidden economy" in the Arab world. See Nazli Choucri, "The Hidden Economy: A New View of Remittances in the Arab World," *World Development* 14, no. 6 (1986): 697–712.

16. Mahmud ʿAbd al-Raziq, "Akhir Saʿa Dakhil Qaryat al-Badaʾiʿ: Nisf Milyun Tilifiziyun Mulawwan maʿ al-ʿAʾidin min al-Kharij!," *Akhir Saʿa*, no. 2492 (28 July 1982): 15.

17. In the summer of 1979, for example, a foreign correspondent for the *New York Times* noted the abundance of electronics inside the cabins of passenger jets carrying Egypt-bound migrants. "The aisles of airliners flying workers home," he observed, "are invariably jammed with radios, cassette recorders, blenders, and television sets." See Christopher Wren, "Egypt's Skilled Workers are Vital for the Other Arabs," *New York Times* (8 July 1979): E4.

18. In 1976, one reporter for *Ruz al-Yusuf* went so far as to assert, "If you ask any Egyptian traveling abroad about what he will buy first, he will immediately answer you: a cassette player." According to the same writer, illustrators lent credence to this phenomenon by often depicting Egyptian returnees with a smile on their face and with two devices in hand: a television and a cassette player. See Iqbal Baraka, "Sharikat Philips Tistaʿid lil-Munafasa al-ʿAlamiyya," *Ruz al-Yusuf*, no. 1396 (17 May 1976): 57–58.

19. In a series of advertisements from 1975, Muhammad Jamil Harun Dahlawa (National's agent) and al-Zaqzuq and al-Matbuli (Toshiba's agent) alerted readers to the presence of cassette players in several different cities across the kingdom, including Mecca, Medina, Jedda, Riyadh, al-Taʾif, and al-Dammam. See "Muntijat Mumtiʿa li-Haya Mumtiʿa—National," *Ruz al-Yusuf*, no. 2439 (10 March 1975): 61; "National," *Ruz al-Yusuf*, no. 2478 (8 December 1975): 63; "Toshiba," *Akhir Saʿa*, no. 2104 (19 February

1975): 24. A second Toshiba advertisement from 1975 notes the existence of another Saudi branch in al-Khobar in the place of al-Ta'if; see "Toshiba," *Ruz al-Yusuf,* no. 2479 (15 December 1975): 22.

20. "Samsung Electronics," *Akhir Sa'a,* no. 2405 (26 November 1980): 31.

21. Ahmad al-Guindi, "Tir Enta," 116 mins. (Egypt: Al-Sharika al-'Arabiyya lil-Intaj wa al-Tawzi' al-Sinima'i, 2009.

22. "National: Ism Tathiq bihi Haythuma Tajiduhu," *Akhir Sa'a,* no. 2330 (20 June 1979): 42; "National: Ism Tathiq bihi Haythuma Tajiduhu," *Akhir Sa'a,* no. 2336 (1 August 1979): 38; "National: Ism Tathiq bihi Haythuma Tajiduhu," *Akhir Sa'a,* no. 2363 (6 February 1980): 2.

23. In 1973, some 60,752 Egyptian migrants found work in Libya. By 1975, this estimate increased to 229,500, with most Egyptian migrant workers in the Middle East (57.7 percent) stationed in Libya. See Farrag, "Migration between Arab Countries," 105; Birks and Sinclair, *International Migration and Development in the Arab Region,* 134.

24. David Ottaway, "Foreign Earnings Transform Egypt's Village Life New Wealth Changes Society in Villages," *Washington Post* (29 January 1985): A1.

25. Louis Eaks, "The new cars, luxuries and food subsidies," *The Guardian* (15 April 1976): 16.

26. This song opened with the lines: "Here came the Libyan, he brought a recorder and it broke." *Libyan,* here, likely refers to Egyptians who spent time abroad in Libya. See Mahmud 'Abd al-Shakur, *Kuntu Sabiyan fi al-Sab'inat* (Cairo: Al-Karama lil-Nashr wa al-Tawzi', 2015), 146.

27. Before the Iran-Iraq War, an estimated seven thousand Egyptians worked in Iraq in 1975. By 1983, there were reportedly more than a million Egyptians in Iraq. See Birks and Sinclair, *International Migration and Development in the Arab Region,* 134; Ralph Sell, "Gone for Good? Egyptian Migration Processes in the Arab World," *Cairo Papers in Social Science* 10, no. 2 (1987): 34.

28. Miller, "Wave of Arab Migration Ending with Oil Boom," 16. Indeed, the pervasive presence of Egyptians in Iraq inspired a joke, in which one Egyptian remarks to another when walking down a popular street in Baghdad: "My goodness, there seem to be a lot of foreigners around here lately," with the implication being that the "foreigners" were "Iraqis." See Camillia Solh, "Egyptian Migrant Peasants in Iraq: A Case-Study of the Settlement Community in Khalsa" (PhD diss., University of London, 1985), 92.

29. Patrick Baz, "Egypt-Gulf War-Refugees" and "Egypt-Gulf War-Egyptian Refugees," Getty Images, 1990, https://www.gettyimages.com/photos/patrick-baz.

30. Based on the time frame of these reports, many, if not most, of the "radios"

mentioned likely doubled as cassette players. See Jane Mayer, "Egyptian Refugees Say They Fled Brutality and Robbery in Kuwait," *Wall Street Journal* (22 August 1990): A6; Joel Brinkley, "Egyptians Tell of Iraqi Rule in Kuwait," *New York Times* (22 August 1990): A12; Deborah Pugh, "Egyptians Stream Back to an Uncertain Future," *The Guardian* (28 August 1990): 2.

31. David Lamb, "Mideast Airlines Struggle as Their High-Flying Days End," *Los Angeles Times* (11 March 1985): E1.

32. Gil Feiler, *Economic Relations between Egypt and the Gulf Oil States, 1967–2000: Petro-Wealth and Patterns of Influence* (Brighton, UK: Sussex Academic Press, 2003), 99.

33. Laythi, "Budun Kalam," *Ruz al-Yusuf*, no. 2230 (8 March 1971): 11.

34. On what the oil boom meant to the United States, see Robert Vitalis, *Oilcraft: The Myths of Scarcity and Security That Haunt U.S. Energy Policy* (Stanford, CA: Stanford University Press, 2020), 57–82.

35. Egyptian critics, for example, regularly lamented what they saw as the "misuse" of remittances on consumer durables as opposed to "productive" investments. See Birks and Sinclair, "Egypt: A Frustrated Labor Exporter?," 302; Ayubi, "Implementation Capability and Political Feasibility of the Open Door Policy in Egypt," 400.

36. "Sharikat 'Abr al-Sharq lil-Turiddat," *Akhir Sa'a*, no. 1851 (15 April 1970): 13.

37. "'Alama Mudi'a fi 'Alam al-Iliktruniyat," *Akhir Sa'a*, no. 2404 (19 November 1980): 55.

38. Mahmud 'Abd al-Hadi, "Mistir Philips fi al-Qahira," *Ruz al-Yusuf*, no. 2484 (19 January 1976): 76–77.

39. "Ajhizat Philips al-Jadida fi al-Tariq Ilayk," *Ruz al-Yusuf*, no. 2477 (1 December 1975): 70.

40. "Philips," *Akhir Sa'a*, no. 2196 (24 November 1976): 28; "Philips," *Ruz al-Yusuf*, no. 2606 (22 May 1978): 67; "Philips," *Ruz al-Yusuf*, no. 2634 (4 December 1978): 20.

41. "National," *Ruz al-Yusuf*, no. 2567 (22 August 1977): 68; "National," *Ruz al-Yusuf*, no. 2568 (29 August 1977): 68; "National," *Akhir Sa'a*, no. 2234 (17 August 1977): 50.

42. "Toshiba," *Akhir Sa'a*, no. 2539 (22 June 1983): 2; "Toshiba," *Akhir Sa'a*, no. 2567 (4 January 1984): 34–5.

43. "Toshiba," *Akhir Sa'a*, no. 2634 (17 April 1985): 2; "Toshiba," *Akhir Sa'a*, no. 2639 (22 May 1985): 2.

44. "Sony," *Ruz al-Yusuf*, no. 2449 (30 September 1981): 68; "Samsung," *Ruz al-Yusuf*, no. 3207 (27 November 1989): 152.

45. "Intahat 'Uzlat al-Sina': Bil-Kabari wa al-Turuq wa al-Matarat," *Akhir Sa'a*, no. 2608 (17 October 1984): 25.

46. Notices for the city's shops regularly promoted luxury goods and underscored their international character. See "Mahalat Intarnashyunal," *Ruz al-Yusuf*, no. 2594 (27 February 1978): 63; "Al-Suq al-Dawli li-Hiltun Bur Sa'id," *Akhir Sa'a*, no. 2517 (19 January 1983): 13.

47. 'Ali Badrakhan, "Ahl al-Qimma," 118 mins. (Egypt: Aflam Jamal al-Laythi, 1981); 'Atif al-Tayyib, "Sawwaq al-Utubis," 108 mins. (Egypt: Al-Subki Film,1983).

48. See, e.g., Steven Cook, *The Struggle for Egypt: From Nasser to Tahrir Square* (New York: Oxford University Press, 2012), 136–39. For one notable exception, see Walter Armbrust, *Mass Culture and Modernism in Egypt* (New York: Cambridge University Press, 1996), esp. chap. 7.

49. William Leach, "Transformations in a Culture of Consumption: Women and Department Stores, 1890–1925," *Journal of American History* 71, no. 2 (1984): 322.

50. Faruq Ibrahim, "'Abd al-Halim Hafiz: Sura wa Sawt wa Nagham fi Qulub al-Malayin," *Akhir Sa'a*, no. 2216 (13 April 1977): 38.

51. Faruq Ibrahim, "Qissat Fannan Ada'at Aghanihi Hayat al-Malayin," *Akhir Sa'a*, no. 2219 (4 May 1977): 40.

52. Tharwat Fahmi, "Ali Isma'il wa Nabila Qandil wa Mawahib Ukhra," *Akhir Sa'a*, no. 2045 (2 January 1974): 49; Muhammad 'Abd al-Rahman, "Rahil 'Imlaq," *Akhir Sa'a*, no. 2433 (10 June 1981): 48–49.

53. In a photo of Farid al-Atrash and his fiancée, Salwa, for instance, a cassette radio rests atop a counter in the singer's upscale, Nile-side apartment in Giza. See "Akhir Sura li-Farid al-Atrash wa Khatibatuhu..wa al-Film Yarwi Asrar Hayatihi!," *Akhir Sa'a*, no. 2411 (7 January 1981): 45.

54. Muhammad Zaki, "I'tirafat 'al-Khatib' Najm al-Ahly: 'Hadhihi Hiya 'Arusati al-Majhula!'" *Akhir Sa'a*, no. 2228 (6 July 1977): 52.

55. 'Ala' Isma'il, "Ha'ula' al-Nujum: Hayatahum al-Khassa," *Akhir Sa'a*, no. 2324 (9 May 1979): 64–65.

56. "Ba'idan 'an al-Kura," *Akhir Sa'a: al-Majalla al-Riyadiyya*, no. 2644 (26 June 1984): 9–10.

57. 'Ala' Isma'il, "Ha'ula' al-Nujum: Hayatahum al-Khassa," *Akhir Sa'a*, no. 2326 (23 May 1979): 64; Rifa't Buhayri, "Ha'ula' al-Nujum: Hayatahum al-Khassa," *Akhir Sa'a*, no. 2331 (27 June 1979): 64–65.

58. "Sony," *Akhir Sa'a*, no. 2436 (1 July 1981): 67; "Sony," *Akhir Sa'a*, no. 2439 (22 July 1981): 2; "Sony," *Akhir Sa'a*, no. 2462 (30 December 1981): 2.

59. Ibrahim's photos of Sadat were later reprinted in a separate volume, see Amir al-Zuhar, *Suwar wa Asrar min Hayat al-Kibar* (Cairo: Akbhar al-Yawm, 1997), 12, 38.

60. Al-Zuhar, 18.

61. As for Sadat's exact preferences when it came to tapes, two foreign observers, who were critical of the president's luxurious lifestyle, claimed that he enjoyed waking to a cassette recording of the Qur'an before transitioning to "his favourite Arabic singers" when he went off to wash. See David Hirst and Irene Beeson, *Sadat* (London: Faber and Faber, 1981), 213.

62. According to one of Nasser's confidants, the prolific journalist Mohamed Hassanein Heikal, the voice of Umm Kulthum "whether on records or on tapes was a companion for him at all times." See Yusuf al-Qa'id, *Mohamed Hassanein Heikal Yatadhakkar 'Abd al-Nasser wa al-Muthaqqafun wa al-Thaqafa* (Cairo: Al-Hay'a al-'Amma al-Misriyya lil-Kitab, 2013), 96.

63. Muhammad 'Abd al-Rahman, "Ba'd 32 Alf Sa'a Fauq al-Sahab: Al-Nisr al-'Ajuz bila Ajniha!," *Akhir Sa'a*, no. 2239 (21 September 1977): 25; Tharwat Fahmi, "Yahia Shahin Yajib 'ala Hadha al-Su'al: Azmat al-Sinima Limadha?," *Akhir Sa'a*, no. 2335 (25 July 1979): 51; Osama 'Agag, "Shati' Zamrara: Lamsa Jadida bil-Alwan," *Akhir Sa'a*, no. 2418 (25 February 1981): 46.

64. Ahmad Amin, *Hayati* (Cairo: Matba'at Lajnat al-Ta'lif wa al-Tarjama wa al-Nashr, 1950), 16.

65. Muhammad al-Hinawi, "Tahqiq Dakhil Hadha al-Rajul," *Ruz al-Yusuf*, no. 2430 (6 January 1975): 17.

66. "Sharikat al-Azya' al-Haditha," *Akhir Sa'a*, no. 2698 (9 July 1986): 46.

67. "Toshiba," *Akhir Sa'a*, no. 2104 (19 February 1975): 24.

68. "Rubi," *Ruz al-Yusuf*, no. 2478 (8 December 1975): 45.

69. "Omar Effendi," *Ruz al-Yusuf*, no. 2566 (15 August 1977): 57.

70. "Sednaoui," *Akhir Sa'a*, no. 2823 (30 November 1988): 32–33.

71. Notably, this discussion of the modern home significantly departs from other inquiries into what it meant to be "modern" in Egypt's historiography, where scholars have focused on "modern citizens," especially in the context of the *efendiyya*. See Lucie Ryzova, *The Age of the Efendiyya: Passages to Modernity in National-Colonial Egypt* (New York: Oxford University Press, 2014); Israel Gershoni and James Jankowski, *Redefining the Egyptian Nation, 1930–1945* (New York: Cambridge University Press, 1995); Lisa Pollard, *Nurturing the Nation: The Family Politics of Modernizing, Colonizing and Liberating Egypt (1805–1923)* (Berkeley: University of California Press, 2005); Wilson C. Jacob, *Working Out Egypt: Effendi Masculinity and Subject Formation in Colonial Modernity, 1870–1940* (Durham, NC: Duke University Press, 2011).

72. Stuart Ewen, *Captains of Consciousness: Advertising and the Social Roots of the Consumer Culture* (New York: McGraw-Hill, 1976), 109.

73. See, e.g., "National," *Akhir Saʻa*, no. 2699 (16 July 1986): 63.

74. "National," *Akhir Saʻa*, no. 1391 (22 December 1971): 30; "National," *Akhir Saʻa*, no. 2119 (4 June 1975): 49.

75. Ramadan print advertisements for cassette players may be read as an extension of Ramadan riddles on Egyptian television, which also endorsed material products, including cassette players, and contributed to what Walter Armbrust has called the "Christmasization of Ramadan." See "The Riddle of Ramadan: Media, Consumer Culture, and the 'Christmasization' of a Muslim Holiday," in *Everyday Life in the Muslim Middle East*, ed. Donna Lee Bowen and Evelyn A. Early (Bloomington: Indiana University Press, 2002), 335, 338.

76. "National," *Akhir Saʻa*, no. 2234 (17 August 1977): 50.

77. "Telimisr," *Akhir Saʻa*, no. 2386 (16 July 1980): 39.

78. Mirvat Fahmi, "Man Yashtari al-Tilifiziyun al-Mulawwan wa al-Fidyu Kasit?," *Ruz al-Yusuf*, no. 2820 (28 June 1982): 66.

79. In a collection of interviews with Egyptian women in the late 1970s, for example, a lower-class housekeeper and aspiring bride-to-be expressed her desire to furnish a home with what her interlocutor called "all the modern conveniences now available in Egypt to anyone who can pay for them." The consumer goods envisioned by the woman in her future abode included "a refrigerator, washing machine, television, and radio-cassette player," among other items. See Nayra Atiya, *Khul-Khaal: Five Egyptian Women Tell Their Stories* (Syracuse, NY: Syracuse University Press, 1982), xxvi–vii.

80. Beth Baron, *Egypt as a Woman: Nationalism, Gender, and Politics* (Berkeley: University of California Press, 2005), 83–84; Stephen Sheehi, "A Social History of Early Arab Photography or a Prolegomenon to an Archaeology of the Lebanese Imago," *International Journal of Middle East Studies* 39, no. 2 (2007): 178.

81. See, e.g., Stephen Sheehi, *The Arab Imago: A Social History of Portrait Photography, 1860–1910* (Princeton, NJ: Princeton University Press, 2016); Issam Nassar, "Familial Snapshots: Representing Palestine in the Work of the First Local Photographers," *History & Memory* 18, no. 2 (2006): 139–55; Nancy Micklewright, "Late Ottoman Photography: Family, Home, and New Identities," in *Transitions in Domestic Consumption and Family Life in the Modern Middle East: Houses in Motion*, ed. Relli Shechter (New York: Palgrave Macmillan, 2003), 65–84.

82. For one major exception, see the following special issue: "Local Histories of

Photography in the Middle East," *Middle East Journal of Culture and Communication* 9, nos. 2–3 (2015).

83. Lucie Ryzova, "Boys, Girls, and Kodaks: Peer Albums and Middle-Class Personhood in Mid-Twentieth-Century Egypt," *Middle East Journal of Culture and Communication* 8, no. 2/3 (2015): 215–55. See also Lucie Ryzova, *The Age of the Efendiyya*, 207–10.

84. For one exception that focuses on upper-class actors, see Magda Baraka, *The Egyptian Upper Class between Revolutions, 1919–1952* (Reading, NY: Ithaca Press, 1998), esp. 163–207. On the lack of attention paid by historians to the subject of pleasure in Middle East studies, see Walter Armbrust, "Audiovisual Media and History of the Arab Middle East," in *Middle East Historiographies: Narrating the Twentieth Century*, ed. Israel Gershoni, Amy Singer, and Y. Hakan Erdem (Seattle: University of Washington Press, 2011), 306.

85. "National," *Akhir Sa'a*, no. 1939 (22 December 1971): 30.

86. For a selected assortment of studies, see Marsha Posusney, *Labor and the State in Egypt: Workers, Unions, and Economic Restructuring* (New York: Columbia University Press, 1997); John Chalcraft, *The Striking Cabbies of Cairo and Other Stories: Crafts and Guilds in Egypt, 1863–1914* (Albany: State University of New York Press, 2004); Robert Tignor, *Egyptian Textiles and British Capital 1930–1956* (Cairo: American University in Cairo Press, 1989); Samer Shehata, *Shop Floor Culture and Politics in Egypt* (Albany: State University of New York Press, 2009); Ellis Goldberg, *Tinker, Tailor, Textile Worker: Class and Politics in Egypt, 1930–1952* (Berkeley: University of California Press, 1986); Joel Beinin and Zachary Lockman, *Workers on the Nile: Nationalism, Communism, Islam, and the Egyptian Working Class, 1882–1954* (Princeton, NJ: Princeton University Press, 1987); Joel Beinin, *Workers and Peasants in the Modern Middle East* (New York: Cambridge University Press, 2001).

87. This impression is not limited to Middle East scholarship. For a similar point on work and workers in literature on America and Europe, see Mary Louise Roberts, "Gender, Consumption, and Commodity Culture," *American Historical Review* 103, no. 3 (1998): 820.

88. For studies on Egypt, see Omar Foda, *Egypt's Beer: Stella, Identity, and the Modern State* (Austin: University of Texas Press, 2019); Nancy Y. Reynolds, *A City Consumed: Urban Commerce, the Cairo Fire, and the Politics of Decolonization in Egypt* (Stanford, CA: Stanford University Press, 2012); Relli Shechter, *Smoking, Culture, and Economy in the Middle East: The Egyptian Tobacco Market, 1850–2000* (Cairo: American University in Cairo Press, 2006); Mona Abaza, *The Changing Consumer Cultures of Modern Egypt*

(Boston: Brill, 2006); Mona Russell, *Creating the New Egyptian Woman: Consumerism, Education, and National Identity, 1863–1922* (New York: Palgrave Macmillan, 2004). For studies covering other Middle Eastern settings, see Toufoul Abou-Hodeib, *A Taste for Home: The Modern Middle Class in Ottoman Beirut* (Stanford, CA: Stanford University Press, 2017); James Grehan, *Everyday Life & Consumer Culture in 18th-Century Damascus* (Seattle: University of Washington Press, 2007); Donald Quataert, ed., *Consumption Studies and the History of the Ottoman Empire, 1550–1922: An Introduction* (Albany: State University of New York Press, 2000).

89. Tarek Osman, *Egypt on the Brink: From Nasser to the Muslim Brotherhood*, rev. ed. (New Haven, CT: Yale University Press, 2013), 128–39; Anthony McDermot, *Egypt from Nasser to Mubarak: A Flawed Revolution* (New York: Croom Helm, 1988), 51–52, 132–34.

2. DESIRING

1. "National," *Akhir Saʿa*, no. 1939 (22 December 1971): 30.

2. During Sadat's rule, electricity was not available to every citizen. According to the population census from 1974–1975, an estimated 18 percent of "rural households" and 77 percent of "urban households" had electricity. By not requiring an electrical outlet to operate, cassette players were all the more desirable from the perspective of Egyptian consumers residing across the country. See Nadia Khouri-Dagher, *Food and Energy in Cairo: Provisioning the Poor* (report prepared for the United Nations Food-Energy Nexus Programme, United Nations, Cairo, 1986), 46.

3. For advertisements from other commercial enterprises that similarly highlighted the mobility and portability of cassette players, see, e.g., "Sony," *Akhir Saʿa*, no. 2203 (12 January 1977): 26; "Toshiba," *Ruz al-Yusuf*, no. 2606 (22 May 1978): 68; "Philips," *Ruz al-Yusuf*, no. 2529 (29 November 1976): 37; "Philips," *Ruz al-Yusuf*, no. 2634 (4 December 1978): 20.

4. *Sabah al-Khayr*, no. 1128 (18 August 1977): 1.

5. Osama Mahmud Bakr, "Misaharati Mudirn," *Ruz al-Yusuf*, no. 3126 (9 May 1988): 42.

6. *Miki*, no. 1388 (26 November 1987): 1.

7. For scholarship on the illegal movement of narcotics, see Liat Kozma, "White Drugs in Interwar Egypt: Decadent Pleasures, Emaciated Fellahin, and the Campaign against Drugs," *Comparative Studies of South Asia, Africa and the Middle East* 33, no. 1 (2013): 89–101; Cyrus Schayegh, "The Many Worlds of ʿAbud Yasin; or, What Narcotics Trafficking in the Interwar Middle East Can Tell Us about Territorialization," *Amer-*

ican Historical Review 116, no. 2 (2011): 273–306; Haggai Ram, "Traveling Substances and Their Human Carriers: Hashish-Trafficking in Mandatory Palestine," in *A Global Middle East: Mobility, Materiality and Culture in the Modern Age, 1880–1940*, ed. Cyrus Schayegh, Liat Kozma, and Avner Wishnitzer (New York: I. B. Tauris, 2015), 201–28; Ryan Gingeras, *Heroin, Organized Crime, and the Making of Modern Turkey* (New York: Oxford University Press, 2014), esp. 82–127.

8. The bread riots unfolded after Sadat's regime, acting on the advice of the International Monetary Fund, cut government subsidies on essential goods. Over the course of two days in January 1977, public order broke down before the army intervened. According to official figures, the riots resulted in some 80 dead, 560 injured, and 1,200 arrested, numbers that may very well be underestimates. On the bread riots, also commonly called the food riots, see Nayera Abdelrahman Soliman, "Remembering the 1977 Bread Riots in Suez: Fragments and Ghosts of Resistance," *International Review of Social History* 66, no. S29 (2021): 23–40; Mark Cooper, *The Transformation of Egypt* (Baltimore: Johns Hopkins University Press, 1982), 235–46. On rising Islamic militancy, see Hamied Ansari, *Egypt: The Stalled Society* (Albany: State University of New York Press, 1986), 211–30; Gilles Kepel, *Muslim Extremism in Egypt: The Prophet and Pharaoh* (Berkeley: University of California Press, 1986), 70–102.

9. For a more detailed discussion of motor vehicles and their history in Egypt, especially during Sadat's rule, see On Barak, "Gridlock Politics: Auto(im)mobility in Sadat's Egypt," *Comparative Studies of South Asia, Africa and the Middle East* 39, no. 1 (2019): 116–30.

10. For a personal account of the private passenger car and its popularization in Egypt, see Galal Amin, *Whatever Happened to the Egyptians?: Changes in Egyptian Society from 1950 to the Present* (Cairo: American University in Cairo Press, 2000), 102–7.

11. During this period, taxis in Egypt reportedly rose from 21,267 in 1970 to 169,170 in 1985, nearly an eightfold increase. See Yasser Taha, "Technology Transfer by Multinational Firms: The Case of the Car Industry in Egypt" (PhD diss., Kingston University, 2002), 156.

12. Here, it is worth noting that the growth of cars in Cairo was likely even greater than this statistic suggests, since it recognizes only *registered* vehicles. See Khouri-Dagher, *Food and Energy in Cairo*, 50.

13. Henry Tanner, "Egypt, Crowded and Poor, Looking Ahead with Hope," *New York Times* (25 October 1975): 22. The number of automobiles imported into Egypt allegedly climbed from 1,400 in 1966–1967 to 40,000 in 1975–1976, only to then increase to 74,000 in 1982. See Gil Feiler, "Scope and Some Effects of Remittances of Egyptian

Migrant Workers in the Arab Oil-Producing Countries, 1973–1984," *Asian and African Studies* 21 (1987): 320.

14. With the onset of the auto boom in the 1970s, traffic and traffic noise frequently captivated foreigners and frustrated local authorities, who sought to restore order to Egypt's streets. See, e.g., G. R. Penzer, "Egypt," in *Noise: Reports from Overseas Posts* (London: Department of Industry, 1979), 9; Gerald McLaughlin, "Infitah in Egypt: An Appraisal of Egypt's Open-Door Policy for Foreign Investment," *Fordham Law Review* 46, no. 5 (1978): 891; "In Noisy Cairo, a General Declares War on Auto-Horn 'Musicians,'" *New York Times* (25 June 1978): 12.

15. On the noise generated by both car horns and cassettes in motion, one writer for the *Egyptian Gazette*, a local English-language newspaper, report-edly observed how drivers routinely refused to cease honking or turn down their tapes, prompting them to ask: "But why do we think so little about other people's feelings? Why have we lost the sense to enjoy peace and quiet?" See Alan Cowell, "Constant Din Is Getting Cairo Residents Down," *New York Times* (25 March 1990): 11.

16. One article in *Ruz al-Yusuf* identifies a "vast kingdom" of spare car parts in downtown Cairo, where "the conscience of the trader . . . and the cleverness of the consumer" were the only mechanisms in place to regulate purchases. See 'Isam 'Abd al-'Aziz and Ibrahim Khalil, "Mamlakat Qita' Ghiyar al-Sayarat," *Ruz al-Yusuf*, no. 3076 (25 May 1987): 26–29.

17. Faiza Sa'd, "Thamaniyat 'Ashr Yawman fi al-Islahiyya Ja'aluni Mujriman," *Ruz al-Yusuf*, no. 2745 (19 January 1981): 62.

18. For other cases of car theft involving cassette players and tapes, see Ali Shalabi, "Saqata Lis Shara'it al-Kasit min al-Sayarat Amam al-Matar," *Akhir Sa'a*, no. 2485 (9 June 1982), 7; Zaki Badr, "Ijra' 'Amaliyat Sariqa fi Madinat al-Sahafiyyin," *Ruz al-Yusuf*, no. 3116 (29 February 1988): 4; "Lusus Shik Yasruqun al-Zalamukat," *Ruz al-Yusuf*, no. 3252 (8 October 1990): 26–28. For a report on the theft of cassette stereos from cars outside of Cairo, see the following editorial on Port Sa'id: Muhsin Lutfi, "Al-Tahrib fi Madinat al-Alf Sanf," *Ruz al-Yusuf*, no. 2613 (10 July 1978): 26. With regard to the overall number of car thefts occurring in and outside of Cairo, exact figures are difficult to determine. But according to one report, 191 thefts took place across Cairo in the first six months of 1990 alone. This number, which in all likelihood was far greater, since people did not report every crime to the police, signaled a dramatic increase from the 202 car thefts transpiring in Cairo in all of 1989. See "Lusus Shik Yasruqun al-Zalamukat," 26.

19. Raymond H. Anderson, "Egypt's Premier Places Economy on a War Footing," *New York Times* (24 January 1972): 1.

20. Ra'fat Butrus, "Arba'a fi Qa' al-Madina," *Akhir Sa'a*, no. 2310 (31 January 1979): 62.

21. Unni Wikan, "Living Conditions among Cairo's Poor: A View from Below," *Middle East Journal* 39, no. 1 (1985): 8.

22. Wikan, 14.

23. Homa Hoodfar, *Between Marriage and the Market: Intimate Politics and Survival in Cairo* (Berkeley: University of California Press, 1997), 205.

24. Ra'fat Butrus, "Lughz 'al-Basma' al-Sadisa Wara' Akbar 'Amaliyat Nasb," *Akhir Sa'a*, no. 2409 (24 December 1980): 60.

25. For different takes on these categories, see Sawsan El-Messiri, *Ibn Al-Balad: A Concept of Egyptian Identity* (Leiden: E. J. Brill, 1978); Walter Armbrust, *Mass Culture and Modernism in Egypt* (New York: Cambridge University Press, 1996); Farha Ghannam, *Remaking the Modern: Space, Relocation, and the Politics of Identity in a Global Cairo* (Los Angeles: University of California Press, 2002).

26. Ra'fat Butrus, "'Sanatur' la Yasruq ila Naharan," *Akhir Sa'a*, no. 1960 (17 May 1972): 40; "Lusus Shik Yasruqun al-Zalamukat": 27.

27. Ra'fat Butrus, "Ma'rid bi-Thalathat Malayin Junayh Dakhil Mudirat Amn al-Qahira," *Akhir Sa'a*, no. 2752 (22 July 1987): 8.

28. Ra'fat Butrus, "Al-Dala' Sabab Musibati," *Akhir Sa'a*, no. 2372 (9 April 1980): 60; Amal Fikar, "Lusus 'Nus' al-Layl," *Ruz al-Yusuf*, no. 2751 (2 March 1981): 61.

29. Hikmat 'Abd al-Hakim, "Harakat al-Aswaq ba'd Takhfid al-As'ar," *Akhir Sa'a* (4 November 1970): 5–6.

30. On this front, Sadat's inspiration may well have been Nasser, who invested in and wielded the radio to promote his views. See Adeed Dawisha, *Arab Nationalism in the Twentieth Century: From Triumph to Despair* (Princeton, NJ: Princeton University Press, 2003), 147–8.

31. 'Abd al-Hakim, "Harakat al-Aswaq ba'd Takhfid al-As'ar," 6.

32. "Ajhizat Philips al-Jadida fi al-Tariq Ilayk," *Ruz al-Yusuf*, no. 2477 (1 December 1975): 70.

33. "Philips," *Ruz al-Yusuf*, no. 2476 (24 November 1975).

34. Two weeks after Philips's announcement, a store in downtown Cairo showcased a variety of consumer goods, including cassette radios, which could be purchased in installments. See "Midhat al-Masri," *Ruz al-Yusuf*, no. 2479 (15 December 1975): 31. The acquisition of cassette players and other consumer goods on credit also

extended to Egypt's villages. See Elizabeth Taylor, "Egyptian Migration and Peasant Wives," *MERIP Reports*, no. 124 (1984): 6–7.

35. For sketches depicting black market traders, see, e.g., "Hal Hinak Siyasa lil-As'ar fi Misr?," *Ruz al-Yusuf*, no. 2437 (24 February 1975): 12; "Al-Suq al-Sawda'," *Ruz al-Yusuf*, no. 2474 (19 January 1976): 29; "Talawuth al-Bi'a," *Ruz al-Yusuf*, no. 3047 (3 November 1986): 55.

36. Samia 'Ali, "Mahzala al-Jamarik fi Matar al-Qahira," *Ruz al-Yusuf*, no. 2990 (30 September 1985): 58–59.

37. Ahmad Bassyuni, "Radd min al-Jamarik," *Ruz al-Yusuf*, no. 2977 (18 November 1985): 40.

38. Muhga 'Uthman, "Dawar al-Jaw alladhi Yusib al-Musafir fi Matar al-Qahira," *Ruz al-Yusuf*, no. 2243 (7 June 1971): 24.

39. 'Isam 'Abd al-'Aziz and 'Isam Abu Haram, "'Awdat al-Misriyyin: Bil-Ahdan ya Jamarik," *Ruz al-Yusuf*, no. 3236 (18 June 1990): 30.

40. Nagi, "Thuqub fi Jidar Wizarat al-Siyaha," *Ruz al-Yusuf*, no. 2656 (7 May 1979): 60.

41. 'Abd al-'Aziz and Abu Haram, "'Awdat al-Misriyyin: Bil-Ahdan ya Jamarik": 32.

42. "Tahrib Jumruki fi Himayat al-Qanun," *Ruz al-Yusuf*, no. 2757 (13 April 1981): 28; Gawad, "Jamarik," *Ruz al-Yusuf*, no. 2887 (10 October 1983): 29.

43. Gawad, "Jamarik," 28; "Yawm Tawil fi Ghabat al-Jamarik," *Ruz al-Yusuf*, no. 2228 (23 December 1974): 20; "Jamarik," *Ruz al-Yusuf*, no. 2544 (14 March 1977): 23.

44. Gawad, "Jamarik," 29.

45. Faiza Sa'd, "Dalil al-Rajul al-Dhaki wa al-Mar'a al-Dhakiyya fi Suq al-Tahrib," *Ruz al-Yusuf*, no. 2207 (28 September 1970): 12.

46. Sa'd, 12.

47. For a discussion of suitcase traders in a single village, see the following report on Egyptians bringing goods from the Gulf into the town of Nabrawa: 'Adil al-Bilk, "Laysa al-Fasikh wa Lakinahu Shai' Akhar fi al-Nabrawa!," *Ruz al-Yusuf*, no. 2152 (21 January 1976): 42–45.

48. For a detailed discussion of this practice in relation to Alexandria's port, see Sultan Mahmud, "Haraka Ghayr 'Adiya fi al-Iskandariyya: Hadhihi al-Shanta al-Baida' Tanfa' al-Suq al-Sawda'," *Akhir Sa'a*, no. 2102 (5 February 1975): 11–13; Sultan Mahmud, "Al-Shanta Tijara Awanta!," *Akhir Sa'a*, no. 2136 (1 October 1975): 42–45.

49. Magdi Mihna, "Thaqab fi Jidar Wizarat al-Siyaha!," *Ruz al-Yusuf*, no. 2656 (7 May 1979): 60.

50. Faiza Sa'd, "Tujjar al-Shanta Yabia'un al-Asmant," *Ruz al-Yusuf*, no. 2543 (7 March 1977): 12.

51. Zaynab Hamdi and Susan al-Gayyar, "Tahrib Jumruki fi Himayat al-Qanun," *Ruz al-Yusuf*, no. 2757 (13 April 1981): 28.

52. Asma Rashid, "Hal Tatahawwul al-Iskandariyya ila Madinat al-Butikat?," *Ruz al-Yusuf*, no. 2773 (3 August 1981): 16–17.

53. 'Abd al-Sattar al-Tawila, "Al-Wajh al-Akhar lil-Tahrib fi al-Bur Sa'id," *Ruz al-Yusuf*, no. 2768 (29 June 1981): 25. For a letter to the editors addressing the problem of counterfeit goods in Port Sa'id, see Muhammad 'Abd al-Maqsud al-Mugi, "Matlub Riqaba 'ala al-Riqaba fi Bur Sa'id," *Akhir Sa'a*, no. 2273 (17 May 1978): 66.

54. 'Ali Badrakhan, "Ahl al-Qimma," 118 mins. (Egypt: Aflam Jamal al-Laythi, 1981).

55. Amal Fikar, "Qadiyya Tahrib min Bur Sa'id," *Ruz al-Yusuf*, no. 2645 (19 February 1979): 60.

56. Muhsin Lutfi, "Al-Tahrib fi Madinat al-Alf Sanf," *Ruz al-Yusuf*, no. 2613 (10 July 1978): 26.

57. Fikar, "Qadaya Tahrib min Bur Sa'id," 60.

58. Muhsin Lutfi, "Madina Siyahiyya 'Alamiya fi Bur Sa'id," *Ruz al-Yusuf*, no. 2621 (4 September 1978): 38.

59. Jean Hureau, *L'Égypte aujourd'hui* (Paris: Editions J.A., 1977), 168.

60. Shawarbi Street derives its name from Muhammad al-Shawarbi Pasha (b. 1841), a politician, philanthropist, and landowner from the Delta.

61. *Nagel's Encyclopedia-Guide: Egypt* (Paris: Nagel Publishers, 1976), 754, 758–60; Hureau, *L'Égypte aujourd'hui*, 253; Kay Showker, *Fodor's Egypt 1978*, ed. Eugene Fodor and Robert Fisher (David McKay Co., 1978), 156–59.

62. With regard to traffic, in the 1990s, Shawarbi underwent a transition from a vehicular street to a pedestrian mall, one of the earliest interventions of its kind in downtown Cairo. For more on this project, see Basil Kamel, Sherine Wahba, and Aly Kandil, "Reclaiming Streets as Public Spaces for People: Promoting Pedestrianization Schemes in Al-Shawarbi Commercial Street—Downtown Cairo" (paper presented at the 1st International Conference on Towards a Better Quality of Life, El Gouna, Egypt, 24–26 November 2017), https://dx.doi.org/10.2139/ssrn.3170365.

63. Ra'fat Butrus, "Anta Zubun idhan fa-anta Qatil fi al-Shawarbi," *Akhir Sa'a*, no. 2156 (18 February 1976).

64. On the enduring presence of audiotapes on Shawarbi Street, one need only consider two guidebooks. The first, from 2003, directs travelers searching for cassettes containing "Arab pop music" to the street; the second, from 2007, notes how it was "full of shops selling jeans and jackets and loud with pop soundtracks emanating from half a dozen music cassette stores." See Joey Shabot, *Let's Go: Egypt* (New York:

St. Martin's Press, 2003), 142; Andrew Humphreys, *Egypt* (Washington, DC: National Geographic, 2007), 86. Outside of audiotapes, Shawarbi also served as a key market for a second recorded product in Cairo: VHS tapes.

65. In addition to these figures, local playwrights underscored the connection between smuggling and Shawarbi Street. At one point in *The School of Troublemakers* (*Madrasat al-Mushaghibin*), for instance, the principal, 'Abd al-Mu'ati (played by Hassan Mustafa), rifles through the belongings of Bahgat al-Abasiri (played by 'Adil Imam), a student who brings in a suitcase filled with imported goods. After sorting through the possessions, which include a giant bra, a bottle of whiskey, and Kent cigarettes, the administrator asks Bahgat whether he is a "student" or a "suitcase trader" and shouts that "the School of Commendable Morals" has become "the School of Shawarbi Street Porters." See Galal al-Sharqawi, *Madrasat al-Mushaghibin*, 251 mins. (Egypt, 1971).

66. Gumla, "Shawarbi," *Ruz al-Yusuf*, no. 2489 (23 February 1976): 22–23.

67. 'Isam Abu Haram, "Imbraturiyyat al-Matar: Tahrib al-Bada'i' Dakhil Sanadiq al-Qimama," *Ruz al-Yusuf*, no. 2561 (11 July 1977): 32. In some cases, airport employees may have joined commuters in purchasing goods from the Duty Free and smuggling them past customs agents in Cairo's airport. See 'Isam Abu Haram, "Hal Nu'llij al-Tahrib min al-Jamarik," *Ruz al-Yusuf*, no. 2644 (12 February 1979): 17.

68. Madiha, "Tahiyati ila Zawjik al-'Aziz," *Ruz al-Yusuf*, no. 2402 (24 June 1974): 47–48; Madiha, "Tahiyati ila Zawjik al-'Aziz," *Ruz al-Yusuf*, no. 2488 (16 February 1976): 64.

69. National Archives, FCO 93/625, DAS Gladstone, "Internal Security," (6 January 1975), 1.

70. Ahmad Higazi, "Hadhihi al-Harb al-Qadhira," *Ruz al-Yusuf*, no. 2339 (9 April 1973): 1.

71. On more than one occasion, Higazi dealt with "wrongdoers" in his caricatures. See Khalid 'Azab, ed., *Ruz Al-Yusuf 80 Sana Sahafa* (Alexandria: Bibliotheca Alexandrina, 2006), 373.

3. CENSURING

This chapter draws on material published in the following article: Simon, A., "Censuring Sounds: Tapes, Taste, and the Creation of Egyptian Culture," *International Journal of Middle East Studies* 51, no. 2 (2019), 233–56. © Cambridge University Press 2019.

1. Menna Farouk, "Egypt Bans 'Music of the Slums,'" *Al-Monitor* (20 February 2020); Wafa' Yahiyya, "Al-Ta'lim Tahzar Aghani al-Mahraganat..wa Mudiriyyat al-Qahira

224   NOTES

Tuhaddid al-Mudirin bil-Fasl," *Al-Masry al-Youm* (17 February 2020); "Al-Na'ib Salah Hasballah: Talabt min Hani bil-Thabat fi Muwajahatihi li-Zahira Mutribi al-Mahraganat," YouTube video, 2:48, posted by "Sada Elbalad," 16 February 2020, https://www.youtube.com/watch?v=ASLWwFhGgQ4.

2. Farid al-Atrash (d. 1974), Umm Kulthum (d. 1975), and ʿAbd al-Halim Hafiz (d. 1977), three leading emblems of state-sanctioned culture, all passed away within a few years of one another. As for state-controlled radio's decreased productions, see, e.g., Tuhami Muntasir, "ʿAmr Batisha fi Shahada ʿala al-ʿAsr: Al-Aghani al-Habita Sababha Ghiyab al-Idhaʿa, Hikayati maʿ al-Mikrofone..wa ʿAlam al-Shiʿr," *Akhir Saʿa*, no. 2853 (28 June 1989): 35.

3. When the Cairo Opera House opened once more in 1988, it surfaced a couple miles away from the venue's original site. In the place of the original opera house is a high-rise parking garage called the Opera Garage. For a documentary on the burning of Cairo Opera House, see Kamal ʿAbd al-ʿAziz, "Harq Ubra al-Qahira," 39 mins. (Egypt: Cadrage Productions, 2009).

4. *Shaʿbi*, in Arabic, means "popular" or "of the people." *Shaʿbi*, likewise, is a particular musical genre that gained traction in Egypt courtesy of cassette-tape technology and its manifold users in the mid- to late twentieth century, inspiring no shortage of criticism from local cultural gatekeepers in the process. Not all *shaʿbi* music was popular, and not all popular music was *shaʿbi*. Accordingly, to be as clear as possible in this chapter, I use the term *shaʿbi*, rather than *popular*, to refer to the singers and songs comprising this genre. In the case of some artists, like Ahmad ʿAdawiya, a *shaʿbi* singer who enjoyed a large fan base, both adjectives are applicable. For more on *shaʿbi* as an idea and a musical genre in Egyptian culture, see, e.g., Chihab El Khachab, "The Sobky Recipe and the Struggle over 'the Popular' in Egypt," *Arab Studies Journal* 27, no. 1 (2019): 35–62; Joel Gordon, "Singing the Pulse of the Egyptian-Arab Street: Shaaban Abd Al-Rahim and the Geo-Pop-Politics of Fast Food," *Popular Music* 22, no. 1 (2003): 73–88.

5. The ability of audiotapes to transcend illiteracy in Egypt was significant. According to one estimate, less than 50 percent of Egyptians were literate between the 1970s and the early 1990s. Notably, this figure masks even lower literacy rates among women and among those living in rural areas in Egypt. See UNESCO Institute for Statistics, "Country Profiles: Egypt," http://www.uis.unesco.org/Data Centre/Pages/country profile.aspx?code=EGY&regioncode=40525.

6. "Cairo Is Abuzz over New Rule Curbing Noise," *New York Times* (30 November 1980): 19.

7. *Ruz al-Yusuf,* no. 2607 (29 May 1978): 50.

8. *Ruz al-Yusuf,* no. 2895 (5 December 1983): 62.

9. "Ziyadat Intishar al-Aghani al-Habita," *Ruz al-Yusuf,* no. 2860 (4 April 1983).

10. For the complete lyrics to this poem, see Bayram al-Tunsi, *Al-A'mal al-Kamila li-Bayram al-Tunsi* (Cairo: Maktabat Madbuli, 2002), 163–64. Notably, a fellow Alexandrian, Fadi Iskander, recorded and performed al-Tunsi's poem on one of his cassette tapes in the mid-1980s. For a copy of the artist's cassette recording of al-Tunsi's poem, see "Ya Ahl al-Maghna—Fadi Iskander," YouTube video, 4:41, posted by "Ahlawy-Daiman," 18 October 2013, https://www.youtube.com/watch?v=0Ob9nboTRoI.

11. For additional illustrations depicting "vulgar" cassettes as a source of noise, see, e.g., Taha Yasin, *Ruz al-Yusuf,* no. 3147 (10 October 1988): 51; *Ruz al-Yusuf,* no. 3152 (7 November 1988): 53; "Masrahiyat al-Isbu'," *Ruz al-Yusuf,* no. 3215 (22 January 1990): 27.

12. R. Murray Schafer, *The Tuning of the World* (New York: Knopf, 1977).

13. Ragab Sa'd al-Sayyid, *Al-Harb didd al-Talawuth,* Kitabak (Cairo: Dar al-Ma'arif, 1978), 74.

14. "Wa'ad Muhammad 'Abd al-Wahhab li-Majlis al-Shura!," *Ruz al-Yusuf,* no. 3111 (25 January 1988): 47.

15. Tal'at Ramih, "Al-Udhun al-Misriyya fi Dhimmat Allah," *Ruz al-Yusuf,* no. 3034 (4 August 1986): 41–42.

16. Ibrahim 'Ali, "Hadhihi al-Aghani: 'Ayb fi Haqq al-Mujtama'," *Akhir Sa'a,* no. 2378 (21 May 1980): 74.

17. Osama al-Mansi, "Al-Wajh al-Akhar li-l-Kasit," *Ruz al-Yusuf,* no. 2773 (3 August 1981): 54.

18. "Al-Mutriba al-Maghribiyya Layla Ghufran: Khalaqtu li-l-Ghina'," *Ruz al-Yusuf,* no. 3196 (11 September 1989): 54.

19. Ahmad Muhammad, "Tijarat al-Ghina' wa 'Abd al-Halim Hafiz!," *Ruz al-Yusuf,* no. (29 August 1988): 55.

20. Faiza Sa'd and 'Adil Hammuda, "Afwan: Hadhihi Qilat Dhawq—2: Wabur Zalat fi Sharit Kasit!," *Ruz al-Yusuf,* no. 2826 (9 August 1982): 27.

21. This idea, to be certain, found fertile ground in still other illustrations surfacing in the popular Egyptian press years later, including one titled "Cassette Chaos," in which two producers record a man asleep at work, snoring, and remark that the resulting tape "will truly dominate the market!!," and a second drawing captioned "The New Child Singer," in which a smiling man holds a wailing baby before a sign reading: "Cassette Phone presents the child singer 'wa-wa.'" See *Ruz al-Yusuf,* no. 3034 (4 August 1986): 51; *Ruz al-Yusuf,* no. 3173 (3 April 1989): 45.

22. "Raghm Najah Min Ghayr Layh: Iflas Tujjar al-Kasit!," *Ruz al-Yusuf*, no. 3214 (15 January 1990): 60.

23. 'Ala' 'Abd al-Karim, "'Akhir Sa'a' Taftah Malaf Qadiyya Fanniyya Khatira: Mafia al-Kasitat al-Mamnu'a wa al-Shara'it al-Habita!," *Akhir Sa'a*, no. 2788 (30 March 1988): 24.

24. Muhammad Hani, "Tujjar al-Muharramat al-Fanniyya!," *Ruz al-Yusuf*, no. 3255 (29 October 1990): 46.

25. 'Abd al-Karim, "'Akhir Sa'a' Taftah Malaf Qadiyya Fanniyya Khatira," 29.

26. Kamal al-Nigmi, *Al-Ghina' al-Misri: Mutribun wa-Mustami'un* (Cairo: Dar al-Hilal, 1993), 420.

27. Kamal al-Nigmi, *Turath Al-Ghina' al-'Arabi* (Cairo: Al-Hay'a al-'Amma li-Qusur al-Thaqafa, 2015), 180–81.

28. Muhammad Qabil, *Mawsu'at al-Ghina' fi Misr* (Cairo: Dar al-Shuruq, 2006), 13.

29. For a series of contemporary cartoons that skillfully distill some of these criticisms, see Ra'uf, "Aghani wa Ta'bani," *Ruz al-Yusuf*, no. 2680 (5 March 1986): 26.

30. Tarek Osman, *Egypt on the Brink: From Nasser to the Muslim Brotherhood* (New Haven, CT: Yale University Press, 2013), 127–39; Kirk Beattie, *Egypt during the Sadat Years* (New York: Palgrave, 2000), 134–60; Mohamed Hassanein Heikal, *Autumn of Fury: The Assassination of Sadat* (New York: Random House, 1983), 84–89.

31. Ali Jihad Racy, "Musical Change and Commercial Recording in Egypt, 1904–1932" (PhD diss., University of Illinois at Urbana-Champaign, 1977), esp. 79–123; Joel Gordon, *Revolutionary Melodrama: Popular Film and Civic Identity in Nasser's Egypt* (Chicago: Middle East Documentation Center, 2002); Virginia Danielson, *The Voice of Egypt: Umm Kulthum, Arabic Song, and Egyptian Society in the 20th Century* (Chicago: University of Chicago Press, 1997).

32. Sa'id al-'Aynayn, "Wazir al-Thaqafa fi Hiwar Sarih: Mujat al-Hubut Bada'at Tanhasir," *Akhir Sa'a*, no. 2681 (12 March 1986): 36, my emphasis.

33. Tharwat 'Ukasha, *Mudhakkirati fi al-Siyasa wa al-Thaqafa* (Cairo: Dar al-Hilal, 1990), 1:506.

34. Jihan al-Maghribi, "Al-Thaqafa al-Jamahiriyya fi Mawqif la Tuhsad 'alayhi," *Ruz al-Yusuf*, no. 2749 (16 February 1981): 50.

35. 'Izz al-Din Kamil, *Sa'd Kamil: Al-Thaqafa al-Jamahiriyya* (Cairo: Al-Majlis al-A'la lil-Thaqafa, 2010), 240.

36. For commentaries on the success, or lack thereof, of Public Culture, see Ahmad Salah, "Khittat al-Thaqafa Sanat 71," *Akhir Sa'a*, no. 1888 (30 December 1970); "Al-Fallah la Yadkhul Qasr al-Thaqafa," *Ruz al-Yusuf*, no. 2188 (18 May 1970): 15; 'Ali al-Ra'i,

"Thaqafat al-Qahira wa Thaqafat al-Aqalim," *Ruz al-Yusuf*, no. 2220 (28 December 1970): 31; "4 Buyut Thaqafiyya fi Sina'," *Ruz al-Yusuf*, no. 2585 (26 December 1977): 43; Fathi Khalil, "Nadthariyya al-Zakah fi Wizarat al-Thaqafa," *Ruz al-Yusuf*, no. 2227 (15 February 1971): 53.

37. Al-Majlis al-A'la lil-Thaqafa, *Al-Thaqafa fi 'Ahd al-Sadat* (Cairo: Al-Hay'a al-Misriyya al-'Amma lil-Kitab, 1981), 195.

38. Tariq al-Shinawi, "Saddiq aw la Tusaddiq: Kadre Umm Kulthum wa 'Abd al-Wahhab wa 'Abd al-Halim fi al-Idha'a," *Ruz al-Yusuf*, no. 2479 (15 December 1975): 41.

39. "Su'al Muhayyir fi Lajnat al-Istima': Ma Huwa al-Mustawa?," *Ruz al-Yusuf*, no. 2847 (3 January 1983): 52.

40. Tariq al-Shinawi, "Al-Ughniyya fi Ma'zak wa Khamsat Alaf Mu'allif 'ala Bab al-Idha'a," *Ruz al-Yusuf*, no. 2879 (15 August 1983): 50.

41. For a telling look inside this selection process during an earlier time, see the following account of the day 'Abd al-Wahhab discovered 'Abd al-Halim when screening songs for the radio: Iris Nazmi, "Safahat Saqatat min Dhikrayatihim," *Akhir Sa'a*, no. 2193 (3 November 1976): 40. On the "closure" of the radio's doors to certain artists, see Muhammad Taha, "Ma'sat Sawt Jadid: Mutrib Sayyi' al-Hadth," *Akhir Sa'a*, no. 2504 (20 October 1982): 42–43.

42. Notably, radio sets far exceeded televisions in Egypt during the final decades of the twentieth century. See B. R. Mitchell, *International Historical Statistics: Africa, Asia & Oceania, 1750–1993* (London: Macmillan Reference, 1998), 814. For an insightful glimpse into the widespread presence of radios in even an "isolated" village in Egypt, see Salwa al-Khatib, "Al-Radiyu fi Abu Tisht: Madtha Fa'al?," *Sabah al-Khayr*, no. 1241 (18 October 1979): 41.

43. *Idha'at al-Jumhuriyya al-'Arabiyya al-Muttahida fi 'Amiha al-Sabi' 'Ashr ba'd al-Thawra* (Cairo: Hay'at Idha'at al-Jumhuriyya al-'Arabiyya al-Muttahida, 1969), 7, 2.

44. Tuhami Muntasir, "Ra'is al-Idha'a al-Jadid Amin Bassyuni: La Makan lil-Aghani al-Habita wa Munafasa ma' al-Tilifiziyun," *Akhir Sa'a*, no. 2791 (20 April 1988): 64.

45. Tariq al-Shinawi, "Al-Nukta allati Aghdabat 'Abd al-Nasser," *Ruz al-Yusuf*, no. (25 July 1983): 48.

46. Osama al-Mansi, "Hiwar ma' Fahmi 'Amr Ra'is al-Idha'a: Hal Tatahaqqaq Ahlam al-Mudhi'a al-Qadim?," *Ruz al-Yusuf*, no. 2851 (31 January 1983): 57.

47. Osama al-Mansi, "Wada'an lil-Ughniyya al-Tafiha," *Ruz al-Yusuf*, no. 2650 (26 March 1979): 52.

48. Fannan, "'Ayb!," *Ruz al-Yusuf*, no. 2638 (1 January 1979): 46.

49. Fannan, "'Ayb!," *Ruz al-Yusuf*, no. 2666 (16 July 1979): 44.

50. Fannan, "'Ayb!," *Ruz al-Yusuf,* no. 2711 (26 May 1980): 58.

51. Fathi Mansur, "Kasit bila Riqaba: Limadha," *Akhir Sa'a,* no. 2758 (2 September 1987): 62.

52. "I'adat al-Nadthar fi Qawanin al-Riqaba!," *Ruz al-Yusuf,* no. 2695 (4 February 1980): 48.

53. Muharram Fu'ad, "Nahnu wa al-Ughniyya," *al-Funun* 1, no. 5 (1980): 109.

54. Perhaps one of the first to propose the creation of a "cassette room" in print, Fu'ad was not the last to suggest a new apparatus for censoring certain voices in the name of protecting public taste. Hilmi Bakr, an accomplished composer, seconded the formation of a cassette room in 1981 and, two years later, called for a different tripartite committee to regulate cassettes. See "Ghurfa li-Sina'at al-Kasit," *Ruz al-Yusuf,* no. 2745 (19 January 1981): 48; "Al-Riqaba wa al-Niqaba wa al-Jam'iya li-Himayat Mustawat al-Ughniyya," *Ruz al-Yusuf,* no. 2848 (10 January 1983): 57.

55. "Al-Majalis al-Qawmiyya Tatasada lil-Kasit al-Habit," *Ruz al-Yusuf,* no. 2861 (11 April 1983): 52.

56. Osama al-Mansi, "Al-Majalis al-Qawmiyya al-Mutakhasissa Tu'lin al-Harb 'ala al-Kasit!," *Ruz al-Yusuf,* no. 2872 (27 June 1983): 47.

57. 'Abd al-Karim, "'Akhir Sa'a' Taftah Malaf Qadiyya Fanniya Khatira," 26.

58. 'Abd al-Karim, 27; Muhammad Taha, "Ziham, Ziham fi Tajdid al-Ughniyya al-Misriyya," *Akhir Sa'a,* no. 2479 (28 April 1982): 42.

59. "Al-Riqaba Tarfud Aghani 'Kaburya,'" *Ruz al-Yusuf,* no. 3251 (1 October 1990); Muhammad 'Itman, "Akhir Ra'i," *Ruz al-Yusuf,* no. 3253 (15 October 1990): 39.

60. Muhammad Hani, "Tujjar al-Muharramat al-Fanniyya!," *Ruz al-Yusuf,* no. 3255 (29 October 1990): 46.

61. Muhammad 'Itman, "Al-Hurub al-Riqabiyya," *Ruz al-Yusuf,* no. 3219 (19 February 1990): 53.

62. Mahmud Burhan, "Al-Aghani Mir'at al-Shu'ub!," *Ruz al-Yusuf,* no. 2301 (29 November 1978); "Ja'iza li-Ahsan Mu'allif Ughniyya," *Ruz al-Yusuf,* no. 3013 (10 March 1986): 52; Taha, "Ziham, Ziham fi Tajdid al-Ughniyya al-Misriyya," *Akhir Sa'a,* no. 2479 (28 April 1982): 42.

63. 'Abd al-Halim, *Ruz al-Yusuf,* no. 2495 (5 April 1976): 75; Ra'uf, "Aghani wa Ta'bani," *Ruz al-Yusuf,* no. 2680 (5 March 1986): 26; Ra'uf, "Tala'a al-Nujum," *Akhir Sa'a,* no. 2568 (11 January 1984): 26.

64. Ta Alif, "Kayf al-Hurub min Madrasa 'Adawiya?," *Ruz al-Yusuf,* no. 2629 (30 October 1978): 56.

65. "Asrar wa Khabaya Ahmad 'Adawiya Yakshifuha Mufid Fawzi 3/3," YouTube

video, 32:40, posted by "Dream TV Egypt," 28 February 2014, https://www.youtube. com/watch?v=PoWIe1NBwvc.

66. Sayyid Mahmud Hassan, "Ahmad 'Adawiya wa al-Mut'a Kharij Nasqiyyat al-Na-khbawi wa al-Sha'bawi: Qira'a min mandhur al-Naqd al-Thaqafi," in *Al-Tarikh wa al-Musiqa: Dirasat fi Tarikh al-Musiqa fi Misr Wa Swisra*, ed. Mahmud 'Afifi and Nahla Matar (Giza: Ein lil-Dirasat wa al-Buhuth al-Insaniyya wa al-Ijtima'iyya, 2013), 93.

67. For two excellent accounts of Muhammad 'Ali Street and its history, see Nicolas Puig, *Farah: Musiciens de noces et scènes urbaines au Caire* (Paris: Sindbad, 2010); Karin van Nieuwkerk, "The Performers of Muhammad 'Ali Street in Cairo," in *The Garland Encyclopedia of World Music*, vol. 6, *The Middle East*, ed. Virginia Danielson, Dwight Reynolds, and Scott Marcus (New York: Routledge, 2002), 615–22.

68. Tharwat Fahmi, "Sirr 'Adawiya Mazala Ghamidan," *Akhir Sa'a*, no. 2857 (26 July 1989): 39.

69. In "al-Sah al-Dah Ambu," 'Adawiya sings about two individuals seeking to quench their "thirst": a man looking for a lover and a baby crying on the ground. The song's title, which does not lend itself easily to translation, has a nursery-rhyme quality to it and features words frequently used by adults with children, including *al-Dah*, or "something nice," and *ambu*, or "water." In these regards, the musical number's use of colloquial Egyptian Arabic, combined with its sexually suggestive content, likely both contributed to contemporary criticisms of it in Egypt.

70. Tariq al-Shinawi, "'Adawiya al-Ustura wa al-Ghaybuba," *Ruz al-Yusuf*, no. 3188 (17 July 1989): 70.

71. Samia 'Attallah, "Sultan al-Ghina' al-Sha'bi Yaqlib al-Ma'ida," *Ruz al-Yusuf*, no. 2461 (11 August 1975): 52.

72. "Muharram Fu'ad fi al-Kasino," *Ruz al-Yusuf*, no. 2567 (29 August 1977): 41.

73. "Al-Shaykh Kishk: Law 'Awiz Tingah fi Masr Ghanni Zay al-Wad Ahmad 'Adaw-iya—Al-Sah al-Dah Ambu," YouTube video, 4:48, posted by "Qanat al-Shaykh Kishk," 6 June 2015, https://www.youtube.com/watch?v=w5LQffcUiwE.

74. Fahmi, "Sirr 'Adawiya Mazala Ghamidan," 39; Muhammad al-Dasuqi, "Naguib Mahfouz al-Sami'a," *Majallat al-Fann* (11 July 1994).

75. Iris Nazmi, "Safahat Saqatat min Dhikrayatihim," *Akhir Sa'a*, no. 2195 (17 No-vember 1976): 47.

76. "Hal Yahtakir 'Abd al-Wahhab wa 'Abd al-Halim Sawt 'Adawiya," *Ruz al-Yusuf*, no. 2486 (2 February 1976): 64.

77. "'Abd al-Halim Hafiz Yughanni al-Sah al-Dah Ambu!!," *Ruz al-Yusuf*, no. 2488 (16 February 1976): 47.

78. Al-Shinawi, "'Adawiya al-Ustura wa al-Ghaybuba," 70.

79. "Mahmud al-Sharif, Kamal al-Tawil, Muhammad al-Mugi, and Munir Murad Yulahinun li-Ahmad 'Adawiya," *Ruz al-Yusuf*, no. 2518 (13 September 1976): 49; "Sayyid Mikkawi Yulahin li-'Adawiya," *Ruz al-Yusuf*, no. 2550 (23 April 1977).

80. "Sira' bayna Muharram wa Ahmad 'Adawiya," *Ruz al-Yusuf*, no. 2559 (27 June 1977): 40.

81. Du'a' Yusri, "Yu'adhibuni 'Aqli wa Dhaka'i," *Ruz al-Yusuf*, no. 3170 (13 March 1989): 49.

82. For more on 'Adil Imam and the vulgarization of one of his productions, see Walter Armbrust, *Mass Culture and Modernism in Egypt* (New York: Cambridge University Press, 1996), 165–73.

83. 'Adil Hammuda, "'Iyun Jari'a," *Ruz al-Yusuf*, no. 3018 (14 April 1986): 51.

84. Hilmi Hilali, "Akhbarihum Kama 'Arifuha," *Ruz al-Yusuf*, no. 2475 (17 November 1975).

85. Daniel Gilman, *Cairo Pop: Youth Music in Contemporary Egypt* (Minneapolis: University of Minnesota Press, 2014), 75.

86. If not for audiotapes, Sayyid Mikkawi once speculated, 'Adawiya's name would be unknown and his songs confined to "wedding celebrations" and "alleyways." See Tariq al-Shinawi, "Al-Misaharati Sayyid Mikkawi Yaqul," *Ruz al-Yusuf*, no. 2519 (20 September 1976): 50.

87. Muhammad 'Itman, "Inqilab fi al-Dhawq," *Ruz al-Yusuf*, no. 3149 (17 October 1988): 51.

88. Al-Shinawi, "'Adawiya al-Ustura wa al-Ghaybuba," 70.

89. Both men and women traditionally take the masculine pronoun in Arabic songs.

90. Faiza Sa'd and 'Adil Hammuda, "Afwan: Hadhihi Qilat Dhawq—2," 29.

91. "1976: 'Amm 'Adawiya!," *Ruz al-Yusuf*, no. 2534 (3 January 1977).

92. Nasir Husayn, "Kayfa Yabi' al-Fannan 2 Milyun Kasit?," *Ruz al-Yusuf*, no. 2740 (15 December 1980): 54.

93. Hilmi Hilali, "Jumhur al-Kalimat al-Ghariba," *Ruz al-Yusuf*, no. 2861 (11 April 1983): 50.

94. 'Ali Badrakhan, "Ahl al-Qimma," 118 mins. (Egypt: Aflam Jamal al-Laythi, 1981).

95. Ministry of Information, *Al-I'lam al-Misri wa al-Alfiyya al-Thalitha* (Cairo: Al-Majmu'a al-Thaqafiyya al-Misriyya, 1999), 174, 177.

96. Ministry of Information, 182, 184.

97. Ministry of Information, 179–81, 183.

98. *Saharat Musiqiyya* (Cairo: Sharikat Sawt al-Qahira lil-Sawtiyat wa Mar'iyat), n.d.

99. *Kataluj al-Kasit lil-Munawwaʿat al-Ghinaʾiyya* (Cairo: Sharikat Sawt al-Qahira lil-Sawtiyat wa Mariyat, 2004).

100. This cassette recording does not appear to be unique. Another tape intended for children, mentioned in a Sawt al-Qahira advertisement in the popular comic *Miki* in 1987, features the beloved radio host Nagwa Ibrahim ("Mama Nagwa") discussing important ideas, including manners, intelligence, cleanliness, justice, friendship, trust, and love. See "Sharikat Sawt al-Qahira," *Miki*, no. 1388 (26 November 1987): 29.

101. *Qurʾan Karim: Qiraʾa Mujawwada bi-Aswat Mashahir al-Qurraʾ* (Cairo: Sharikat Sawt al-Qahira lil-Sawtiyat wa Mar'iyat, n.d.).

102. Charles Hirschkind, *The Ethical Soundscape: Cassette Sermons and Islamic Counterpublics* (New York: Columbia University Press, 2006).

103. "Kasit wa Katib li-Qawalib al-Ghinaʾ al-ʿArabi," *Ruz al-Yusuf*, no. 2855 (28 February 1983): 52.

104. "Al-Abnudi wa Abu Duma fi Sharit Kasit li-Sarhan!," *Ruz al-Yusuf*, no. 3199 (2 October 1989): 58. Notably, it appears that poets were not the only Egyptian writers to break into the cassette market. Both Yusuf Idris and Ihsan ʿAbd al-Quddus, for instance, agreed to record their stories on tapes for one label. See "Qissas Ihsan wa Yusuf ʿala Sharaʾit Kasit!," *Ruz al-Yusuf*, no. 3010 (17 February 1986): 47.

105. The military mind behind these cassette recordings was ʿAbd al-Ghaffar Higazi, a major general, who selected Aynas Gawher. Before working with al-Sharq al-Awsat, Gawher began her career as a broadcaster in the "Hebrew Department" (*al-qism al-ʿibri*) of Egyptian radio. See "Taʿlim al-ʿIbriyya ʿala Sharaʾit Kasit," *Sabah al-Khayr*, no. 1253 (10 January 1980): 50.

106. Notably, this cassette commending Egypt's new peace was part and parcel of a broader effort to applaud Sadat's signing of the treaty with Israel. The director of Egyptian radio, for example, met with writers and composers to discuss how they, too, could honor this historic agreement. This gathering, reportedly, inspired several songs to be broadcast upon Sadat's return to Egypt. See Osama al-Mansi, "Ayna Yaqif al-Fann min Qadiyyat al-Salam?," *Ruz al-Yusuf*, no. 2651 (2 April 1979): 48. On the Ministry of Culture's subsequent cassette tape recordings, see "'Nahj al-Burda' wa Funnunana al-Shaʿbiyya ʿala Kasit Thaqafi," *Ruz al-Yusuf*, no. 2888 (17 October 1983): 54; "Wizarat al-Thaqafa Tuntij Sharaʾit Kasit li-Qimam al-Musiqa," *Ruz al-Yusuf*, no. 2931 (13 August 1984): 47; Osama al-Mansi, "Al-Kitab al-Masmuʿ Yabdaʾ bi-ʿAbd al-Wahhab!,"

Ruz al-Yusuf, no. 2903 (30 January 1984): 54; "Hayat 'Abd al-Wahhab fi Kitab Masmu'," *Ruz al-Yusuf,* no. 2991 (7 October 1985): 53.

107. Douglas Kennedy, *Beyond the Pyramids: Travels in Egypt* (New York: Henry Holt and Co., 1988), 42, 44, 57, 79, 80, 122, 141, 180, 215.

108. Armbrust, *Mass Culture and Modernism in Egypt,* esp. 165–220.

109. "Hi'..Hi' fi Ustuwanat," *Ruz al-Yusuf,* no. 1982 (6 June 1966): 39; Muhammad Hamza, "Jarima . . . Ismuha al-Fulklur," *Ruz al-Yusuf,* no. 2180 (23 March 1970): 32; Amal al-Shamma', "Idha'at al-Shata'im fi al-Tilifiziyun wa al-Idha'a," *Akhir Sa'a,* no. 2326 (23 May 1979).

110. 'Isam Zakariyya, "Durus Masrahiyya fi Qilat al-Adab!," *Ruz al-Yusuf,* no. 3252 (8 October 1990): 44; "Imna'u Hadhihi al-Aflam al-Habita," *Akhir Sa'a,* no. 2255 (11 January 1978); Sayyid 'Abd al-Qadir, "Sahir Khatir Yaqtahim Kul Bayt: Ismuhu 'al-Fidyu'!," *Akhir Sa'a,* no. 2568 (11 January 1984): 28.

111. Here, it is worth noting that another name for *mahraganat* in Egypt is *electro sha'bi.*

112. Freemuse, "Egypt: Radio Station Bans Mahraganat Song," 2016; "Mahraganat: Cairo's Music Revolution," YouTube video, 12:07, posted by "DW (English)," 13 April 2014, https://www.youtube.com/watch?v=wGbYG41-6wU&t=634s.

113. "Asrar wa Khabaya Ahmad 'Adawiya Yakshifuha Mufid Fawzi 3/3," YouTube video, 12:11, posted by "Dream TV Egypt," 28 February 2014, https://www.youtube.com/watch?v =PoWIe1NBwvc.

4. COPYING

1. Sharif 'Arafa, "Halim," 155 mins. (Egypt: Al-Sharika al-'Arabiyya lil-Intaj wa al-Tawzi' al-Sinima'i, 2006).

2. Muhammad Qabil, *Mawsu'at al-Ghina' fi Misr* (Cairo: Dar al-Shuruq, 2006), 138–39.

3. "Arqam fi al-Fann," *Ruz al-Yusuf,* no. 2531 (13 December 1976): 41.

4. "Arqam fi al-Fann," *Ruz al-Yusuf,* no. 2532 (20 December 1976): 40.

5. Mirvat Fahmy, "'Abd al-Wahhab wa 'Abd al-Halim Yakhsaran al-Qadiyya," *Ruz al-Yusuf,* no. 2537 (24 January 1977): 41.

6. "Arqam fi al-Fann," *Ruz al-Yusuf,* no. 2582 (5 December 1977): 43.

7. "Al-Fannanun fi Kawalis al-Mahakim," *Ruz al-Yusuf,* no. 2584 (19 December 1977): 44.

8. Tariq al-Shinawi, "Istiqalat Muhammad 'Abd al-Wahhab," *Ruz al-Yusuf,* no. 2605 (15 May 1978): 47.

9. "Matlub min 'Abd al-Wahhab Mi'at Alf Junayh," *Ruz al-Yusuf,* no. 2673 (3 September 1979): 43.

10. Tariq al-Shinawi, "Muhakama," *Ruz al-Yusuf,* no. 2731 (13 October 1980): 50.

11. "'Abd al-Wahhab wa Sayyid Isma'il wa Ughniyyat al-Thalathinat," *Ruz al-Yusuf,* no. 2856 (7 March 1983): 52.

12. For select accounts of state-sanctioned artists see Virginia Danielson, *The Voice of Egypt: Umm Kulthum, Arabic Song, and Egyptian Society in the Twentieth Century* (Chicago: University of Chicago Press, 1997); Sa'd Ramadan, ed., *Umm Kulthum: Sawt fi Tarikh al-Umma* (Tunis: Ma'had al-Musiqa al-'Arabiyya, 2000); Laura Lohman, *Umm Kulthum: Artistic Agency and the Shaping of an Arab Legend* (Middletown, CT: Wesleyan University Press, 2010); Mahmud 'Awad, *Muhammad 'Abd al-Wahhab alladhi la Ya'rifuhu Ahad* (Cairo: Dar al-Ma'arif, 1991); Walter Armbrust, *Mass Culture and Modernism in Egypt* (New York: Cambridge University Press, 1996), esp. 63–93; Joel Gordon, "The Nightingale and the Ra'is: 'Abd Al-Halim Hafız and Nasserist Longings," in *Rethinking Nasserism: Revolution and Historical Memory in Modern Egypt,* ed. Elie Podeh and Onn Winckler (Gainesville: University Press of Florida, 2004), 307–23.

13. "Ghurfa li-Sina'at al-Kasit," *Ruz al-Yusuf,* no. 2745 (19 January 1981): 48; Tariq al-Shinawi, "Shurut al-Idha'a li-Qubul al-Hadaya," *Ruz al-Yusuf,* no. 2749 (16 February 1981): 46.

14. "Raghm Najah Min Ghayr Layh: Iflas Tujjar al-Kasit!," *Ruz al-Yusuf,* no. 3214 (15 January 1990): 60.

15. "'Abd al-Wahhab: Yaqud Himla li-Mukafahat Tazwir al-Kasit," *Ruz al-Yusuf,* no. 2652 (9 April 1979): 46.

16. Tariq al-Shinawi, "Shurta Mutakhasissa li-Muharibat Qarsanat al-Kasit!," *Ruz al-Yusuf,* no. 2658 (13 October 1980): 50.

17. "Arqam fi al-Fann," *Ruz al-Yusuf,* no. 2664 (2 July 1979): 43.

18. Al-Shinawi, "Shurta Mutakhasissa li-Muharibat Qarsanat al-Kasit!," 50.

19. "Tazwir al-Kasit Raghm Himlat al-Shurta!," *Ruz al-Yusuf,* no. 2714 (16 June 1980): 51, my emphasis.

20. "Al-Tiknulujiyya Tuhaddid Huquq al-Mu'alifin!," *Ruz al-Yusuf,* no. 2738 (1 December 1980): 46.

21. Nasir Husayn, "Suq al-Kasit..Ma Zala fi Khatar!," *Ruz al-Yusuf,* no. 2756 (6 April 1981): 53.

22. Nasir Husayn, "Al-Indharat la Tufid!," *Ruz al-Yusuf,* no. 2757 (13 April 1981): 54, my emphasis.

23. Jan al-Kisan, "Al-Ughniyya al-'Arabiyya 'ala al-Rasif," *al-Majalla al-Musiqiyya* 1977, 11.

24. Two types of "cocktail" cassettes existed in Egypt. The first contained direct and unsanctioned reproductions of existing recordings, while the second featured people performing the songs of artists without their permission. For an example of the second sort of "cocktail" tape, which contained several hit songs subsequently sung by unknown individuals, see "Jaysh Ghina'i!," *Ruz al-Yusuf,* no. 3211 (25 December 1989): 55.

25. "Imsik Harami: Qarasinat al-Kasit Yasruqun fi Wadih al-Nahar!," *al-Nujum* 8, no. 373 (27 November 1999): 36.

26. Muhammad Darwish, "Nutalib bi-Muraqabat Masani' al-Sharit al-Kham," *al-Nujum* 8, no. 373 (27 November 1999): 36; Magdi al-'Amrusi, "Musta'idun li-Shira' Sayarat Haditha li-Shurtat al-Musanifat," *al-Nujum* 8, no. 373 (27 November 1999): 37. The Society for Cassette Producers allegedly approved this project nine years earlier, see 'Isam Zakariyya, "Lusus al-Sawt wa al-Sura," *Ruz al-Yusuf,* no. 3230 (7 May 1990): 57.

27. A somber-faced Midhat Salih, a smiling 'Amr Diab, a denim-clad Anushka, and a singing Hisham 'Abbas all appear on the sleeves of their respective recordings: Midhat Salih, *Tindahini* (Egypt: Sawt al-Hubb, EMI); 'Amr Diab, *'Awiduni* (Egypt: Sawt al-Delta); Anushkha, *Nadani* (Egypt: Al-Awtar al-Dhahabiyya); Hisham 'Abbas, *Ard al-Sharq 2000* (Egypt: Free Music).

28. For examples of elaborate cassette covers, see Ihab Tawfiq, *Ahla Minhum* (Egypt: 'Alam al-Fann); 'Ali al-Higar, *Hawwa wa Adam* (Lebanon: ArabicaMusic); Samira Sa'id, *Yawm Wara Yawm* (Egypt: 'Alam al-Fann).

29. Nadia Mustafa, *Ma Takhafsh 'Alaya* (Egypt: 'Alam al-Fann).

30. For a second *'Alam al-Fann* cassette to feature the same disclaimer, see Ragheb 'Allama, *Farq Kabir Sayidati al-Jamila* (Egypt: 'Alam al-Fann).

31. *High Quality al-Juz' al-Sabi'* (Egypt: High Quality).

32. Ihab, *Habib al-'Alb* (Egypt: High Quality); Hamada Hilal, *Dar al-Zaman* (Egypt: High Quality).

33. 'Amr Khalid, *Ikhlas* (Egypt: Sharikat al-Nur lil-Intaj al-I'lami wa al-Tawzi').

34. Tariq al-Shinawi, "Suq al-Kasit Madmunat al-Ribh..wa Lakin!," *Ruz al-Yusuf* no. 2775 (17 August 1981): 54.

35. Zakariyya, "Lusus al-Sawt wa al-Sura," 56–59.

36. Such was the case with a cassette recording featuring Danna International, a Mizrahi singer who inspired no shortage of controversy in Egypt in the 1990s. In the case of this cassette and others, religious packaging served two purposes. It concealed

not only pirated recordings but also those considered to be "vulgar" by local cultural gatekeepers. See Ted Swedenburg, "Saida Sultan/Danna International: Transgender Pop and the Polysemiotics of Sex, Nation, and Ethnicity on the Israeli-Egyptian Border," *Musical Quarterly* 81, no. 1 (1997): 91.

37. Zakariyya, "Lusus al-Sawt wa al-Sura," 57.

38. 'Isam Zakariyya, "Jam'iyat 'Ali Baba wa al-Arba'in Harami!," *Ruz al-Yusuf* no. 3231 (14 May 1990): 56.

39. Mahmud Lutfi, "Al-Shurta lam Tuqim bi ay 'Amal Muhimm," *Al-Nujum* 8, no. 373 (27 November 1999): 38–39.

40. I acquired these tapes from a juice vendor in the Cairo district of Garden City who asked his neighbors to bring him their cassettes in March 2015.

41. This was the case in the summer of 1975, when Anwar Zaytun, a popular artist, heard one of his compositions on Hikmat al-Shirbini's radio program *Makeup and without Makeup (Makiyaj wa Budun Makiyaj)*. The score, one penned by Zaytun eight years prior and recorded on a cassette with Muhammad al-Kahlawi, supported a second tune by Shadia. Whether or not al-Shirbini was aware that Shadia copied the arrangement is difficult to know, but it is clear from Zaytun's letter to the editors of *Akhir Sa'a* that the singer's unauthorized performance of his work did not belong on the radio. See Anwar Zaytun, "Idbat..Ughniyyat Shadia min Talhini Ana!," *Akhir Sa'a*, no. 2119 (4 June 1975): 48.

42. Shuhayb 'Abd al-Qadir, "Asrar 'Izbat al-Idha'a," *Ruz al-Yusuf*, no. 2510 (19 July 1976): 34–36.

43. Tariq Hamdi, "Tasjilat Nadira lil-Bay'!," *Akhir Sa'a*, no. 2396 (24 September 1980): 74.

44. Tariq al-Shinawi, "'Abd al-Wahhab Yas'al 'an Huquq Umm Kulthum!," *Ruz al-Yusuf* no. 3116 (29 February 1988): 43.

45. "Balagh min al-Kahlawi didd Sawt al-Qahira," *Ruz al-Yusuf*, no. 2671 (20 August 1979): 42.

46. "The Daily Diary of President Jimmy Carter," Washington, DC (29 November 1977): 2. For a list of the Egyptian delegation's members, see Jimmy Carter Presidential Library and Museum, "Appendix 'B': Photo Opportunity with Sheikh Abdul Hamid Mahoud [sic] and Members of His Official Party," Washington, DC (29 November 1977), 1.

47. Jimmy Carter Presidential Library and Museum, "Contact Sheets" (29 November 1977).

48. "Hadiya min al-Shaykh al-Husari ila Carter," *Akhir Sa'a*, no. 2254 (4 January 1978): 13.

49. Iqbal al-Siba'i, "Qurra' al-Qur'an Yutalibun bi Haqq al-Ada' al-'Alani," *Ruz al-Yusuf*, no. 2917 (7 May 1984): 38–39.

50. "Idbat: Sharika Italiyya!," *Ruz al-Yusuf*, no. 2564 (1 August 1977): 41.

51. "Tunis Tashkur 'Abd al-Wahhab," *Ruz al-Yusuf*, no. 3217 (5 February 1990): 46.

52. Osama al-Mansi, "Al-Kitab al-Masmu' Yabda' bi-'Abd al-Wahhab!," *Ruz al-Yusuf*, no. 2903 (30 January 1984): 54.

53. "Hayat 'Abd al-Wahhab fi Kitab Masmu'," *Ruz al-Yusuf*, no. 2991 (7 October 1985): 53.

54. I purchased 'Abd al-Wahhab's audiobook from a merchant in Zamalek.

55. EMI Group Archive Trust, Alexandria, January–May 1909, K. Fr. Vogel, "Vogel's Report on Turkey," 17 March 1909, 6–7; EMI Group Archive Trust, Alexandria: January–May 1909, #3265, The Gramophone Company Ltd., 17 April 1909, 2; EMI Group Archive Trust, Alexandria 1909, #37379, K. F. Vogel, 17 November 1909, 11–12.

56. EMI Group Archive Trust, Alexandria, June–September 1909, #18417, K. Fr. Vogel, 17 July 1909, 1–3; EMI Group Archive Trust, Alexandria, June–September 1909, #18264, The Gramophone Company Ltd., "Copyright on Records," 24 July 1909, 2.

57. "Sharikat Astawanat Iraniyya Tasriq Aghani al-Qahira," *Ruz al-Yusuf*, no. 1910 (18 January 1965): 45; Nasir Husayn, "Min al-Mas'ul 'an Tahrib al-Aghani," *Ruz al-Yusuf*, no. 1978 (9 May 1966): 43. On the seizure of twenty-five thousand pirated records in Egypt at an even later date, in 1981, see Alex Sayf Cummings, *Democracy of Sound: Music Piracy and the Remaking of American Copyright in the Twentieth Century* (New York: Oxford University Press, 2013), 179, 190.

5. SUBVERTING

1. "Akhbar al-Sabah," *al-Ahram* (8 June 1995): 30.

2. "Al-Baqa' lil-Lah," *al-Ahram* (9 June 1995): 31.

3. Saudi Arabia, Syria, Israel, and Jordan were the four other stops on Nixon's tour.

4. On 20 April 1974, Sadat personally approved Hermann Eilts as the first US ambassador to Egypt since the 1967 war. See "U.S. Role Praised in Egypt: Sadat Lauds Nixon Policy at Ceremony," *Washington Post* (21 April 1974): 1.

5. "Nixon Yatasil bil-Bayt al-Abiad," *al-Jumhuriyya* (14 June 1974): 1; "Ma' Nixon fi Ziyaratihi," *al-Ahram* (13 June 1974). US media also devoted significant resources to covering Nixon's journey across the Atlantic. ABC, CBS, and NBC each spent an estimated $500,000 on sending over the necessary equipment and personnel. See Les Brown, "Covering Nixon in Arab Lands Runs Up Costs for the Networks," *New York Times* (14 June 1974): 67.

6. Richard Nixon, "Text of the 'Principles of Relations and Cooperation Between Egypt and the United States,'" 14 June 1974. Online by Gerhard Peters and John T. Woolley, *The American Presidency Project*, http://www.presidency.ucsb.edu/ws/?pid=4251.

7. Sadat accepted Nixon's invitation and later announced his plan to visit the United States on 25 September 1974. See Samir 'Izat, "Ziyarat al-Ra'is li-Amrika fi Khamsa wa 'Ishrin Sibtambir," *Ruz al-Yusuf*, no. 2401 (17 June 1974): 8.

8. Elie Podeh, *The Politics of National Celebrations in the Arab Middle East* (New York: Cambridge University Press, 2011).

9. Laurie Brand, *Official Stories: Politics and National Narratives in Egypt and Algeria* (Stanford, CA: Stanford University Press, 2014).

10. Podeh, *The Politics of National Celebrations in the Arab Middle East*, 4.

11. Brand, *Official Stories*, 20.

12. "Al-Sadat wa Nixon Yabda'an Muhadithatihim bi-Jalsa Mughlaqa fi 'Asr al-Tahara," *al-Ahram* (13 June 1974): 5.

13. "Istiqbal Sha'bi wa Rasmi Kabir li-Nixon Fi al-Qahira," *al-Ahram* (13 June 1974): 1.

14. "Mawkab al-Ra'isayn Istaghraq Sa'a," *al-Jumhuriyya* (13 June 1974): 11.

15. Richard Reston, "Nixon Cheered by Huge Cairo Crowd," *Los Angeles Times* (13 June 1974): 16. On Nasser's funeral, see Raymond Anderson, "Nasser Funeral Is Disrupted by Frenzy of Millions," *New York Times* (2 October 1970): 1.

16. "Behind All the Hoopla," *Newsweek* (24 June 1974): 23; "Kayfa Kharija al-Sha'b ba'd Harb Uktubir li-Istiqbal Awwal Ra'is Amrika Yazur Misr?," *al-Jumhuriyya* (13 June 1974).

17. "Yawm Salam Tarikhi fi Istiqbal Nixon," *al-Jumhuriyya* (13 June 1974): 1; Frank Starr, "Cairo's Wild about Nixon," *Chicago Tribune* (13 June 1974): 1; John Herbers, "Cheering Cairo Throngs Greet Nixon," *New York Times* (13 June 1974): 3.

18. For photographs of these musicians, see database entries named "Richard Nixon's Visit to Egypt June 1974, and a Meeting with President Anwar Sadat," from Memory of Modern Egypt website, Library of Alexandria, http://modernegypt.bibalex.org/collections/Images.

19. "'Nixo-on Welcome!,'" *Newsweek* (24 June 1974): 20.

20. "Isti'idat Kabira fi Washingtun wa al-Qahira li-Ziyarat Nixon," *al-Jumhuriyya* (10 June 1974): 1. Notably, the US embassy in Cairo described the extensive preparations for Nixon's welcome as "the most lavish display of ceremony given to any foreign dignitary within the memory of this embassy." See #04219, American Embassy Cairo, "Cairo on Day of President Nixon's Arrival" (12 June 1974), US National Archives, https://aad.archives.gov/aad/index.jsp.

21. For images of these displays, see database entries named "Richard Nixon's Visit to Egypt June 1974, and a Meeting with President Anwar Sadat," from Memory of Modern Egypt website, Library of Alexandria, http://modernegypt.bibalex.org/ collections/Images; "Presidents Nixon and Sadat Wave from a Motorcade Driving through Alexandria, Egypt, 1974," photograph, Corbis, http://www.corbisimages.com/ Search#mlt=WL001148&mla= 11135066.

22. Database entry "Richard Nixon's Visit to Egypt June 1974, and a Meeting with President Anwar Sadat," from Memory of Modern Egypt website, Library of Alexandria, http://modernegypt.bibalex.org/collections/Images.

23. Otto Bettmann, photographer, "Crowd Waving at Nixon and Anwar Sadat," Corbis, http://www.corbisimages.com/Search#p=1&q=Nixon+in+Cairo&s=100.

24. "Hashud Kabira ala al-Mahatat Tistaqbil Qatar al-Ra'isayn," al-Ahram (14 June 1974): 8.

25. Wally McNamee, "Richard Nixon Visiting Egypt" (1974), Getty Images.

26. Dirck Halstead, "US Pres Richard Nixon and Egyptian Pres Anwar Sadat" (1974), Getty Images.

27. Wally McNamee, "Nixon in Egypt" (1974), Dolph Briscoe Center for American History.

28. Frank Starr, "Nile Throngs Hail Nixon; Sadat Will Visit US," Chicago Tribune (14 June 1974): 1.

29. "A Triumphant Middle East Hegira." Time, no. 25 (24 June 1974): 19.

30. 'Aziz Baqtr, "Malayin al-Muwatinin Tahtashad li-Tahiya al-Sadat wa Nixon 'ala Tul al-Tariq ila al-Iskandariyya," al-Jumhuriyya (14 June 1974): 3.

31. Salah Hafız, Mustafa al-Hussein, Samir Azzat, and Mahmoud Dhini, "Nixon: Min Watergate ila al-Qahira," Ruz al-Yusuf, no. 2401 (17 June 1974): 3; Wally McNamee, in Newsweek (24 June 1974): 21.

32. Photographs of Nixon receiving some of these awards appeared in the Egyptian press. See, e.g., "Khitabayn lil-Ra'isayn fı Haflat al-'Isha'," al-Ahram (13 June 1974): 3.

33. Al-Ahram (14 June 1974): 5; al-Ahram (14 June 1974); al-Ahram (13 June 1974): 4; "Yurahab Sha'b al-Iskandariyya," al-Ahram (13 June 1974): 9; "Sha'b al-Iskandariyya," al-Jumhuriyya (13 June 1974): 9.

34. Al-Jumhuriyya (13 June 1974): 10; al-Jumhuriyya (6 June 1974):6.

35. No shortage of ink has been spilled on Umm Kulthum, Muhammad 'Abd al-Wahhab, and 'Abd al-Halim Hafız, three of Imam's contemporaries. For a list of representative works on these musicians, see Gabriel Rosenbaum, "Nasser and Nasserism as Perceived in Modern Egyptian Literature through Allusions to Songs," in

Rethinking Nasserism: Revolution and Historical Memory in Modern Egypt, ed. Elie Podeh and Onn Winckler (Gainesville: University Press of Florida, 2004), 338–39. On Nigm and his poetry, see, e.g., Kamal Abdel-Malek, *A Study of the Vernacular Poetry of Ahmad Fu'ad Nigm* (Leiden: E. J. Brill, 1990).

36. See, e.g., the following entry on Shaykh Imam in a recent encyclopedia: Muhammad Qabil, *Mawsu'at al-Ghina' fi Misr*, 56–57.

37. Ayman al-Hakim, *Sanawat al-Fann wa al-Sijn wa al-Dumu': Mudhakkirat al-Shaykh Imam* (Cairo: Dar al-Ahmadi lil-Nashr, 2001), 22–23.

38. Al-Hakim, 22.

39. Al-Hakim, 25.

40. According to Imam, the establishment's administrators deemed the radio a gateway to "unbelief, immorality, and disobedience." Al-Hakim, 31.

41. Al-Hakim, 34.

42. Al-Hakim, 40.

43. Al-Hakim, 37.

44. It is worth noting that Imam and Nigm briefly appeared on Egyptian radio in the late 1960s, prior to being banned from state-controlled airwaves. Sawt al-'Arab promoted the artists on a program lasting less than one year—*With Shaykh Imam's Compositions (Ma' Alhan al-Shaykh Imam)*—in 1968. On the broadcast, Imam performed sentimental and nationalist songs penned by Nigm and a few other poets. Significantly, the duo's more critical works, which easily circulated on audiocassette tapes, did not sound on the radio show. Recordings of the Sawt al-'Arab program are exceedingly difficult to locate in formal archives, but certain segments have been uploaded to platforms like Facebook and SoundCloud by Esmat al-Nimr, a friend of Imam in Cairo, and to YouTube by Ayesh Abed, a Shaykh Imam fan in the West Bank. See, e.g., "Ma' Alhan al-Shaykh Imam: Idha'at Sawt al-'Arab 1968 ha [*sic*] 1," YouTube video, posted by "Ayesh Abed," 27 February 2016, https://www.youtube.com/watch?v=k9H2xGj1h7I.

45. The Egyptian poet and songwriter Gamal Bikhayt goes so far as to claim that cassettes paved the way for two important affairs in the 1970s: "the Nigm-Imam phenomenon" and the Iranian Revolution. See Sayyid 'Inaba, *Al-Shaykh Imam: 'Ushaq Bahiyya* (Cairo: Maktabat Jazirat al-Ward, 2010), 89.

46. Amir al-'Umri, *Al-Shaykh Imam fi 'Asr al-Thawra wa al-Ghadab* (Cairo: Maktabat Madbuli, 2010), 78.

47. Sayyid 'Inaba, personal communication, 14 July 2015.

48. In an interview with Imam in 1975, the journalist Safinaz Kazim voiced her

desire for the singer and his fans to meet face-to-face rather than only by way of "cassettes, half of which are muddled." See "Hiwar Nadir lil-Shaykh Imam ma' al-Katiba Safinaz Kazim 7 wa al-Akhir," YouTube video, 12:41, posted by "Ahmad Fawzi," 21 July 2012, https://www.youtube.com/watch?v=dOCIdsvhDAY.

49. Henry Tanner, "No Voice of Dissent to Mar Nixon Visit," *New York Times* (14 June 1974): 10.

50. A *zar* is primarily a lower- to middle-class phenomenon. For a recent ethnographic treatment of this spiritual practice in modern Egypt, see Hager El Hadidi, *Zar: Spirit Possession, Music, and Healing Rituals in Egypt* (New York: Oxford University Press, 2016).

51. For more on *mulids*, carnivalesque events that often piqued the attention and the anxiety of Egyptian authorities, see Samuli Schielke, *The Perils of Joy: Contesting Mulid Festivals in Contemporary Egypt* (Syracuse, NY: Syracuse University Press, 2013).

52. Ahdaf Soueif, *In the Eye of the Sun* (London: Bloomsbury, 1992), 496.

53. Soueif, 496.

54. Soueif, 497–98.

55. Soueif, 499.

56. Sayyid 'Inaba, "Haflat al-Maadi bi-Maktab Anas al-Manufi 31 December 1991," home video.

57. Al-Hashimi Bin Faraj reflects on this experience in a recent documentary, see Sharif al-Maghazi, "Imam..Tunis," 71 mins. (Al-Jazeera al-Watha'iqiyya, 2018).

58. Shaykh Imam, *Le Cheikh Imam chante Negm* (Le Chant du Monde, 1976).

59. Sayyid 'Inaba, *Hikayat Shaykh Imam* (Cairo: Maktabat Jazirat al-Ward, 2013), 99.

60. Other vinyl records, released abroad, showcasing Shaykh Imam, include *Hommage à mon pays!* (1980), *Réveille-toi l'Egypte!* (1982), *Les nuits des amandiers, volume 1* (1984), and *Les nuits des amandiers, volume 2* (1984). Collectively, these official albums stand in stark contrast to Imam's unofficial recordings in Egypt. See https://www.discogs.com/artist/3319851-الشيخ-إمام.

61. For more on the mobility of Imam's cassettes, which "went here and there," see an interview with the Egyptian artist 'Azza Balba': Banning Eyre, "Program: Egypt 5: Revolution Songs," *Afropop Worldwide*, interview with 'Azza Balba', 2012, http://www.afropop.org/wp/1955/azza-balba.

62. Al-Hakim, *Sanawat al-Fann wa al-Sijn wa al-Dumu'*, 51; Ahmad Fu'ad Nigm, *Kalb al-Sit: Al-Diwan al-Thalith* (Cairo: Maktabat Madbuli al-Saghir, 1999), 76.

63. Faith Petric, "Speak Out Freely, Speak Out! Egypt's El Sheikh Imam," *Sing Out! The Folk Song Magazine* (1980): 18.

64. The National Archives, FCO 93/380, DAS Gladstone, "Egypt Internal—September 1974," (30 September 1974), 2.

65. "Barnamij Watha'iqi fi al-Tilifiziyun al-Jaza'iri: Al-Halaqa al-Sadisa," YouTube video, posted by "al-Shaykh Imam 'Isa," 19 July 2011, https://www.youtube.com/watch?v=ZhI1hApzoiE&t=923s.

66. "Barnamij Watha'iqi fi al-Tilifiziyun al-Jaza'iri: Al-Halaqa al-Tasi'a," YouTube video, posted by "al-Shaykh Imam 'Isa," 27 July 2011, https://www.youtube.com/watch?v=g14TMvsAk6E&list=PLBOgA1uvNldmYMht37BNQ-ZOA2x3s07mH&index=20.

67. "Sharaft ya Nixon Baba ma' Nawwar," YouTube video, posted by "salim85799," 16 May 2011, https://www.youtube.com/watch?v=gTRzdHstBbk; "Nixon Baba (al-Shaykh Imam)—Urkestra al-Mawhubin," YouTube video, posted by "TalentsOrchestra," 15 November 2013, https://www.youtube.com/watch?v=K-dNRFysuPo; "Bil-Video..Shahid 'Nixon Baba' bi-Sawt Maryam Salih 'ala Masrah al-Falaki," YouTube video, posted by "VideoYoum7," 30 November 2013, https://www.youtube.com/watch?v=agIDj1PKBpw. Still other YouTube videos creatively incorporate "Nixon Baba" as a soundtrack to level political statements. In one such upload, the track plays as images of Barack Obama's visit to Egypt in 2009 stream, see "Sharaft ya Nixon Baba—Al-Shaykh Imam," YouTube video, posted by "CheKhal6d," 2 May 2011, https://www.youtube.com/watch?v=JRm-f3AvRhyE.

68. Antika, "Ziyarat al-Ra'is al-Amriki Richard Nixon ila Misr 'Amm 74," Facebook, April 2, 2020, https://www.facebook.com/AntiqueArabia/photos/3083807184976919.

69. For Imam Facebook groups, see, e.g., Shaykh Imam, https://www.facebook.com/Sheikh-Imam-64438575709-امام-شيخ/; Al-Shaykh Imam 'Isa, https://www.facebook.com/0813 21150742223-عيسى-امام-الشيخ. For offline performances, see "Ihtifal bil-Dhikra al-17 li-Wafat al-Shaykh Imam bi-Maktabat al-Kabina bil-Iskandariyya," al-Shuruq (2012); Amjad Mustafa, "Yehya Khalil Yughanni lil-Shaykh Imam..wa Yassif al-Baradi'i bi-Muharrir al-'Abid," al-Shuruq (2012); "Al-Fannan 'Abdullah Rif'at Yughanni lil-Shaykh Imam wa Sayyid Darwish bi-Maktabat Akmal Misr," al-Shuruq (2011); "Al-Ihtifal bi-Dhikrat al-Shaykh Imam bi-Markaz Sa'd Zaghlul al-Thaqafi Ghadan," al-Shuruq (2012); "'Azza Balba' Tughanni lil-Shaykh Imam bi-Saqiyat al-Sawi," al-Shuruq (2012). For Imam associations, see, e.g., Jam'iyat Muhibi al-Shaykh Imam, https://www.facebook. com/-محبي-جمعية 1586279964949188امام-الشيخ/info/?tab=page_info.

70. Hana' Fathi, "Sayyid Mikkawi fi Mal'ab al-Shaykh Imam," Ruz al-Yusuf, no. 3118 (14 March 1988): 57.

71. Fathi, 57.

72. Fathi, 57.

73. Indeed, Imam's "Nixon Baba" continued to circulate and sound long after Sadat strove to personally downplay the very spectacle over which he presided in Egypt. In his autobiography, *In Search of Identity*, published four years after Nixon's visit and subsequent resignation, Sadat devotes a single sentence to his guest's stay. He simply acknowledges that the trip took place and preceded America's entrance into a "terrible whirlpool" of political turmoil. See Anwar Sadat, *Al-Bahth 'an al-Dhat: Qissat Hayati* (Cairo: Al-Maktab al-Misri al-Hadith, 1978), 391.

74. Jim Hoagland, "Arabs to Seek Tradeoff," *Washington Post* (10 June 1974): 1.

75. "A Triumphant Middle East Hegira": 12; "'Nixo-on Welcome!'": 18.

76. Salah Hafiz, Mustafa al-Husayn, Samir 'Izat, and Mahmud Dhini, "Nixon: Min Watergate ila al-Qahira," *Ruz al-Yusuf*, no. 2401 (17 June 1974): 5; "Nasr Sahafi 'Alami: Ruz al-Yusuf Da'iman Asdaq," *Ruz al-Yusuf*, no. 2409 (12 August 1974): 5.

77. Ibrahim 'Izat, "Nixon Yu'rid Istiqalatihi," *Ruz al-Yusuf*, no. 2408 (5 August 1974): 3.

78. Sonallah Ibrahim, *Zaat*, trans. Anthony Calderbank (New York: American University in Cairo Press, 2001), 13. Notably, this remark regarding the cassette being "far more radical and subversive" than Imam's tapes is not present in the original Arabic text, leading one to wonder whether Ibrahim, the novel's author and a signatory of Imam's revised obituary, cited at the start of this chapter, would agree. See Sonallah Ibrahim, *Dhat* (Cairo: Dar al-Mustaqbil al-'Arabi, 1992), 20.

79. Ibrahim, 13.

80. See, e.g., "Roundtable: Toward New Histories of the Left," *International Journal of Middle East Studies* 51, no. 2 (2019): 301–319; Sune Haugbolle and Manfred Sing, "New Approaches to Arab Left Histories," *Arab Studies Journal* 24, no. 1 (2016): 90–97.

81. Such was the case with "You Are My Life" ("Enta 'Umri"), a famous collaboration between Umm Kulthum and Muhammad 'Abd al-Wahhab. See Sa'd Ramadan, ed., *Umm Kulthum: Sawt fi Tarikh al-Umma* (Tunis: Ma'had al-Musiqa al-'Arabiyya, 2000), 147.

82. Afaf Lutfi Al-Sayyid Marsot, "Survey of Egyptian Works of History," *American Historical Review* 96, no. 5 (1991): 1425.

83. Anwar Sadat, *Safahat Majhula* (Cairo: Dar al-Tahrir lil-Tiba'a wa al-Nashr, 1954). Notably, the material found in *Unknown Pages* first appeared in 1954 in *al-Jumhuriyya*, a daily Egyptian newspaper (founded in 1953), where Sadat published a series of articles and served as editor.

84. Sadat, *Al-Bahth 'an al-Dhat*.

6. ARCHIVING

1. Unlike Nasser, Barih does not surface in Egypt's historical record, and outside of this cassette recording, which simply acknowledges her passing, Barih's life remains very much a mystery.

2. This approach draws inspiration from select historians, who have effectively utilized ethnographic methods to reveal a more nuanced picture of the Middle East's past through the personal experiences of particular individuals, and from certain anthropologists, who have harnessed oral interviews to write imaginative histories of the region. See, e.g., Eric Tagliacozzo, *The Longest Journey: Southeast Asians and the Pilgrimage to Mecca* (New York: Oxford University Press, 2013); Engseng Ho, *The Graves of Tarim: Genealogy and Mobility across the Indian Ocean* (Berkeley: University of California Press, 2006); Michael Meeker, *A Nation of Empire: The Ottoman Legacy of Turkish Modernity* (Berkeley: University of California Press, 2002); Andrew Shryock, *Nationalism and the Genealogical Imagination: Oral History and Textual Authority in Tribal Jordan* (Berkeley: University of California Press, 1997). (footnote 3 has been deleted).

3. Lila Ellen Gray, *Fado Resounding: Affective Politics and Urban Life* (Durham, NC: Duke University Press, 2013); Maureen Jackson, *Mixing Musics: Turkish Jewry and the Urban Landscape of a Sacred Song* (Stanford, CA: Stanford University Press, 2013); Lise Waxer, *The City of Musical Memory: Salsa, Record Grooves, and Popular Culture in Cali, Colombia* (Middletown, CT: Wesleyan University Press, 2002).

4. Donald Reid, *Whose Pharaohs? Archaeology, Museums, and Egyptian National Identity from Napoleon to World War I* (Berkeley: University of California Press, 2002); Donald Reid, *Cairo University and the Making of Modern Egypt* (New York: Cambridge University Press, 1990).

5. Laila Parsons, "Micro-Narrative and the Historiography of the Modern Middle East," *History Compass* 9, no. 1 (2011): 85.

6. For two insightful discussions of preservation politics in the case of one iconic singer's legacy and private art collections in Egypt, see Laura Lohman, "Preservation and Politicization: Umm Kulthum's National and International Legacy," *Popular Music and Society* 33, no. 1 (2010): 45–60; Jessica Winegar, *Creative Reckonings: The Politics of Art and Culture in Contemporary Egypt* (Stanford, CA: Stanford University Press, 2006), 225–67.

7. ʿImad al-Muhsin, Samar al-Mutalaq, Susan Kamil, Hana Saʿid, *Al-Thaqafa: Dauʾ ʿala Wajh al-Watan 1987–1997* (Cairo: Sunduq al-Tanmiya al-Thaqafiyya, 1997).

8. ʿAbbas Muhammad Salama, personal communication, July 2015.

9. Cairo Opera Press, "Music Library: Al-Maktaba al-Musiqiyya," n.d.

10. Mark Katz, *Capturing Sound: How Technology Has Changed Music* (2004; Berkeley: University of California Press, 2010), 213.

11. Mansur 'Abd al-'Al, personal communication, July 2015.

12. My interest in music, it seems, assuaged any suspicions that I was researching "politics."

13. 'Ala' 'Abd al-Karim, "'Akhir Sa'a' Taftah Malaf Qadiyya Fanniyya Khatira: Mafia al-Kasitat al-Mamnu'a wa al-Shara'it al-Habita!," *Akhir Sa'a*, no. 2788 (30 March 1988): 24.

14. 'Abd al-Karim, 26.

15. 'Abd al-Karim, 26.

16. 'Abd al-Karim, 25.

17. Malika Zeghal, "Religion and Politics in Egypt: The Ulema of Al-Azhar, Radical Islam, and the State (1952–94), *International Journal of Middle East Studies* 31, no. 3 (1999): 394.

18. Hirschkind refers to the Islamic Research Academy as the "Council on Islamic Research." These places are one and the same. See Charles Hirschkind, *The Ethical Soundscapes: Cassettes Sermons and Islamic Counterpublics* (New York: Columbia University Press, 2006), 59–60.

19. Hany Shams al-Din, personal communication, June 2019.

20. Ahmad Muhammad Ibrahim, personal communication, July 2019.

21. 'Ali al-Asali, personal communication, July 2019.

22. Christopher Wren, "Blind Cairo Sheik Rallies Poor with Fiery Islamic Creed," *New York Times* (28 November 1979): 2.

23. Abu al-Shayma', "Qisat Hayat al-Shaykh (('Antar Sa'id Mussallam)) wa Ma'aha Mufaja'a (Tafaddulu)," Ahlalalm, https://www.ahlalalm.org/vb/showthread.php?t=3873.

24. The ease with which ordinary Egyptians recorded Shaykh 'Antar's recitations on audiocassettes stands in especially stark contrast to the top-down creation of the first standardized recording of the Qur'an in its entirety, which surfaced on a series of records in the summer of 1961 and featured the voice of another Egyptian reciter, Shaykh Mahmud Khalil al-Husari (chapter 4). For more on the making of this recording, the outcome of a highly centralized process that took two years to complete in Egypt, involved no fewer than five government ministries in addition to al-Azhar, and was led by Labib Sa'id, the then president of the General Association for the Preservation of the Glorious Qur'an, see Labib Sa'id, *The Recited Koran: A History of the First*

Recorded Version, trans. Bernard Weiss, M. A. Rauf, and Morroe Berger (Princeton, NJ: Darwin Press, 1975), esp. chaps. 5 and 6.

25. Mahmud al-Saʿadni, *Alhan al-Sama'* (Cairo: Akhbar al-Yawm, 1996), 118–19.

26. Al-Saʿadni, 117.

27. Here, the Qur'anic passage under discussion is the beginning of verse 126, chapter 2.

28. Al-Saʿadni, *Alhan al-Sama'*, 118.

29. Al-Saʿadni, 118.

30. Al-Idthaʿa al-Qur'aniyya lil-Tilawat al-Kashiʿa wa al-Nadiyya, https://www.facebook.com/ Quranic.radio.station/posts/1620334628268338/.

31. Al-Idthaʿa al-Qur'aniyya lil-Tilawat al-Kashiʿa wa al-Nadiyya, https://www.facebook.com/ Quranic.radio.station/posts/1620334628268338/.

32. Al-Saʿadni, *Alhan al-Sama'*, 119.

33. Al-Idthaʿa al-Qur'aniyya lil-Tilawat al-Kashiʿa wa al-Nadiyya, https://www.facebook.com/ Quranic.radio.station/posts/1620334628268338/.

34. All these videos are available on Mohamed's YouTube channel, at https://www.youtube.com/ channel/UC5EoIYNXWmG59PdUbvV6soQ/videos.

35. See https://www.instagram.com/p/vWolHNIeos/.

36. Deborah Cowley, *Cairo—A Practical Guide* (Cairo: American University in Cairo Press, 1975), 75.

37. Heba Yossry, *Situ Zad: Awwal 'Ishq*, 82 mins. (Egypt: Misr International Films, 2011).

38. Heba Yossry, personal communication, June 2015.

39. This practice, it appears, was commonplace. A 2015 pamphlet from Mobilnil, a major communications company in Egypt, highlights the historical movement of audiotapes in the mail. "In the past, letters were like this," the leaflet gestures to a blank tape above an open envelope, but "today you can send a Voice SMS (an audio message) to anyone, anywhere in the world." See "Zaman al-Rasa'il Kanat Kida" (Cairo: Mobilnil, 2015).

40. Farha Ghannam, *Remaking the Modern: Space, Relocation, and the Politics of Identity in a Global Cairo* (Los Angeles: University of California Press, 2002), 142–44, 146, 148–51, 155; Soraya Duval De Dampierre, "Gulf and Gender: Migration and Women's New Roles in Rural Egypt" (PhD diss., Lund University, 1996), 87, 90, 115, 172.

41. "The Letter You Sent," YouTube video, 8:32, posted by "Mada Masr," 18 April 2020, https://www.youtube.com/watch?v=z9tsbHjgnpg&feature=emb_logo.

42. According to UNESCO statistics, less than 50 percent of Egyptian adults were

literate between the 1970s and early 1990s, a figure that masks even lower literacy rates among women and those residing in rural areas. See UNESCO Institute for Statistics, "Country Profiles: Egypt," United Nations Educational, Scientific, and Cultural Organization, http://www.uis.unesco.org/DataCentre/Pages/countryprofile.aspx?code=-EGY&regioncode=40525 (3 August 3 2016).

43. Notably, sending personal messages on audiotapes was not unique to Egypt and Egyptians. David McMurray observes how Moroccan migrants in Europe similarly exchanged audiotapes with loved ones back home in Morocco, while Anh Longva calls attention to the audiotapes traveling between migrants in Kuwait and their families elsewhere. Ahmad Ghossein, likewise, introduces the personal messages his mother began to record on cassettes in Lebanon in the late 1970s for his father, who was working abroad in the Gulf, in a 2011 documentary. See David McMurray, *In and Out of Morocco: Smuggling and Migration in a Frontier Boomtown* (Minneapolis: University of Minnesota Press, 2001), 28; Anh Longva, *Walls Built on Sand: Migration, Exclusion and Society in Kuwait* (Boulder, CO: Westview Press, 1997), 36, 162, 164; Ahmad Ghossein, *My Father Is Still a Communist*," 32 mins. (Lebanon, 2011).

44. Notably, al-Nimr attributes his passion for Egypt's musical heritage and its preservation to Shaykh Imam, a friend and mentor. See Esmat al-Nimr and 'Alaa al-Mislimani, "'An Misrfone," Misrfone, https://www.misrfone.net/?page_id=26.

45. Aladdin Fattah, "Radio Misrfone Need Help," *Indiegogo*, https://www.indiegogo.com/projects/ radio-misrfone-need help?fbclid=IwAR3C2ClMxLL4ZlCi3VXNmw2t-1PCoi4D6qKEqRp293X PFu1XQwbSpAfxXitA#/.

46. Discogs, "About Discogs," https://www.discogs.com/about.

47. "AnalogPlanet Interviews Discogs Founder Kevin Lewandowski," YouTube video, 25:32, posted by "Analog Planet," 29 April 2019, https://www.youtube.com/watch?time_continue=392&v=rSntbjpLnvE.

48. During one visit to eBay in September 2019, for example, cassette tape recordings carrying Egyptian performers were posted by sellers based in Egypt, Israel, Morocco, Canada, the United Kingdom, the United States, and the United Arab Emirates.

49. Doreen Lee, *Activist Archives: Youth Culture and the Political Past in Indonesia* (Durham, NC: Duke University Press, 2016), 5.

CONCLUSION

1. To listen to this recording, see "Ramy Essam—Album Manshourat," SoundCloud, posted by "MFekki," https://soundcloud.com/mohamed-elfiky/sets/ramy-essam-al-bum-manshourat.

2. For one such performance, see "Ughniyya Irhal min Midan al-Tahrir—Ramy Essam—Protestors singing in Tahrir Square—Erhal," YouTube video, 3:03, posted by "Ibrahim Khalid," 5 February 2011, https://www.youtube.com/watch?v=wFTwl-cEnE4.

3. Mark M. Smith, *Sensing the Past: Seeing, Hearing, Smelling, Tasting, and Touching in History* (Berkeley: University of California Press, 2007), 117, 121–23.

4. For a selection of this artist's inventive work with audiotapes, see @erika_iris_art, at Instagram, https://www.instagram.com/erika_iris_art/?hl=en.

5. See, e.g., Alan Mikhail, *The Animal in Ottoman Egypt* (New Haven, CT: Yale University Press, 2014); Nükhet Varlik, *Plague and Empire in the Early Modern Mediterranean World: The Ottoman Experience, 1347–1600* (New York: Cambridge University Press, 2015); Secil Yilmaz, "Love in the Time of Syphilis: Medicine and Sex in the Ottoman Empire, 1860–1922" (PhD diss., City University of New York, 2016); Febe Armanios and Boğaç Ergene, *Halal Food: A History* (New York: Oxford University Press, 2018); Yaron Ayalon, *Natural Disasters in the Ottoman Empire: Plague, Famine, and Other Misfortunes* (New York: Oxford University Press, 2015).

APPENDIX

1. All translations in this appendix are my own.

2. Imam performs much of this song in a French accent, particularly the italicized words.

3. Imam pronounces Arabiyya ("Arab") with an *alif* instead of an *'ayn*.

Bibliography

ARCHIVAL COLLECTIONS

British National Archives, London

Moshe Dayan Center Arabic Press Archives, Tel Aviv

The Netherlands-Flemish Institute in Cairo

ARABIC PERIODICALS

Al-Ahram

Akhir Sa'a

Al-Funun

Al-Jumhuriyya

Al-Majalla al-Musiqiyya

Majallat al-Fann

Miki

Al-Nujum

Ruz al-Yusuf

Sabah al-Khayr

Al-Shuruq

ENGLISH PERIODICALS

Ahram Online

Chicago Tribune

The Guardian

Los Angeles Times

New York Times

Newsweek

Time

Wall Street Journal

Washington Post

AUDIOCASSETTE CATALOGS

Kataluj al-Kasit lil-Munawwaʻat al-Ghinaʼiyya. Sharikat Sawt al-Qahira lil-Sawtiyat wa Marʼiyat, 2004.

Kataluj ʻUmumi Kamil li-Kafat al-Tasjilat al-ʻArabiyya 1977. Athens: EMI Greece, 1977.

Qurʼan Karim: Qiraʼa Mujawwada bi-Aswat Mashahir al-Qurraʼ. Cairo: Sharikat Sawt al-Qahira lil-Sawtiyat wa Mariʼyat, n.d.

Saharat Musiqiyya. Cairo: Sharikat Sawt al-Qahira lil-Sawtiyat wa Mariʼyat, n.d.

FILMS, GUIDEBOOKS, MEMOIRS, NOVELS, OPERATING INSTRUCTIONS

ʻAbd al-ʻAziz, Kamal. *Harq Ubra al-Qahira.* 39 mins. Egypt: Cadrage Productions, 2009.

ʻAbd al-Shakur, Mahmud. *Kuntu Sabiyan fi al-Sabʻinat.* Cairo: Al-Karama lil-Nashr wa al-Tawziʻ, 2015.

Amin, Ahmad. *Hayati.* Cairo: Matbaʻat Lajnat al-Taʼlif wa al-Tarjama wa al-Nashr, 1950.

Amin, Galal. *Whatever Happened to the Egyptians? Changes in Egyptian Society from 1950 to the Present.* Cairo: American University in Cairo Press, 2000.

Badrakhan, ʻAli. *Ahl Al-Qimma.* 118 mins. Egypt: Aflam Jamal al-Laythi, 1981.

Cowley, Deborah. *Cairo—A Practical Guide.* Cairo: American University in Cairo Press, 1975.

Ghossein, Ahmad. *My Father Is Still a Communist.* 32 mins. Lebanon, 2011.

al-Guindi, Ahmad. *Tir Enta.* 116 mins. Egypt: Al-Sharika al-ʻArabiyya lil-Intaj wa al-Tawziʻ al-Sinimaʼi, 2009.

al-Hakim, Ayman. *Sanawat al-Fann wa al-Sijn wa al-Dumuʻ: Mudhakkirat al-Shaykh Imam.* Cairo: Dar al-Ahmadi lil-Nashr, 2001.

Humphreys, Andrew. *Egypt.* Washington, DC: National Geographic, 2007.

Hureau, Jean. *L'Égypte aujourd'hui.* Paris: Éditions JA, 1977.

Ibrahim, Sonallah. *Dhat.* Cairo: Dar al-Mustaqbil al-ʻArabi, 1992.

Kamil, ʻIzz al-Din. *Saʻd Kamil: Al-Thaqafa al-Jamahiriyya.* Cairo: Al-Majlis al-Aʻla lil-Thaqafa, 2010.

Kennedy, Douglas. *Beyond the Pyramids: Travels in Egypt.* New York: Henry Holt and Co., 1988.

al-Maghazi, Sharif. *Imam..Tunis.* 71 mins. Al-Jazeera al-Watha'iqiyya, 2018.

Nagel's Encyclopedia-Guide: Egypt. Paris: Nagel Publishers, 1976.

Philips Operating Instructions: EL-3300.

Sadat, Anwar. *Al-Bahth 'an al-Dhat: Qissat Hayati.* Cairo: Al-Maktab al-Masri al-Hadith, 1978.

———. *Safahat Majhula.* Cairo: Dar al-Tahrir lil-Tiba'a wa al-Nashr, 1954.

Shabot, Joey. *Let's Go: Egypt.* New York: St. Martin's Press, 2003.

Sharqawi, Galal. *Madrasat al-Mushaghibin.* 251 mins. Egypt, 1971.

Showker, Kay. *Fodor's Egypt 1978.* Edited by Eugene Fodor and Robert Fisher. New York: David McKay Co., 1978.

Soueif, Ahdaf. *In the Eye of the Sun.* London: Bloomsbury, 1992.

Taylor, Zack. *Cassette: A Documentary Mixtape.* 87 mins. United States, 2016.

al-Tayyib, 'Atif. *Sawwaq al-Utubis.* 108 mins. Egypt: Al-Subki Film, 1983.

'Ukasha, Tharwat. *Mudhakkirati fi al-Siyasa wa al-Thaqafa.* Vol. 1. Cairo: Dar al-Hilal, 1990.

Yossry, Heba. *Situ Zad: Awwal 'Ishq.* 82 mins. Egypt: Misr International Films, 2011.

al-Yusuf, Fatima. *Dhikrayat.* 2nd ed. Cairo: Mu'assasat Ruz al-Yusuf, 1976.

ARTICLES, BOOKS, DISSERTATIONS, REPORTS

Abaza, Mona. *The Changing Consumer Cultures of Modern Egypt.* Boston: Brill, 2006.

Abdel-Malek, Kamal. *A Study of the Vernacular Poetry of Ahmad Fu'ad Nigm.* Leiden: E. J. Brill, 1990.

'Abduh, Ibrahim. *Tarikh bila Watha'iq.* Cairo: Mu'assasat Sajil al-'Arab, 1975.

Abou-El-Fadl, Reem. *Foreign Policy as Nation Making: Turkey and Egypt in the Cold War.* New York: Cambridge University Press, 2019.

Abou-Hodeib, Toufoul. *A Taste for Home: The Modern Middle Class in Ottoman Beirut.* Stanford, CA: Stanford University Press, 2017.

Abu-Lughod, Lila. "Bedouins, Cassettes and Technologies of Public Culture." *Middle East Report,* no. 159 (1989): 7–11, 47.

———. *Dramas of Nationhood: The Politics of Television in Egypt.* Chicago: University of Chicago Press, 2005.

Abul-Magd, Zeinab. *Militarizing the Nation: The Army, Business, and Revolution in Egypt.* New York: Columbia University Press, 2018.

Adams, Richard, Jr. "Worker Remittances and Inequality in Rural Egypt." *Economic Development and Cultural Change* 38, no. 1 (1989): 45–71.

Allman, Jean. "Phantoms of the Archive: Kwame Nkrumah, a Nazi Pilot Named Hanna, and the Contingencies of Postcolonial History-Writing." *American Historical Review* 118, no. 1 (2013): 104–29.

'Inaba, Sayyid. *Hikayat Shaykh Imam*. Cairo: Maktabat Jazirat al-Ward, 2013.

———. *Al-Shaykh Imam: 'Ushaq Bahiyya*. Cairo: Maktabat Jazirat al-Ward, 2010.

Anderson, Tim. *Making Easy Listening: Material Culture and Postwar American Recording*. Minneapolis: University of Minnesota, 2006.

Ansari, Hamied. *Egypt: The Stalled Society*. Albany: State University of New York Press, 1986.

Antoun, Richard. *Muslim Preacher in the Modern World: A Jordanian Case Study in Comparative Perspective*. Princeton, NJ: Princeton University Press, 1989.

Armanios, Febe, and Boğaç Ergene. *Halal Food: A History*. New York: Oxford University Press, 2018.

Armanios, Febe, and Andrew Amstutz. "Emerging Christian Media in Egypt: Clerical Authority and the Visualization of Women in Coptic Video Films." *International Journal of Middle East Studies* 45, no. 3 (2013): 513–33.

Armbrust, Walter. "Audiovisual Media and History of the Arab Middle East." In *Middle East Historiographies: Narrating the Twentieth Century*, edited by Israel Gershoni, Amy Singer, and Y. Hakan Erdem, 288–313. Seattle: University of Washington Press, 2011.

———. *Mass Culture and Modernism in Egypt*. New York: Cambridge University Press, 1996.

———. "The Riddle of Ramadan: Media, Consumer Culture, and the 'Christmasization' of a Muslim Holiday." In *Everyday Life in the Muslim Middle East*, edited by Donna Lee Bowen and Evelyn A. Early, 335–48. Bloomington: Indiana University Press, 2002.

Atiya, Nayra. *Khul-Khaal: Five Egyptian Women Tell Their Stories*. Syracuse, NY: Syracuse University Press, 1982.

'Awad, Mahmud. *Muhammad 'Abd al-Wahhab alladhi la Ya'rifuhu Ahad*. Cairo: Dar al-Ma'arif, 1991.

Ayalon, Ami. *The Press in the Arab Middle East: A History*. New York: Oxford University Press, 1995.

Ayalon, Yaron. *Natural Disasters in the Ottoman Empire: Plague, Famine, and Other Misfortunes*. New York: Oxford University Press, 2015.

Ayubi, Nazih. "Implementation Capability and Political Feasibility of the Open Door Policy in Egypt." In *Rich and Poor States in the Middle East: Egypt and the New Arab Order*, edited by Malcolm Kerr and El Sayed Yassin, 349–414. Boulder, CO: Westview Press, 1982.

'Azab, Khalid, ed. *Ruz Al-Yusuf 80 Sana Sahafa*. Alexandria: Bibliotheca Alexandrina, 2006.

Barak, On. "Gridlock Politics: Auto(im)mobility in Sadat's Egypt." *Comparative Studies of South Asia, Africa and the Middle East* 39, no. 1 (2019): 116–30.

———. *On Time: Technology and Temporality in Modern Egypt*. Berkeley: University of California Press, 2013.

Baraka, Magda. *The Egyptian Upper Class between Revolutions, 1919–1952*. Reading, NY: Ithaca Press, 1998.

Baron, Beth. *Egypt as a Woman: Nationalism, Gender, and Politics*. Berkeley: University of California Press, 2005.

———. *The Women's Awakening in Egypt: Culture, Society, and the Press*. New Haven, CT: Yale University Press, 1994.

Beattie, Kirk. *Egypt during the Sadat Years*. New York: Palgrave, 2000.

Beinin, Joel. *Workers and Peasants in the Modern Middle East*. New York: Cambridge University Press, 2001.

Beinin, Joel, and Zachary Lockman. *Workers on the Nile: Nationalism, Communism, Islam, and the Egyptian Working Class, 1882–1954*. Princeton, NJ: Princeton University Press, 1987.

Belli, Mériam. *An Incurable Past: Nasser's Egypt Then and Now*. Gainesville: University Press of Florida, 2013.

Bier, Laura. *Revolutionary Womanhood: Feminisms, Modernity, and the State in Nasser's Egypt*. Stanford, CA: Stanford University Press, 2011.

Bijsterveld, Karin. *Mechanical Sound: Technology, Culture, and Public Problems of Noise in the Twentieth Century*. Cambridge, MA: MIT Press, 2008.

Birks, J. S., and C. A. Sinclair. "Egypt: A Frustrated Labor Exporter?" *Middle East Journal* 33, no. 3 (1979): 288–303.

———. *International Migration and Development in the Arab Region*. Geneva: International Labour Office, 1980.

Booth, Marilyn. "Fiction's Imaginative Archive and the Newspaper's Local Scandals: The Case of Nineteenth-Century Egypt." In *Archive Stories: Facts, Fictions, and the Writing of History*, edited by Antoinette Burton, 274–95. Durham, NC: Duke University Press, 2005.

Brand, Laurie. *Official Stories: Politics and National Narratives in Egypt and Algeria*. Stanford, CA: Stanford University Press, 2014.

Brinton, Jacquelene. *Preaching Islamic Renewal: Religious Authority and Media in Contemporary Egypt*. Oakland: University of California Press, 2016.

Bruton, Henry. "Egypt's Development in the Seventies." *Economic Development and Cultural Change* 31, no. 4 (1983): 679–704.

Bsheer, Rosie. *Archive Wars: The Politics of History in Saudi Arabia*. Stanford, CA: Stanford University Press, 2020.

Bull, Michael, and Les Back, ed. *The Auditory Culture Reader*. Oxford, UK: Berg, 2003.

Bunt, Gary R. *iMuslims: Rewiring the House of Islam*. Chapel Hill: University of North Carolina Press, 2009.

Burns, Kathryn. *Into the Archive: Writing and Power in Colonial Peru*. Durham, NC: Duke University Press, 2010.

Cairo Opera Press. "Music Library: Al-Maktaba al-Musiqiyya." N.d.

Castelo-Branco S., El-Shawan. "Some Aspects of the Cassette Industry in Egypt." *World of Music* 29, no. 2 (1987): 32–45.

Chalcraft, John. *The Striking Cabbies of Cairo and Other Stories: Crafts and Guilds in Egypt, 1863–1914*. Albany: State University of New York Press, 2004.

Cherribi, Sam. *Fridays of Rage: Al-Jazeera, the Arab Spring, and Political Islam*. New York: Oxford University Press, 2017.

Choucri, Nazli. "The Hidden Economy: A New View of Remittances in the Arab World." *World Development* 14, no. 6 (1986): 697–712.

———. "The New Migration in the Middle East: A Problem for Whom?" *International Migration Review* 11, no. 4 (1977): 421–443.

Colla, Elliott. *Conflicted Antiquities: Egyptology, Egyptomania, Egyptian Modernity*. Durham, NC: Duke University Press, 2007.

Connor, Steven. "Edison's Teeth: Touching Hearing." In *Hearing Cultures: Essays on Sound, Listening, and Modernity*, edited by Veit Erlmann, 153–72. Oxford, UK: Berg Press, 2004.

Cook, Steven. *The Struggle for Egypt: From Nasser to Tahrir Square*. New York: Oxford University Press, 2012.

Cooper, Mark. *The Transformation of Egypt*. Baltimore: Johns Hopkins University Press, 1982.

Corbin, Alain. *Village Bells: Sound and Meaning in the 19th-Century French Countryside*. Translated by Martin Thom. New York: Columbia University Press, 1998.

Originally published as *Les cloches de la terre: Paysage sonore et culture sensible dans les campagnes au XIXe siècle.* Paris: A. Michel, 1994.

Cummings, Alex Sayf. *Democracy of Sound: Music Piracy and the Remaking of American Copyright in the Twentieth Century.* New York: Oxford University Press, 2013.

Danielson, Virginia. *The Voice of Egypt: Umm Kulthum, Arabic Song, and Egyptian Society in the Twentieth Century.* Chicago: University of Chicago Press, 1997.

Daughtry, J. Martin. *Listening to War: Sound, Music, Trauma, and Survival in Wartime Iraq.* New York: Oxford University Press, 2015.

Davis, Natalie Zemon. *Fiction in the Archives: Pardon Tales and Their Tellers in Sixteenth-Century France.* Stanford, CA: Stanford University Press, 1987.

Dawisha, Adeed. *Arab Nationalism in the Twentieth Century: From Triumph to Despair.* Princeton, NJ: Princeton University Press, 2003

Dessouki, Ali. "The Shift in Egypt's Migration Policy: 1952–1978." *Middle Eastern Studies* 18, no. 1 (1982): 53–68.

Di-Capua, Yoav. *Gatekeepers of the Arab Past: Historians and History Writing in Twentieth-Century Egypt.* Berkeley: University of California Press, 2009.

Doumani, Beshara. *Rediscovering Palestine: Merchants and Peasants in Jabal Nablus, 1700–1900.* Berkeley: University of California Press, 1995.

Duval De Dampierre, Soraya. "Gulf and Gender: Migration and Women's New Roles in Rural Egypt." PhD diss., Lund University, 1996.

Edgerton, David. *The Shock of the Old: Technology and Global History since 1900.* New York: Oxford University Press, 2007.

Eickelman, Dale, and Jon Anderson, ed. *New Media in the Muslim World: The Emerging Public Sphere.* Bloomington: Indiana University Press, 1999.

El Hadidi, Hager. *Zar: Spirit Possession, Music, and Healing Rituals in Egypt.* New York: American University in Cairo Press, 2016.

El Khachab, Chihab. "The Sobky Recipe and the Struggle Over 'The Popular' in Egypt." *Arab Studies Journal* 27, no. 1 (2019): 35–62.

El Shakry, Omnia. "'History without Documents': The Vexed Archives of Decolonization in the Middle East." *The American Historical Review* 120, no. 3 (2015): 920–34.

El-Messiri, Sawsan. *Ibn Al-Balad: A Concept of Egyptian Identity.* Leiden: E. J. Brill, 1978.

Ewen, Stuart. *Captains of Consciousness: Advertising and the Social Roots of the Consumer Culture.* New York: McGraw-Hill, 1976.

Ezzat, Dina. "65 Years Later: The 'Cairo Fire' of 1952 Revisited." *Ahram Online* (2017).

Fahmy, Khaled. "How Do We Write Our Military History?" *Ahram Online* (2013).

Fahmy, Ziad. "Early Egyptian Radio: From Media-Capitalism to Media-Etatism, 1925–1934." *Middle East Journal of Culture and Communication* [Forthcoming].

———. *Street Sounds: Listening to Everyday Life in Modern Egypt.* Stanford, CA: Stanford University Press, 2020.

———. "Coming to Our Senses: Historicizing Sound and Noise in the Middle East." *History Compass* 11, no. 4 (2013): 305–15.

———. *Ordinary Egyptians: Creating the Modern Nation through Popular Culture.* Stanford, CA: Stanford University Press, 2011.

———. "Media-Capitalism: Colloquial Mass Culture and Nationalism in Egypt, 1908–18." *International Journal of Middle East Studies* 42, no. 1 (2010): 83–103.

Faris, David. *Dissent and Revolution in a Digital Age: Social Media, Blogging and Activism in Egypt.* New York: I. B. Tauris, 2013.

Farrag, Abdelmegid. "Migration between Arab Countries." In *Manpower and Employment in Arab Countries Some Critical Issues*, 84–108. Geneva: International Labour Office, 1976.

Feiler, Gil. *Economic Relations Between Egypt and the Gulf Oil States, 1967–2000: Petro-Wealth and Patterns of Influence.* Brighton, UK: Sussex Academic Press, 2003.

———. "Scope and Some Effects of Remittances of Egyptian Migrant Workers in the Arab Oil-Producing Countries, 1973–1984." *Asian and African Studies* 21 (1987): 305–25.

Ferris, Jesse. *Nasser's Gamble: How Intervention in Yemen Caused the Six-Day War and the Decline of Egyptian Power.* Princeton, NJ: Princeton University Press, 2013.

Foda, Omar. *Egypt's Beer: Stella, Identity, and the Modern State.* Austin: University of Texas Press, 2019.

Frishkopf, Michael. "Mediated Qur'anic Recitation and the Contestation of Islam in Contemporary Egypt." In *Music and the Play of Power in the Middle East*, edited by Laudan Nosshin, 75–114. Farnham, UK: Ashgate, 2009.

———. "Tarab ('Enchantment') in the Mystic Sufi Chant of Egypt." In *Colors of Enchantment: Theater, Dance, Music, and the Visual Arts of the Middle East*, edited by Sherifa Zuhur, 239–76. Cairo: American University in Cairo Press, 2001.

Frishkopf, Michael, and Federico Spinetti, eds. *Music, Sound, and Architecture in Islam.* Austin: University of Texas Press, 2017.

Gade, Anna M. *Perfection Makes Practice: Learning, Emotion, and the Recited Qur'an in Indonesia.* Honolulu: University of Hawai'i Press, 2004.

Gaffney, Patrick. *The Prophet's Pulpit: Islamic Preaching in Contemporary Egypt.* Berkeley: University of California Press, 1994.

Gasper, Michael Ezekiel. *The Power of Representation: Publics, Peasants, and Islam in Egypt*. Stanford, CA: Stanford University Press, 2009.

Gaytán, Marie Sarita. *¡Tequila! Distilling the Spirit of Mexico*. Stanford, CA: Stanford University Press, 2014.

Gerges, Fawaz. *Making the Arab World: Nasser, Qutb, and the Clash That Shaped the Middle East*. Princeton, NJ: Princeton University Press, 2018.

Gershoni, Israel, and James Jankowski. *Redefining the Egyptian Nation, 1930–1945*. New York: Cambridge University Press, 1995.

Ghannam, Farha. *Remaking the Modern: Space, Relocation, and the Politics of Identity in a Global Cairo*. Los Angeles: University of California Press, 2002.

Gilman, Daniel. *Cairo Pop: Youth Music in Contemporary Egypt*. Minneapolis: University of Minnesota Press, 2014.

Gingeras, Ryan. *Heroin, Organized Crime, and the Making of Modern Turkey*. New York: Oxford University Press, 2014.

Gitelman, Lisa. *Always Already New: Media, History, and the Data of Culture*. Cambridge, MA: MIT Press, 2006.

Goldberg, Ellis. *Tinker, Tailor, Textile Worker: Class and Politics in Egypt, 1930–1952*. Berkeley: University of California Press, 1986.

Gordon, Joel. *Nasser's Blessed Movement: Egypt's Free Officers and the July Revolution*. New York: Oxford University Press, 1992.

———. "The Nightingale and the Ra'is: 'Abd Al-Halim Hafiz and Nasserist Longings." In *Rethinking Nasserism: Revolution and Historical Memory in Modern Egypt*, edited by Elie Podeh and Onn Winckler, 307–23. Gainesville: University Press of Florida, 2004.

———. *Revolutionary Melodrama: Popular Film and Civic Identity in Nasser's Egypt*. Chicago: Middle East Documentation Center, 2002.

———. "Singing the Pulse of the Egyptian-Arab Street: Shaaban Abd Al-Rahim and the Geo-Pop-Politics of Fast Food." *Popular Music* 22, no. 1 (2003): 73–88.

Gorman, Anthony. *Historians, State, and Politics in Twentieth Century Egypt: Contesting the Nation*. New York: Routledge, 2003.

Gray, Lila Ellen. *Fado Resounding: Affective Politics and Urban Life*. Durham, NC: Duke University Press, 2013.

Green, Nile. "Journeymen, Middlemen: Travel, Transculture, and Technology in the Origins of Muslim Printing." *International Journal of Middle East Studies* 41, no. 2 (2009): 203–24.

Grehan, James. *Everyday Life & Consumer Culture in 18th-Century Damascus.* Seattle: University of Washington Press, 2007.

Halliday, Fred. "Migration and the Labour Force in the Oil Producing States of the Middle East." *Development and Change* 8, no. 3 (1977): 263–291.

Hassan, Sayyid Mahmud. "Ahmad 'Adawiya wa al-Mut'a Kharij Nasqiyyat al-Nakhbawi wa al-Sha'bawi: Qira'a min mandhur al-Naqd al-Thaqafi." In *Al-Tarikh wa al-Musiqa: Dirasat fi Tarikh al-Musiqa fi Misr Wa Swisra*, edited by Mahmud 'Afifi and Nahla Matar, 75–94. Giza: Ein lil-Dirasat wa al-Buhuth al-Insaniyya wa al-Ijtima'iyya, 2013.

Heikal, Mohamed Hassanein. *Autumn of Fury: The Assassination of Sadat.* New York: Random House, 1983.

Herrera, Linda. *Revolution in the Age of Social Media: The Egyptian Popular Insurrection and the Internet.* New York: Verso, 2014.

Hirschkind, Charles. *The Ethical Soundscape: Cassette Sermons and Islamic Counterpublics.* New York: Columbia University Press, 2006.

———. "Experiments in Devotion Online: The YouTube Khutba." *International Journal of Middle East Studies* 44, no. 1 (2012): 5–21.

Hirst, David, and Irene Beeson. *Sadat.* London: Faber and Faber, 1981.

Ho, Engseng. *The Graves of Tarim: Genealogy and Mobility across the Indian Ocean.* Berkeley: University of California Press, 2006.

Hoodfar, Homa. *Between Marriage and the Market: Intimate Politics and Survival in Cairo.* Berkeley: University of California Press, 1997.

Horning, Susan Schmidt. *Chasing Sound: Technology, Culture, and the Art of Studio Recording from Edison to the LP.* Baltimore: Johns Hopkins University Press, 2013.

Howard, Philip, and Muzammil Hussain. *Democracy's Fourth Wave? Digital Media and the Arab Spring.* New York: Oxford University Press, 2013.

Howes, David. "Charting the Sensorial Revolution." *Senses & Society* 1, no. 1 (2006): 113–28.

Hroub, Khaled, ed. *Religious Broadcasting in the Middle East.* New York: Columbia University Press, 2012.

Ibrahim, Saad Eddin. "Oil, Migration and the New Arab Social Order." In *Rich and Poor States in the Middle East: Egypt and the New Arab Order*, edited by Malcolm Kerr and El Sayed Yassin, 17–70. Boulder, CO: Westview Press, 1982.

Idha'at al-Jumhuriyya al-'Arabiyya al-Muttahida fi 'Amiha al-Sabi' 'Ashr ba'd al-Thawra. Cairo: Hay'at Idha'at al-Jumhuriyya al-'Arabiyya al-Muttahida, 1969.

Ipsen, Carl. *Fumo: Italy's Love Affair with the Cigarette*. Stanford, CA: Stanford University Press, 2016.

Jackson, Maureen. *Mixing Musics: Turkish Jewry and the Urban Landscape of a Sacred Song*. Stanford, CA: Stanford University Press, 2013.

Jacob, Wilson C. *Working Out Egypt: Effendi Masculinity and Subject Formation in Colonial Modernity, 1870–1940*. Durham, NC: Duke University Press, 2011.

Jones, Toby. *Desert Kingdom: How Oil and Water Forged Modern Saudi Arabia*. Cambridge, MA: Harvard University Press, 2010.

Jouili, Jeanette, and Annelies Moors. "Introduction: Islamic Sounds and the Politics of Listening." *Anthropological Quarterly* 87, no. 4 (2014): 977–88.

Kamel, Basil, Sherine Wahba, and Aly Kandil. "Reclaiming Streets as Public Spaces for People: Promoting Pedestrianization Schemes in Al-Shawarbi Commercial Street—Downtown Cairo." Paper presented at the 1st International Conference on Towards a Better Quality of Life, El Gouna, Egypt, 24–26 November 2017, 1–12.

Katz, Mark. *Capturing Sound: How Technology Has Changed Music*. Berkeley: University of California Press, 2010.

Kenney, William. *Recorded Music in American Life: The Phonograph and Popular Memory, 1890–1945*. New York: Oxford University Press, 2003.

Kepel, Gilles. *Muslim Extremism in Egypt: The Prophet and Pharaoh*. Translated by Jon Rothschild. Berkeley: University of California Press, 1986.

Khafagy, Fatma. "Women and Labor Migration: One Village in Egypt." *MERIP Reports*, no. 124 (1984): 17–21.

Khazeni, Arash. *Sky Blue Stone: The Turquoise Trade in World History*. Berkeley: University of California Press, 2014.

Kholoussy, Hanan. *For Better, for Worse: The Marriage Crisis That Made Modern Egypt*. Stanford, CA: Stanford University Press, 2010.

Khouri-Dagher, Nadia. *Food and Energy in Cairo: Provisioning the Poor*. Report prepared for the United Nations Food-Energy Nexus Programme. Cairo: United Nations, 1986.

Kopytoff, Igor. "The Cultural Biography of Things: Commoditization as Process." In *The Social Life of Things: Commodities in Cultural Perspective*, edited by Arjun Appadurai, 64–92. New York: Cambridge University Press, 1986.

Kozma, Liat. "White Drugs in Interwar Egypt: Decadent Pleasures, Emaciated Fellahin, and the Campaign against Drugs." *Comparative Studies of South Asia, Africa and the Middle East* 33, no. 1 (2013): 89–101.

Kraidy, Marwan. *Reality Television and Arab Politics: Contention in Public Life*. New York: Cambridge University Press, 2010.

Kuntsman, Adi, and Rebecca Stein. *Digital Militarism: Israel's Occupation in the Social Media Age*. Stanford, CA: Stanford University Press, 2015.

Larsson, Göran. *Muslims and the New Media: Historical and Contemporary Debates*. Burlington, VT: Ashgate, 2011.

LaTowsky, Robert. "Egyptian Labor Abroad: Mass Participation and Modest Returns." *MERIP Reports*, no. 123 (1984): 11–18.

Leach, William. "Transformations in a Culture of Consumption: Women and Department Stores, 1890–1925." *Journal of American History* 71, no. 2 (1984): 319–42.

Lee, Doreen. *Activist Archives: Youth Culture and the Political Past in Indonesia*. Durham, NC: Duke University Press, 2016.

LeVine, Mark. *Heavy Metal Islam: Rock, Resistance, and the Struggle for the Soul of Islam*. New York: Three Rivers Press, 2008.

Lohman, Laura. "Preservation and Politicization: Umm Kulthum's National and International Legacy." *Popular Music and Society* 33, no. 1 (2010): 45–60.

———. *Umm Kulthum: Artistic Agency and the Shaping of an Arab Legend*. Middletown, CT: Wesleyan University Press, 2010.

Longva, Anh. *Walls Built on Sand: Migration, Exclusion and Society in Kuwait*. Boulder, CO: Westview Press, 1997.

Lynch, Marc. *Voices of the New Arab Public: Iraq, Al-Jazeera, and Middle East Politics Today*. New York: Columbia University Press, 2006.

Al-Majlis al-A'la lil-Thaqafa. *Al-Thaqafa fi 'Ahd al-Sadat*. Cairo: Al-Hay'a al-Misriyya al-'Amma lil-Kitab, 1981.

Malmström, Maria. *The Streets Are Talking to Me: Affective Fragments in Sisi's Egypt*. Berkeley: University of California Press, 2019.

Manuel, Peter. *Cassette Culture: Popular Music and Technology in North India*. Chicago: University of Chicago Press, 1993.

Marcus, Scott. *Music in Egypt: Experiencing Music, Expressing Culture*. New York: Oxford University Press, 2007.

Marsot, Afaf Lutfi Al-Sayyid. "Survey of Egyptian Works of History." *American Historical Review* 96, no. 5 (1991): 1422–34.

McDermot, Anthony. *Egypt from Nasser to Mubarak: A Flawed Revolution*. New York: Croom Helm, 1988.

McLaughlin, Gerald. "Infitah in Egypt: An Appraisal of Egypt's Open-Door Policy for Foreign Investment." *Fordham Law Review* 46, no. 5 (1978): 885–906.

McMurray, David. *In and out of Morocco: Smuggling and Migration in a Frontier Boomtown*. Minneapolis: University of Minnesota Press, 2000.

Meeker, Michael. *A Nation of Empire: The Ottoman Legacy of Turkish Modernity*. Berkeley: University of California Press, 2002.

Messick, Brinkley. "Media Muftis: Radio Fatwas in Yemen." In *Islamic Legal Interpretation: Muftis and Their Fatwas*, edited by Khalid Muhammad Masud, Brinkley Messick, and David S. Powers, 310–23. Cambridge, MA: Harvard University Press, 1996.

Micklewright, Nancy. "Late Ottoman Photography: Family, Home, and New Identities." In *Transitions in Domestic Consumption and Family Life in the Modern Middle East: Houses in Motion*, edited by Relli Shechter, 65–84. New York: Palgrave Macmillan, 2003.

Mikhail, Alan. *The Animal in Ottoman Egypt*. New Haven, CT: Yale University Press, 2014.

Miles, Hugh. *Al-Jazeera: The Inside Story of the Arab News Channel That Is Challenging the West*. New York: Grove Press, 2005.

Miller, Flagg. *The Audacious Ascetic: What Osama Bin Laden's Sound Archive Reveals About Al-Qa'ida*. New York: Oxford University Press, 2015.

———. *The Moral Resonance of Arab Media: Audiocassette Poetry and Culture in Yemen*. Cambridge, MA: Harvard Center for Middle Eastern Studies, 2007.

Minawi, Mostafa. *The Ottoman Scramble for Africa: Empire and Diplomacy in the Sahara and the Hijaz*. Stanford, CA: Stanford University Press, 2016.

Ministry of Information. *Al-I'lam al-Misri wa al-Alfiyya al-Thalitha*. Cairo: Al-Majmu'a al-Thaqafiyya al-Misriyya, 1999.

Mitchell, B. R. *International Historical Statistics: Africa, Asia & Oceania, 1750–1993*. London: Macmillan Reference, 1998.

Moll, Yasmin. "Islamic Televangelism: Religion, Media and Visuality." *Arab Media & Society*, no. 10 (2010): 1–27.

Morton, David. *Off the Record: The Technology and Culture of Sound Recording in America*. New Brunswick, NJ: Rutgers University Press, 1999.

Mottahedeh, Negar. *#iranElection: Hashtag Solidarity and the Transformation of Online Life*. Stanford, CA: Stanford University Press, 2015.

———. *Whisper Tapes: Kate Millet in Iran*. Stanford, CA: Stanford University Press, 2019.

al-Muhsin, 'Imad, Samar al-Mutalaq, Susan Kamil, Hana Sa'id. *Al-Thaqafa: Dau' 'ala Wajh al-Watan 1987–1997*. Cairo: Sunduq al-Tanmiya al-Thaqafiyya, 1997.

Mukerji, Chandra. "Entangled in Questions of Cultural Analysis." *History and Technology* 30, no. 5 (2014): 255.

Nassar, Issam. "Familial Snapshots: Representing Palestine in the Work of the First Local Photographers." *History & Memory* 18, no. 2 (2006): 139–55.

Nelson, Kristina. *The Art of Reciting the Qur'an.* Austin: University of Texas Press, 1985.

Nieuwkerk, Karin van. "Artistic Developments in the Muslim Cultural Sphere: Ethics, Aesthetics, and the Performing Arts." In *Muslim Rap, Halal Soaps, and Revolutionary Theater,* edited by Karin van Nieuwkerk, 1–26. Austin: University of Texas Press, 2011.

———. "The Performers of Muhammad 'Ali Street in Cairo." In *The Garland Encyclopedia of World Music, Volume 6: The Middle East,* edited by Virginia Danielson, Dwight Reynolds, and Scott Marcus, 615–22. New York: Routledge, 2002.

———. *"A Trade Like Any Other": Female Singers and Dancers in Egypt.* Austin: University of Texas Press, 1995.

Nieuwkerk, Karin van, Mark LeVine, and Martin Stokes, eds. *Islam and Popular Culture.* Austin: University of Texas Press, 2016.

Nigm, Ahmad Fu'ad. *Kalb al-Sit: Al-Diwan al-Thalith.* Cairo: Maktabat Madbuli al-Saghir, 1999.

al-Nigmi, Kamal. *Al-Ghina' al-Masri: Mutribun wa Mustami'un.* Cairo: Dar al-Hilal, 1993.

———. *Turath al-Ghina' al-'Arabi.* Cairo: Al-Hay'a al-'Amma li-Qusur al-Thaqafa, 2015.

Nye, David. *Technology Matters: Questions to Live With.* Cambridge, MA: MIT Press, 2006.

Olsson, Susanne. *Preaching Islamic Revival: 'Amr Khaled, Mass Media and Social Change in Egypt.* New York: I. B. Tauris, 2015.

Osborne, Lauren E. "From Text to Sound to Perception: Modes and Relationships of Meaning in the Recited Qur'an." PhD diss., University of Chicago, 2014.

Osman, Tarek. *Egypt on the Brink: From Nasser to the Muslim Brotherhood.* Revised ed. New Haven, CT: Yale University Press, 2013.

Otterbeck, Jonas, and Anders Ackfeldt. "Music and Islam." *Contemporary Islam* 6, no. 3 (2012): 227–33.

Parker, Ann, and Avon Neal. *Hajj Paintings: Folk Art of the Great Pilgrimage.* Cairo: American University in Cairo Press, 2009.

Parsons, Laila. "Micro-Narrative and the Historiography of the Modern Middle East." *History Compass* 9, no. 1 (2011): 84–96.

Penzer, G. R. "Egypt." In *Noise: Reports from Overseas Posts*. London: Department of Industry, 1979.

Petric, Faith. "Speak Out Freely, Speak Out! Egypt's El Sheikh Imam." *Sing Out! The Folk Song Magazine* 1980, 16–19.

Pinch, Trevor, and Karin Bijsterveld, eds. *The Oxford Handbook of Sound Studies*. New York: Oxford University Press, 2012.

Podeh, Elie. *The Politics of National Celebrations in the Arab Middle East*. New York: Cambridge University Press, 2011.

Pollard, Lisa. *Nurturing the Nation: The Family Politics of Modernizing, Colonizing and Liberating Egypt (1805–1923)*. Berkeley: University of California Press, 2005.

Posusney, Marsha. *Labor and the State in Egypt: Workers, Unions, and Economic Restructuring*. New York: Columbia University Press, 1997.

Puig, Nicolas. *Farah: Musiciens de noces et scènes urbaines au Caire*. Paris: Sindbad, 2010.

Qabil, Muhammad. *Mawsuʿat al-Ghinaʾ fi Misr*. Cairo: Dar al-Shuruq, 2006.

al-Qaʾid, Yusuf. *Mohamed Hassanein Heikal Yatadhakkar ʿAbd al-Nasser wa al-Muthaqqafun wa al-Thaqafa*. Cairo: Al-Hayʾa al-ʿAmma al-Misriyya lil-Kitab, 2013.

Quataert, Donald, ed. *Consumption Studies and the History of the Ottoman Empire, 1550–1922: An Introduction*. Albany: State University of New York Press, 2000.

Racy, Ali Jihad. *Making Music in the Arab World: The Culture and Artistry of Tarab*. New York: Cambridge University Press, 2004.

———. "Musical Change and Commercial Recording in Egypt, 1904–1932." PhD diss., University of Illinois at Urbana-Champaign, 1977.

Ram, Haggai. "Traveling Substances and Their Human Carriers: Hashish-Trafficking in Mandatory Palestine." In *A Global Middle East: Mobility, Materiality and Culture in the Modern Age, 1880–1940*, edited by Cyrus Schayegh, Liat Kozma, and Avner Wishnitzer, 201–28. New York: I. B. Tauris, 2015.

Ramadan, Saʿd, ed. *Umm Kulthum: Sawt fi Tarikh al-Umma*. Tunis: Maʿhad al-Musiqa al-ʿArabiyya, 2000.

Rasmussen, Anne K. *Women, the Recited Qurʾan, and Islamic Music in Indonesia*. Berkeley: University of California Press, 2010.

Rath, Richard Cullen. *How Early America Sounded*. Ithaca, NY: Cornell University Press, 2005.

Reid, Donald. *Cairo University and the Making of Modern Egypt*. New York: Cambridge University Press, 1990.

————. *Whose Pharaohs? Archaeology, Museums, and Egyptian National Identity from Napoleon to World War I*. Berkeley: University of California Press, 2002.

Reynolds, Nancy. "Building the Past: Rockscapes and the Aswan High Dam in Egypt." In *Water on Sand: Environmental Histories of the Middle East and North Africa*, edited by Alan Mikhail, 181–205. New York: Oxford University Press, 2013.

————. *A City Consumed: Urban Commerce, the Cairo Fire, and the Politics of Decolonization in Egypt*. Stanford, CA: Stanford University Press, 2012.

Roberts, Mary Louise. "Gender, Consumption, and Commodity Culture." *American Historical Review* 103, no. 3 (1998): 817–44.

Rock-Singer, Aaron. "Censoring the Kishkophone: Religion and State Power in Mubarak's Egypt," *International Journal of Middle East Studies* 49, no. 3 (2017): 437–56.

————. *Practicing Islam in Egypt: Print Media and the Islamic Revival*. New York: Cambridge University Press, 2019.

Roeder, George H., Jr. "Coming to Our Senses." *Journal of American History* 81, no. 3 (1994): 1112.

Rosenbaum, Gabriel. "Nasser and Nasserism as Perceived in Modern Egyptian Literature through Allusions to Songs." In *Rethinking Nasserism: Revolution and Historical Memory in Modern Egypt*, edited by Elie Podeh and Onn Winckler, 324–42. Gainesville: University Press of Florida, 2004.

Rosenfeld, Sophia. "On Being Heard: A Case for Paying Attention to the Historical Ear." *American Historical Review*, no. 116 (2011): 316–34.

Ross, Kerry. *Photography for Everyone: The Cultural Lives of Cameras and Consumers in Early Twentieth-Century Japan*. Stanford, CA: Stanford University Press, 2015.

Roy, Delwin. "Egyptian Emigrant Labor: Domestic Consequences." *Middle Eastern Studies* 27, no. 4 (1991): 551–82.

Rugh, William. *The Arab Press: News Media and Political Process in the Arab World*. 2nd ed. Syracuse, NY: Syracuse University Press, 1987.

Russell, Mona. *Creating the New Egyptian Woman: Consumerism, Education, and National Identity, 1863–1922*. New York: Palgrave Macmillan, 2004.

Ryzova, Lucie. *The Age of the Efendiyya: Passages to Modernity in National-Colonial Egypt*. New York: Oxford University Press, 2014.

————. "Boys, Girls, and Kodaks: Peer Albums and Middle-Class Personhood in Mid-Twentieth-Century Egypt." *Middle East Journal of Culture and Communication* 8, nos. 2–3 (2015): 215–55.

————. "Mourning the Archive: Middle Eastern Photographic Heritage between

Neoliberalism and Digital Reproduction." *Comparative Studies in Society and History* 56, no. 4 (2014): 1027–61.

al-Saʿadni, Mahmud. *Alhan al-Samaʾ*. Cairo: Akhbar al-Yawm, 1996.

Saʿid, Labib. *The Recited Koran: A History of the First Recorded Version*. Translated by Bernard Weiss, M. A. Rauf, and Morroe Berger. Princeton, NJ: Darwin Press, 1975.

Salamandra, Christa. "Moustache Hairs Lost: Ramadan Television Serials and the Construction of Identity in Damascus, Syria." *Visual Anthropology* 10, no. 2–4 (1998): 226–46.

al-Sayyid, Ragab Saʿd. *Al-Harb didd al-Talawwuth*, Kitabak. Cairo: Dar al-Maʿarif, 1978.

Scales, Rebecca. "Subversive Sound: Transnational Radio, Arabic Recordings, and the Dangers of Listening in French Colonial Algeria, 1934–1939." *Comparative Studies in Society and History* 52, no. 2 (2010): 384–417.

Schafer, R. Murray. *The Soundscape: Our Sonic Environment and the Tuning of the World*. Rochester, NY: Destiny Books, 1994.

———. *The Tuning of the World*. New York: Knopf, 1977.

Schayegh, Cyrus. "The Many Worlds of ʿAbud Yasin; or, What Narcotics Trafficking in the Interwar Middle East Can Tell Us about Territorialization." *American Historical Review* 116, no. 2 (2011): 273–306.

Schielke, Samuli. *The Perils of Joy: Contesting Mulid Festivals in Contemporary Egypt*. Syracuse, NY: Syracuse University Press, 2013.

Seikaly, Sherene. "Gaza as Archive." In *Gaza as Metaphor*, edited by Helga Tawil-Souri and Dina Matar, 225–31. London: Hurst & Co., 2016.

Sell, Ralph. "Egyptian International Labor Migration and Social Processes: Toward Regional Integration." *International Migration Review* 22, no. 3 (1988): 87–108.

———. "Gone for Good? Egyptian Migration Processes in the Arab World." *Cairo Papers in Social Science* 10, no. 2 (1987): 1–85.

Seymour, Elizabeth. "Imagining Modernity: Consuming Identities and Constructing the Ideal Nation on Egyptian Television." PhD diss., SUNY Binghamton University, 1999.

Shafik, Fouad Fahmy. "The Press and Politics of Modern Egypt, 1798–1970: A Comparative Analysis of Casual Relationships." PhD diss., New York University, 1981.

Shalabi, Hilmi Ahmad. *Tarikh al-Idhaʿa al-Misriyya: Dirasa Tarikhiyya (1934–1952)*. Cairo: Al-Hayʾa al-ʿAmma al-Misriyya lil-Kitab, 1995.

Shannon, Jonathan H. "Roundtable: Sounding North Africa and the Middle East: Introduction." *International Journal of Middle East Studies* 44, no. 4 (2012): 775-78.

Shechter, Relli. *The Rise of the Egyptian Middle Class: Socio-Economic Mobility and*

Public Discontent from Nasser to Sadat. New York: Cambridge University Press, 2019.

———. *Smoking, Culture, and Economy in the Middle East: The Egyptian Tobacco Market, 1850–2000.* Cairo: American University in Cairo Press, 2006.

Sheehi, Stephen. *The Arab Imago: A Social History of Portrait Photography, 1860–1910.* Princeton, NJ: Princeton University Press, 2016.

———. "A Social History of Early Arab Photography or a Prolegomenon to an Archaeology of the Lebanese Imago." *International Journal of Middle East Studies* 39, no. 2 (2007): 177–208.

Shehata, Samer. *Shop Floor Culture and Politics in Egypt.* Albany: State University of New York Press, 2009.

Shryock, Andrew. *Nationalism and the Genealogical Imagination: Oral History and Textual Authority in Tribal Jordan.* Berkeley: University of California Press, 1997.

Siamdoust, Nahid. *Soundtrack of the Revolution: The Politics of Music in Iran.* Stanford, CA: Stanford University Press, 2017.

Smith, Mark M., ed. *Hearing History: A Reader.* Athens: University of Georgia Press, 2004.

———. *Listening to Nineteenth-Century America.* Chapel Hill: Chapel Hill University Press, 2001.

———. *Sensing the Past: Seeing, Hearing, Smelling, Tasting, and Touching in History.* Berkeley: University of California Press, 2007.

———. "Still Coming to 'Our' Senses: An Introduction." *Journal of American History* 95, no. 2 (2008): 378–80.

Smolin, Jonathan. *Moroccan Noir: Police, Crime, and Politics in Popular Culture.* Bloomington: Indiana University Press, 2013.

Solh, Camillia. "Egyptian Migrant Peasants in Iraq: A Case-Study of the Settlement Community in Khalsa." PhD diss., University of London, 1985.

Soliman, Nayera Abdelrahman. "Remembering the 1977 Bread Riots in Suez: Fragments and Ghosts of Resistance." *International Review of Social History* 66, no. S29 (2021): 23–40.

Spadola, Emilio. *The Calls of Islam: Sufis, Islamists, and Mass Mediation in Urban Morocco.* Bloomington: Indiana University Press, 2014.

Sreberny, Annabelle, and Ali Mohammadi. *Small Media, Big Revolution: Communication, Culture, and the Iranian Revolution.* Minneapolis: University of Minnesota, 1994.

Starkey, Paul. "Modern Egyptian Culture in the Arab World." In *The Cambridge History of Egypt*, edited by M. W. Daly, 394–426. New York: Cambridge University Press, 1998.

Stanton, Andrea. *"This Is Jerusalem Calling": State Radio in Mandate Palestine*. Austin: University of Texas Press, 2013.

Stanton, Andrea, and Carole Woodall. "Roundtable: Bringing Sound into Middle East Studies." *International Journal of Middle East Studies* 48, no. 1 (2016): 113–14.

Sterne, Jonathan. *The Audible Past: Cultural Origins of Sound Reproduction*. Durham, NC: Duke University Press, 2003.

———, ed. *The Sound Studies Reader*. New York: Routledge, 2012.

Stokes, Martin. "'Abd Al-Halim's Microphone." In *Music and the Play of Power in the Middle East, North Africa and Central Asia*, edited by Laudan Nooshin, 55–74. Burlington, VT: Ashgate, 2009.

Stoler, Ann Laura. *Along the Archival Grain: Epistemic Anxieties and Colonial Common Sense*. Princeton, NJ: Princeton University Press, 2009.

Stolz, Daniel. "Positioning the Watch Hand: 'Ulama' and the Practice of Mechanical Timekeeping in Cairo, 1737–1874." *International Journal of Middle East Studies* 47, no. 3 (2015): 489–510.

Stone, Christopher. *Popular Culture and Nationalism in Lebanon: The Fairouz and Rahbani Nation*. New York: Routledge, 2008.

Suisman, David. *Selling Sounds: The Commercial Revolution in American Music*. Cambridge, MA: Harvard University Press, 2012.

Swedenburg, Ted. "Nubian Music in Cairo." In *The Garland Encyclopedia of World Music*, vol. 6, *The Middle East*, edited by Virginia Danielson, Dwight Reynolds, and Scott Marcus, 641–45. New York: Routledge, 2002.

———. "Saida Sultan/Danna International: Transgender Pop and the Polysemiotics of Sex, Nation, and Ethnicity on the Israeli-Egyptian Border." *Musical Quarterly* 81, no. 1 (1997): 81–108.

al-Tabi'i, Huda. "Taqdim." In *Muhammad al-Tabi'i*, edited by Abu al-Majd Sabri, 11–87. Cairo: Mu'assasat Dar al-Ta'awun lil-Tiba'a wa al-Nashr, 1993.

Tagliacozzo, Eric. "Hajj in the Time of Cholera: Pilgrim Ships and Contagion from Southeast Asia to the Red Sea." In *Global Muslims in the Age of Steam and Print*, ed. James Gelvin and Nile Green, 103–20. Berkeley: University of California Press, 2013.

———. *The Longest Journey: Southeast Asians and the Pilgrimage to Mecca*. New York: Oxford University Press, 2013.

Taha, Yasser. "Technology Transfer by Multinational Firms: The Case of the Car Industry in Egypt." PhD diss., Kingston University, 2002.

Taylor, Elizabeth. "Egyptian Migration and Peasant Wives." *MERIP Reports*, no. 124 (1984): 3–10.

Thompson, Emily. *The Soundscape of Modernity: Architectural Acoustics and the Culture of Listening in America, 1900–1933*. Cambridge, MA: MIT Press, 2002.

Tignor, Robert. *Egyptian Textiles and British Capital 1930–1956*. Cairo: American University in Cairo Press, 1989.

Tsourapas, Gerasimos. "Nasser's Educators and Agitators across *al-Watan al-Arabi*: Tracing the Foreign Policy Importance of Egyptian Regional Migration, 1952–1967." *British Journal of Middle Eastern Studies* 43, no. 3 (2016): 324–341.

———. *The Politics of Migration in Modern Egypt: Strategies for Regime Survival in Autocracies*. New York: Cambridge University Press, 2019.

al-Tunsi, Bayram. *Al-A'mal al-Kamila li-Bayram al-Tunsi*. Cairo: Maktabat Madbuli, 2002.

al-'Umri, Amir. *Al-Shaykh Imam fi 'Asr al-Thawra wa al-Ghadab*. Cairo: Maktabat Madbuli, 2010.

Varlik, Nükhet. *Plague and Empire in the Early Modern Mediterranean World: The Ottoman Experience, 1347–1600*. New York: Cambridge University Press, 2015.

Vitalis, Robert. *Oilcraft: The Myths of Scarcity and Security That Haunt U.S. Energy Policy*. Stanford, CA: Stanford University Press, 2020.

Waxer, Lise. *The City of Musical Memory: Salsa, Record Grooves, and Popular Culture in Cali, Colombia*. Middletown, CT: Wesleyan University Press, 2002.

Weiner, Isaac A. "Calling Everyone to Pray: Pluralism, Secularism, and the Adhān in Hamtramck, Michigan." *Anthropological Quarterly* 87, no. 4 (2014): 1049–77.

Weld, Kirsten. *Paper Cadavers: The Archives of Dictatorship in Guatemala*. Durham, NC: Duke University Press, 2014.

Weyland, Petra. *Inside the Third World Village*. New York: Routledge, 1993.

Wikan, Unni. "Living Conditions among Cairo's Poor: A View from Below." *Middle East Journal* 39, no. 1 (1985): 7–26.

Winegar, Jessica. *Creative Reckonings: The Politics of Art and Culture in Contemporary Egypt*. Stanford, CA: Stanford University Press, 2006.

Wise, Lindsay. "'Words from the Heart': New Forms of Islamic Preaching in Egypt." MPhil thesis, Oxford University, 2003.

Wishnitzer, Avner. "Into the Dark: Power, Light, and Nocturnal Life in 18th-Century Istanbul." *International Journal of Middle East Studies* 46, no. 3 (2014): 513–31.

Woodall, Carole. "Sensing the City: Sound, Movement, and the Night in 1920s Istanbul." PhD diss., New York University, 2008.

Yilmaz, Secil. "Love in the Time of Syphilis: Medicine and Sex in the Ottoman Empire, 1860–1922." PhD diss., Graduate Center, City University of New York, 2016.

Zayani, Mohamed. *Networked Publics and Digital Contention: The Politics of Everyday Life in Tunisia*. Oxford: Oxford University Press, 2015.

———, ed. *The Al Jazeera Phenomenon: Critical Perspectives on New Arab Media*. Boulder, CO: Paradigm Publishers, 2005.

Zeghal, Malika. "Religion and Politics in Egypt: The Ulema of Al-Azhar, Radical Islam, and the State (1952–94)." *International Journal of Middle East Studies* 31, no. 3 (1999): 371–99.

al-Zuhar, Amir. *Suwar wa Asrar min Hayat al-Kibar*. Cairo: Akhbar al-Yawm, 1997.

Index

Page numbers in *italics* refer to illustrations.

Ministry of Information, 102, 103, 136

Ministry of Social Affairs, 136

Minshawi, Muhammad Sadiq al-, 165

Mislimani, 'Alaa al-, 175

Misrfone (online radio station), 175

Mutawalli, Salah, 14

mix tapes, 18–22

Modern Egypt Project, 22, 187–88

"modern home," 40–42, 48, 57, 186

motorcycles, in advertisements, 45, 50, 51

Mubarak, Gamal, 165

Mubarak, Husni, 7, 12, 19, 35, 42, 48, 181;
cultural production under, 149; library
construction under, 151; migrant labor
under, 28–29; music piracy under, 122;
repression by, 17–18

Mubarak, Suzanne, 150–52, 153

Mugi, Muhammad al-, 98, 122

Muhammad, Prophet, 140, 144, 165

Muhammad, Su'ad (musician), 91

Muhammad 'Ali Street, 96

Muhammad "Peugeot" (car thief), 60

Murad, Layla, 115, 174

Murad, Munir, 98

Musbah, Ibrahim al-, 91

music, 20, 79–80, 90

musicians, as unofficial spokesmen, 37

Musicians Syndicate, 79, 94, 110

Music Library, 150–56, 177

Mussallam, 'Antar Sa'id 168–72, 175, 182

Mustafa, Hassan, 223n65

Mustafa, Nadia, 120, 124

Nagat (musician), 91, 115

Nagham FM, 110

Naguib, Muhammad, 204–5n41

Nahda (Arab renaissance), 175

Na'na' (thief), 55–56

Nasir (kiosk proprietor), 1, 179, 181

Nasser, Gamal Abdel, 11, 12, 13, 16, 145,
151, 163, 165, 204–5n41; businesses nationalized by, 42; commemoration of,
148; death of, 17, 63, 66, 134; July Laws
enacted by, 34; as pan-Arabist, 146;
pirating under, 129; radio exploited
by, 220n30; Suez Canal nationalized
by, 104

National (Japanese corporation), 30, 35,
43, 45, 50

nationalization, 13, 34, 42, 104

National Union, 207n55

Nawira, 'Abd al-Halim, 104

neoliberalism, 17, 18

Newsweek, 144

"Night Stars" (al-Atrash), 161

Nigm, Ahmad Fu'ad, 131, 137–38, 140–42,
145, 147

Nigmi, Kamal al-, 87

Nimr, Esmat al-, 175

Nixon, Richard, 21, 132–37, 140, 142–46

"Nixon Baba" ("Father Nixon"; Nigm and
Shaykh Imam), 21, 132, 137–46, 193–94

noise, 53, 81, 83–84

Notorious B.I.G., 183

Nur, al- (recording label), 120, 121

Nye, David, 4

October Paper (1974), 17, 55

October War (1973), 17, 28, 104, 133, 163

Office of Art Censorship, 92–95

official stories, 21, 132–34, 136, 140, 142,
146, 182

"Oh, Crowded World!" ('Adawiya), 102

oil exports, 28, 29, 32, 53

Omar Effendi, 41

Orientalism, 43

Osman, Tarek, 88

Ottens, Lou, 3–4, 7

advisers expelled by, 133; trade policy of, 68; traffic and noise targeted by, 81–82

Sadat, Jehan, 38–39

Saʻid, Labib, 244–45n24

Salah, Muhammad, 38

Salama, ʻAbbas Muhammad, 152–55, 176

Salih, Maryam, 143

Salih, Midhat, 123, 234n27

Salih, Nabil, 56

Samsung, 30, 35

Sangam (film), 167

Saudi Arabia, 30, 65, 156, 208nn4–5

Sawt al-Fann (recording label), 97–98, 112–15, 128, 154

Sawt al-Gharbiyya (recording label), 168

Sawt al-Hubb (recording label), 96, 109, 110, 154

Sawt al-Qahira (recording label), 94, 110, 128, 154, 159, 174; "refined" cassettes issued by, 81, 95, 102–5; unauthorized releases by, 125–26

Sayegh, Georgette, 123

Sayyid, Ragab al-, 82–83

Schafer, R. Murray, 8, 82

Scheherazade (singer), 173–74

The School of Troublemakers (al-Sharqawi), 223n65

Sednaoui (retailer), 42

"Senator" (white-collar criminal), 60

senses, 8–9, 23, 183

Senses and Society (journal), 8

Shaʻir, ʻAida al-, 47, 113

Shaʻrawi, Muhammad Mutawalli al-, 174

shaʻbi music, 20, 80–84, 96–106, 109, 110, 125, 155

Shadia (musician), 91, 115, 235n41

"shadow archives," 12–16, 22, 185, 187

Shafiq, Hafiz, 54

Shaker, Hany, 79

Shakosh, Hassan, 79

Shams al-Din, Hany, 164, 168

Shannon, Jonathan, 201–2n27

Shawarbi, al- (street), 71–72, 110, 223n65

Sharif, Mahmud al-, 98

Sharqawi, Galal al-, 223n65

Shaykh Imam, 8, 21, 131–32, 137–47, 182

Shihab, Simsim, 124

Shinawi, ʻAbd al-ʻAziz Muhammad al-, 163

Shinawi, Maʼmun al-, 96

Shirbini, Hikmat al-, 235n41

shopping, 55, 71. See also consumer culture

Shuhayb, ʻAbd al-Qadir, 124

Sidky, ʻAziz, 55

Sidqi, ʻAtif, 152

Sinai, 31, 35, 55

Six Day War (1967), 17, 55

Smith, Mark, 8, 182

smuggling, 19, 30, 51–52, 63, 65–70, 73

The Social Life of Things (Appadurai), 4

social media, 5, 19, 25, 143, 170–72

Society for Authors and Composers, 114, 116–17, 122–23, 125, 127

sonorous spectacle, 21, 130, 132, 136, 142

Sony Corporation, 35, 62

Soueif, Ahdaf, 140–41

soundscapes, 8, 53, 183

sound studies, 82

Specialized National Councils, 94

Stanton, Andrea, 9

Starkey, Paul, 9

Stoler, Ann Laura, 12

Suez Canal, 29, 55, 68, 104

"suitcase carriers" (himal al-shanta), 66–67, 72

"suitcase trader" (tajir al-shanta), 66, 72, 223n65

Sukkar (thief), 55–56, 58, 62

Stanford Studies in Middle Eastern
and Islamic Societies and Cultures

Joel Beinin and Laleh Khalili, editors

EDITORIAL BOARD
Asef Bayat, Marilyn Booth, Laurie Brand, Timothy Mitchell,
Jillian Schwedler, Rebecca L. Stein, Max Weiss

Between Dreams and Ghosts: Indian Migration and Middle Eastern Oil   2021
ANDREA WRIGHT

Bread and Freedom: Egypt's Revolutionary Situation   2021
MONA EL-GHOBASHY

Paradoxes of Care: Children and Global Medical Aid in Egypt   2021
RANIA KASSAB SWEIS

*The Politics of Art: Dissent and Cultural Diplomacy in Lebanon,
Palestine, and Jordan*   2021
HANAN TOUKAN

*The Paranoid Style in American Diplomacy: Oil and Arab
Nationalism in Iraq*   2021
BRANDON WOLFE-HUNNICUTT

Dear Palestine: A Social History of the 1948 War   2021
SHAY HAZKANI

A Critical Political Economy of the Middle East and North Africa   2021
JOEL BEININ, BASSAM HADDAD, AND SHERENE SEIKALY, EDITORS

Archive Wars: The Politics of History in Saudi Arabia   2020
ROSIE BSHEER

Showpiece City: How Architecture Made Dubai   2020
TODD REISZ

The Optimist: A Social Biography of Tawfiq Zayyad   2020
TAMIR SOREK

Graveyard of Clerics: Everyday Activism in Saudi Arabia   2020
PASCAL MENORET

Cleft Capitalism: The Social Origins of Failed Market Making in Egypt   2020
AMR ADLY

The Universal Enemy: Jihad, Empire, and the Challenge of Solidarity   2019
DARRYL LI

Waste Siege: The Life of Infrastructure in Palestine   2019
SOPHIA STAMATOPOULOU-ROBBINS

Heritage and the Cultural Struggle for Palestine   2019
CHIARA DE CESARI

Iran Reframed: Anxieties of Power in the Islamic Republic   2019
NARGES BAJOGHLI

Banking on the State: The Financial Foundations of Lebanon   2019
HICHAM SAFIEDDINE

Familiar Futures: Time, Selfhood, and Sovereignty in Iraq   2019
SARA PURSLEY

Made in United States
North Haven, CT
13 July 2022

21295291R00183